IN BRIGHTEST DAY,
IN BLACKEST NIGHT,
NO EVIL SHALL ESCAPE
MY SIGHT:

LET THOSE WHO
WORSHIP EVIL'S MIGHT
BEWARE MY POWER...

GREEN LANTERN'S
LIGHT!

RON MARZ
CHUCK DIXON
writers

DARRYL BANKS
JEFF JOHNSON
PAUL PELLETIER
DOUGIE BRAITHWAITE
ANTHONY WILLIAMS
SCOT EATON
pencillers

ROB SCHWAGER
LEE LOUGHRIDGE
colorists

CHRIS ELIOPOULOS
JOHN COSTANZA
letterers

TERRY AUSTIN
BOB WIACEK
ROBIN RIGGS
ANDY LANNING
DON HUDSON
inkers

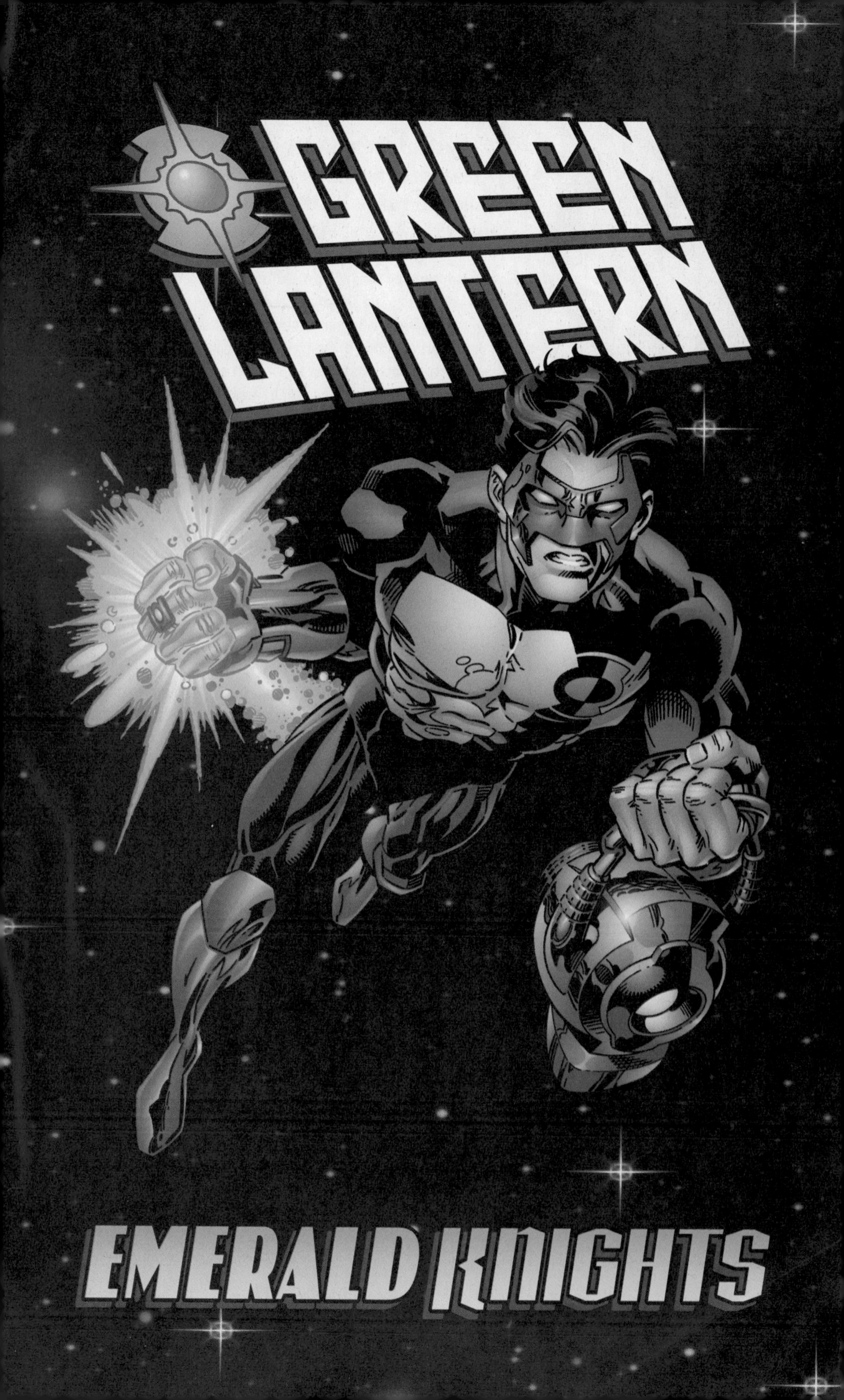
GREEN LANTERN
EMERALD KNIGHTS

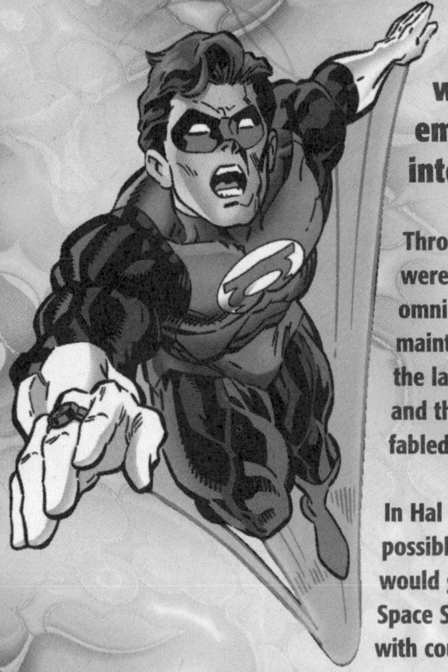

Each of them wears one of the most powerful weapons the universe has ever known: an emerald ring with the ability to focus thought into bright, tangible substance.

Through simple twists of fate, Earthmen Hal Jordan and Kyle Rayner were selected by the self-appointed Guardians of the Universe – nigh-omnipotent aliens who make their home on the distant planet Oa – to maintain order within the universe. One would be their brightest pupil, the latter their last remaining hope; each armed with only his wits and the awesome power rings of the Guardians' agents-at-large: the fabled Green Lantern Corps.

In Hal Jordan, the dying Green Lantern Abin Sur sought out the nearest possible successor and found an individual utterly devoid of fear, who would go on to defend his hometown Coast City and the entirety of Space Sector 2814, of which the Earth was but a small part, with courage and honor.

It was Hal Jordan who defeated the rogue Lantern Sinestro when all others failed. It was Hal Jordan who helped found the mighty Justice League of America. And it was Hal Jordan who supported the Corps in its darkest times.

The destruction of his beloved Coast City changed all that. Grief-stricken, Hal beseeched the Guardians to resurrect his home and loved ones. When his venerable masters refused, Hal usurped their power, leaving a trail of slain Green Lanterns in his wake and decimating the immortal Guardians. As the power-mad Parallax, Hal descended headlong into conflict with Earth's preeminent defenders.

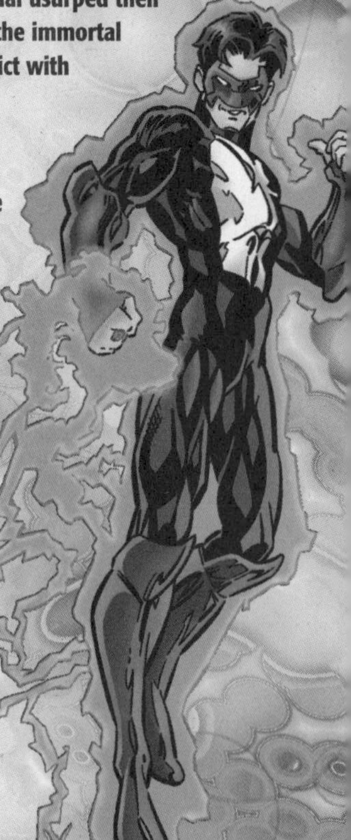

Ultimately, Hal's deeply rooted moral center prevailed, and he returned to the heroic fold in time to reignite Earth's extinguished sun and prevent the deaths of billions. He died a hero.

The Guardians' legacy, however, would survive.

Like Hal Jordan, blind luck changed the destiny of the brash Kyle Rayner. Awarded the sole remaining power ring by the surviving Guardian Ganthet, Kyle became the last Green Lantern. But where Hal Jordan benefited from instruction from veteran Corps members to bolster an already formidable mastery of his ring, Kyle's training has been strictly trial and error...flying utterly solo and often by the seat of his pants.

Surviving his freshman foray into super-heroics, Kyle has more than proved himself worthy of his role as Green Lantern, joining Earth's champions in the JLA and filling the seat once occupied by Hal Jordan. Through sheer force of will, Kyle has finally come into his own.

And now, after an adventure in the 30th century alongside that era's defenders, the young Legion of Super-Heroes, a more confident and self-assured Kyle is returning home, having finally overcome Hal's daunting shadow...

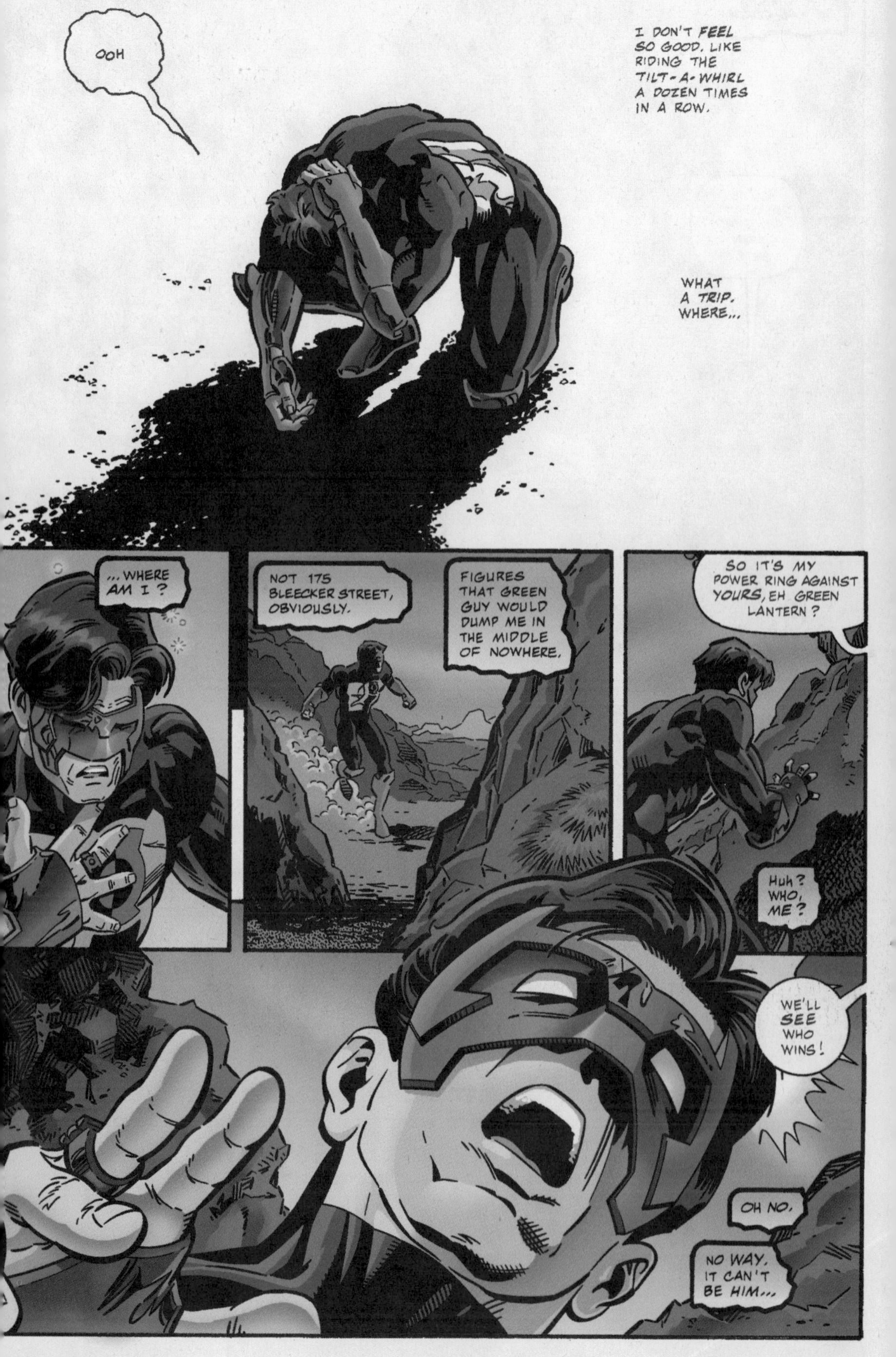
OOH
I DON'T FEEL SO GOOD. LIKE RIDING THE TILT-A-WHIRL A DOZEN TIMES IN A ROW.
WHAT A TRIP. WHERE...
...WHERE AM I?
NOT 175 BLEECKER STREET, OBVIOUSLY.
FIGURES THAT GREEN GUY WOULD DUMP ME IN THE MIDDLE OF NOWHERE.
SO IT'S MY POWER RING AGAINST YOURS, EH GREEN LANTERN?
Huh? WHO, ME?
WE'LL SEE WHO WINS!
OH NO.
NO WAY. IT CAN'T BE HIM...

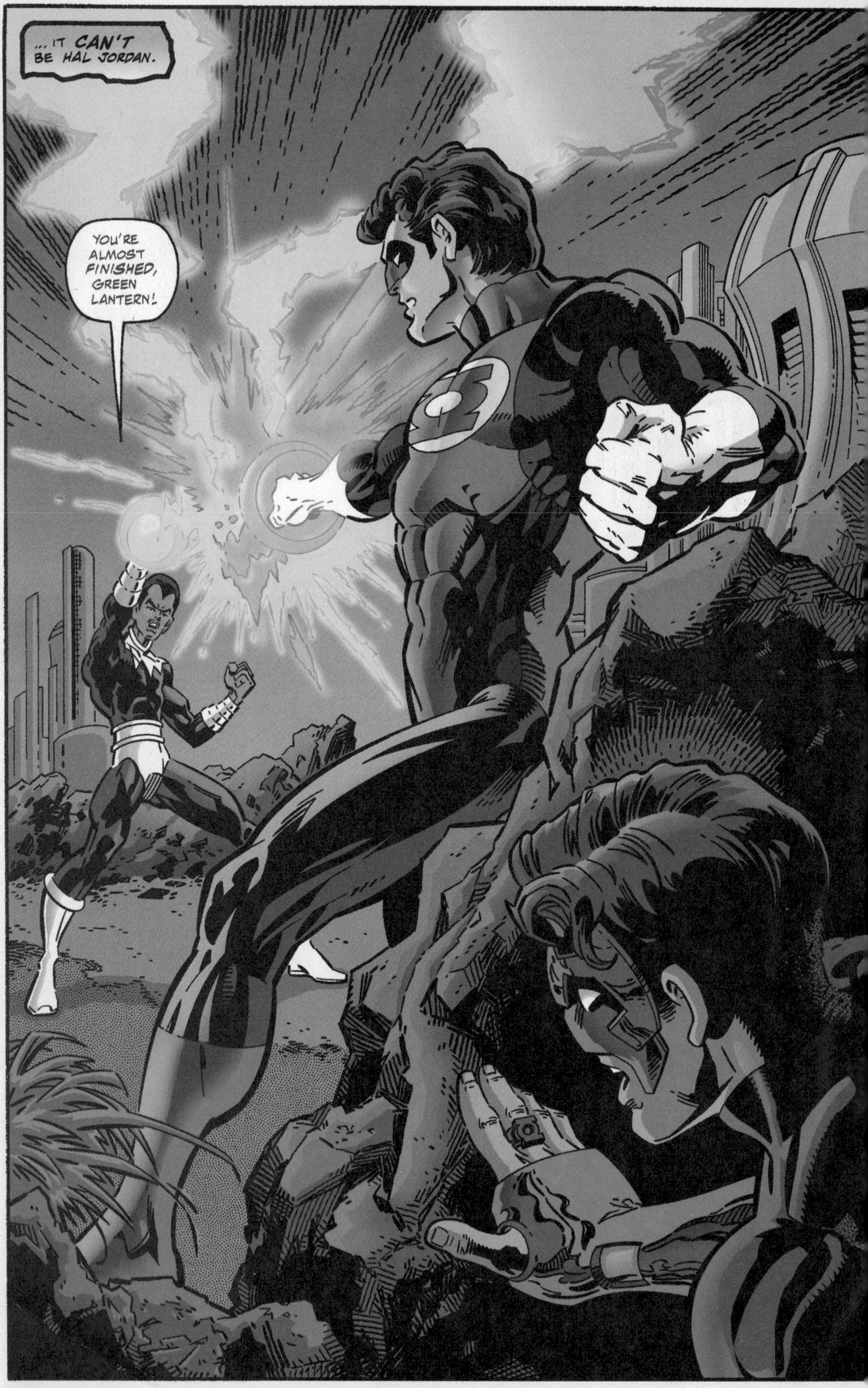
...IT CAN'T BE HAL JORDAN.
YOU'RE ALMOST FINISHED, GREEN LANTERN!

...or so he thinks.

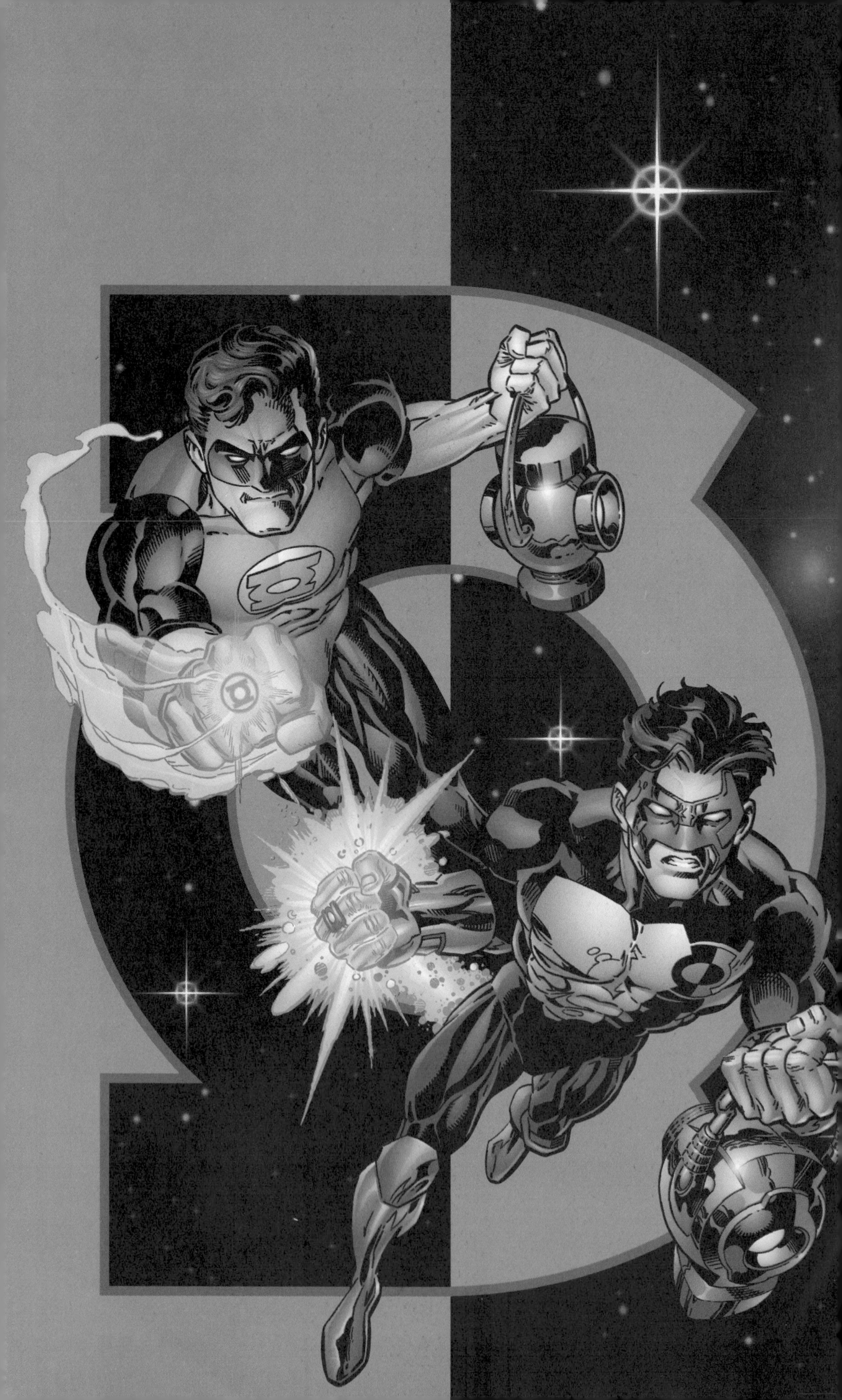

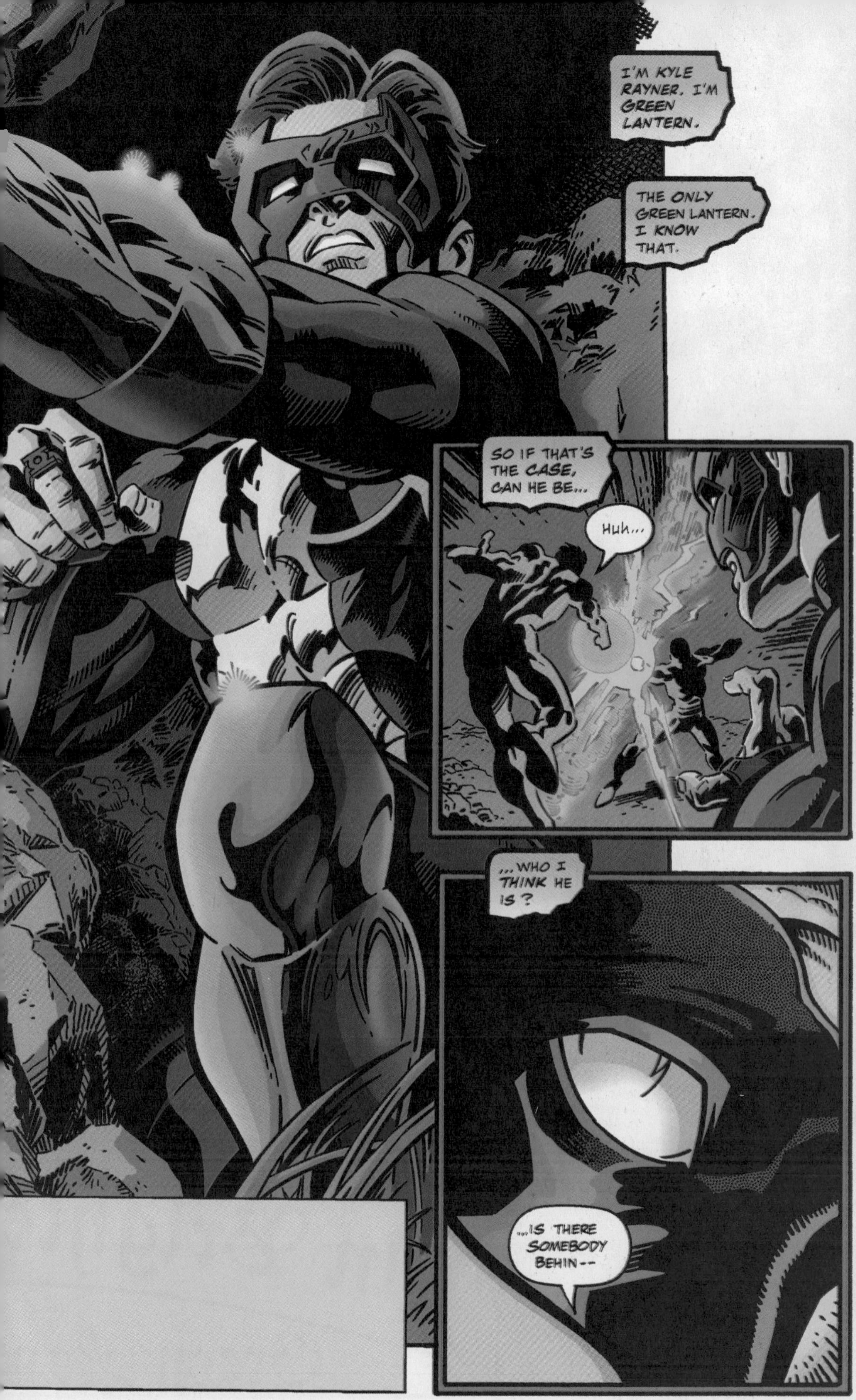
I'M KYLE RAYNER. I'M GREEN LANTERN.
THE ONLY GREEN LANTERN. I KNOW THAT.
SO IF THAT'S THE CASE, CAN HE BE...
Huh...
...WHO I THINK HE IS?
...IS THERE SOMEBODY BEHIN--

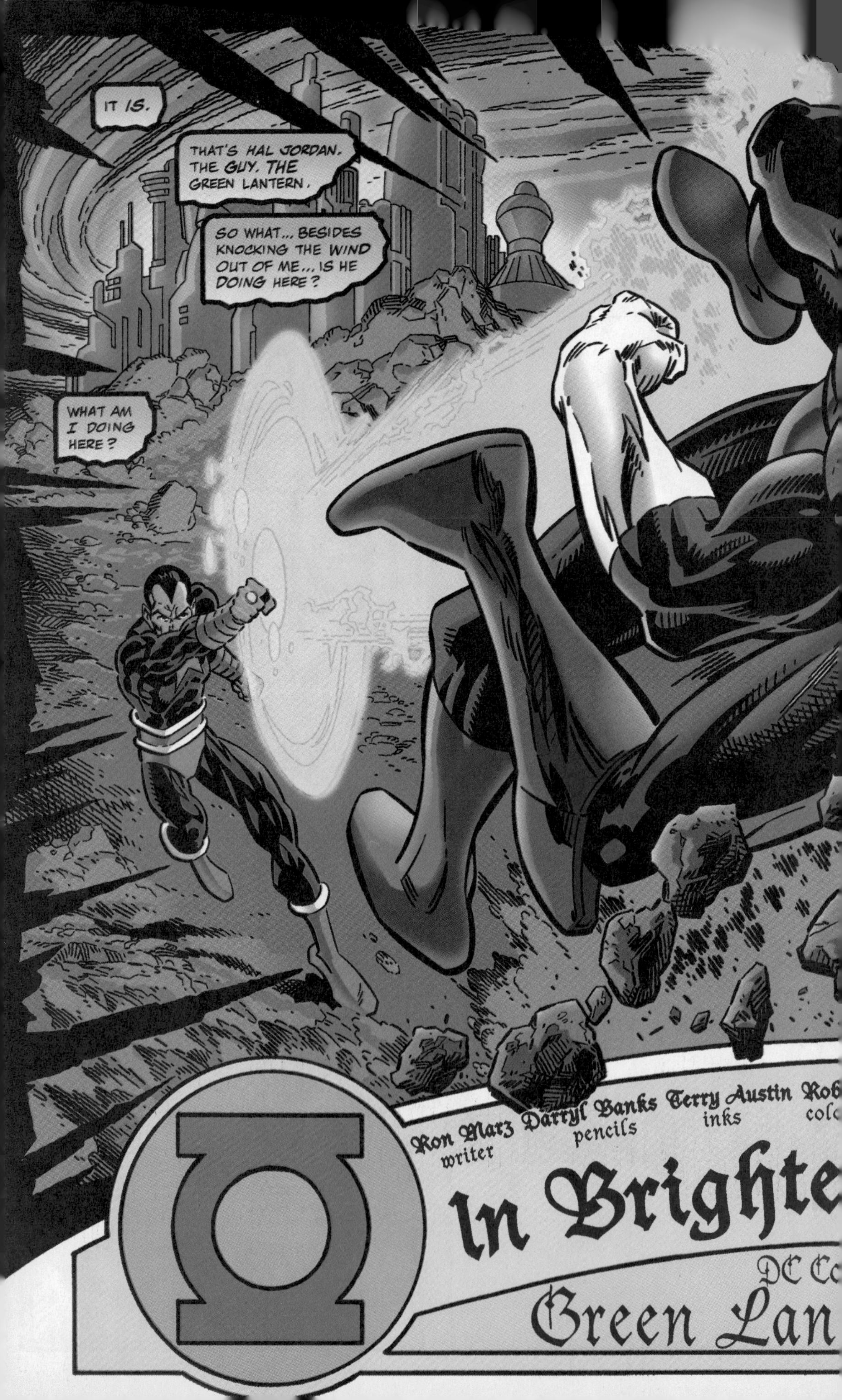

IT IS.
THAT'S HAL JORDAN. THE GUY. THE GREEN LANTERN.
SO WHAT... BESIDES KNOCKING THE WIND OUT OF ME... IS HE DOING HERE?
WHAT AM I DOING HERE?
Ron Marz writer
Darryl Banks pencils
Terry Austin inks
In Brighte
Green Lan

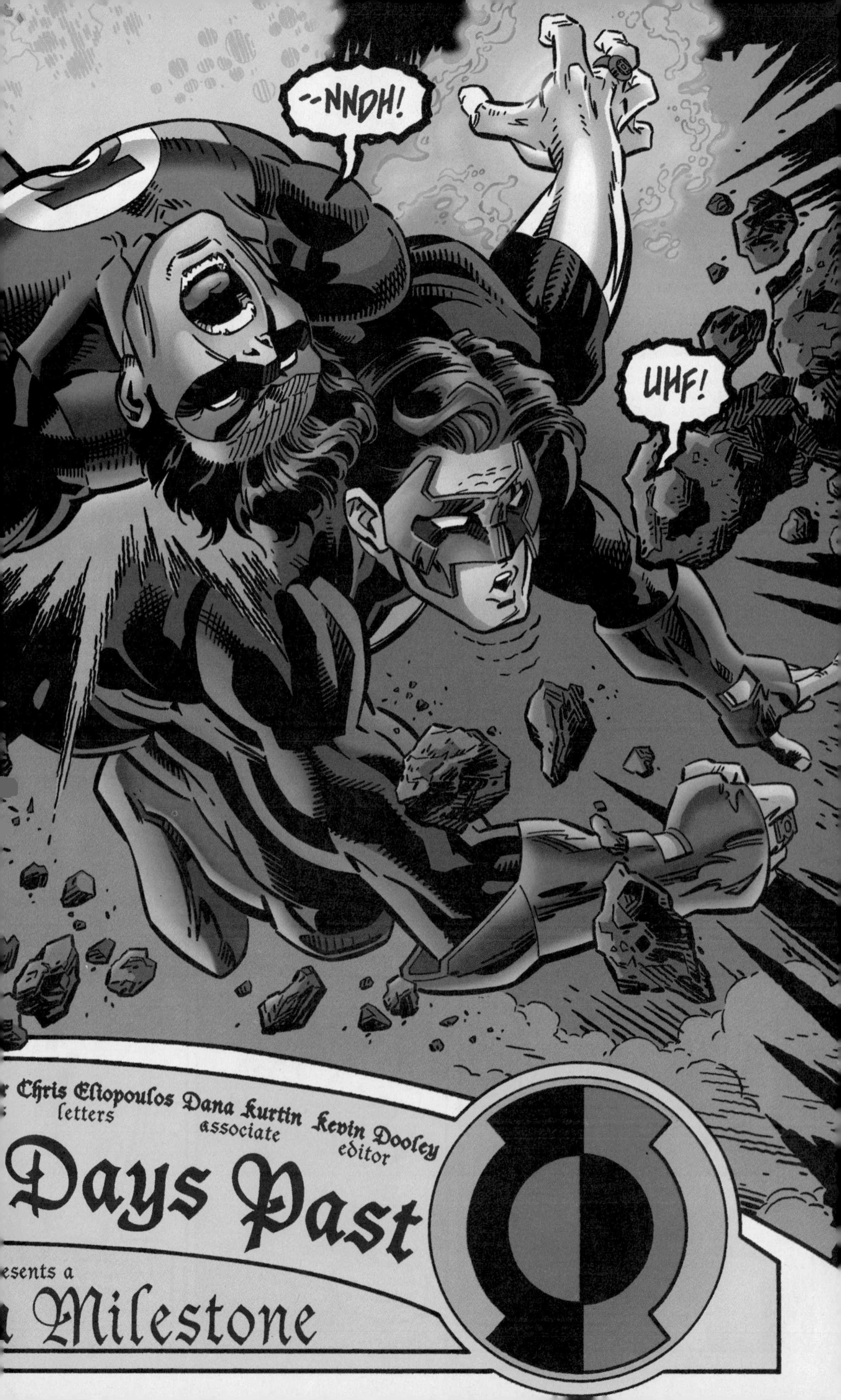

--NNDH!
UHF!
Chris Eliopoulos letters
Dana Kurtin associate
Kevin Dooley editor
Days Past
esents a
Milestone

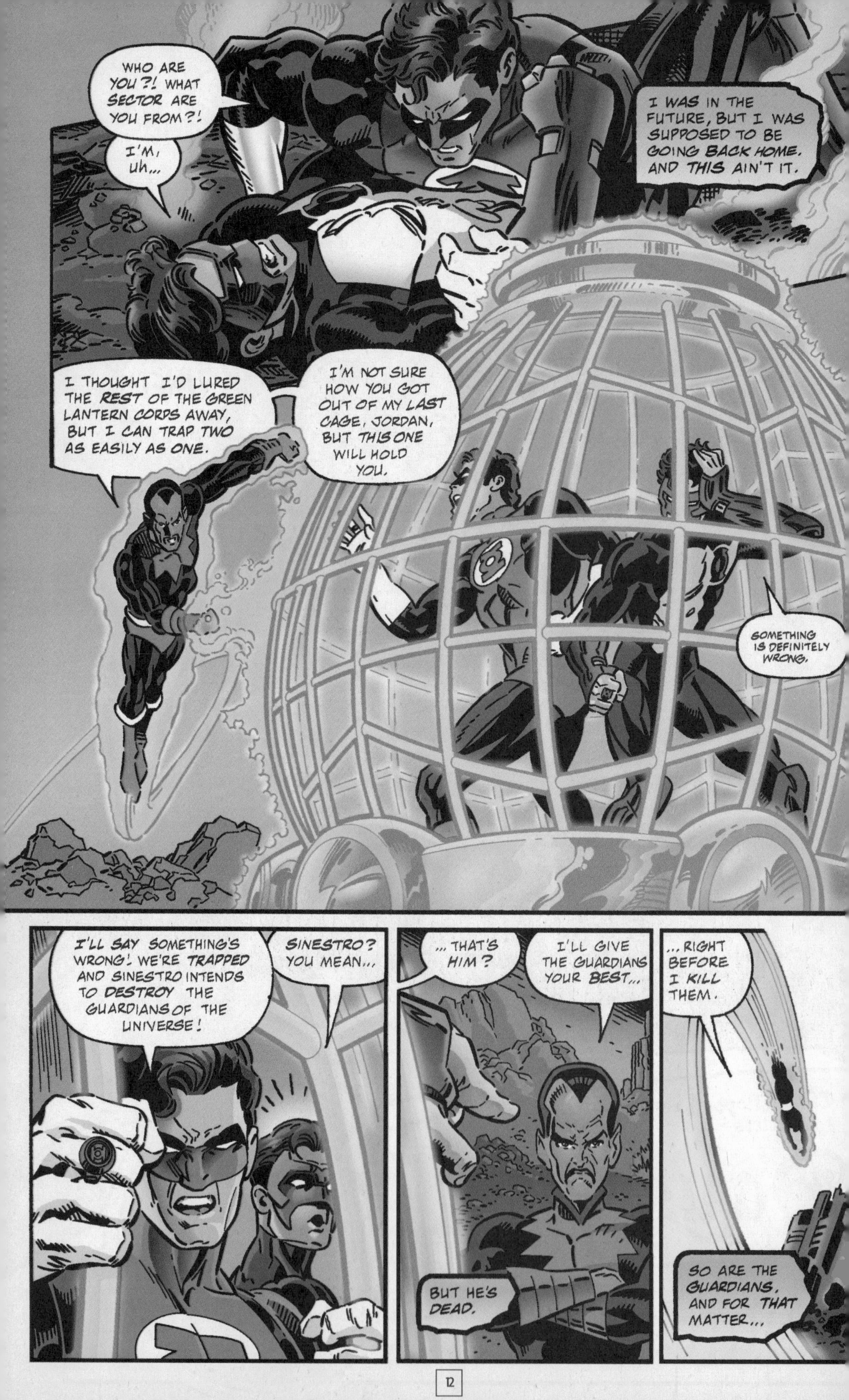

WHO ARE YOU?! WHAT SECTOR ARE YOU FROM?!
I'M, uh...
I WAS IN THE FUTURE, BUT I WAS SUPPOSED TO BE GOING BACK HOME. AND THIS AIN'T IT.
I THOUGHT I'D LURED THE REST OF THE GREEN LANTERN CORPS AWAY, BUT I CAN TRAP TWO AS EASILY AS ONE.
I'M NOT SURE HOW YOU GOT OUT OF MY LAST CAGE, JORDAN, BUT THIS ONE WILL HOLD YOU.
SOMETHING IS DEFINITELY WRONG.
I'LL SAY SOMETHING'S WRONG! WE'RE TRAPPED AND SINESTRO INTENDS TO DESTROY THE GUARDIANS OF THE UNIVERSE!
SINESTRO? YOU MEAN...
...THAT'S HIM?
BUT HE'S DEAD.
I'LL GIVE THE GUARDIANS YOUR BEST...
...RIGHT BEFORE I KILL THEM.
SO ARE THE GUARDIANS, AND FOR THAT MATTER...

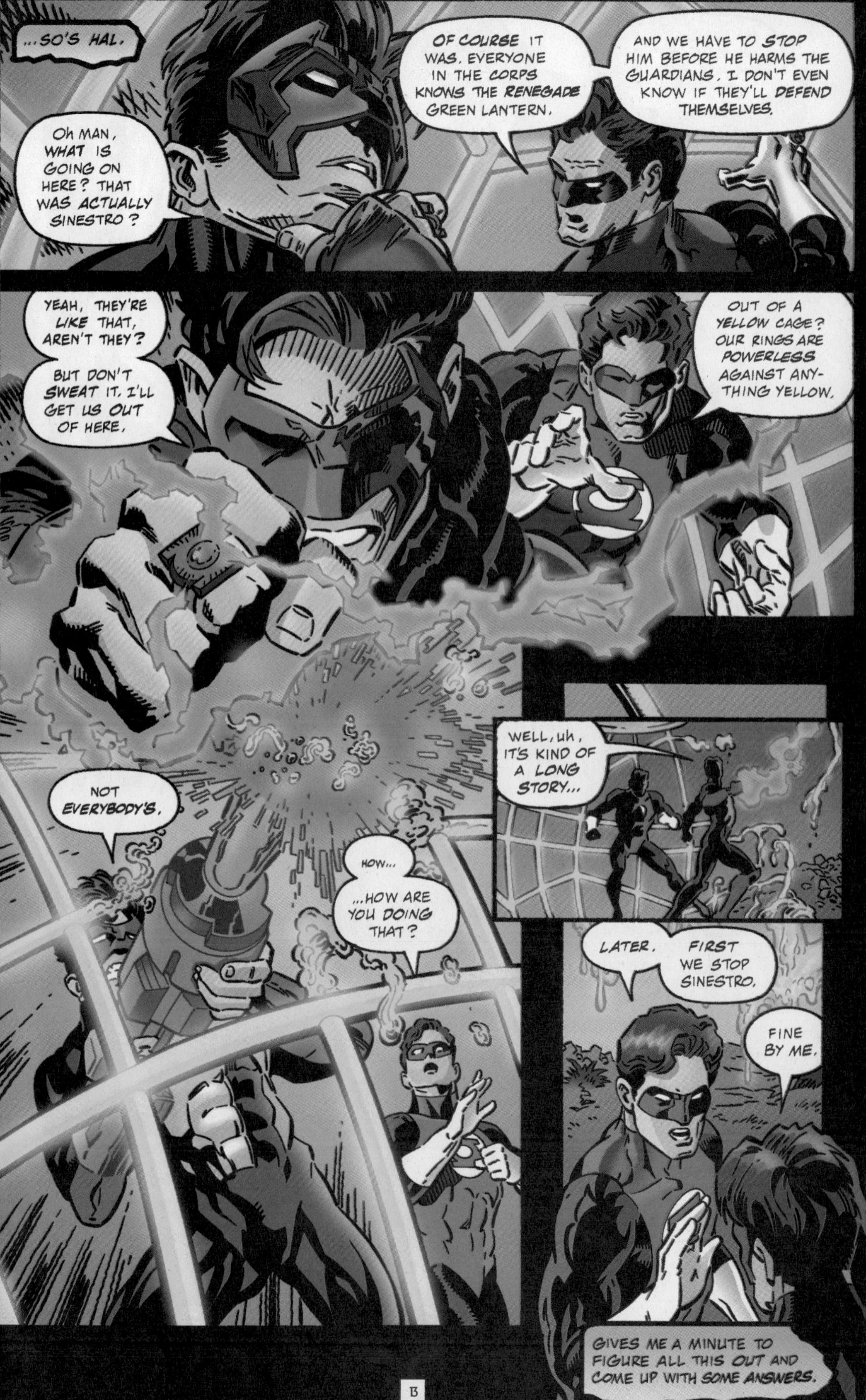
...SO'S HAL.
Oh MAN, WHAT IS GOING ON HERE? THAT WAS ACTUALLY SINESTRO?
OF COURSE IT WAS. EVERYONE IN THE CORPS KNOWS THE RENEGADE GREEN LANTERN.
AND WE HAVE TO STOP HIM BEFORE HE HARMS THE GUARDIANS. I DON'T EVEN KNOW IF THEY'LL DEFEND THEMSELVES.
OUT OF A YELLOW CAGE? OUR RINGS ARE POWERLESS AGAINST ANYTHING YELLOW.
YEAH, THEY'RE LIKE THAT, AREN'T THEY?
BUT DON'T SWEAT IT. I'LL GET US OUT OF HERE.
NOT EVERYBODY'S.
HOW...
...HOW ARE YOU DOING THAT?
WELL, uh, IT'S KIND OF A LONG STORY...
LATER.
FIRST WE STOP SINESTRO.
FINE BY ME.
GIVES ME A MINUTE TO FIGURE ALL THIS OUT AND COME UP WITH SOME ANSWERS.

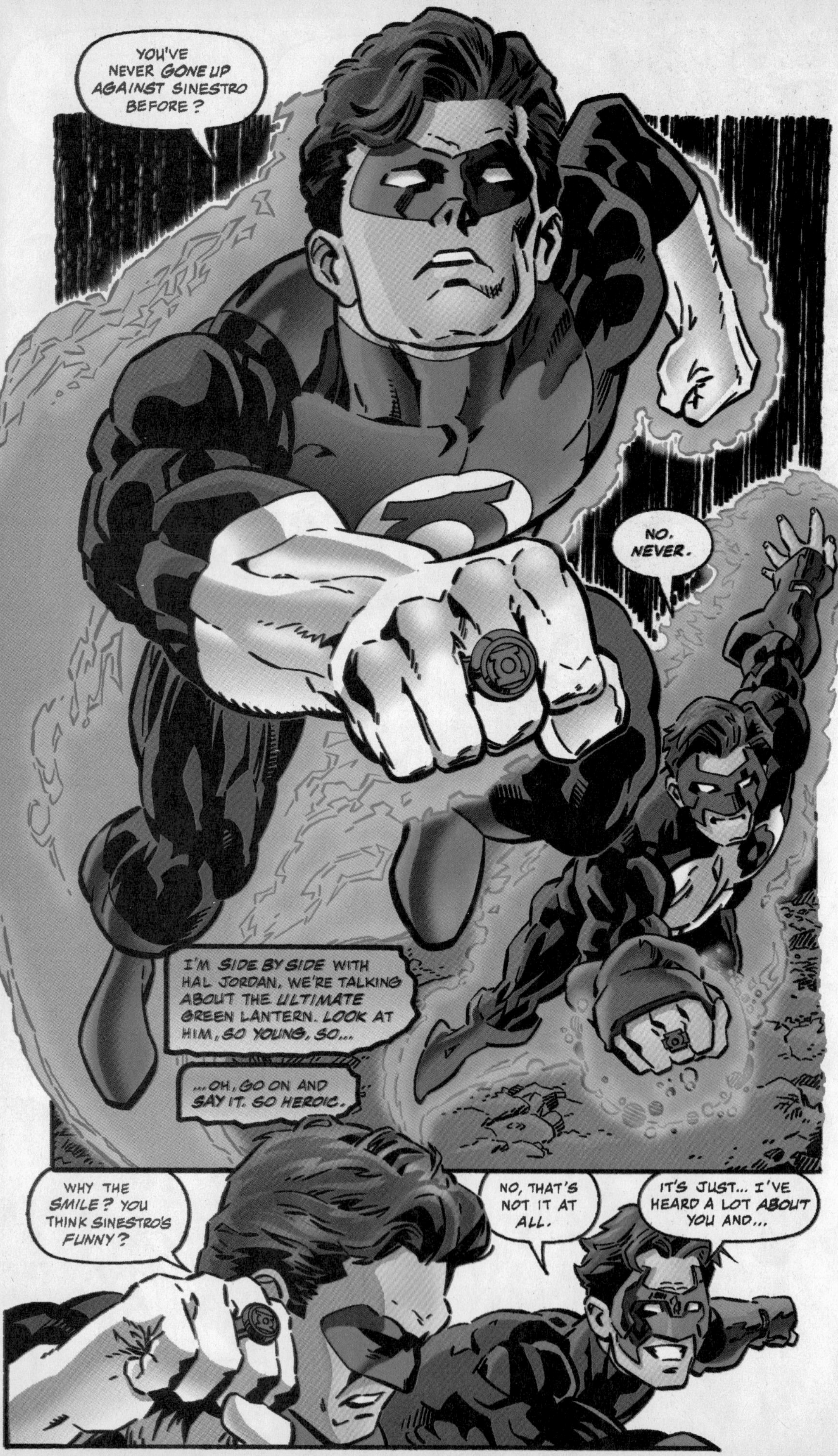

YOU'VE NEVER GONE UP AGAINST SINESTRO BEFORE?
NO. NEVER.
I'M SIDE BY SIDE WITH HAL JORDAN. WE'RE TALKING ABOUT THE ULTIMATE GREEN LANTERN. LOOK AT HIM, SO YOUNG, SO...
...OH, GO ON AND SAY IT. SO HEROIC.
WHY THE SMILE? YOU THINK SINESTRO'S FUNNY?
NO, THAT'S NOT IT AT ALL.
IT'S JUST... I'VE HEARD A LOT ABOUT YOU AND...

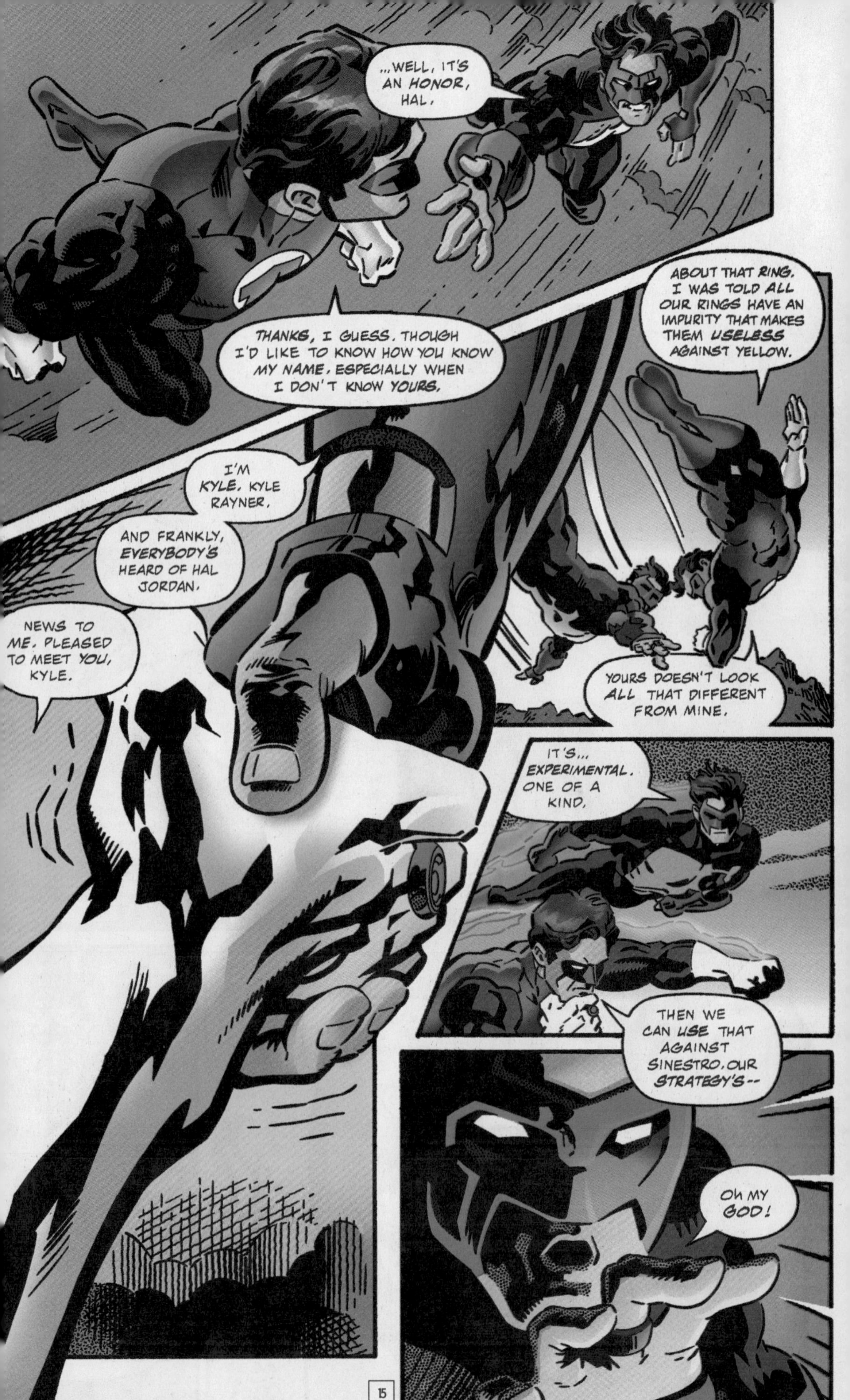
...WELL, IT'S AN HONOR, HAL.
THANKS, I GUESS. THOUGH I'D LIKE TO KNOW HOW YOU KNOW MY NAME, ESPECIALLY WHEN I DON'T KNOW YOURS.
I'M KYLE. KYLE RAYNER.
AND FRANKLY, EVERYBODY'S HEARD OF HAL JORDAN.
NEWS TO ME. PLEASED TO MEET YOU, KYLE.
ABOUT THAT RING. I WAS TOLD ALL OUR RINGS HAVE AN IMPURITY THAT MAKES THEM USELESS AGAINST YELLOW.
YOURS DOESN'T LOOK ALL THAT DIFFERENT FROM MINE.
IT'S... EXPERIMENTAL. ONE OF A KIND.
THEN WE CAN USE THAT AGAINST SINESTRO. OUR STRATEGY'S--
Oh MY GOD!

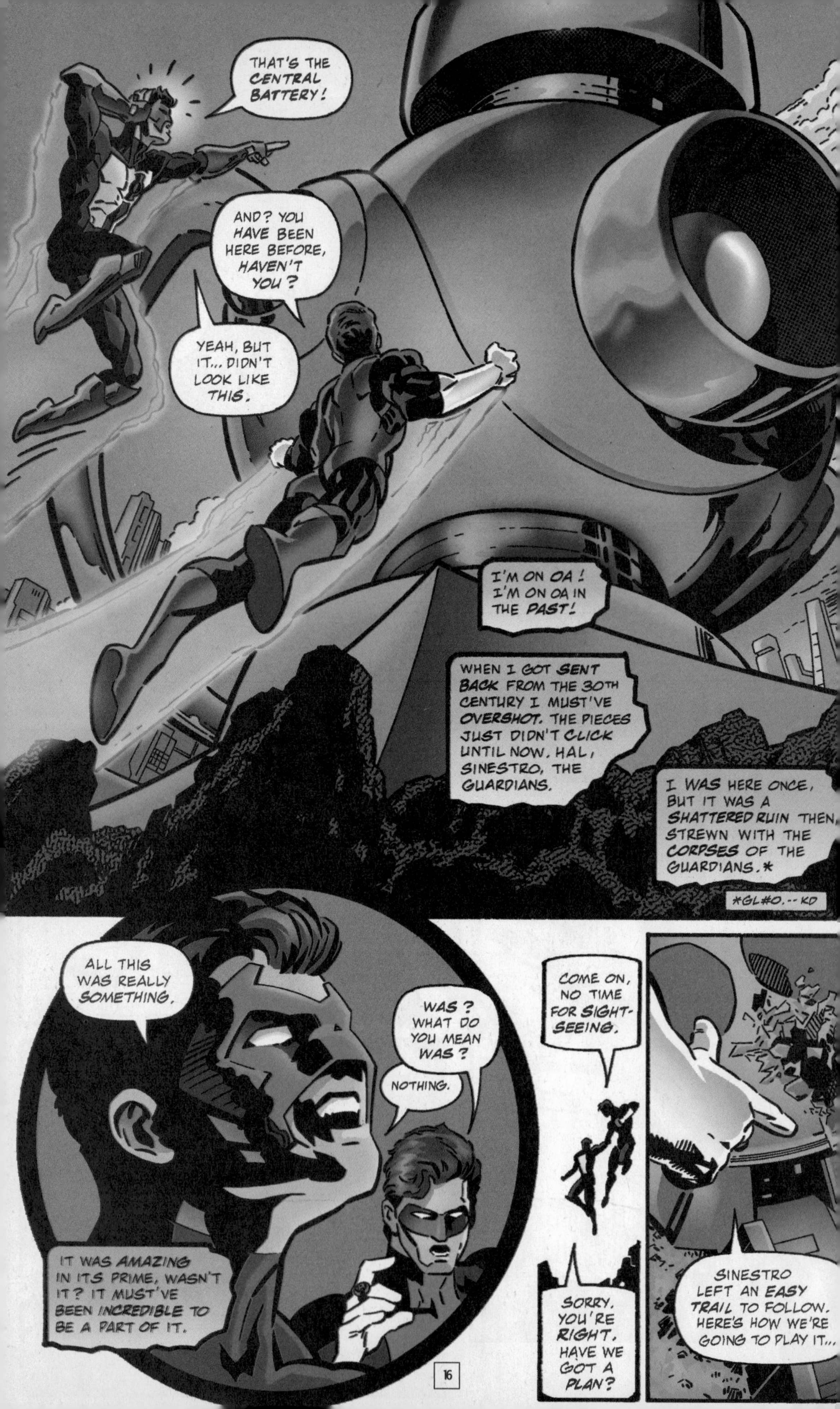
THAT'S THE CENTRAL BATTERY!
AND? YOU HAVE BEEN HERE BEFORE, HAVEN'T YOU?
YEAH, BUT IT... DIDN'T LOOK LIKE THIS.
I'M ON OA! I'M ON OA IN THE PAST!
WHEN I GOT SENT BACK FROM THE 30TH CENTURY I MUST'VE OVERSHOT. THE PIECES JUST DIDN'T CLICK UNTIL NOW. HAL, SINESTRO, THE GUARDIANS.
I WAS HERE ONCE, BUT IT WAS A SHATTERED RUIN THEN, STREWN WITH THE CORPSES OF THE GUARDIANS.*
*GL#0. -- KD
ALL THIS WAS REALLY SOMETHING.
WAS? WHAT DO YOU MEAN WAS?
NOTHING.
IT WAS AMAZING IN ITS PRIME, WASN'T IT? IT MUST'VE BEEN INCREDIBLE TO BE A PART OF IT.
COME ON, NO TIME FOR SIGHT-SEEING.
SORRY. YOU'RE RIGHT. HAVE WE GOT A PLAN?
SINESTRO LEFT AN EASY TRAIL TO FOLLOW. HERE'S HOW WE'RE GOING TO PLAY IT...

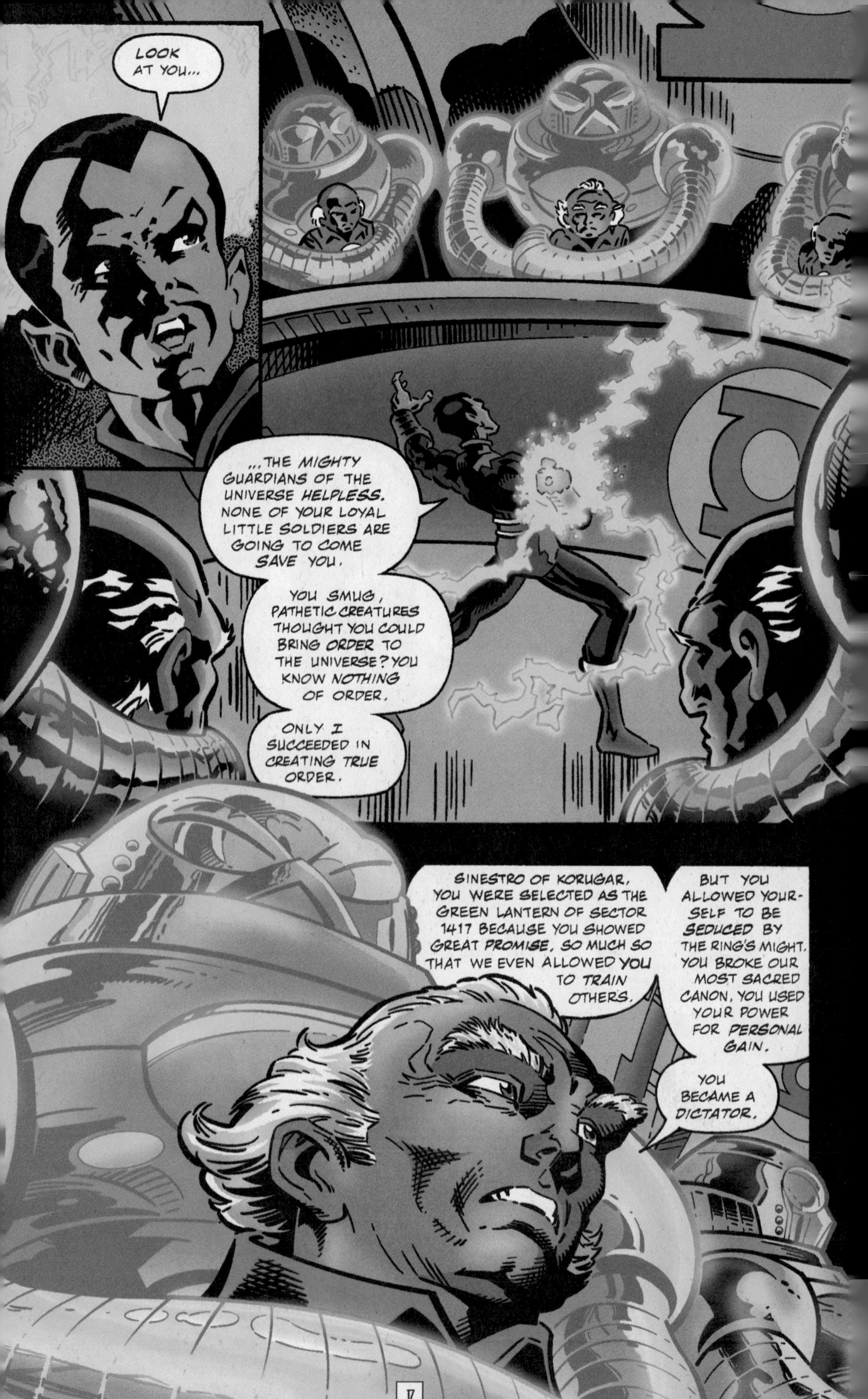
LOOK AT YOU...
...THE MIGHTY GUARDIANS OF THE UNIVERSE HELPLESS. NONE OF YOUR LOYAL LITTLE SOLDIERS ARE GOING TO COME SAVE YOU.
YOU SMUG, PATHETIC CREATURES THOUGHT YOU COULD BRING ORDER TO THE UNIVERSE? YOU KNOW NOTHING OF ORDER.
ONLY I SUCCEEDED IN CREATING TRUE ORDER.
SINESTRO OF KORUGAR, YOU WERE SELECTED AS THE GREEN LANTERN OF SECTOR 1417 BECAUSE YOU SHOWED GREAT PROMISE, SO MUCH SO THAT WE EVEN ALLOWED YOU TO TRAIN OTHERS.
BUT YOU ALLOWED YOURSELF TO BE SEDUCED BY THE RING'S MIGHT. YOU BROKE OUR MOST SACRED CANON. YOU USED YOUR POWER FOR PERSONAL GAIN.
YOU BECAME A DICTATOR.

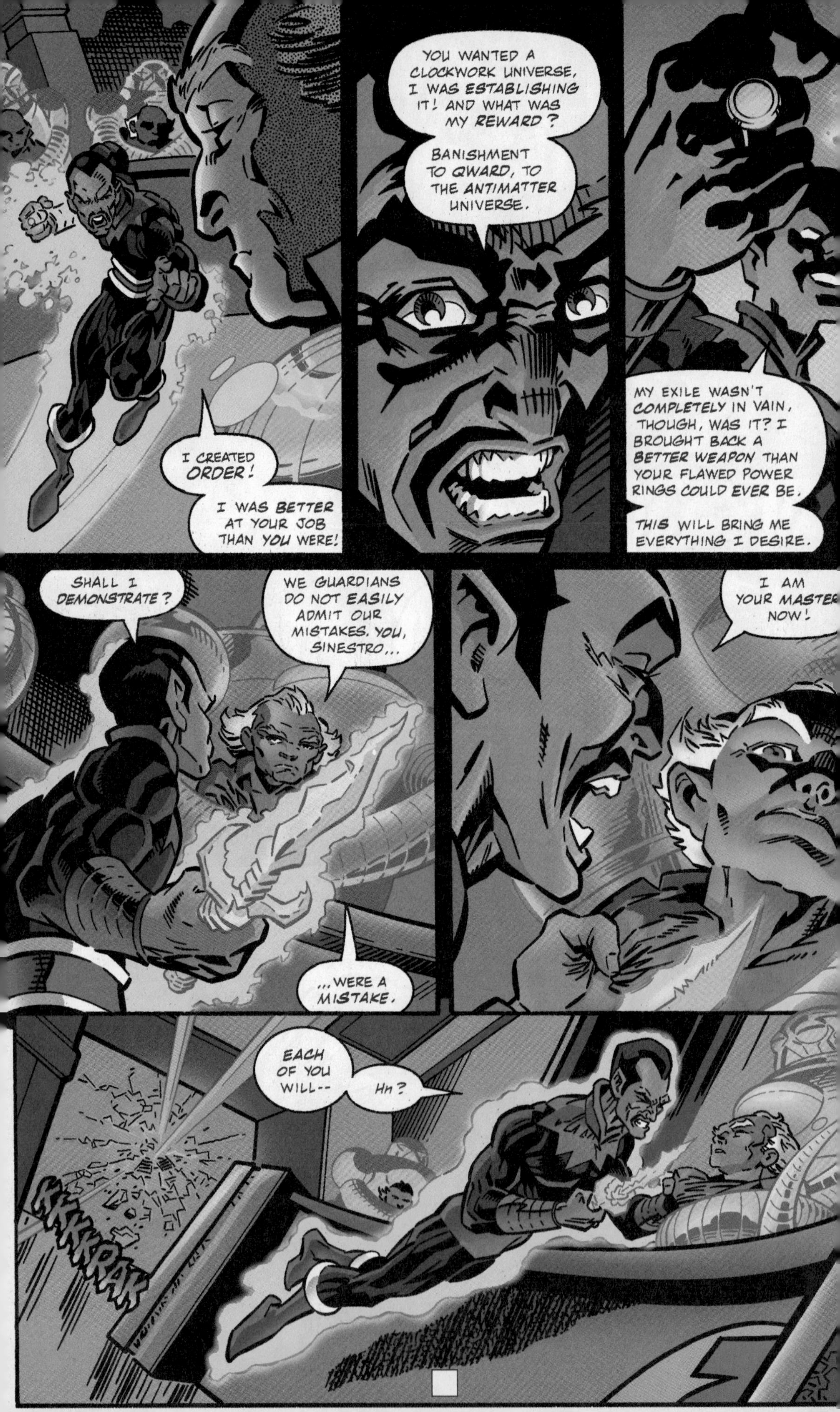
I CREATED ORDER!
I WAS BETTER AT YOUR JOB THAN YOU WERE!
YOU WANTED A CLOCKWORK UNIVERSE, I WAS ESTABLISHING IT! AND WHAT WAS MY REWARD?
BANISHMENT TO QWARD, TO THE ANTIMATTER UNIVERSE.
MY EXILE WASN'T COMPLETELY IN VAIN, THOUGH, WAS IT? I BROUGHT BACK A BETTER WEAPON THAN YOUR FLAWED POWER RINGS COULD EVER BE.
THIS WILL BRING ME EVERYTHING I DESIRE.
SHALL I DEMONSTRATE?
WE GUARDIANS DO NOT EASILY ADMIT OUR MISTAKES. YOU, SINESTRO...
...WERE A MISTAKE.
I AM YOUR MASTER NOW!
EACH OF YOU WILL--
Hn?
SKKRAK

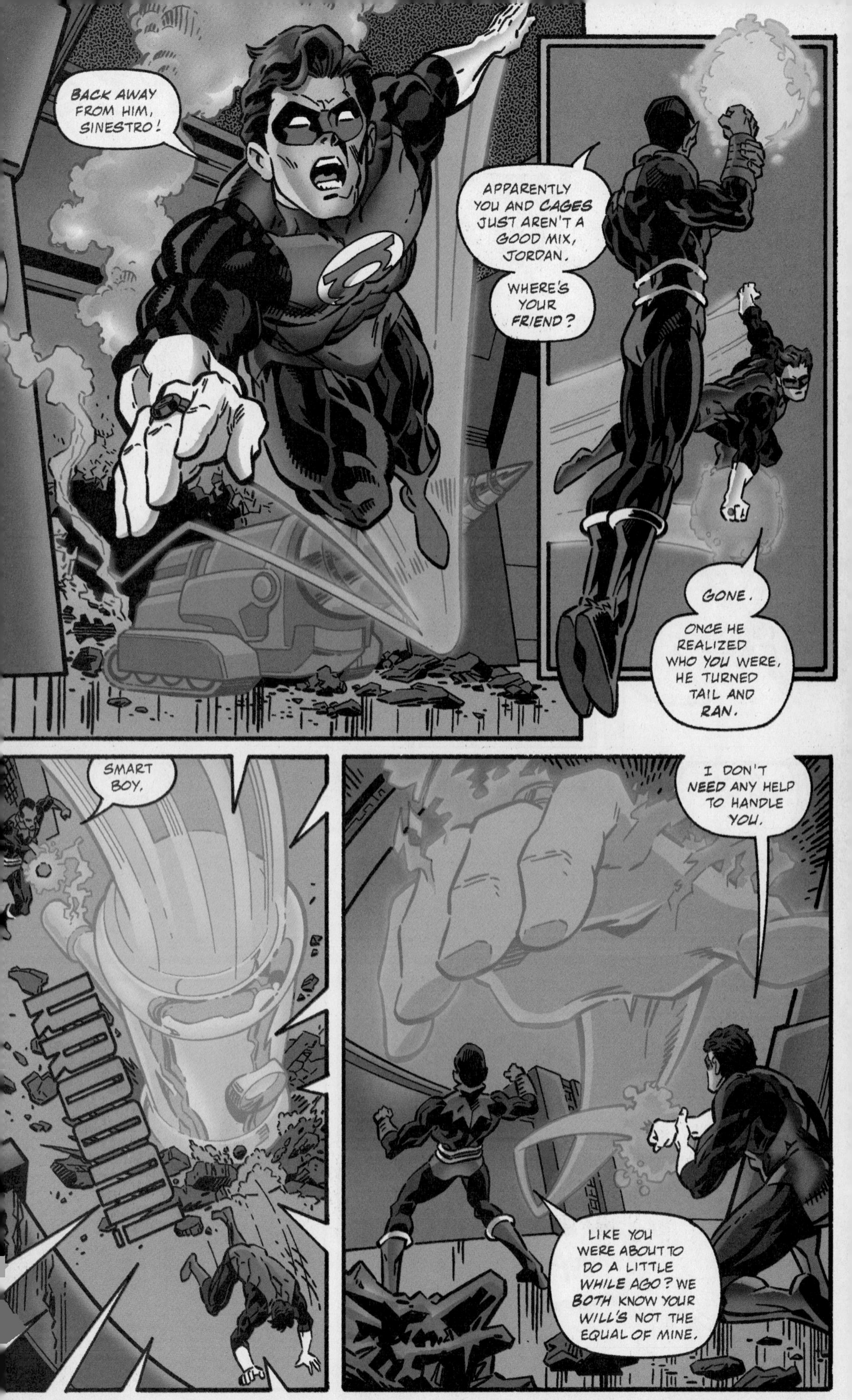

BACK AWAY FROM HIM, SINESTRO!
APPARENTLY YOU AND CAGES JUST AREN'T A GOOD MIX, JORDAN.
WHERE'S YOUR FRIEND?
GONE.
ONCE HE REALIZED WHO YOU WERE, HE TURNED TAIL AND RAN.
SMART BOY.
I DON'T NEED ANY HELP TO HANDLE YOU.
LIKE YOU WERE ABOUT TO DO A LITTLE WHILE AGO? WE BOTH KNOW YOUR WILL'S NOT THE EQUAL OF MINE.

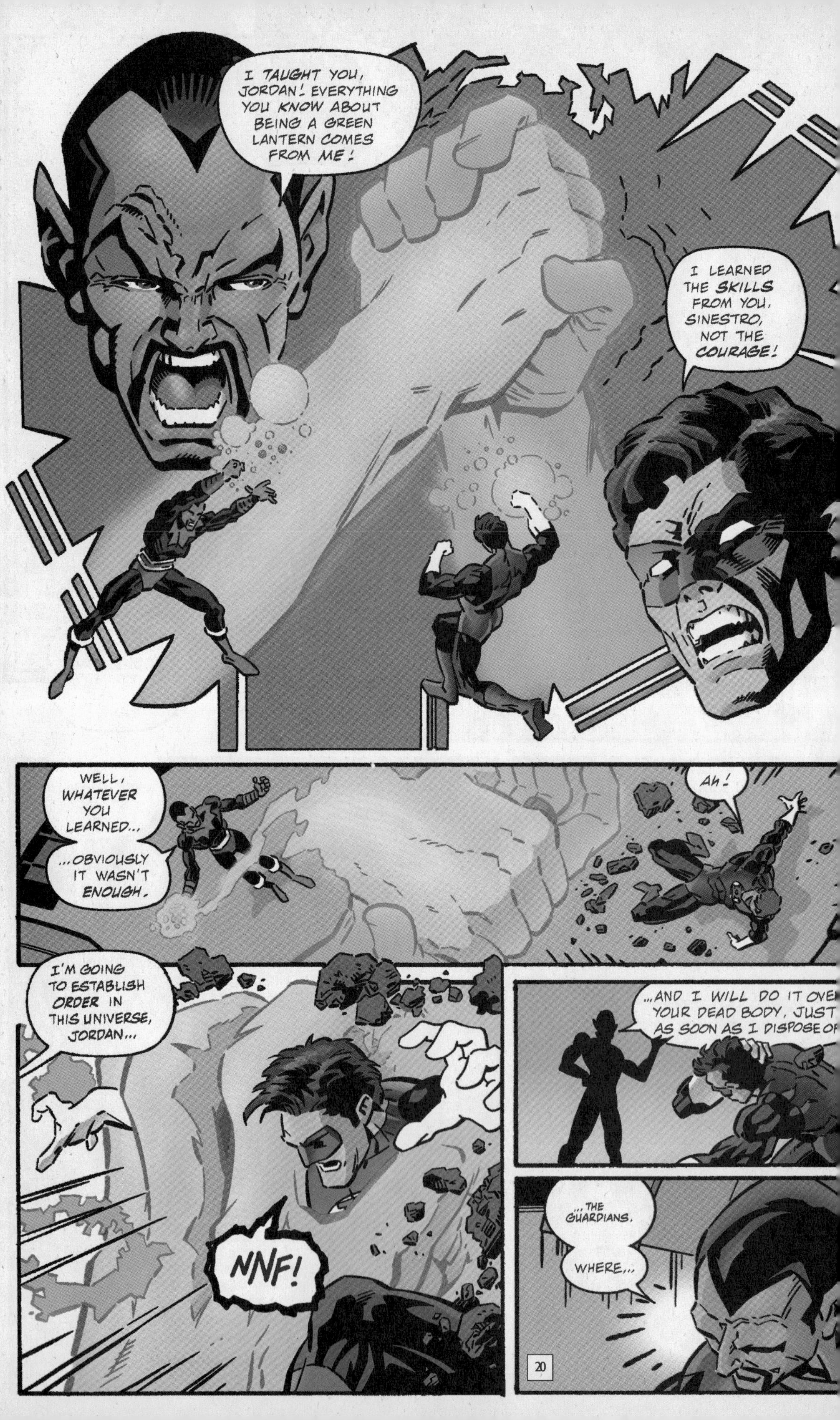

I TAUGHT YOU, JORDAN! EVERYTHING YOU KNOW ABOUT BEING A GREEN LANTERN COMES FROM ME!
I LEARNED THE SKILLS FROM YOU, SINESTRO, NOT THE COURAGE!
WELL, WHATEVER YOU LEARNED...
...OBVIOUSLY IT WASN'T ENOUGH.
AH!
I'M GOING TO ESTABLISH ORDER IN THIS UNIVERSE, JORDAN...
NNF!
...AND I WILL DO IT OVE
YOUR DEAD BODY, JUST
AS SOON AS I DISPOSE OF
...THE GUARDIANS.
WHERE...

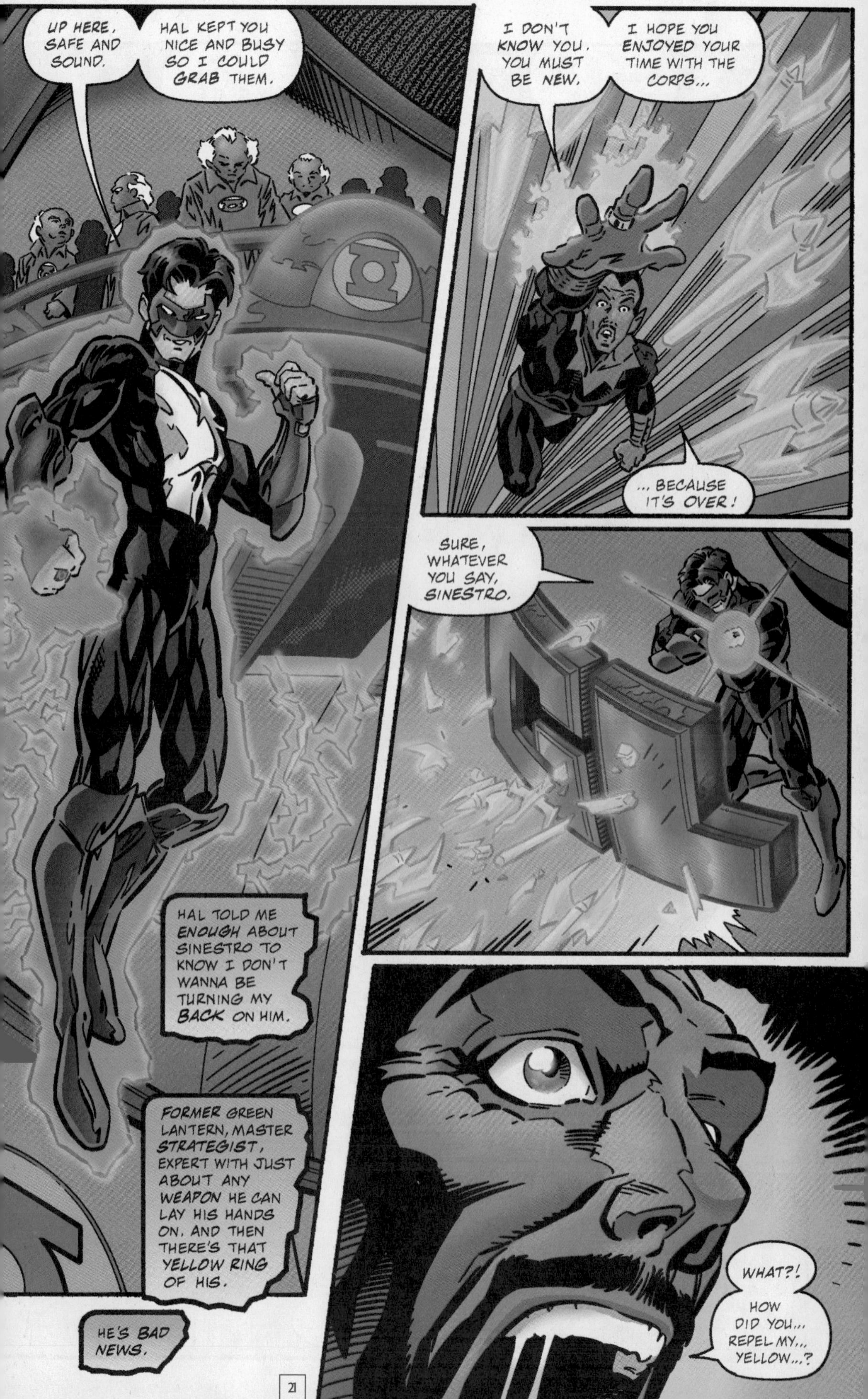
UP HERE. SAFE AND SOUND.
HAL KEPT YOU NICE AND BUSY SO I COULD GRAB THEM.
I DON'T KNOW YOU. YOU MUST BE NEW.
I HOPE YOU ENJOYED YOUR TIME WITH THE CORPS...
...BECAUSE IT'S OVER!
SURE, WHATEVER YOU SAY, SINESTRO.
HAL TOLD ME ENOUGH ABOUT SINESTRO TO KNOW I DON'T WANNA BE TURNING MY BACK ON HIM.
FORMER GREEN LANTERN, MASTER STRATEGIST, EXPERT WITH JUST ABOUT ANY WEAPON HE CAN LAY HIS HANDS ON. AND THEN THERE'S THAT YELLOW RING OF HIS.
HE'S BAD NEWS.
WHAT?!
HOW DID YOU... REPEL MY... YELLOW...?

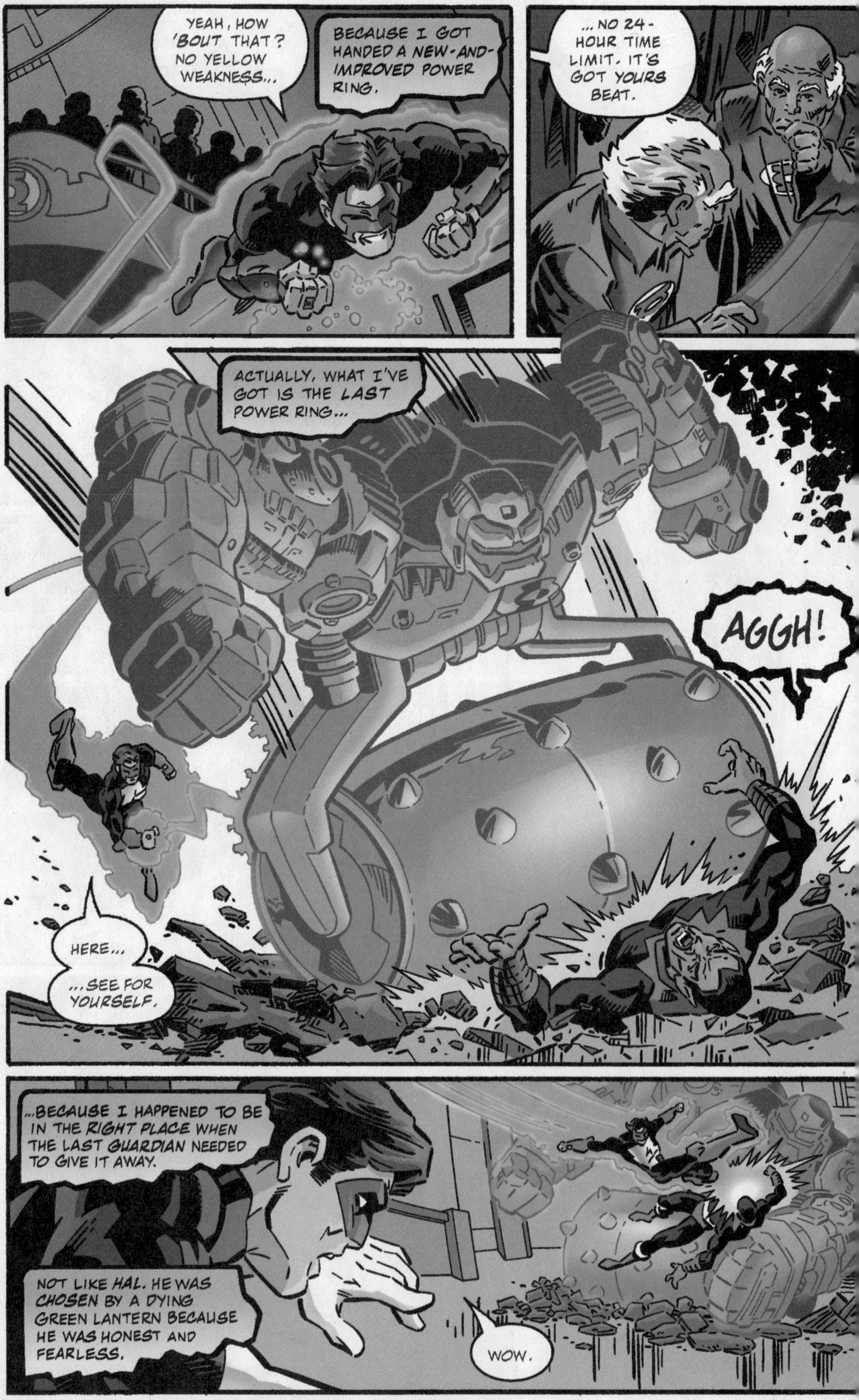
YEAH, HOW 'BOUT THAT? NO YELLOW WEAKNESS...
BECAUSE I GOT HANDED A NEW-AND-IMPROVED POWER RING.
...NO 24-HOUR TIME LIMIT. IT'S GOT YOURS BEAT.
ACTUALLY, WHAT I'VE GOT IS THE LAST POWER RING...
AGGH!
HERE...
...SEE FOR YOURSELF.
...BECAUSE I HAPPENED TO BE IN THE RIGHT PLACE WHEN THE LAST GUARDIAN NEEDED TO GIVE IT AWAY.
NOT LIKE HAL. HE WAS CHOSEN BY A DYING GREEN LANTERN BECAUSE HE WAS HONEST AND FEARLESS.
WOW.

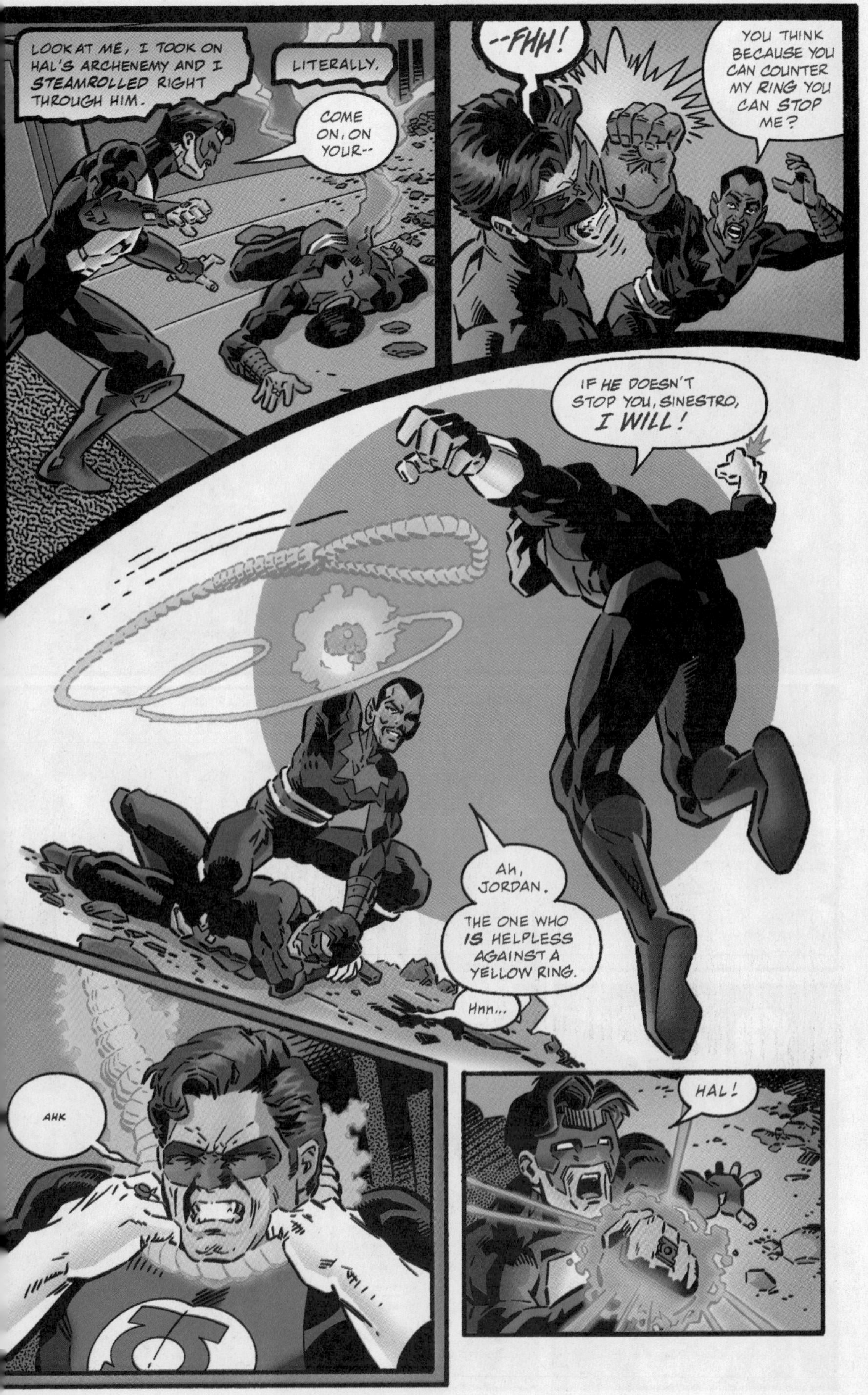
LOOK AT ME, I TOOK ON HAL'S ARCHENEMY AND I STEAMROLLED RIGHT THROUGH HIM.
LITERALLY.
COME ON, ON YOUR--
--FHH!
YOU THINK BECAUSE YOU CAN COUNTER MY RING YOU CAN STOP ME?
IF HE DOESN'T STOP YOU, SINESTRO, I WILL!
Ah, JORDAN.
THE ONE WHO IS HELPLESS AGAINST A YELLOW RING.
Hnn...
AHK
HAL!

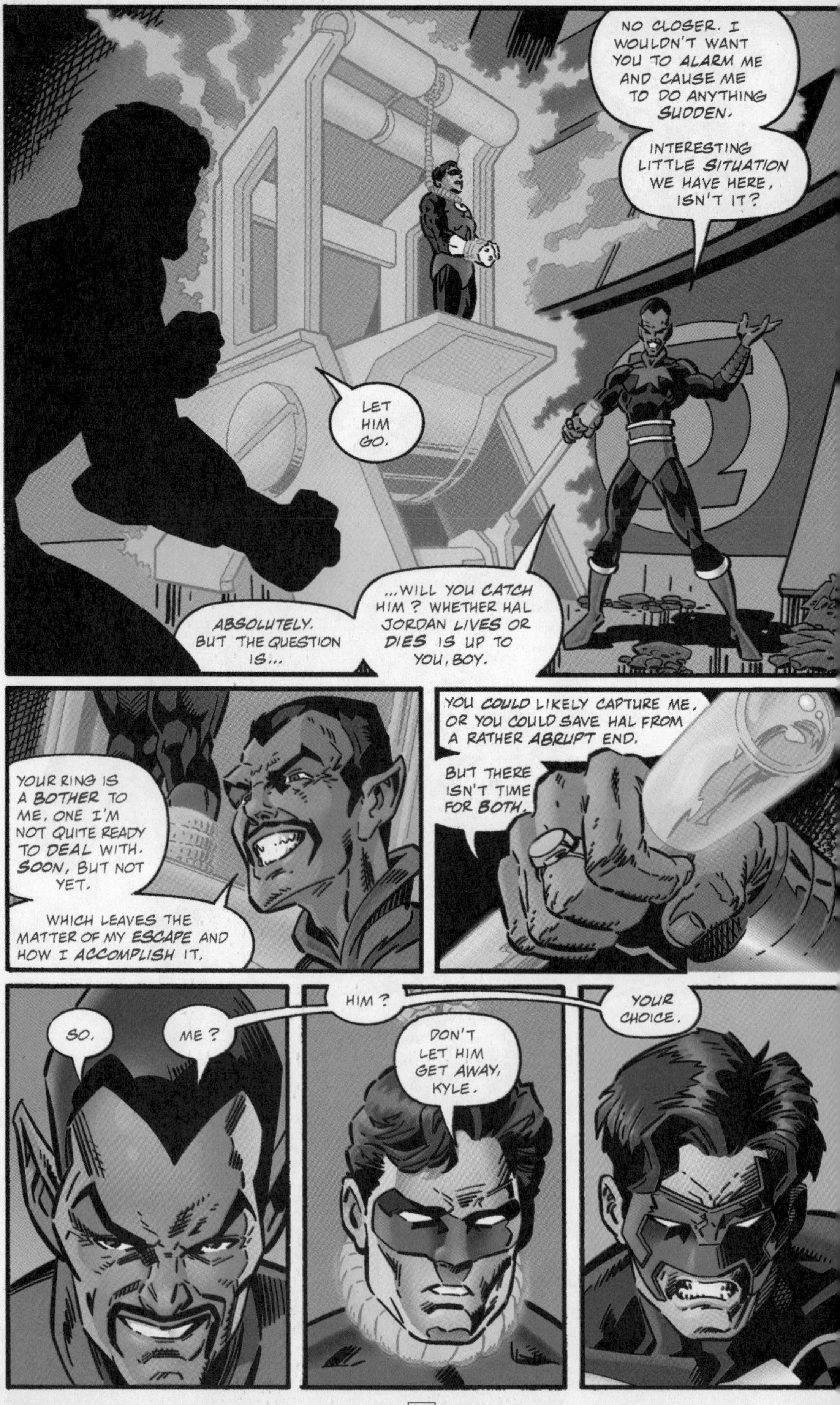

NO CLOSER. I WOULDN'T WANT YOU TO ALARM ME AND CAUSE ME TO DO ANYTHING SUDDEN.
INTERESTING LITTLE SITUATION WE HAVE HERE, ISN'T IT?
LET HIM GO.
ABSOLUTELY. BUT THE QUESTION IS...
...WILL YOU CATCH HIM? WHETHER HAL JORDAN LIVES OR DIES IS UP TO YOU, BOY.
YOUR RING IS A BOTHER TO ME. ONE I'M NOT QUITE READY TO DEAL WITH. SOON, BUT NOT YET.
WHICH LEAVES THE MATTER OF MY ESCAPE AND HOW I ACCOMPLISH IT.
YOU COULD LIKELY CAPTURE ME. OR YOU COULD SAVE HAL FROM A RATHER ABRUPT END.
BUT THERE ISN'T TIME FOR BOTH.
SO.
ME?
HIM?
YOUR CHOICE.
DON'T LET HIM GET AWAY, KYLE.

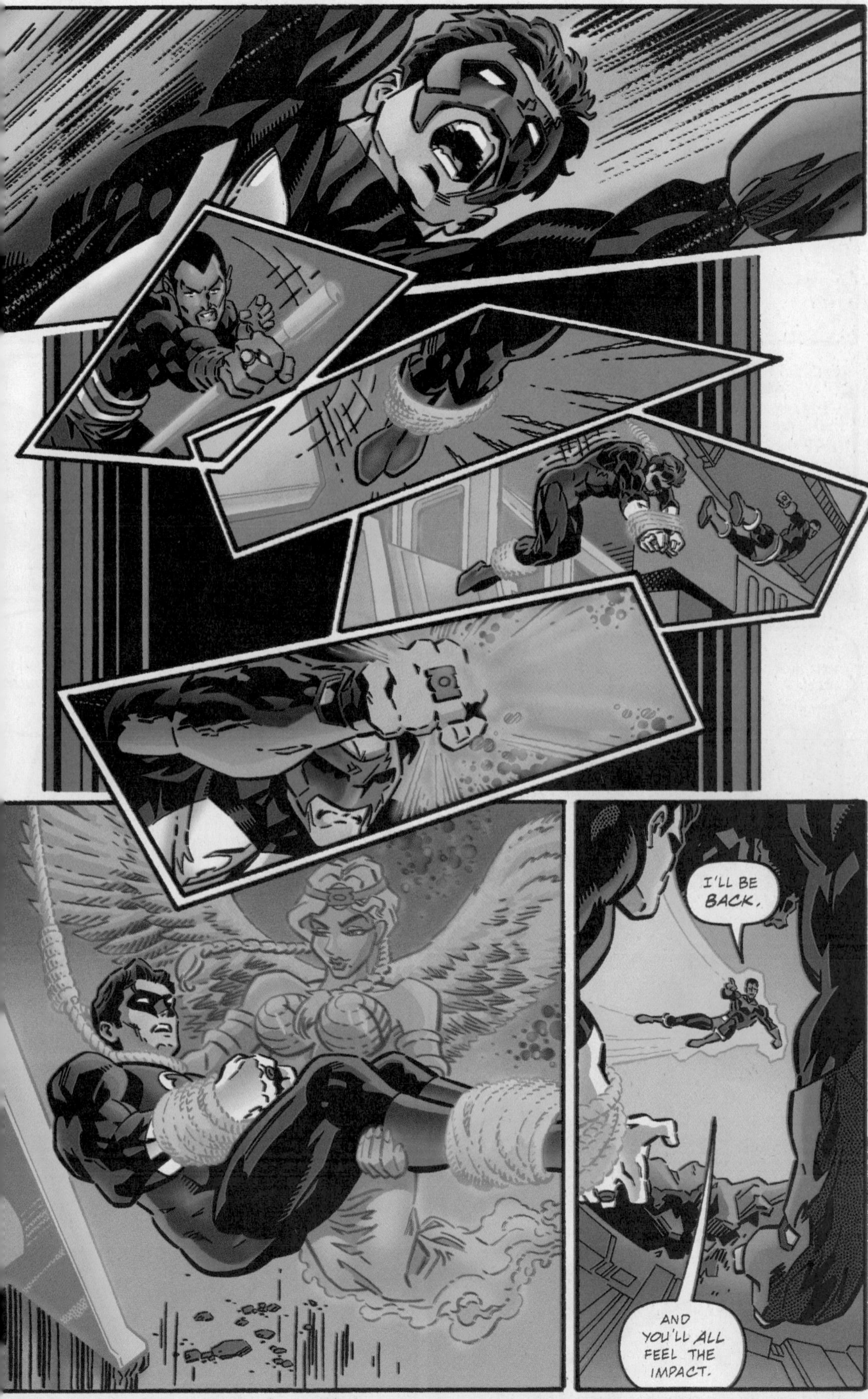
I'LL BE BACK.
AND YOU'LL ALL FEEL THE IMPACT.

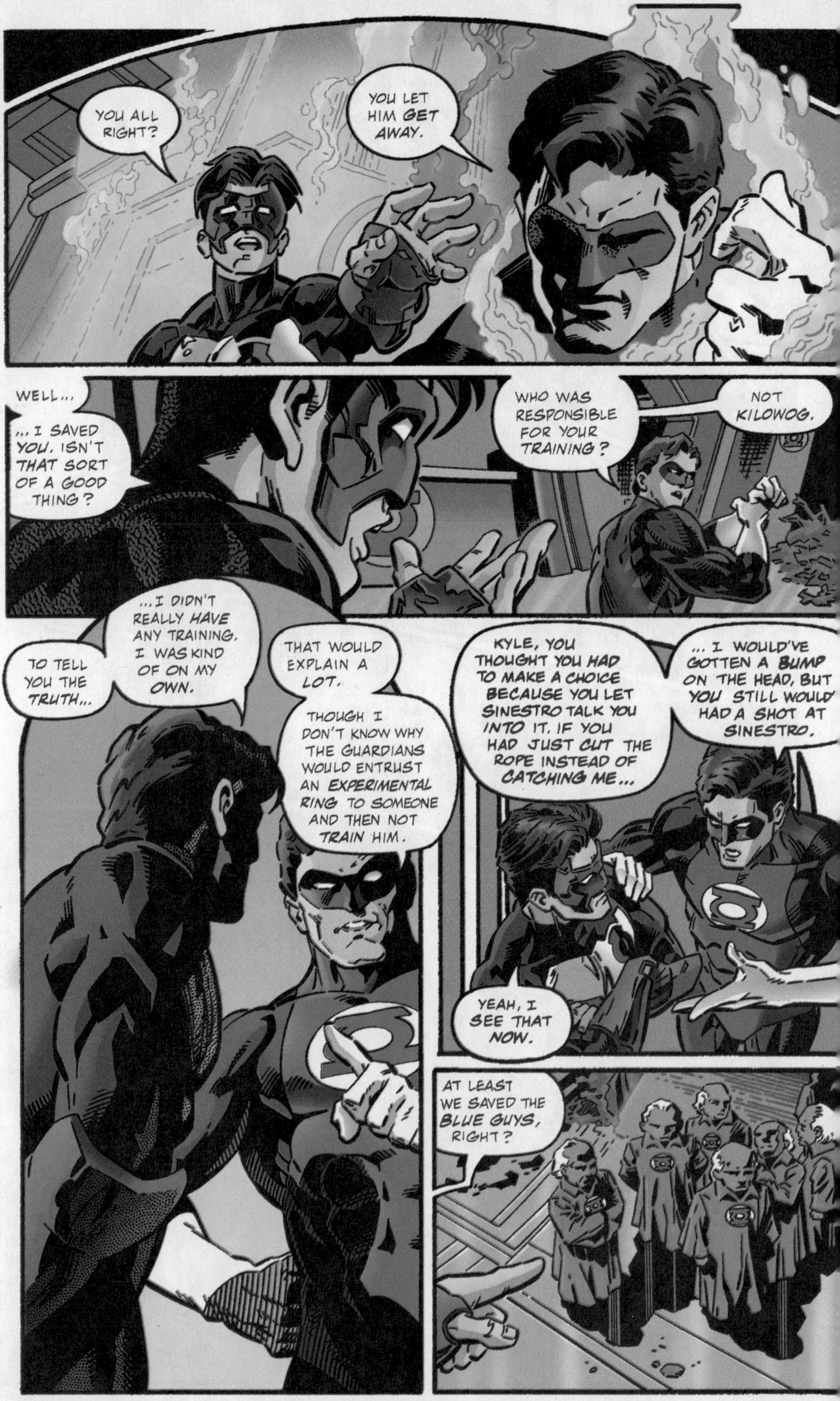

YOU ALL RIGHT?
YOU LET HIM GET AWAY.
WELL...
...I SAVED YOU. ISN'T THAT SORT OF A GOOD THING?
WHO WAS RESPONSIBLE FOR YOUR TRAINING?
NOT KILOWOG.
TO TELL YOU THE TRUTH...
...I DIDN'T REALLY HAVE ANY TRAINING. I WAS KIND OF ON MY OWN.
THAT WOULD EXPLAIN A LOT.
THOUGH I DON'T KNOW WHY THE GUARDIANS WOULD ENTRUST AN EXPERIMENTAL RING TO SOMEONE AND THEN NOT TRAIN HIM.
KYLE, YOU THOUGHT YOU HAD TO MAKE A CHOICE BECAUSE YOU LET SINESTRO TALK YOU INTO IT. IF YOU HAD JUST CUT THE ROPE INSTEAD OF CATCHING ME...
...I WOULD'VE GOTTEN A BUMP ON THE HEAD, BUT YOU STILL WOULD' HAD A SHOT AT SINESTRO.
YEAH, I SEE THAT NOW.
AT LEAST WE SAVED THE BLUE GUYS, RIGHT?

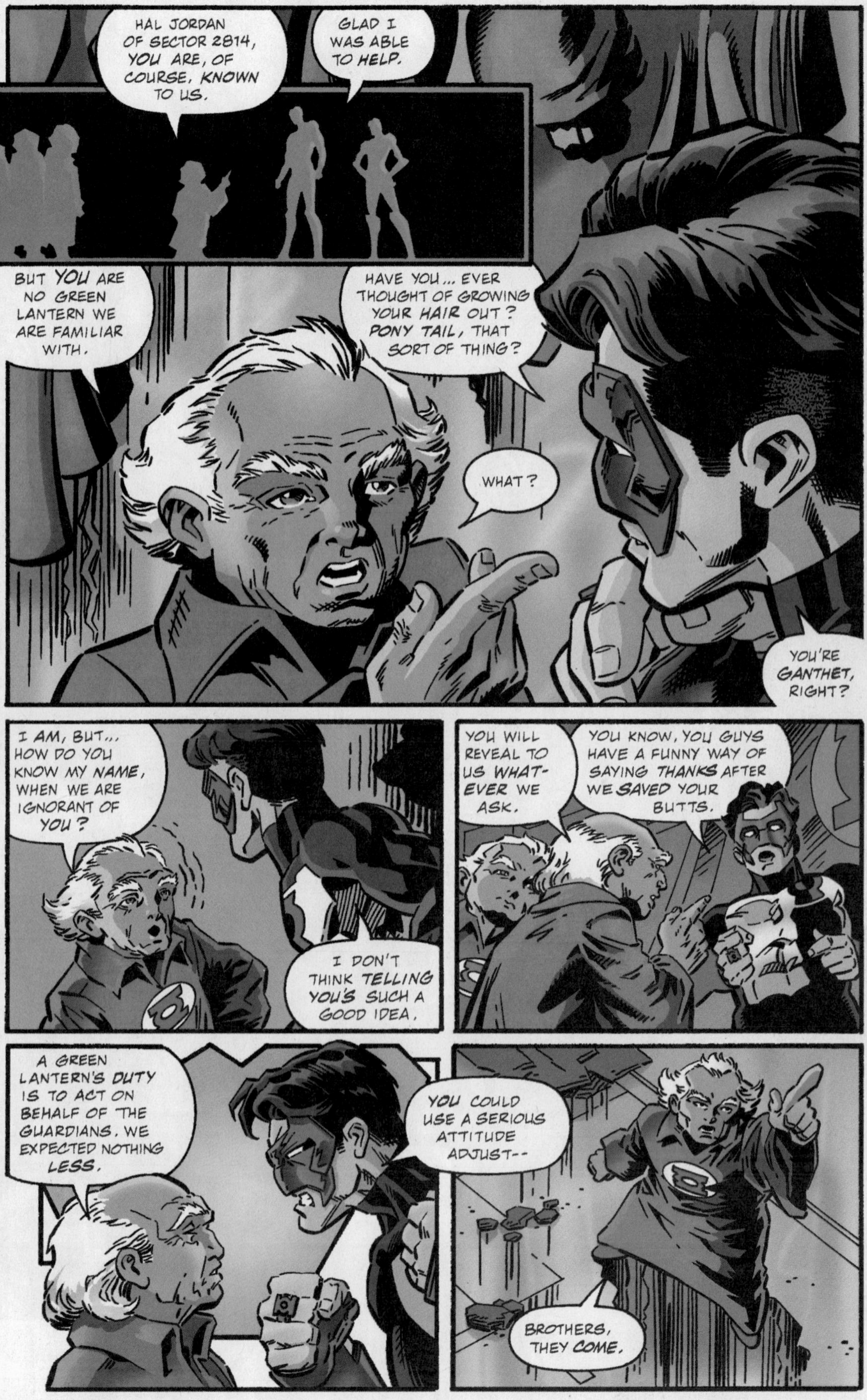
HAL JORDAN OF SECTOR 2814, YOU ARE, OF COURSE, KNOWN TO US.
GLAD I WAS ABLE TO HELP.
BUT YOU ARE NO GREEN LANTERN WE ARE FAMILIAR WITH.
HAVE YOU... EVER THOUGHT OF GROWING YOUR HAIR OUT? PONY TAIL, THAT SORT OF THING?
WHAT?
YOU'RE GANTHET, RIGHT?
I AM, BUT... HOW DO YOU KNOW MY NAME, WHEN WE ARE IGNORANT OF YOU?
I DON'T THINK TELLING YOU'S SUCH A GOOD IDEA.
YOU WILL REVEAL TO US WHATEVER WE ASK.
YOU KNOW, YOU GUYS HAVE A FUNNY WAY OF SAYING THANKS AFTER WE SAVED YOUR BUTTS.
A GREEN LANTERN'S DUTY IS TO ACT ON BEHALF OF THE GUARDIANS. WE EXPECTED NOTHING LESS.
YOU COULD USE A SERIOUS ATTITUDE ADJUST--
BROTHERS, THEY COME.

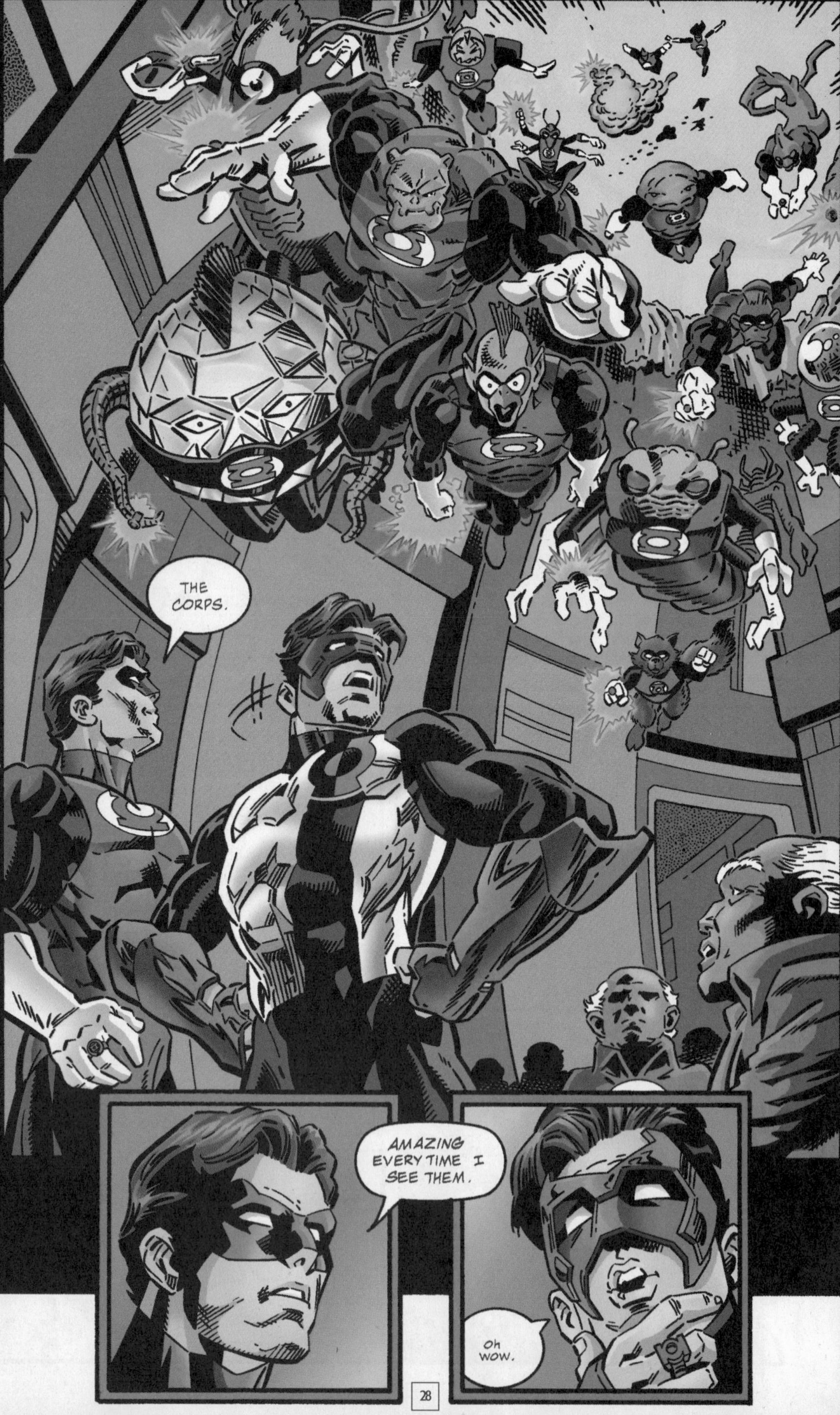
THE CORPS.
AMAZING EVERY TIME I SEE THEM.
Oh WOW.

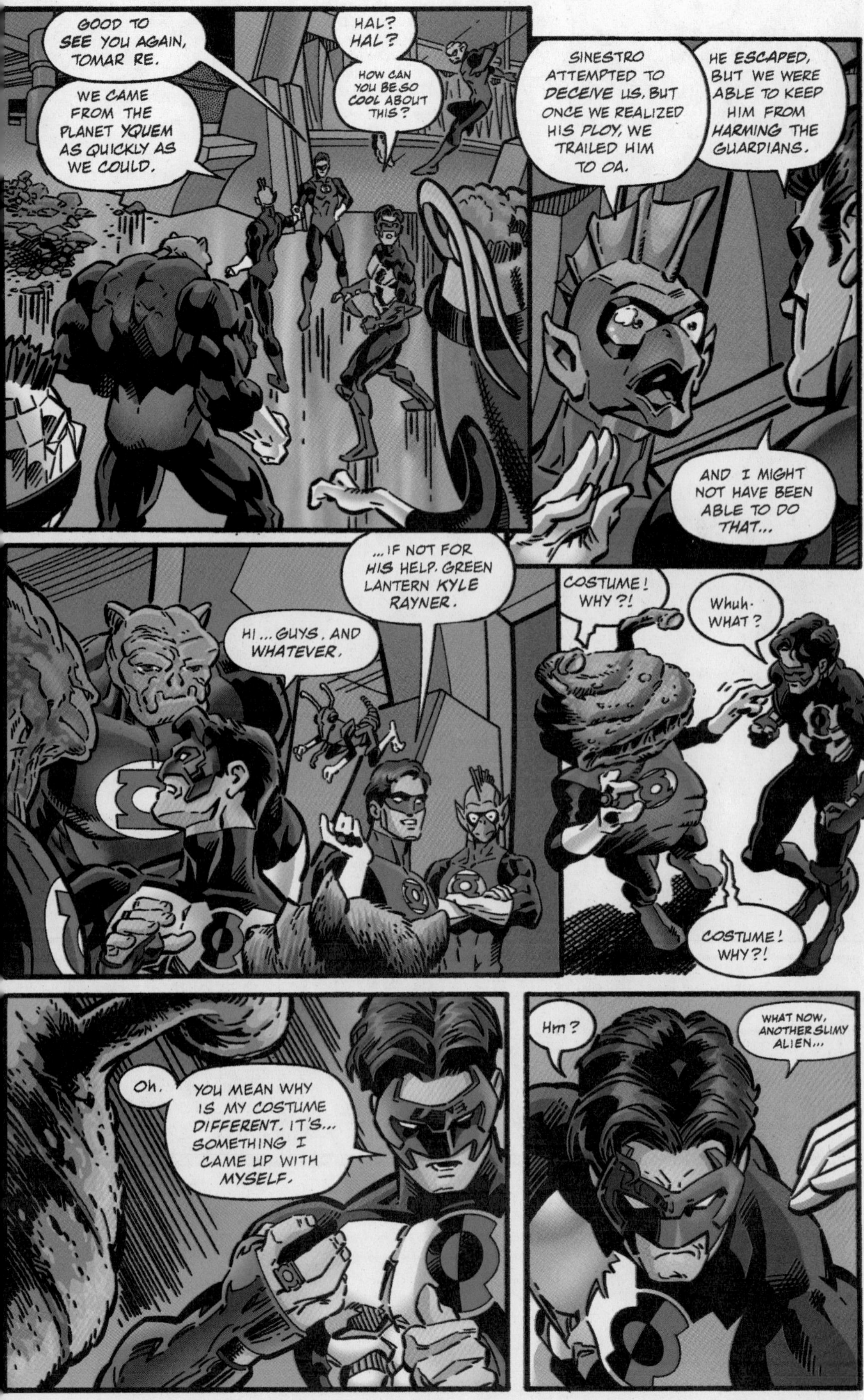
GOOD TO SEE YOU AGAIN, TOMAR RE.
WE CAME FROM THE PLANET YQUEM AS QUICKLY AS WE COULD.
HAL? HAL?
HOW CAN YOU BE SO COOL ABOUT THIS?
SINESTRO ATTEMPTED TO DECEIVE US, BUT ONCE WE REALIZED HIS PLOY, WE TRAILED HIM TO OA.
HE ESCAPED, BUT WE WERE ABLE TO KEEP HIM FROM HARMING THE GUARDIANS.
AND I MIGHT NOT HAVE BEEN ABLE TO DO THAT...
...IF NOT FOR HIS HELP. GREEN LANTERN KYLE RAYNER.
HI ... GUYS, AND WHATEVER.
COSTUME! WHY?!
Whuh. WHAT?
COSTUME! WHY?!
Oh.
YOU MEAN WHY IS MY COSTUME DIFFERENT. IT'S... SOMETHING I CAME UP WITH MYSELF.
Hm?
WHAT NOW, ANOTHER SLIMY ALIEN...

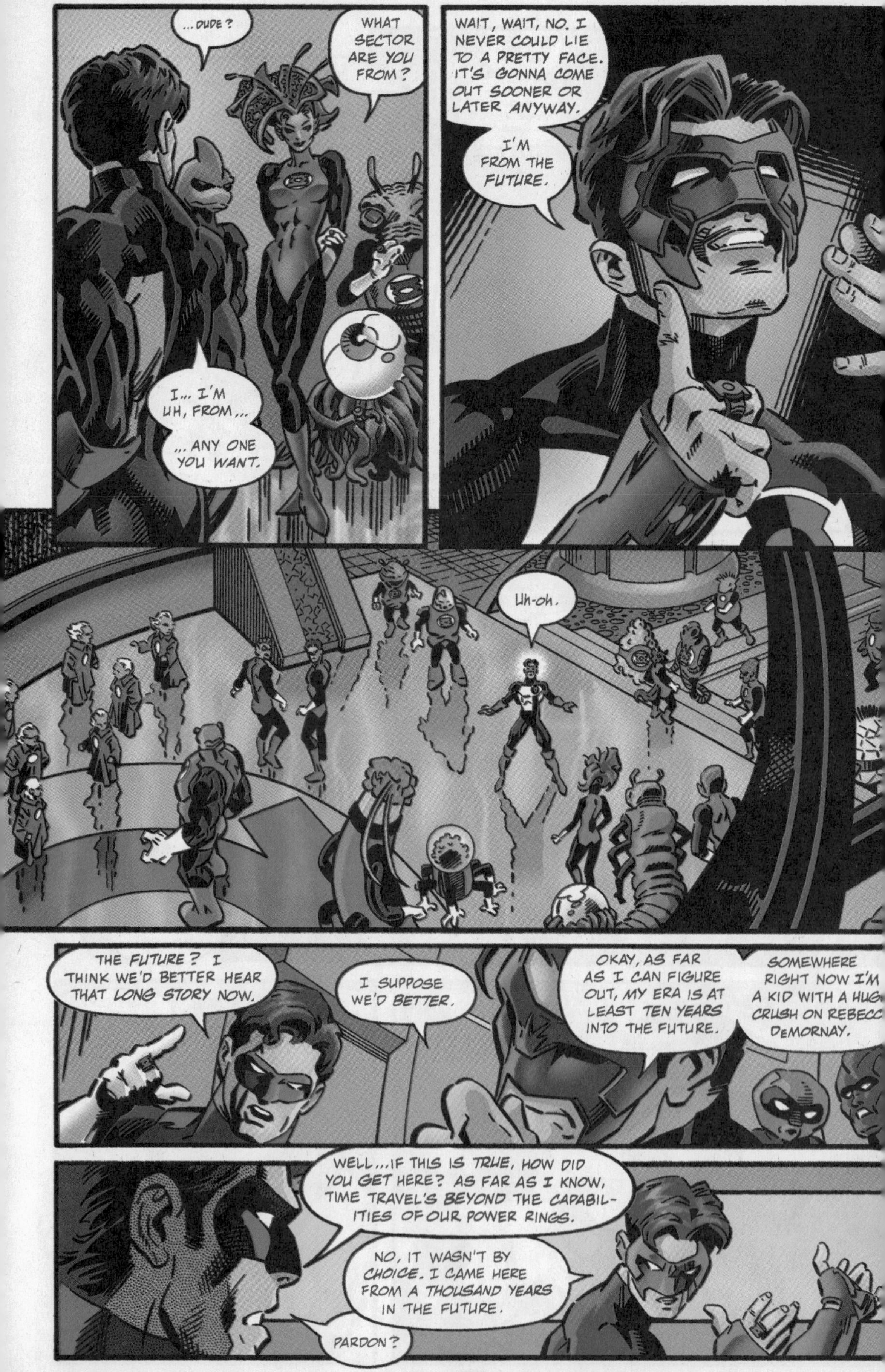
...DUDE?
WHAT SECTOR ARE YOU FROM?
I... I'M UH, FROM...
...ANY ONE YOU WANT.
WAIT, WAIT, NO. I NEVER COULD LIE TO A PRETTY FACE. IT'S GONNA COME OUT SOONER OR LATER ANYWAY.
I'M FROM THE FUTURE.
Uh-oh.
THE FUTURE? I THINK WE'D BETTER HEAR THAT LONG STORY NOW.
I SUPPOSE WE'D BETTER.
OKAY, AS FAR AS I CAN FIGURE OUT, MY ERA IS AT LEAST TEN YEARS INTO THE FUTURE.
SOMEWHERE RIGHT NOW I'M A KID WITH A HUG CRUSH ON REBECC DEMORNAY.
WELL...IF THIS IS TRUE, HOW DID YOU GET HERE? AS FAR AS I KNOW, TIME TRAVEL'S BEYOND THE CAPABIL-ITIES OF OUR POWER RINGS.
NO, IT WASN'T BY CHOICE. I CAME HERE FROM A THOUSAND YEARS IN THE FUTURE.
PARDON?

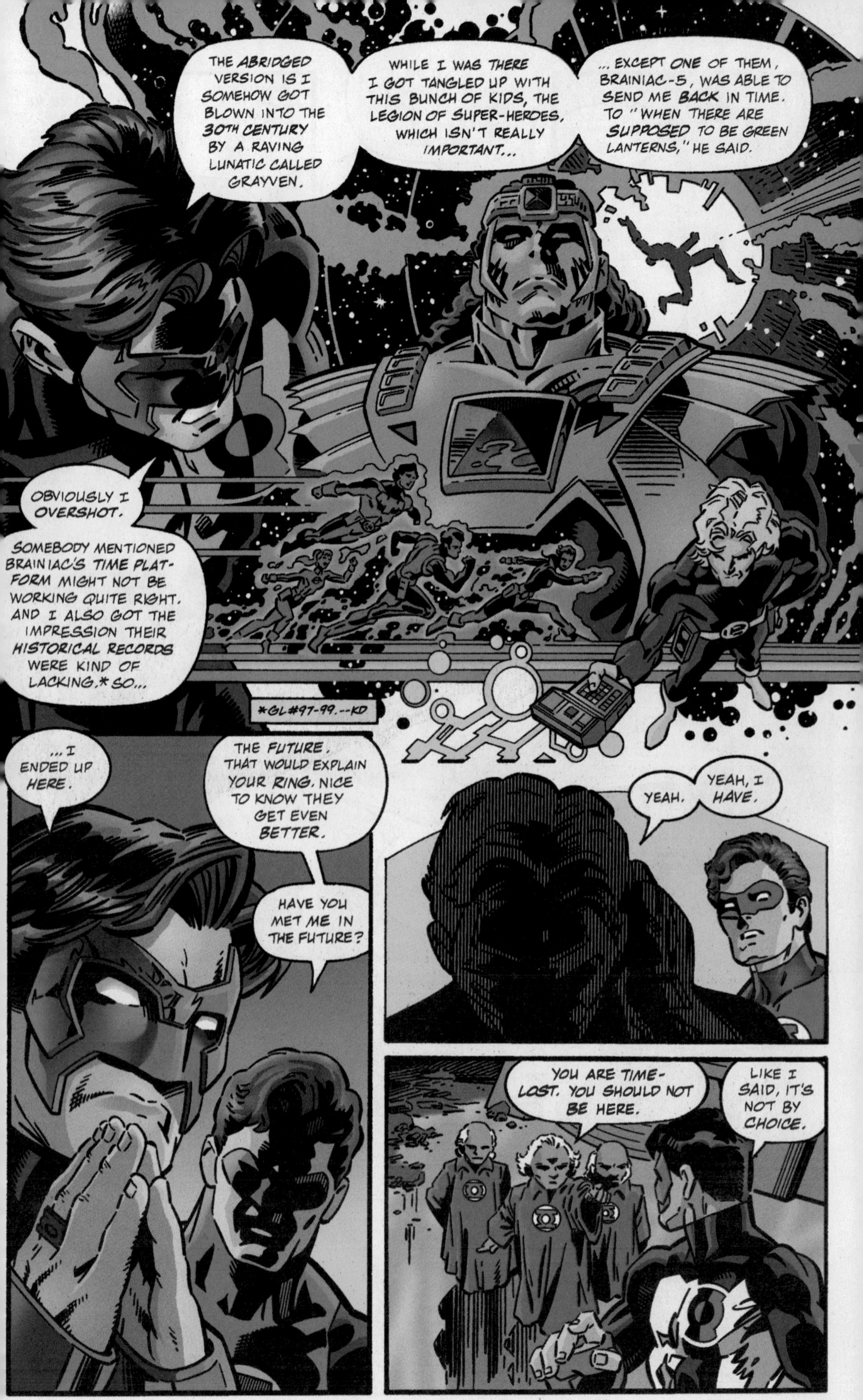
THE ABRIDGED VERSION IS I SOMEHOW GOT BLOWN INTO THE 30TH CENTURY BY A RAVING LUNATIC CALLED GRAYVEN.
WHILE I WAS THERE I GOT TANGLED UP WITH THIS BUNCH OF KIDS, THE LEGION OF SUPER-HEROES, WHICH ISN'T REALLY IMPORTANT...
...EXCEPT ONE OF THEM, BRAINIAC-5, WAS ABLE TO SEND ME BACK IN TIME. TO "WHEN THERE ARE SUPPOSED TO BE GREEN LANTERNS," HE SAID.
OBVIOUSLY I OVERSHOT.
SOMEBODY MENTIONED BRAINIAC'S TIME PLATFORM MIGHT NOT BE WORKING QUITE RIGHT. AND I ALSO GOT THE IMPRESSION THEIR HISTORICAL RECORDS WERE KIND OF LACKING.* SO...
*GL#97-99.--KD
...I ENDED UP HERE.
THE FUTURE. THAT WOULD EXPLAIN YOUR RING. NICE TO KNOW THEY GET EVEN BETTER.
HAVE YOU MET ME IN THE FUTURE?
YEAH.
YEAH, I HAVE.
YOU ARE TIME-LOST. YOU SHOULD NOT BE HERE.
LIKE I SAID, IT'S NOT BY CHOICE.

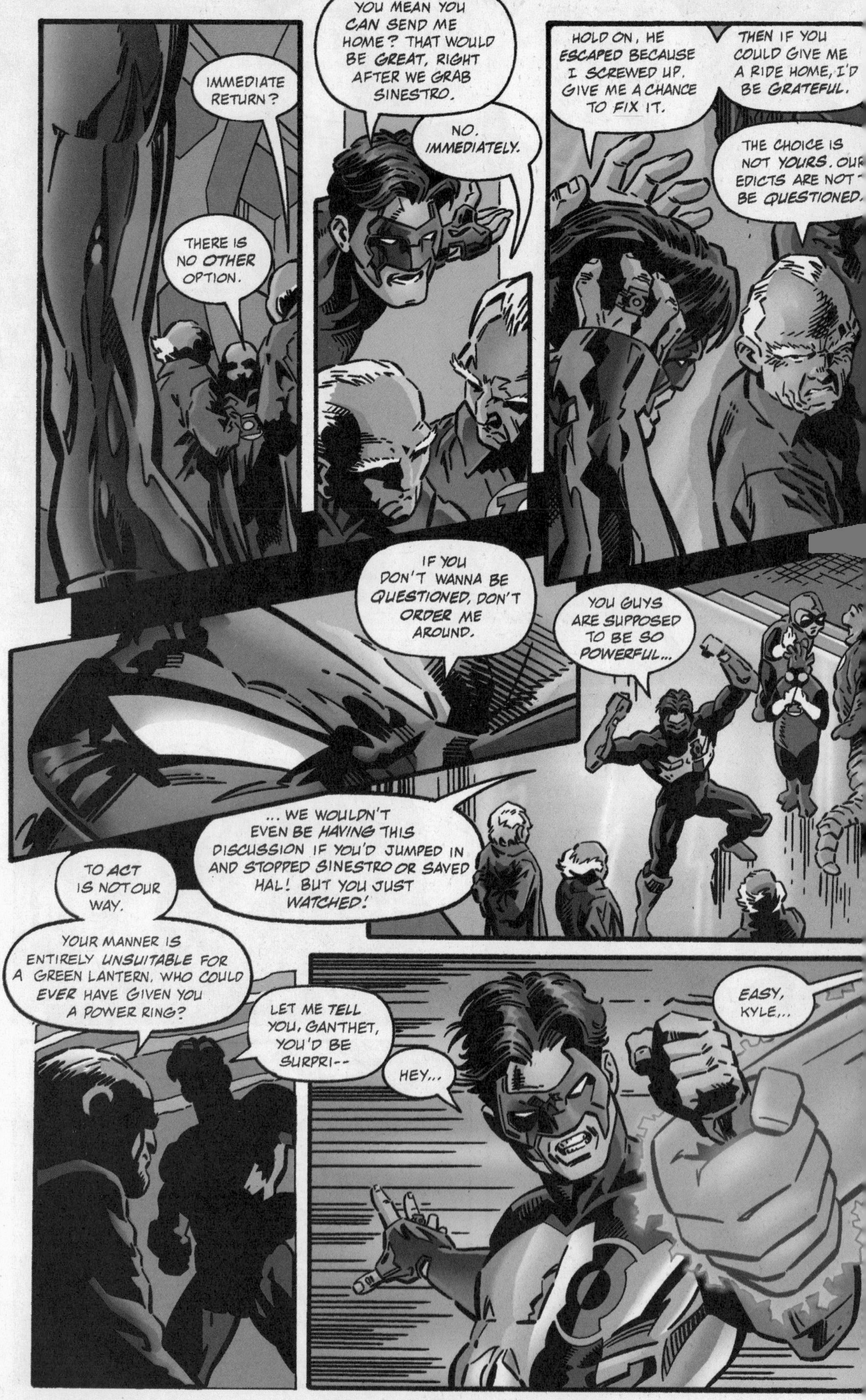
IMMEDIATE RETURN?
THERE IS NO OTHER OPTION.
YOU MEAN YOU CAN SEND ME HOME? THAT WOULD BE GREAT, RIGHT AFTER WE GRAB SINESTRO.
NO. IMMEDIATELY.
HOLD ON, HE ESCAPED BECAUSE I SCREWED UP. GIVE ME A CHANCE TO FIX IT.
THEN IF YOU COULD GIVE ME A RIDE HOME, I'D BE GRATEFUL.
THE CHOICE IS NOT YOURS. OUR EDICTS ARE NOT BE QUESTIONED.
IF YOU DON'T WANNA BE QUESTIONED, DON'T ORDER ME AROUND.
YOU GUYS ARE SUPPOSED TO BE SO POWERFUL...
...WE WOULDN'T EVEN BE HAVING THIS DISCUSSION IF YOU'D JUMPED IN AND STOPPED SINESTRO OR SAVED HAL! BUT YOU JUST WATCHED!
TO ACT IS NOT OUR WAY.
YOUR MANNER IS ENTIRELY UNSUITABLE FOR A GREEN LANTERN. WHO COULD EVER HAVE GIVEN YOU A POWER RING?
LET ME TELL YOU, GANTHET, YOU'D BE SURPRI--
HEY...
EASY, KYLE...

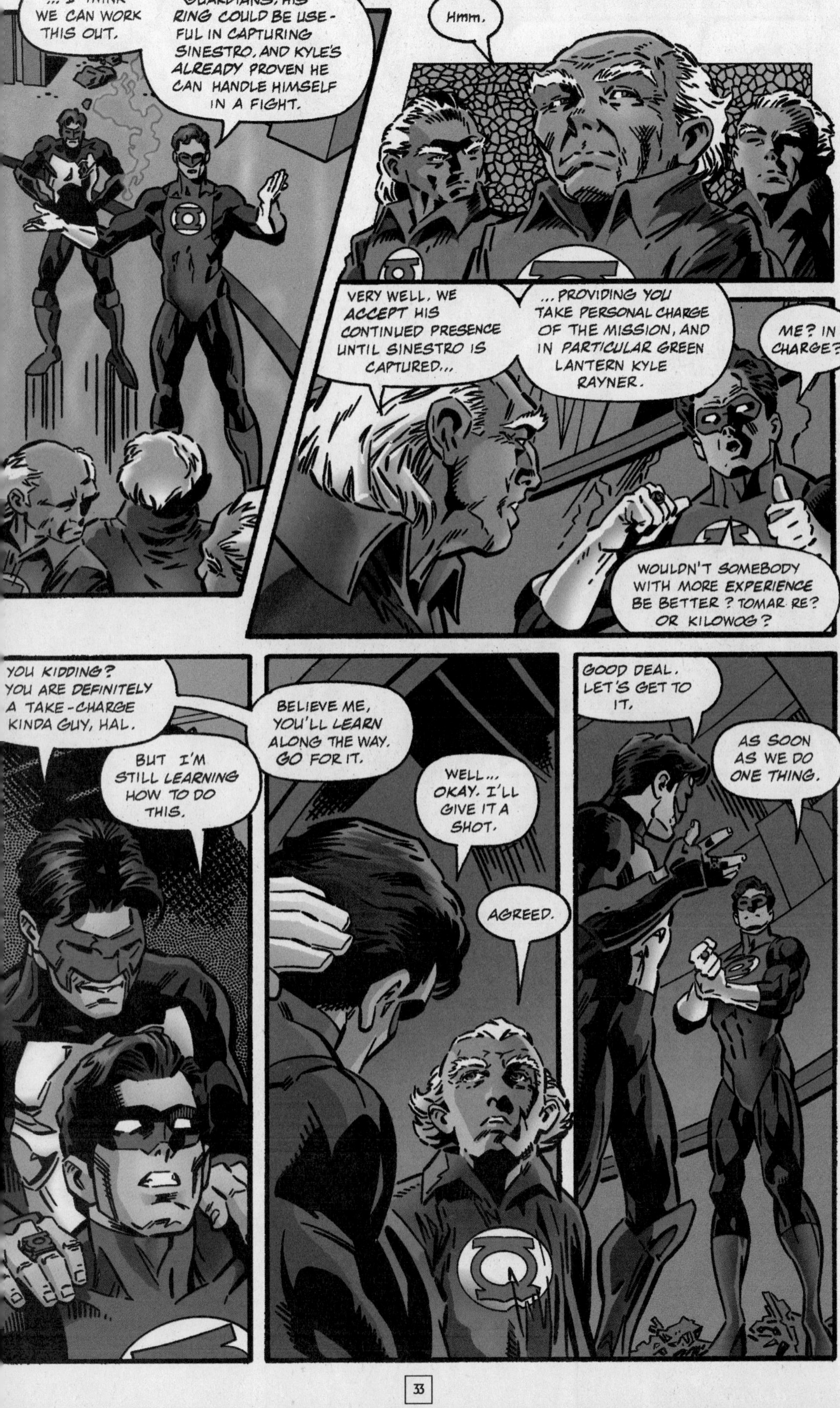

... I THINK WE CAN WORK THIS OUT.
GUARDIANS, HIS RING COULD BE USE-FUL IN CAPTURING SINESTRO, AND KYLE'S ALREADY PROVEN HE CAN HANDLE HIMSELF IN A FIGHT.
Hmm.
VERY WELL. WE ACCEPT HIS CONTINUED PRESENCE UNTIL SINESTRO IS CAPTURED...
... PROVIDING YOU TAKE PERSONAL CHARGE OF THE MISSION, AND IN PARTICULAR GREEN LANTERN KYLE RAYNER.
ME? IN CHARGE?
WOULDN'T SOMEBODY WITH MORE EXPERIENCE BE BETTER? TOMAR RE? OR KILOWOG?
YOU KIDDING? YOU ARE DEFINITELY A TAKE-CHARGE KINDA GUY, HAL.
BUT I'M STILL LEARNING HOW TO DO THIS.
BELIEVE ME, YOU'LL LEARN ALONG THE WAY. GO FOR IT.
WELL... OKAY. I'LL GIVE IT A SHOT.
AGREED.
GOOD DEAL. LET'S GET TO IT.
AS SOON AS WE DO ONE THING.

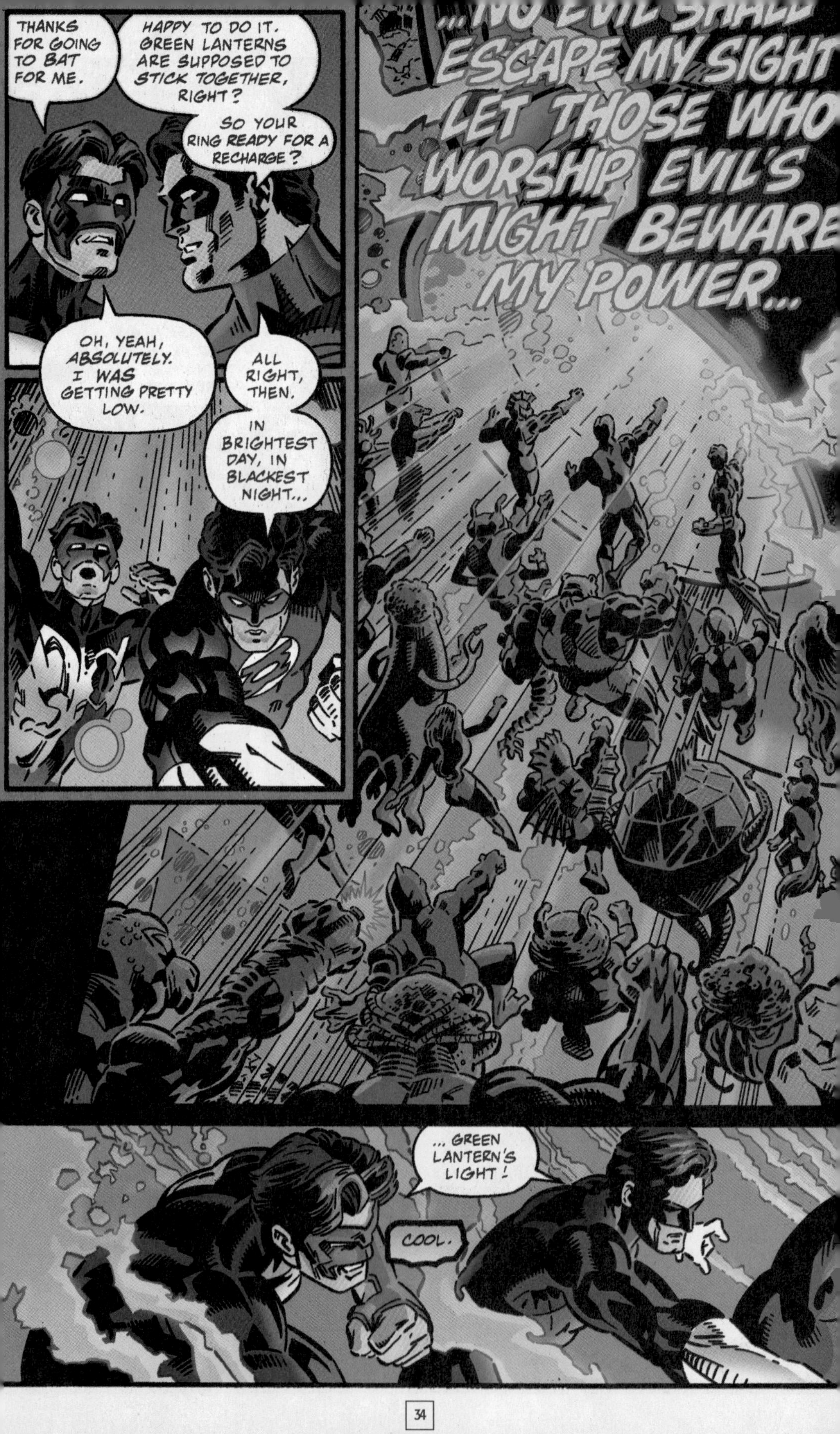
THANKS FOR GOING TO BAT FOR ME.
HAPPY TO DO IT. GREEN LANTERNS ARE SUPPOSED TO STICK TOGETHER, RIGHT?
SO YOUR RING READY FOR A RECHARGE?
OH, YEAH, ABSOLUTELY. I WAS GETTING PRETTY LOW.
ALL RIGHT, THEN.
IN BRIGHTEST DAY, IN BLACKEST NIGHT...
...NO EVIL SHALL ESCAPE MY SIGHT. LET THOSE WHO WORSHIP EVIL'S MIGHT BEWARE MY POWER...
...GREEN LANTERN'S LIGHT!
COOL.

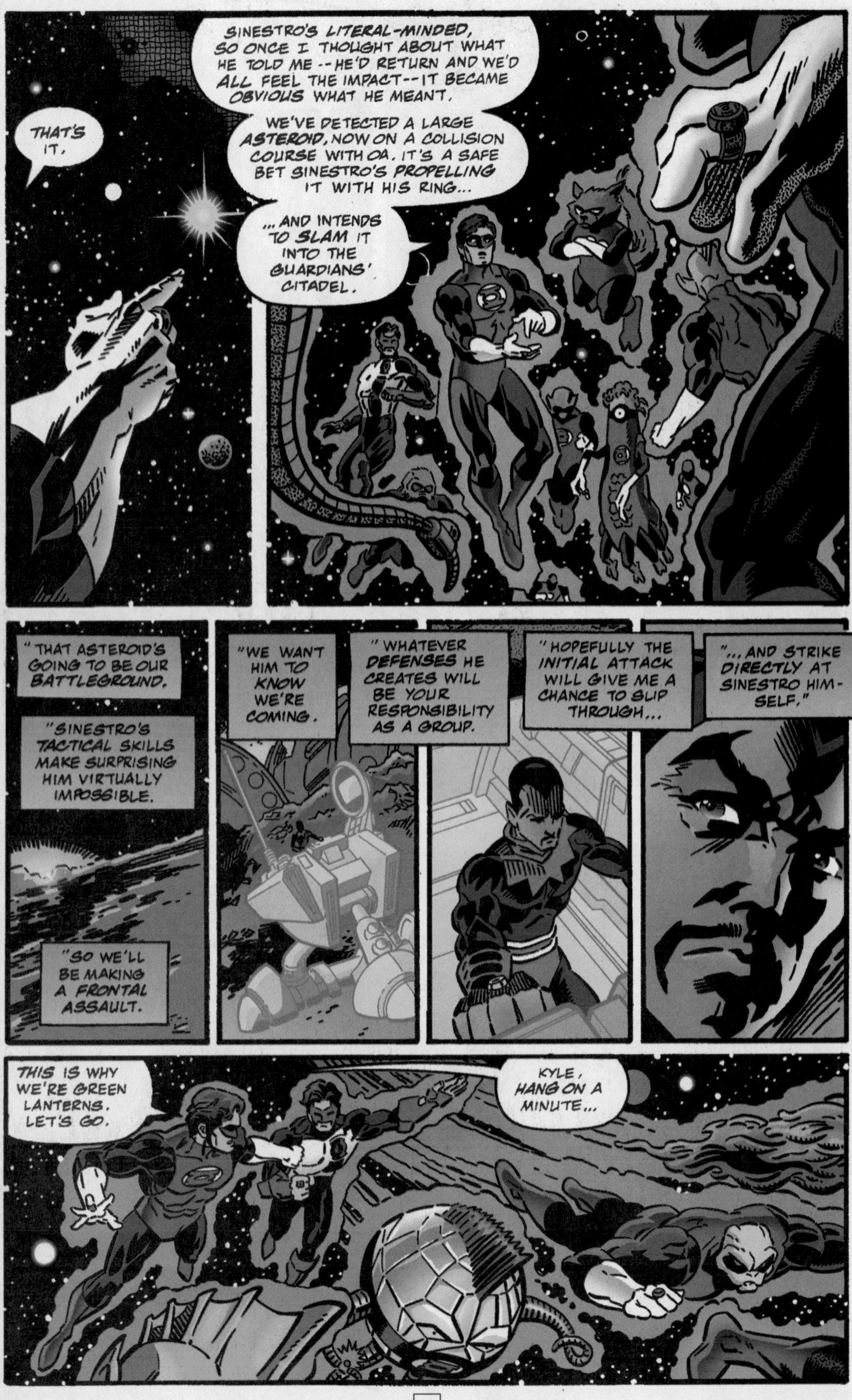
THAT'S IT.
SINESTRO'S LITERAL-MINDED, SO ONCE I THOUGHT ABOUT WHAT HE TOLD ME -- HE'D RETURN AND WE'D ALL FEEL THE IMPACT -- IT BECAME OBVIOUS WHAT HE MEANT.
WE'VE DETECTED A LARGE ASTEROID, NOW ON A COLLISION COURSE WITH OA. IT'S A SAFE BET SINESTRO'S PROPELLING IT WITH HIS RING...
...AND INTENDS TO SLAM IT INTO THE GUARDIANS' CITADEL.
"THAT ASTEROID'S GOING TO BE OUR BATTLEGROUND.
"SINESTRO'S TACTICAL SKILLS MAKE SURPRISING HIM VIRTUALLY IMPOSSIBLE.
"SO WE'LL BE MAKING A FRONTAL ASSAULT.
"WE WANT HIM TO KNOW WE'RE COMING.
"WHATEVER DEFENSES HE CREATES WILL BE YOUR RESPONSIBILITY AS A GROUP.
"HOPEFULLY THE INITIAL ATTACK WILL GIVE ME A CHANCE TO SLIP THROUGH...
"...AND STRIKE DIRECTLY AT SINESTRO HIMSELF."
THIS IS WHY WE'RE GREEN LANTERNS. LET'S GO.
KYLE, HANG ON A MINUTE...

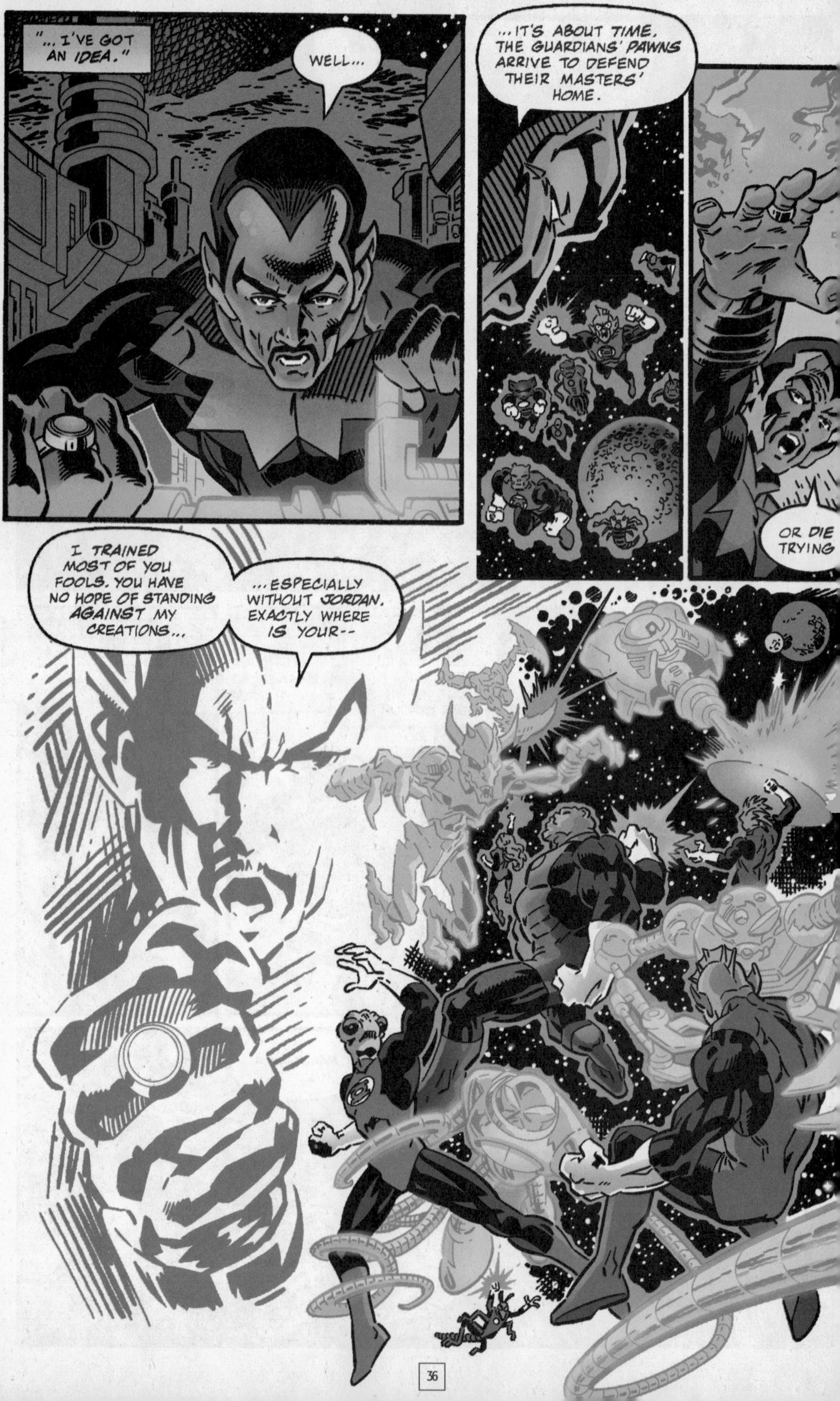
"... I'VE GOT AN IDEA."
WELL...
... IT'S ABOUT TIME. THE GUARDIANS' PAWNS ARRIVE TO DEFEND THEIR MASTERS' HOME.
OR DIE TRYING
I TRAINED MOST OF YOU FOOLS. YOU HAVE NO HOPE OF STANDING AGAINST MY CREATIONS...
... ESPECIALLY WITHOUT JORDAN. EXACTLY WHERE IS YOUR--

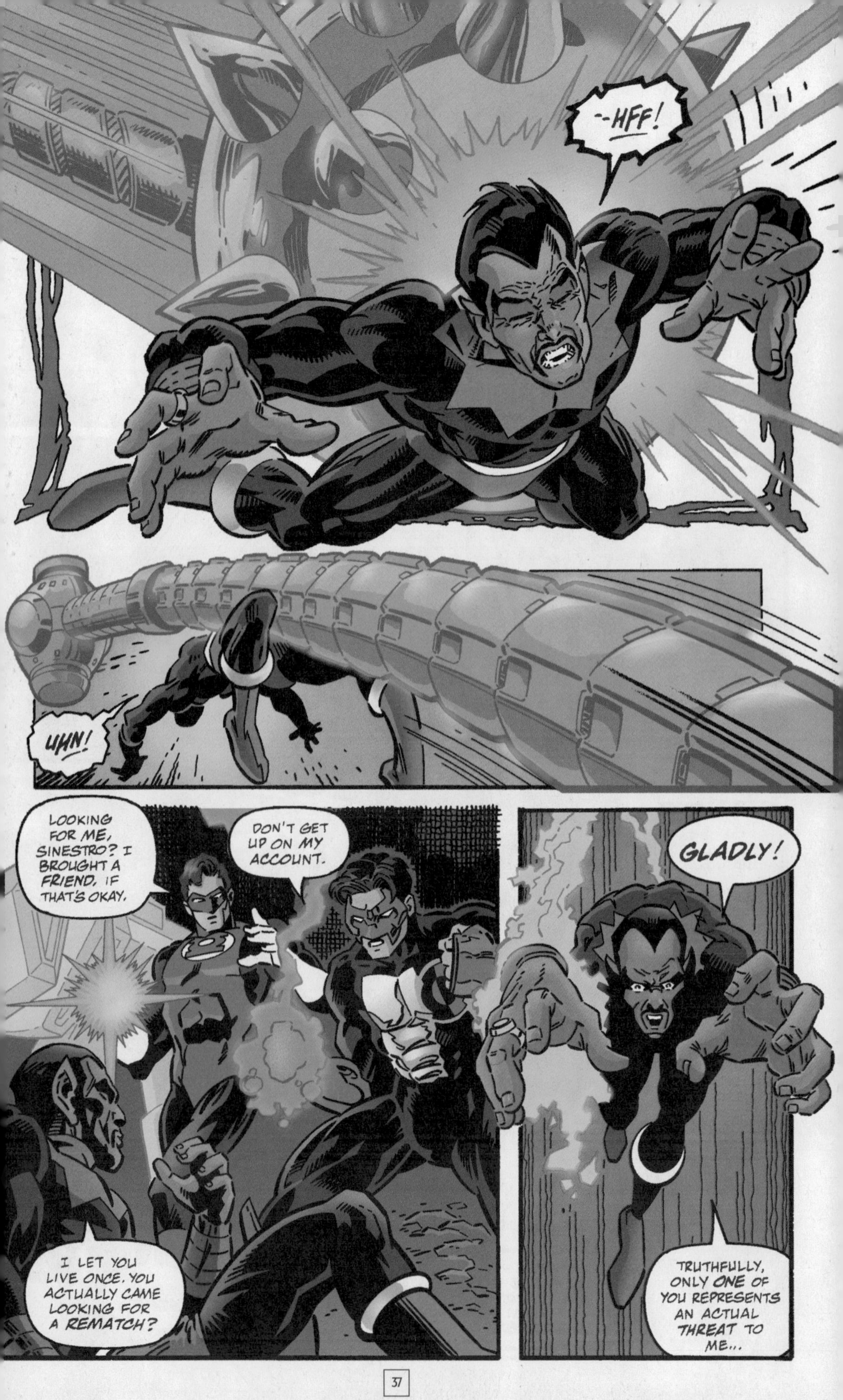

--HFF!
UHN!
LOOKING FOR ME, SINESTRO? I BROUGHT A FRIEND, IF THAT'S OKAY.
DON'T GET UP ON MY ACCOUNT.
I LET YOU LIVE ONCE. YOU ACTUALLY CAME LOOKING FOR A REMATCH?
GLADLY!
TRUTHFULLY, ONLY ONE OF YOU REPRESENTS AN ACTUAL THREAT TO ME...

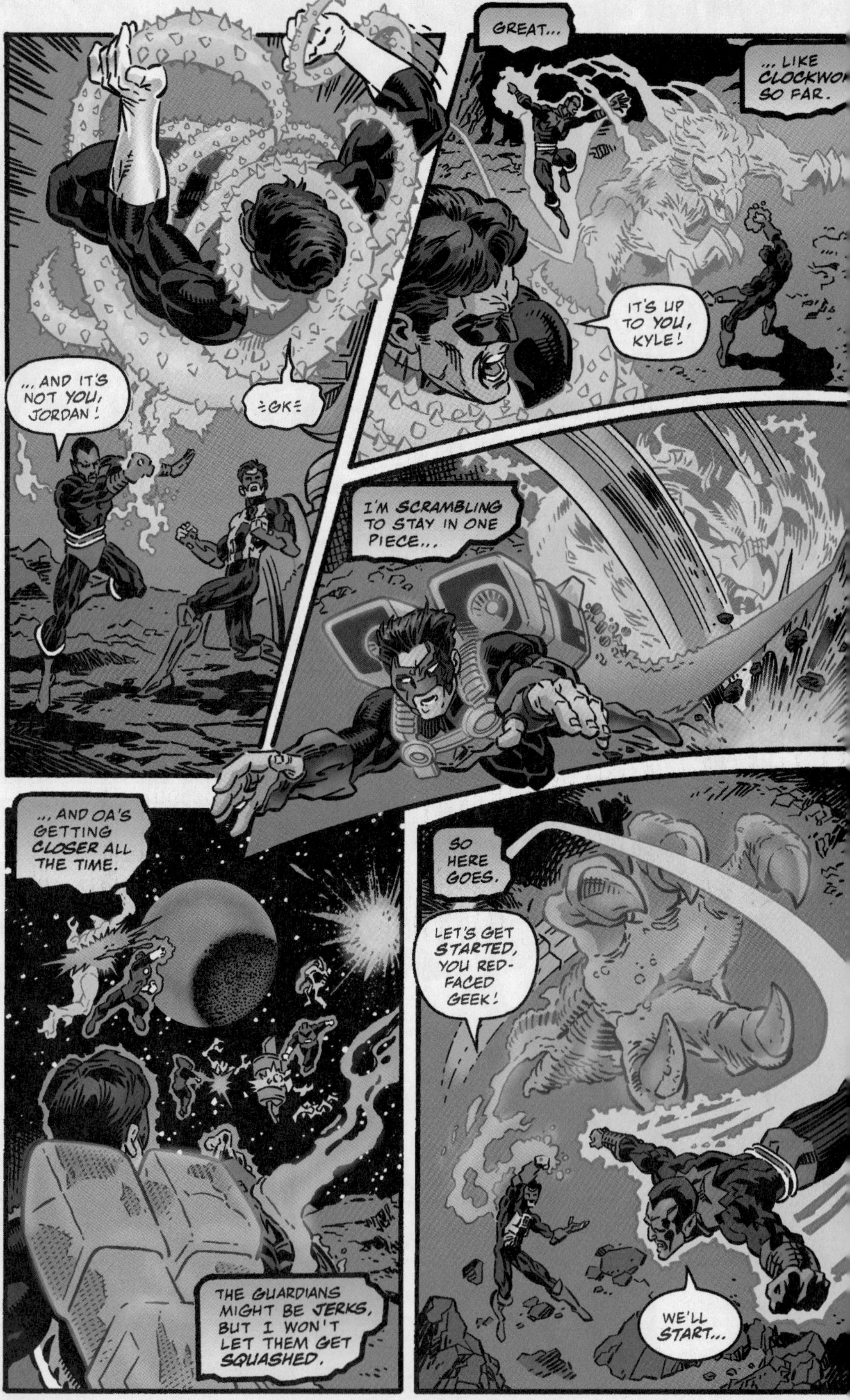

...AND IT'S NOT YOU, JORDAN!
GK
GREAT...
...LIKE CLOCKWO
SO FAR.
IT'S UP TO YOU, KYLE!
I'M SCRAMBLING TO STAY IN ONE PIECE...
...AND OA'S GETTING CLOSER ALL THE TIME.
THE GUARDIANS MIGHT BE JERKS, BUT I WON'T LET THEM GET SQUASHED.
SO HERE GOES.
LET'S GET STARTED, YOU RED-FACED GEEK!
WE'LL START...

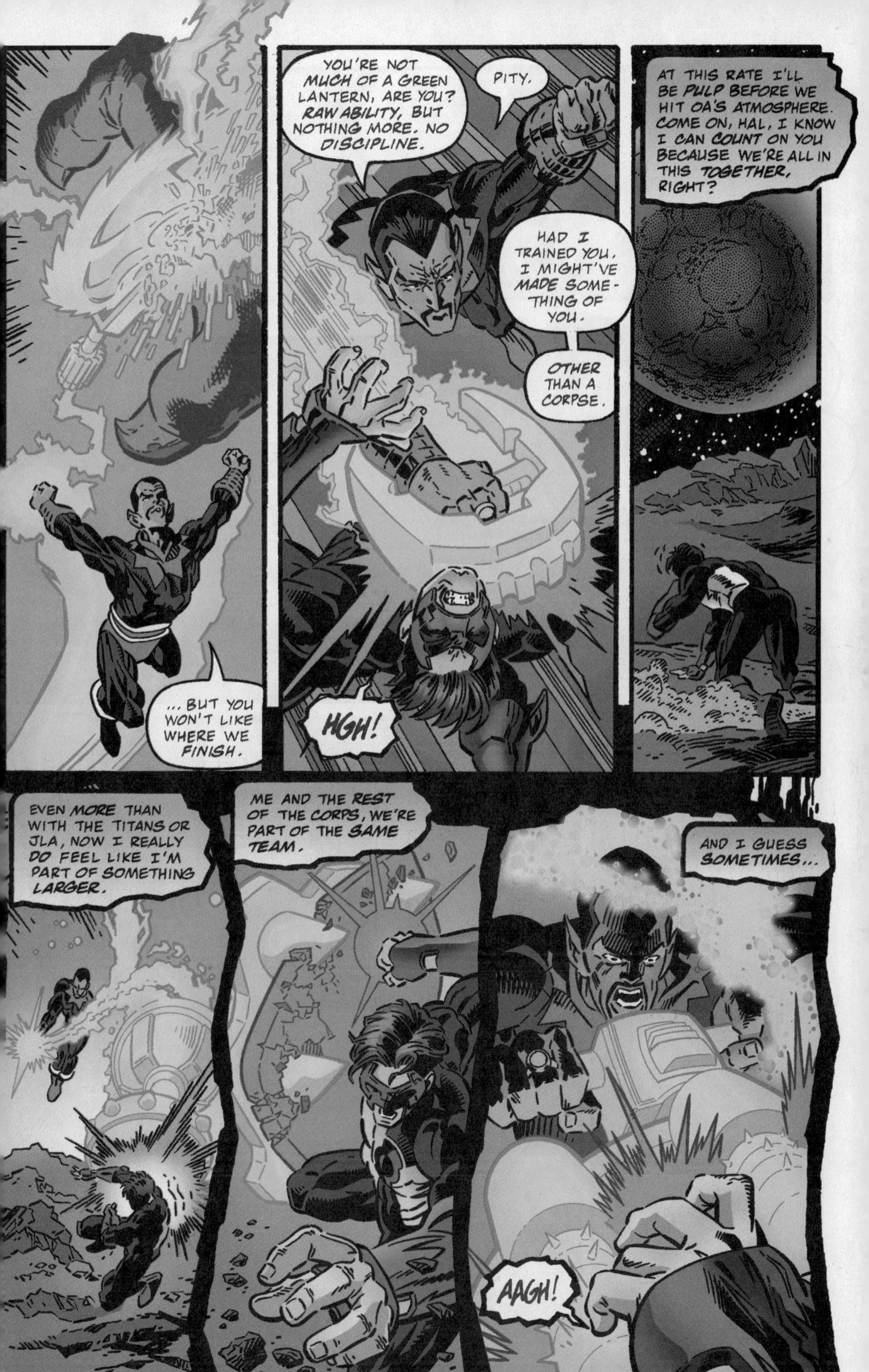

... BUT YOU WON'T LIKE WHERE WE FINISH.
YOU'RE NOT MUCH OF A GREEN LANTERN, ARE YOU? RAW ABILITY, BUT NOTHING MORE. NO DISCIPLINE.
PITY.
HAD I TRAINED YOU, I MIGHT'VE MADE SOME-THING OF YOU.
OTHER THAN A CORPSE.
HGH!
AT THIS RATE I'LL BE PULP BEFORE WE HIT OA'S ATMOSPHERE. COME ON, HAL, I KNOW I CAN COUNT ON YOU BECAUSE WE'RE ALL IN THIS TOGETHER, RIGHT?
EVEN MORE THAN WITH THE TITANS OR JLA, NOW I REALLY DO FEEL LIKE I'M PART OF SOMETHING LARGER.
ME AND THE REST OF THE CORPS, WE'RE PART OF THE SAME TEAM.
AND I GUESS SOMETIMES...
AAGH!

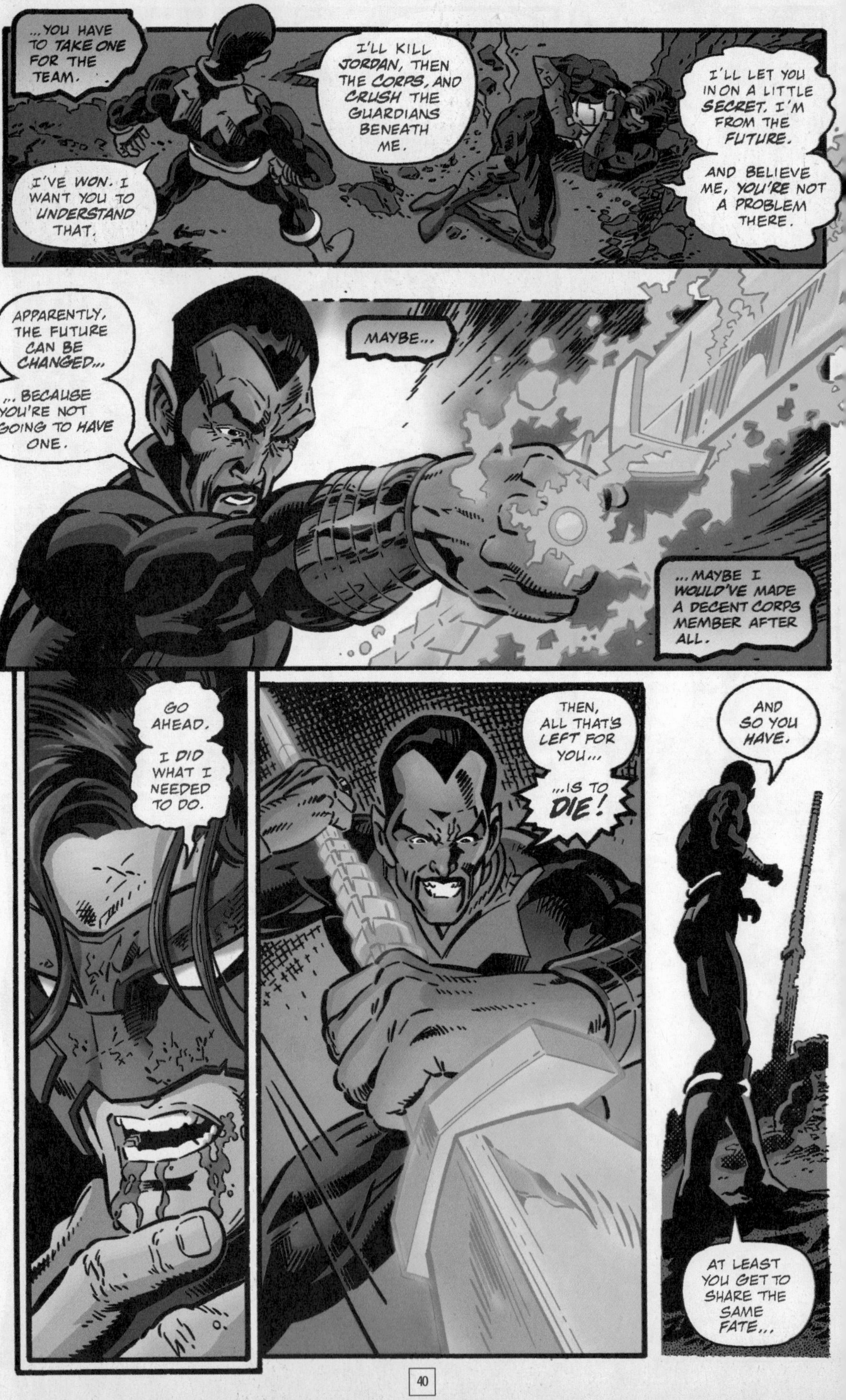

...YOU HAVE TO TAKE ONE FOR THE TEAM.
I'VE WON. I WANT YOU TO UNDERSTAND THAT.
I'LL KILL JORDAN, THEN THE CORPS, AND CRUSH THE GUARDIANS BENEATH ME.
I'LL LET YOU IN ON A LITTLE SECRET. I'M FROM THE FUTURE.
AND BELIEVE ME, YOU'RE NOT A PROBLEM THERE.
APPARENTLY, THE FUTURE CAN BE CHANGED...
...BECAUSE YOU'RE NOT GOING TO HAVE ONE.
MAYBE...
...MAYBE I WOULD'VE MADE A DECENT CORPS MEMBER AFTER ALL.
GO AHEAD.
I DID WHAT I NEEDED TO DO.
THEN, ALL THAT'S LEFT FOR YOU...
...IS TO DIE!
AND SO YOU HAVE.
AT LEAST YOU GET TO SHARE THE SAME FATE...

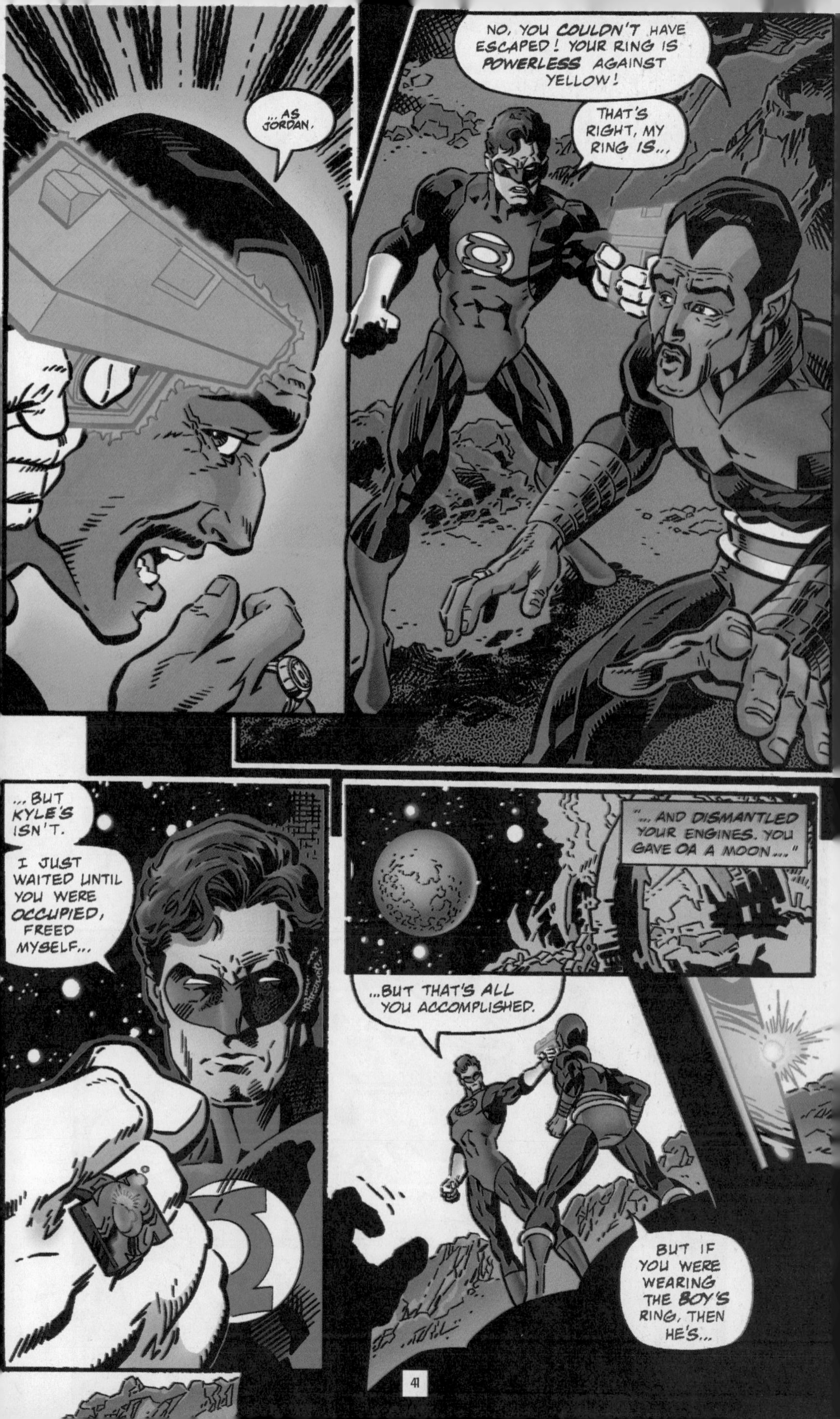
...AS JORDAN.
NO, YOU COULDN'T HAVE ESCAPED! YOUR RING IS POWERLESS AGAINST YELLOW!
THAT'S RIGHT, MY RING IS...
...BUT KYLE'S ISN'T.
I JUST WAITED UNTIL YOU WERE OCCUPIED, FREED MYSELF...
"...AND DISMANTLED YOUR ENGINES. YOU GAVE OA A MOON..."
...BUT THAT'S ALL YOU ACCOMPLISHED.
BUT IF YOU WERE WEARING THE BOY'S RING, THEN HE'S...

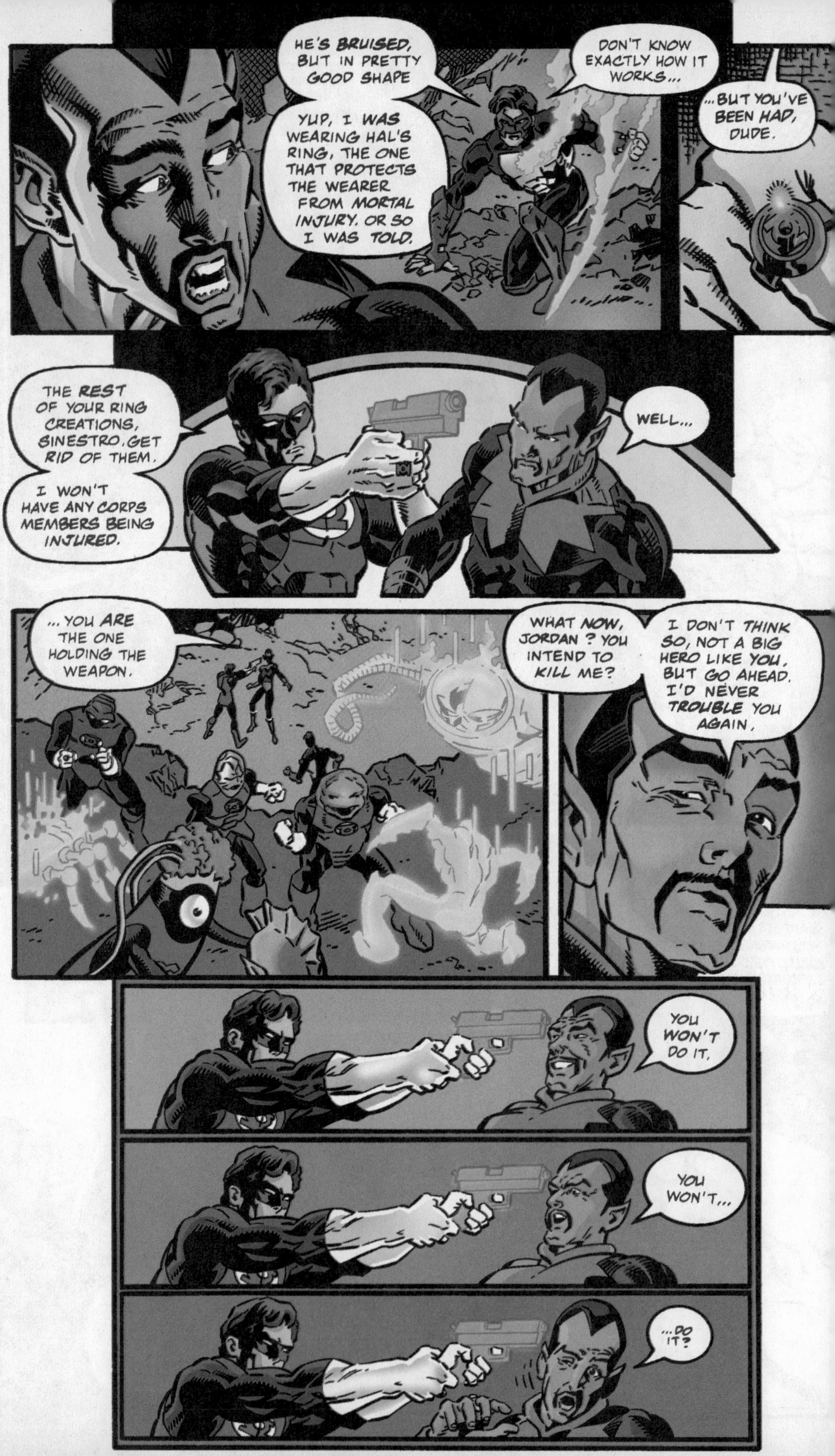
HE'S BRUISED, BUT IN PRETTY GOOD SHAPE
YUP, I WAS WEARING HAL'S RING, THE ONE THAT PROTECTS THE WEARER FROM MORTAL INJURY. OR SO I WAS TOLD.
DON'T KNOW EXACTLY HOW IT WORKS...
...BUT YOU'VE BEEN HAD, DUDE.
THE REST OF YOUR RING CREATIONS, SINESTRO. GET RID OF THEM.
I WON'T HAVE ANY CORPS MEMBERS BEING INJURED.
WELL...
...YOU ARE THE ONE HOLDING THE WEAPON.
WHAT NOW, JORDAN ? YOU INTEND TO KILL ME?
I DON'T THINK SO, NOT A BIG HERO LIKE YOU. BUT GO AHEAD. I'D NEVER TROUBLE YOU AGAIN.
YOU WON'T DO IT.
YOU WON'T...
...DO IT?

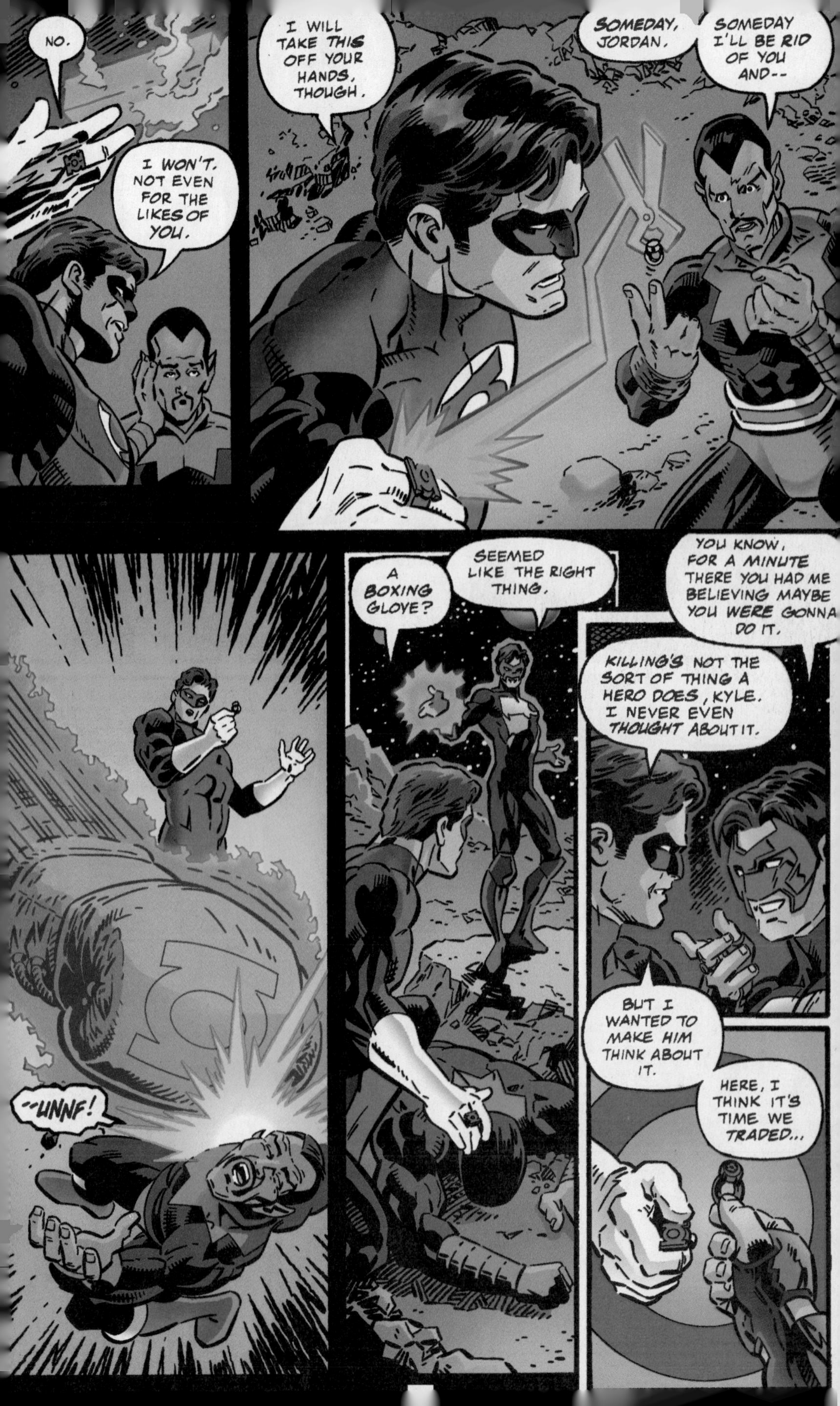

NO.
I WON'T. NOT EVEN FOR THE LIKES OF YOU.
I WILL TAKE THIS OFF YOUR HANDS, THOUGH.
SOMEDAY, JORDAN.
SOMEDAY I'LL BE RID OF YOU AND--
--UNNF!
A BOXING GLOVE?
SEEMED LIKE THE RIGHT THING.
YOU KNOW, FOR A MINUTE THERE YOU HAD ME BELIEVING MAYBE YOU WERE GONNA DO IT.
KILLING'S NOT THE SORT OF THING A HERO DOES, KYLE. I NEVER EVEN THOUGHT ABOUT IT.
BUT I WANTED TO MAKE HIM THINK ABOUT IT.
HERE, I THINK IT'S TIME WE TRADED...

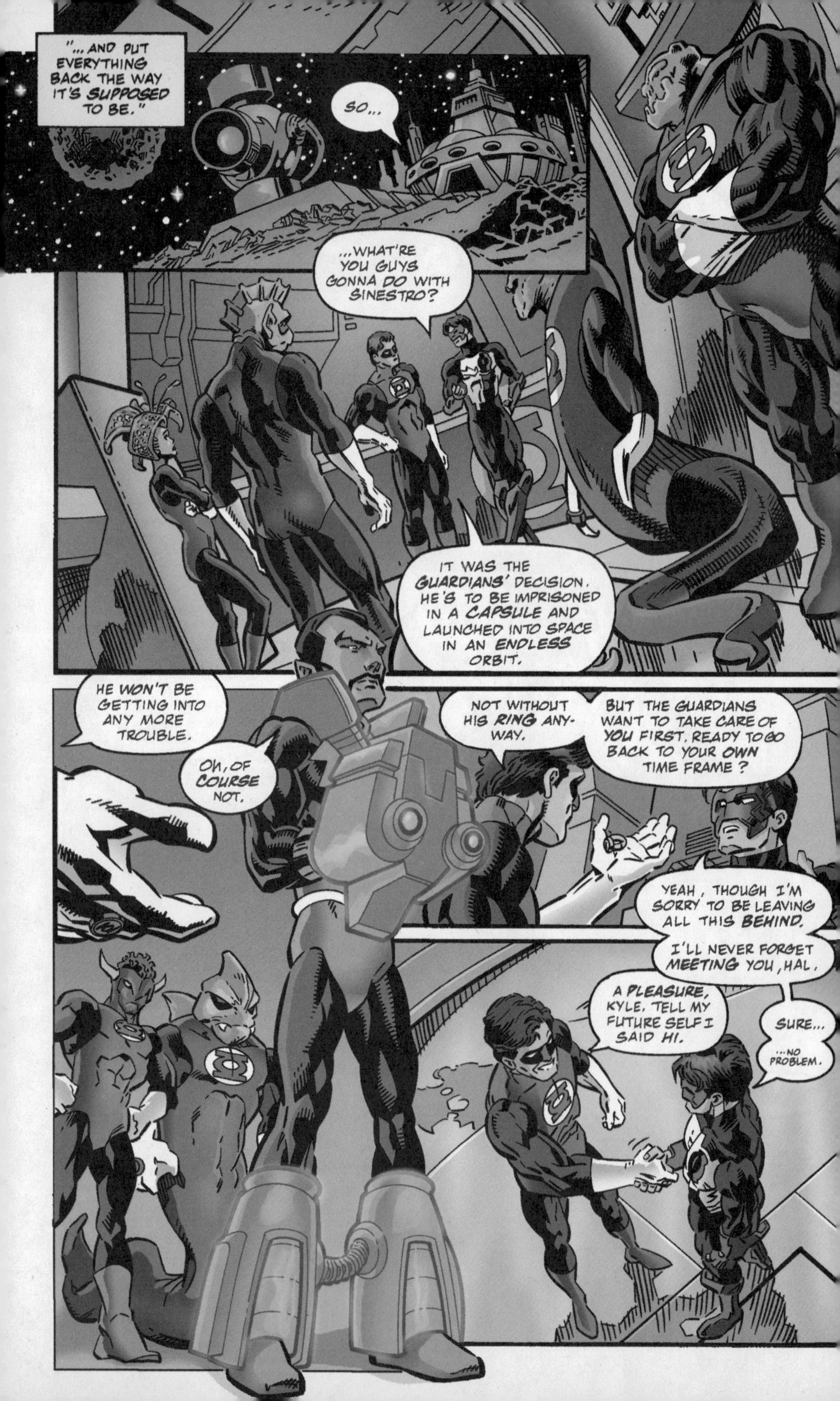
"...AND PUT EVERYTHING BACK THE WAY IT'S SUPPOSED TO BE."
SO...
...WHAT'RE YOU GUYS GONNA DO WITH SINESTRO?
IT WAS THE GUARDIANS' DECISION. HE'S TO BE IMPRISONED IN A CAPSULE AND LAUNCHED INTO SPACE IN AN ENDLESS ORBIT.
HE WON'T BE GETTING INTO ANY MORE TROUBLE.
Oh, OF COURSE NOT.
NOT WITHOUT HIS RING ANY-WAY.
BUT THE GUARDIANS WANT TO TAKE CARE OF YOU FIRST. READY TO GO BACK TO YOUR OWN TIME FRAME?
YEAH, THOUGH I'M SORRY TO BE LEAVING ALL THIS BEHIND.
I'LL NEVER FORGET MEETING YOU, HAL.
A PLEASURE, KYLE. TELL MY FUTURE SELF I SAID HI.
SURE...
...NO PROBLEM.

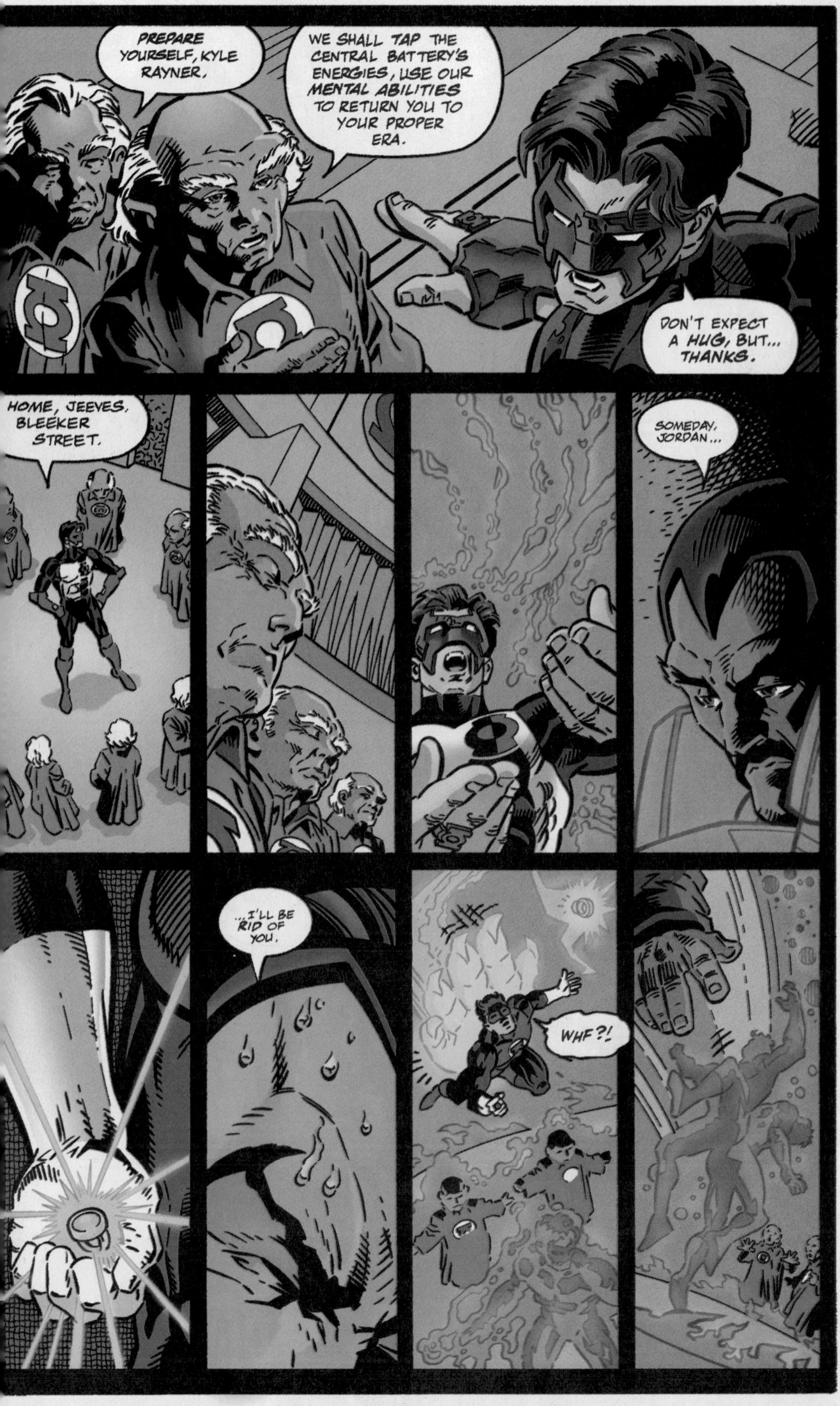
PREPARE YOURSELF, KYLE RAYNER.
WE SHALL TAP THE CENTRAL BATTERY'S ENERGIES, USE OUR MENTAL ABILITIES TO RETURN YOU TO YOUR PROPER ERA.
DON'T EXPECT A HUG, BUT... THANKS.
HOME, JEEVES. BLEEKER STREET.
SOMEDAY, JORDAN...
...I'LL BE RID OF YOU.
WHF?!

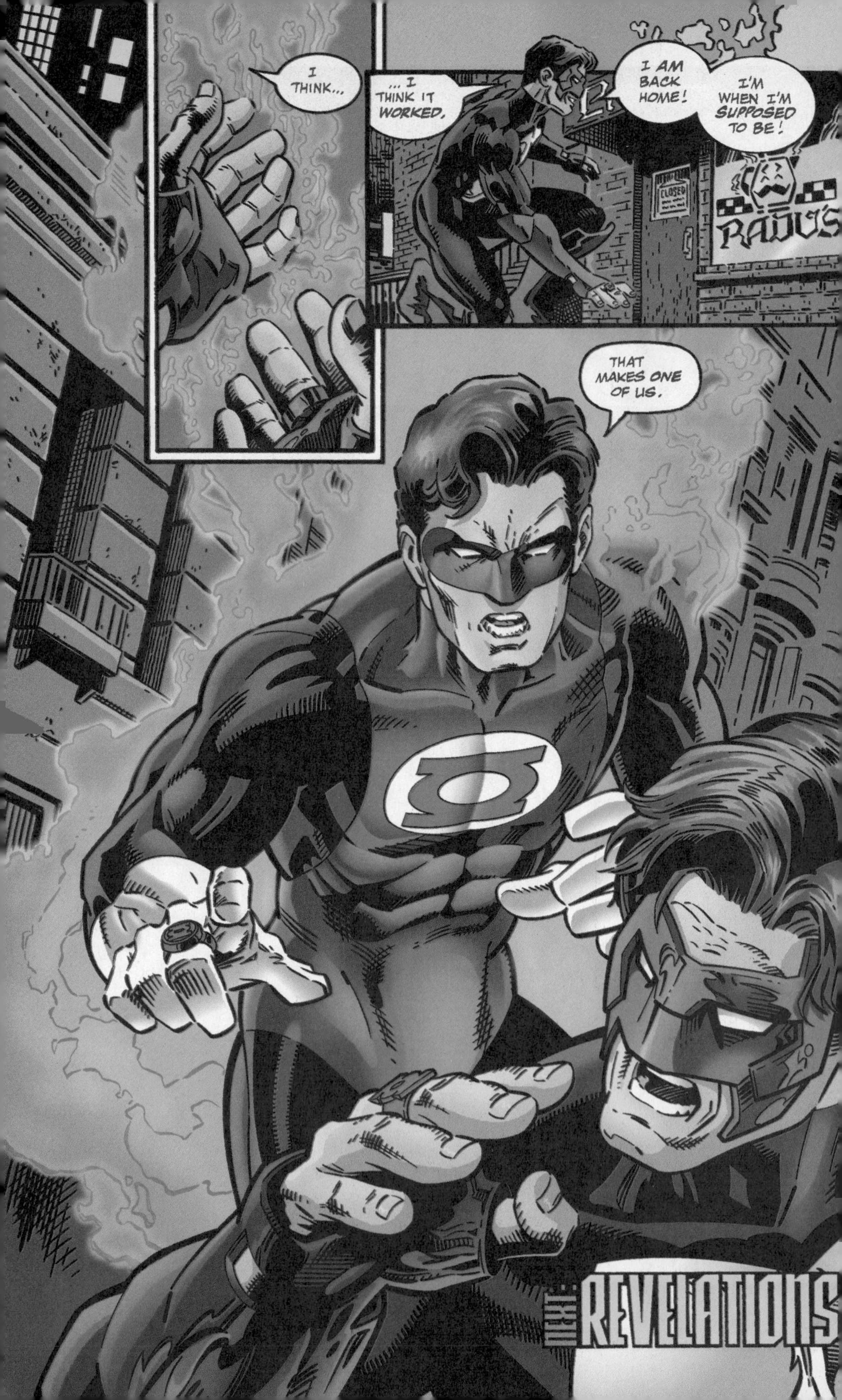

I THINK...
...I THINK IT WORKED.
I AM BACK HOME!
I'M WHEN I'M SUPPOSED TO BE!
CLOSED
RADU'S
THAT MAKES ONE OF US.
NEXT: REVELATIONS

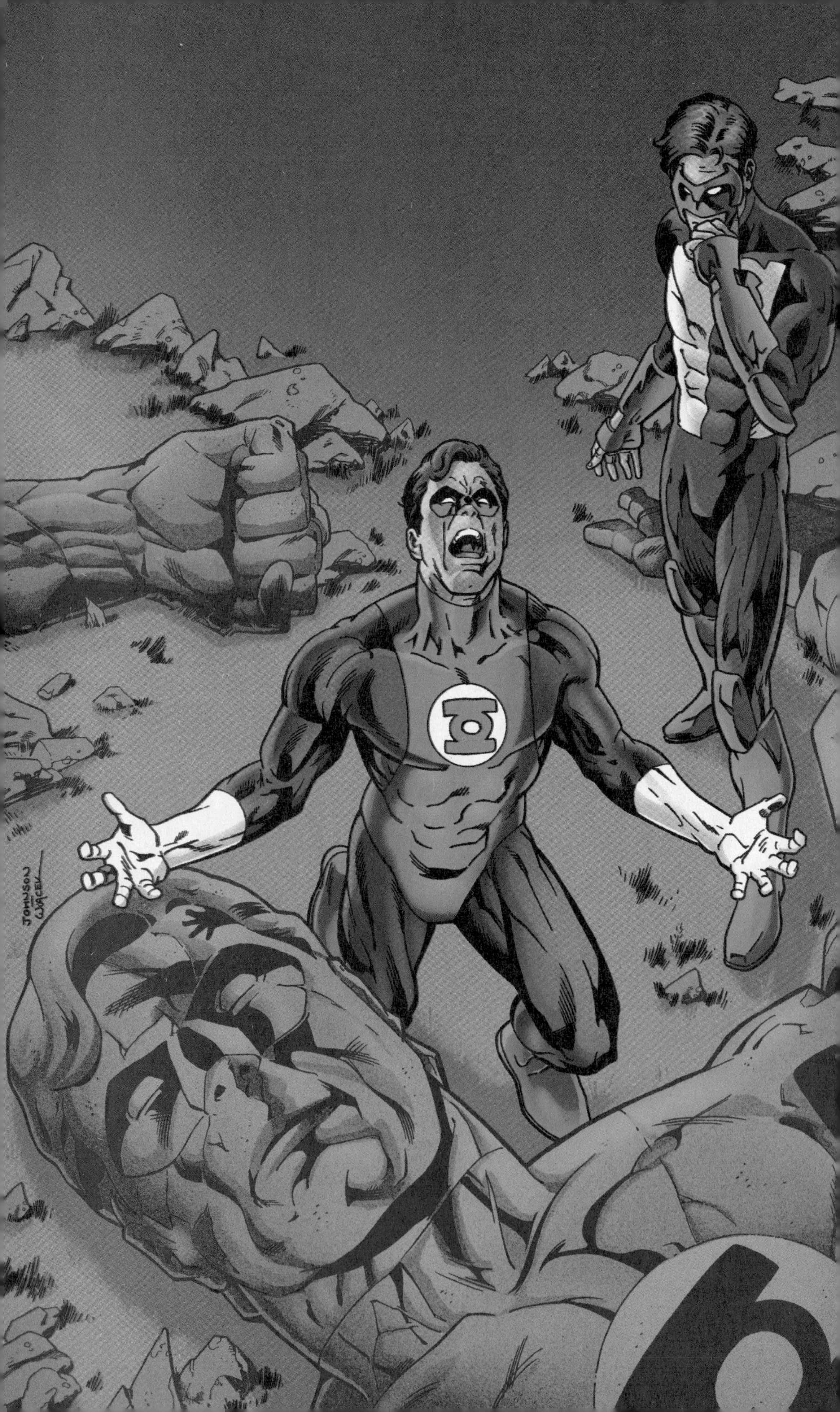
JOHNSON
WIACEK

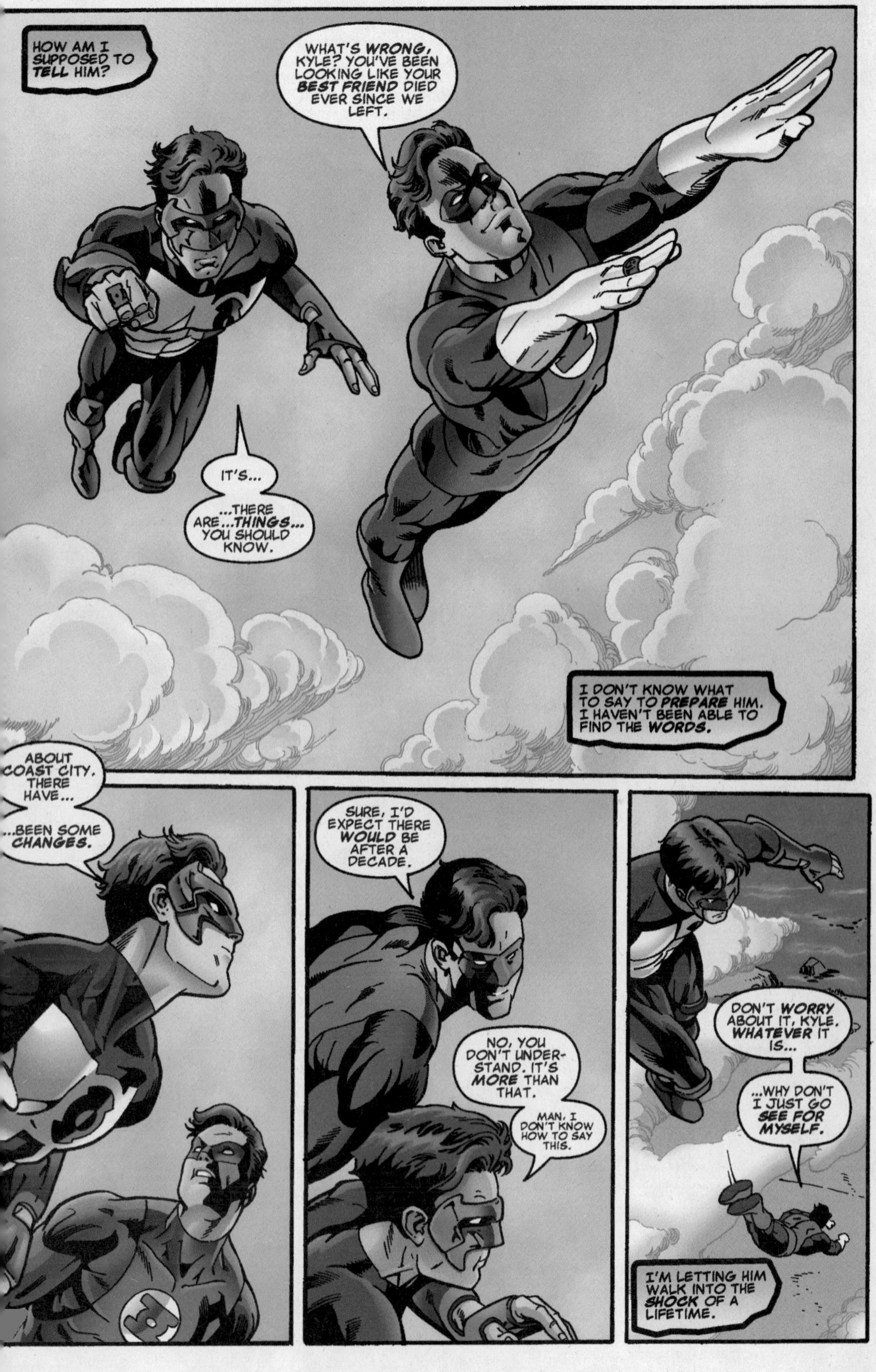

HOW AM I SUPPOSED TO TELL HIM?
WHAT'S WRONG, KYLE? YOU'VE BEEN LOOKING LIKE YOUR BEST FRIEND DIED EVER SINCE WE LEFT.
IT'S...
...THERE ARE...THINGS... YOU SHOULD KNOW.
I DON'T KNOW WHAT TO SAY TO PREPARE HIM. I HAVEN'T BEEN ABLE TO FIND THE WORDS.
ABOUT COAST CITY. THERE HAVE...
...BEEN SOME CHANGES.
SURE, I'D EXPECT THERE WOULD BE AFTER A DECADE.
NO, YOU DON'T UNDER-STAND. IT'S MORE THAN THAT.
MAN, I DON'T KNOW HOW TO SAY THIS.
DON'T WORRY ABOUT IT, KYLE. WHATEVER IT IS...
...WHY DON'T I JUST GO SEE FOR MYSELF.
I'M LETTING HIM WALK INTO THE SHOCK OF A LIFETIME.

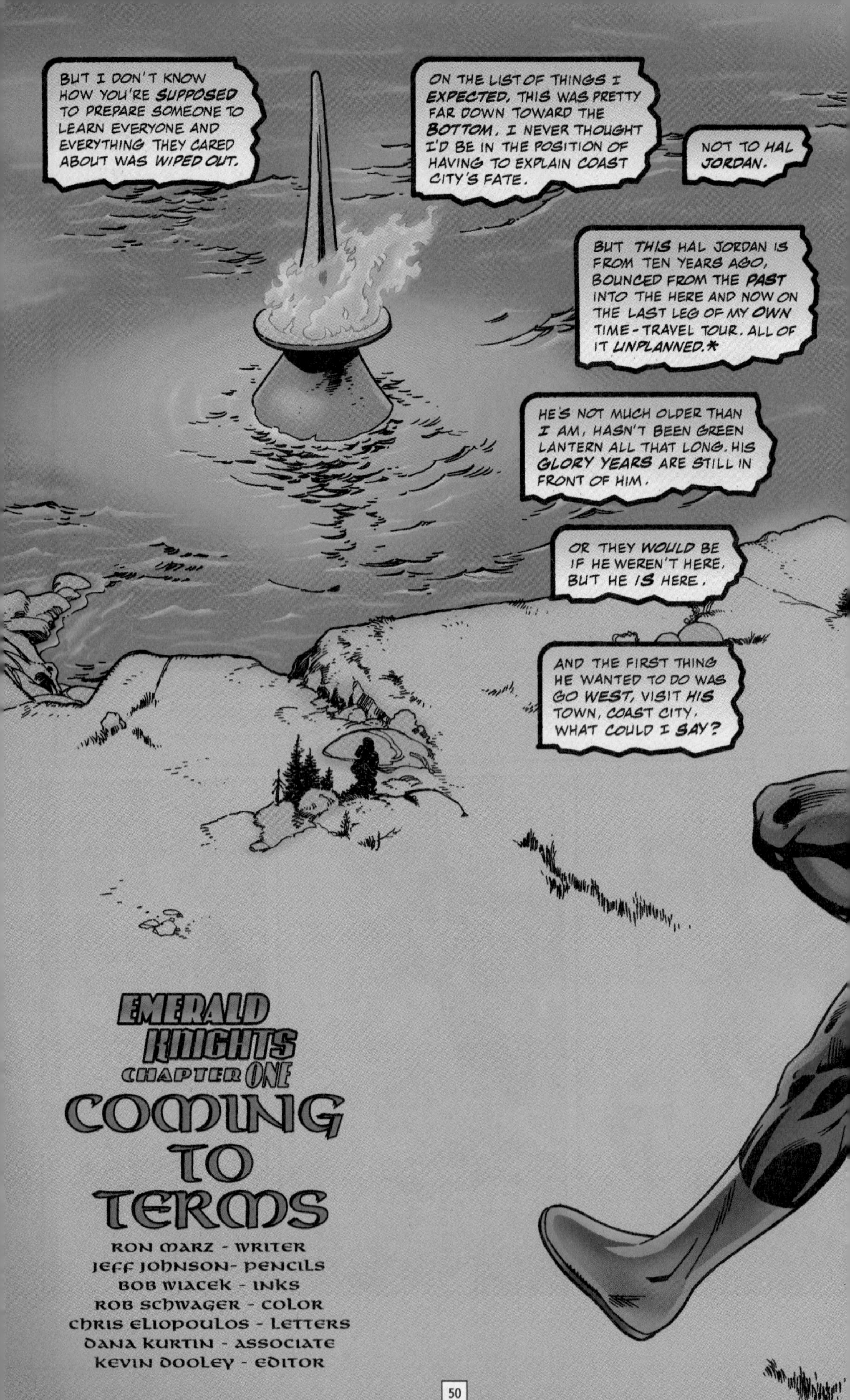
BUT I DON'T KNOW HOW YOU'RE SUPPOSED TO PREPARE SOMEONE TO LEARN EVERYONE AND EVERYTHING THEY CARED ABOUT WAS WIPED OUT.
ON THE LIST OF THINGS I EXPECTED, THIS WAS PRETTY FAR DOWN TOWARD THE BOTTOM. I NEVER THOUGHT I'D BE IN THE POSITION OF HAVING TO EXPLAIN COAST CITY'S FATE.
NOT TO HAL JORDAN.
BUT THIS HAL JORDAN IS FROM TEN YEARS AGO, BOUNCED FROM THE PAST INTO THE HERE AND NOW ON THE LAST LEG OF MY OWN TIME-TRAVEL TOUR. ALL OF IT UNPLANNED.*
HE'S NOT MUCH OLDER THAN I AM, HASN'T BEEN GREEN LANTERN ALL THAT LONG. HIS GLORY YEARS ARE STILL IN FRONT OF HIM.
OR THEY WOULD BE IF HE WEREN'T HERE. BUT HE IS HERE.
AND THE FIRST THING HE WANTED TO DO WAS GO WEST, VISIT HIS TOWN, COAST CITY. WHAT COULD I SAY?
EMERALD KNIGHTS
CHAPTER ONE
COMING TO TERMS
RON MARZ - WRITER
JEFF JOHNSON- PENCILS
BOB WIACEK - INKS
ROB SCHWAGER - COLOR
CHRIS ELIOPOULOS - LETTERS
DANA KURTIN - ASSOCIATE
KEVIN DOOLEY - EDITOR

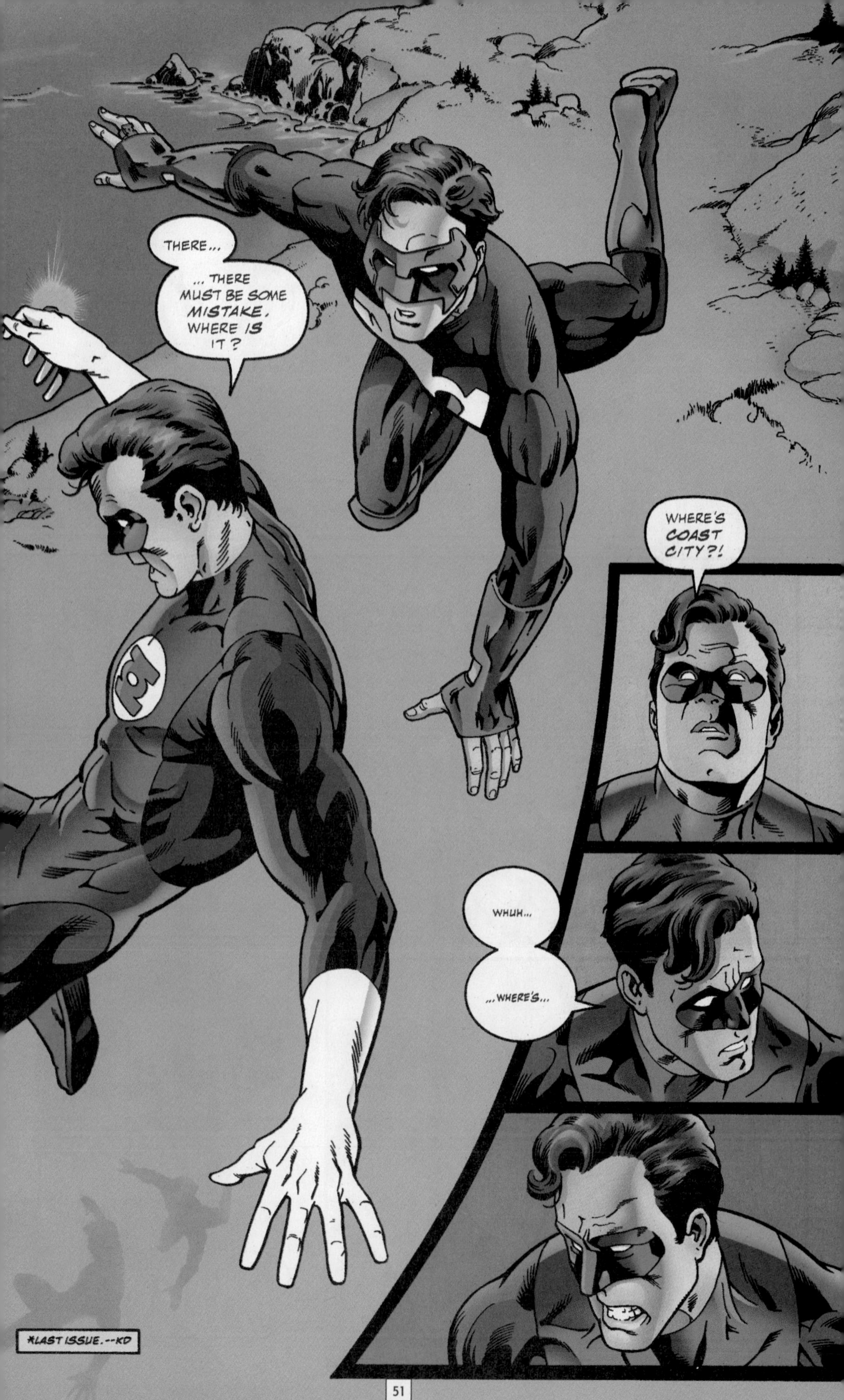
THERE...
... THERE MUST BE SOME MISTAKE. WHERE IS IT?
WHERE'S COAST CITY?!
WHUH...
...WHERE'S...
*LAST ISSUE.--KD

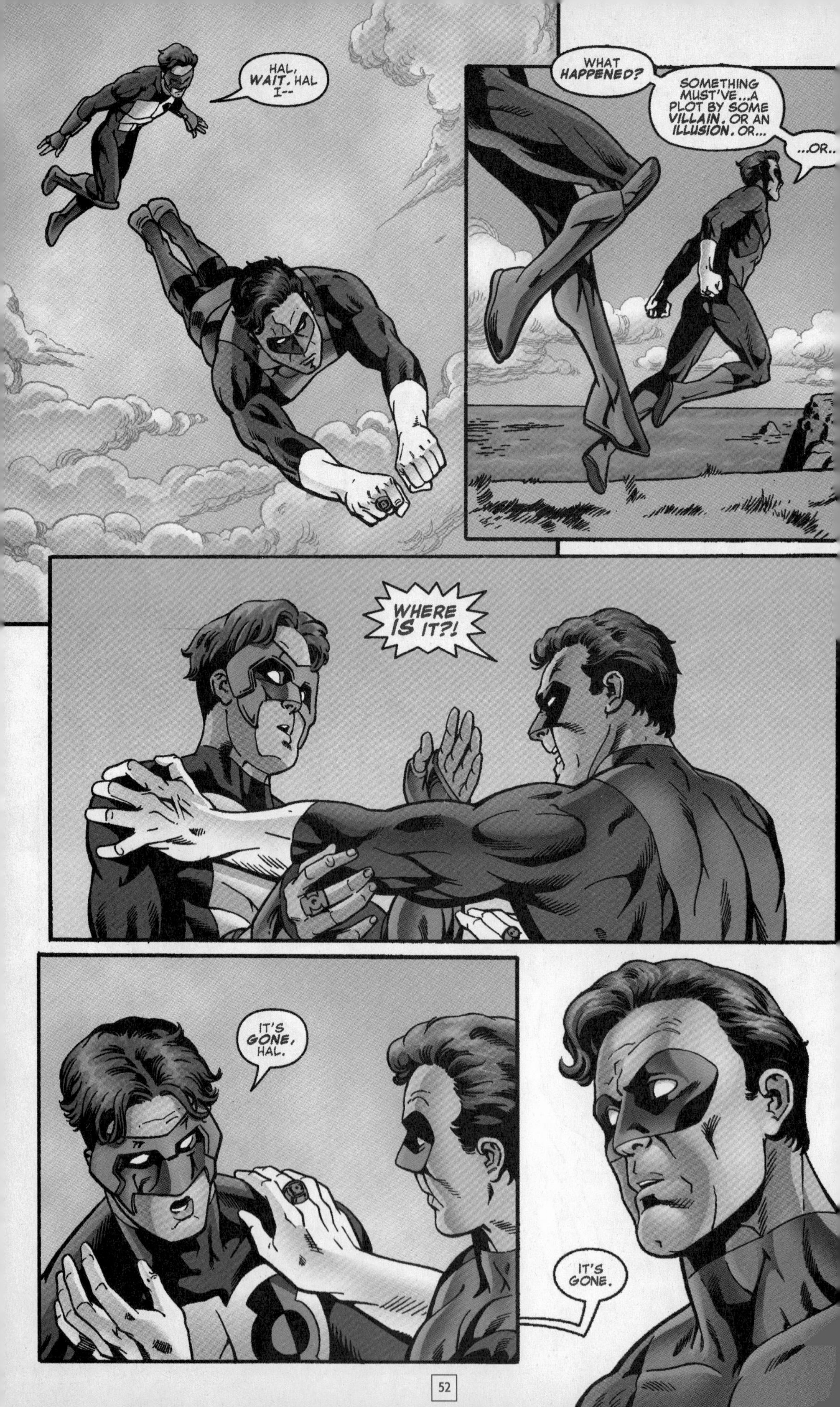
HAL, WAIT. HAL I--
WHAT HAPPENED?
SOMETHING MUST'VE...A PLOT BY SOME VILLAIN. OR AN ILLUSION. OR...
...OR...
WHERE IS IT?!
IT'S GONE, HAL.
IT'S GONE.

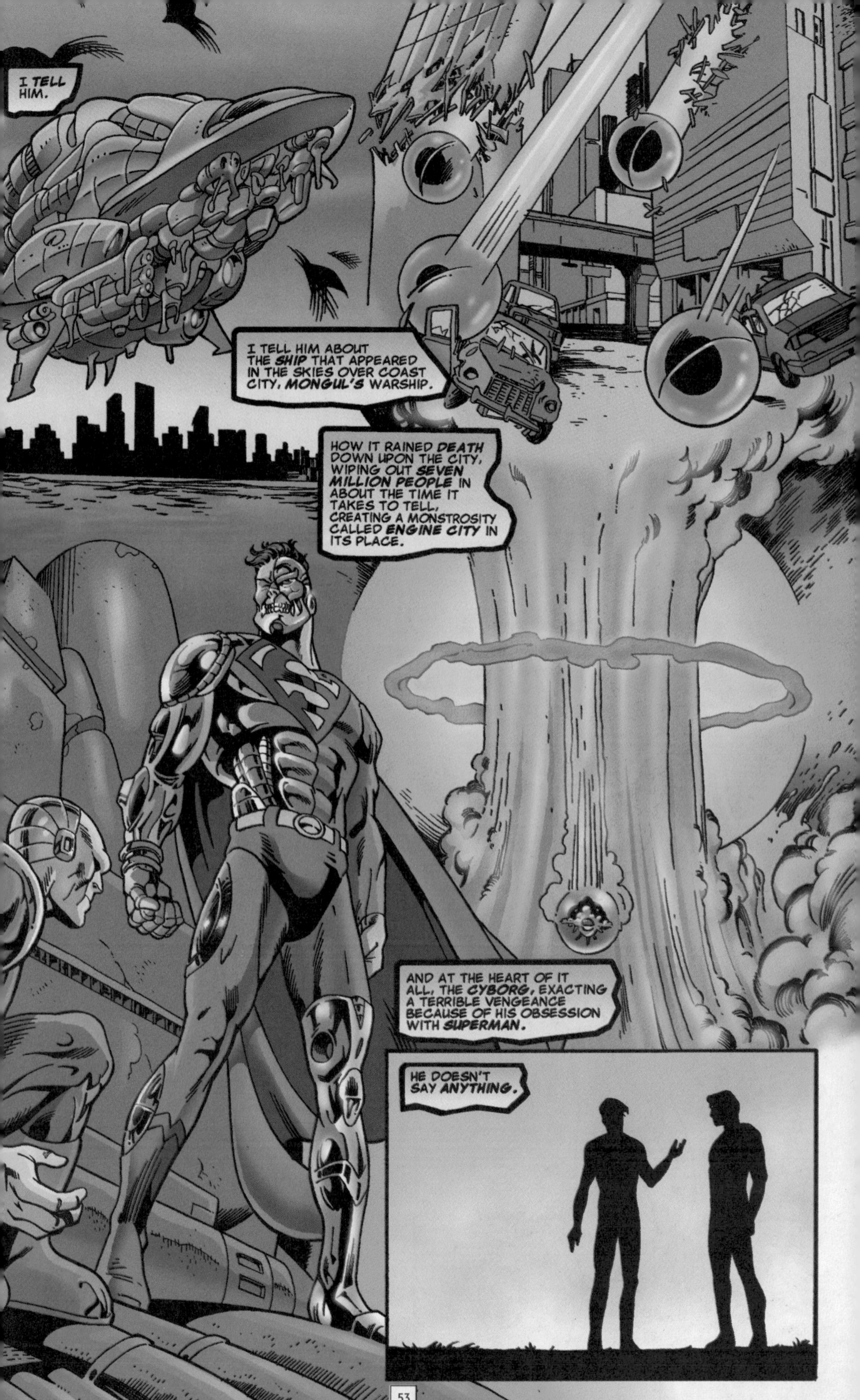
I TELL HIM.
I TELL HIM ABOUT THE SHIP THAT APPEARED IN THE SKIES OVER COAST CITY. MONGUL'S WARSHIP.
HOW IT RAINED DEATH DOWN UPON THE CITY, WIPING OUT SEVEN MILLION PEOPLE IN ABOUT THE TIME IT TAKES TO TELL, CREATING A MONSTROSITY CALLED ENGINE CITY IN ITS PLACE.
AND AT THE HEART OF IT ALL, THE CYBORG, EXACTING A TERRIBLE VENGEANCE BECAUSE OF HIS OBSESSION WITH SUPERMAN.
HE DOESN'T SAY ANYTHING.

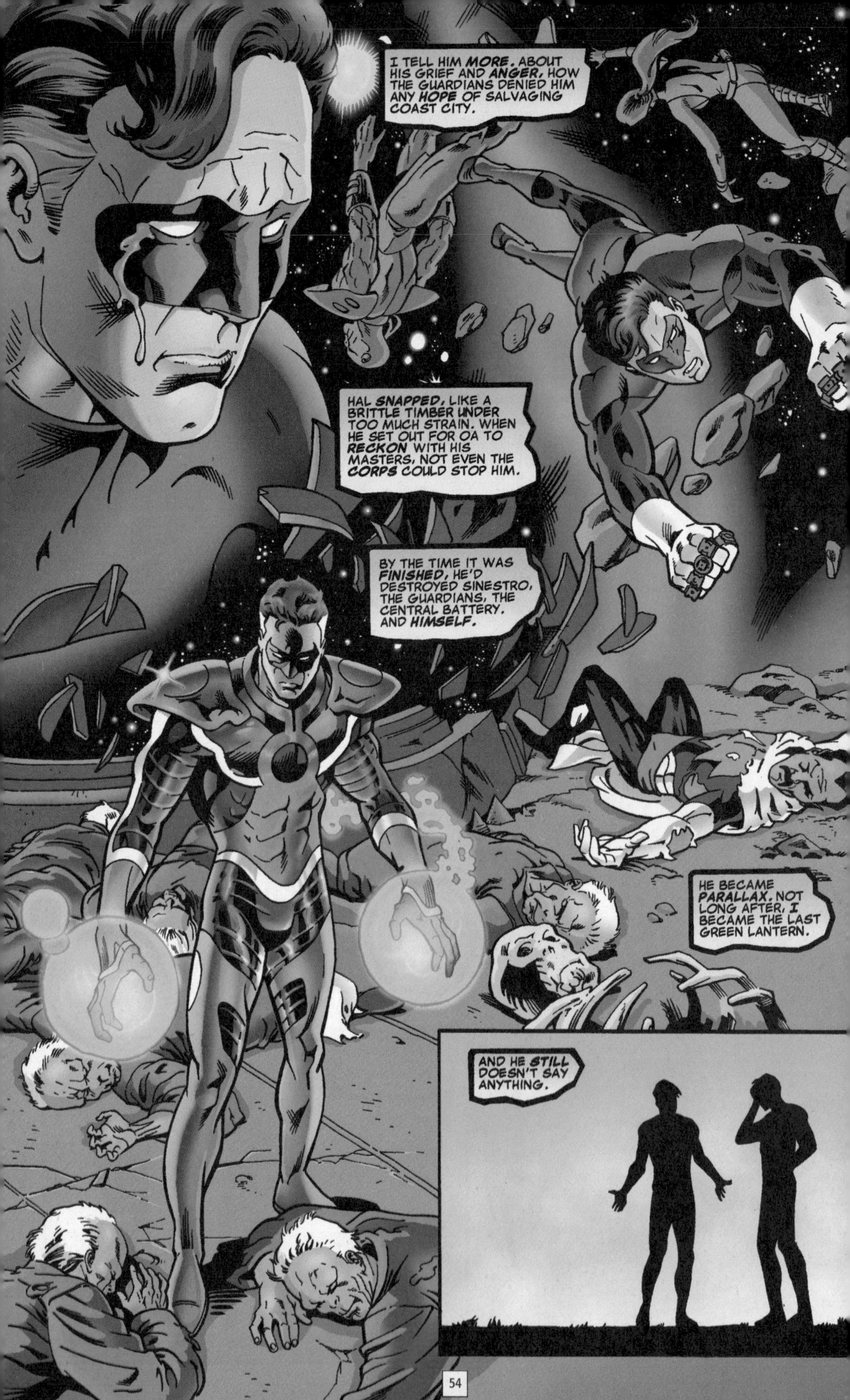
I TELL HIM MORE. ABOUT HIS GRIEF AND ANGER. HOW THE GUARDIANS DENIED HIM ANY HOPE OF SALVAGING COAST CITY.
HAL SNAPPED, LIKE A BRITTLE TIMBER UNDER TOO MUCH STRAIN. WHEN HE SET OUT FOR OA TO RECKON WITH HIS MASTERS, NOT EVEN THE CORPS COULD STOP HIM.
BY THE TIME IT WAS FINISHED, HE'D DESTROYED SINESTRO, THE GUARDIANS, THE CENTRAL BATTERY. AND HIMSELF.
HE BECAME PARALLAX. NOT LONG AFTER, I BECAME THE LAST GREEN LANTERN.
AND HE STILL DOESN'T SAY ANYTHING.

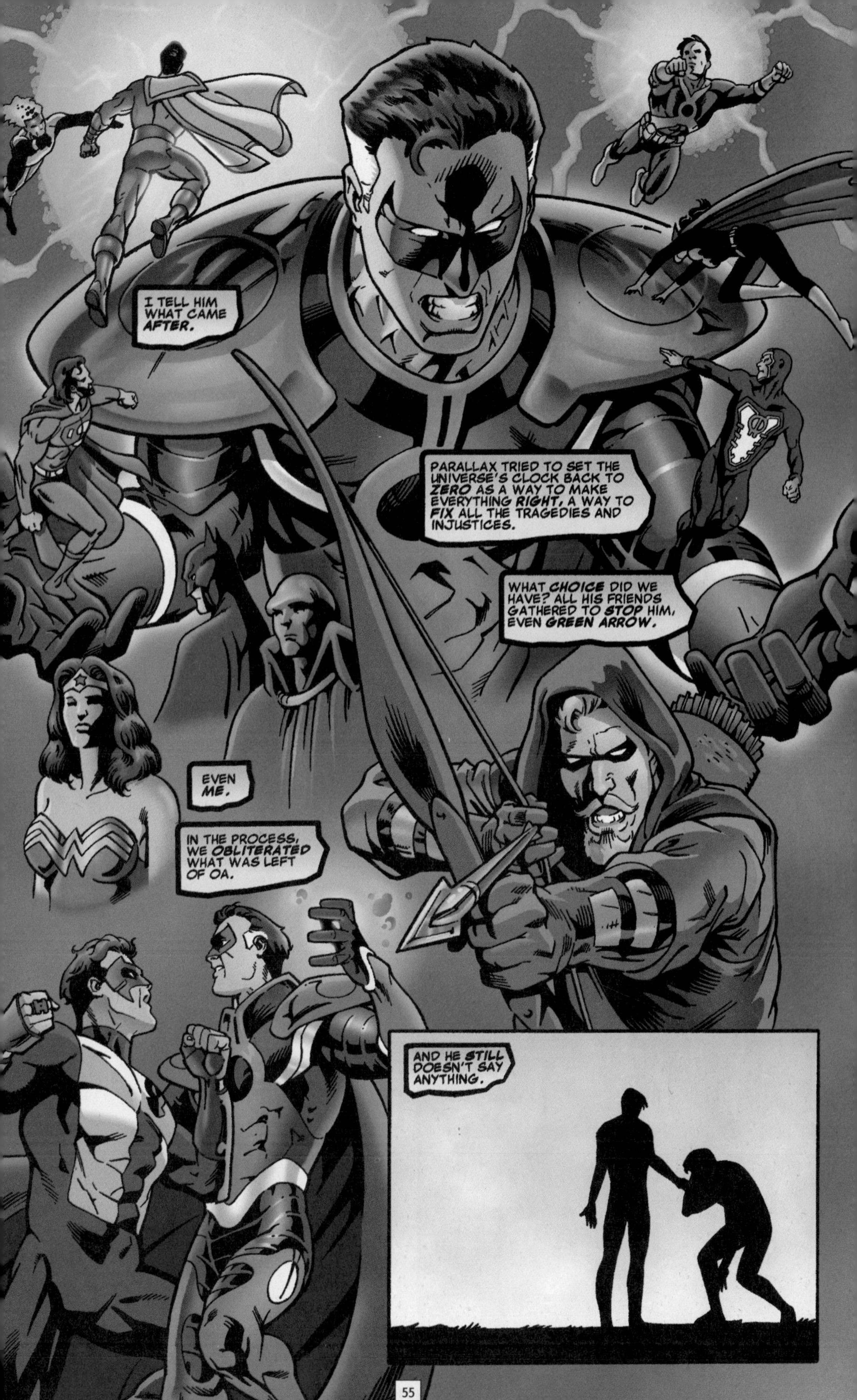
I TELL HIM WHAT CAME AFTER.
PARALLAX TRIED TO SET THE UNIVERSE'S CLOCK BACK TO ZERO AS A WAY TO MAKE EVERYTHING RIGHT, A WAY TO FIX ALL THE TRAGEDIES AND INJUSTICES.
WHAT CHOICE DID WE HAVE? ALL HIS FRIENDS GATHERED TO STOP HIM, EVEN GREEN ARROW.
EVEN ME.
IN THE PROCESS, WE OBLITERATED WHAT WAS LEFT OF OA.
AND HE STILL DOESN'T SAY ANYTHING.

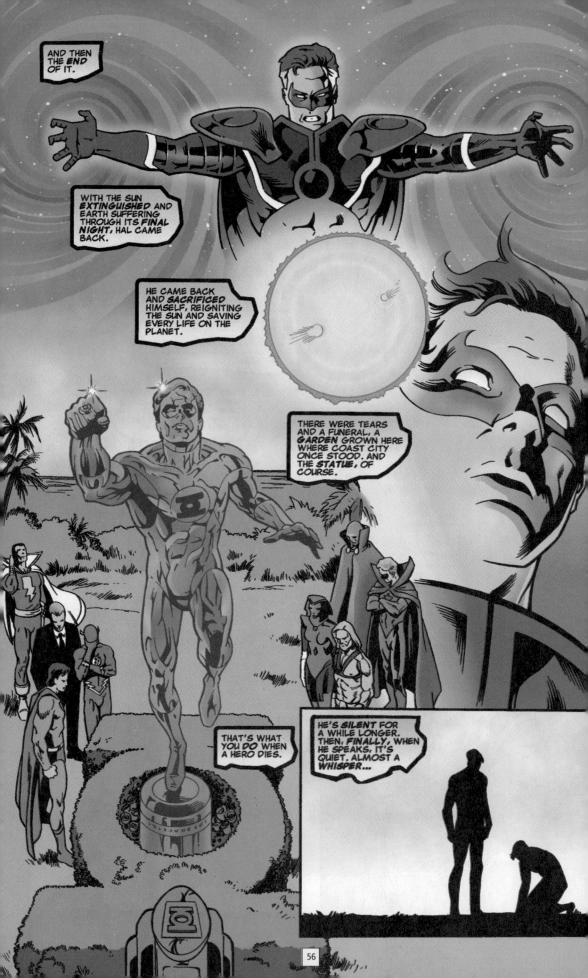

AND THEN THE *END* OF IT.

WITH THE SUN *EXTINGUISHED* AND EARTH SUFFERING THROUGH ITS *FINAL NIGHT,* HAL CAME BACK.

HE CAME BACK AND *SACRIFICED* HIMSELF, REIGNITING THE SUN AND SAVING EVERY LIFE ON THE PLANET.

THERE WERE TEARS AND A FUNERAL, A *GARDEN* GROWN HERE WHERE COAST CITY ONCE STOOD. AND THE *STATUE,* OF COURSE.

THAT'S WHAT YOU *DO* WHEN A HERO DIES.

HE'S *SILENT* FOR A WHILE LONGER. THEN, *FINALLY,* WHEN HE SPEAKS, IT'S QUIET, ALMOST A *WHISPER...*

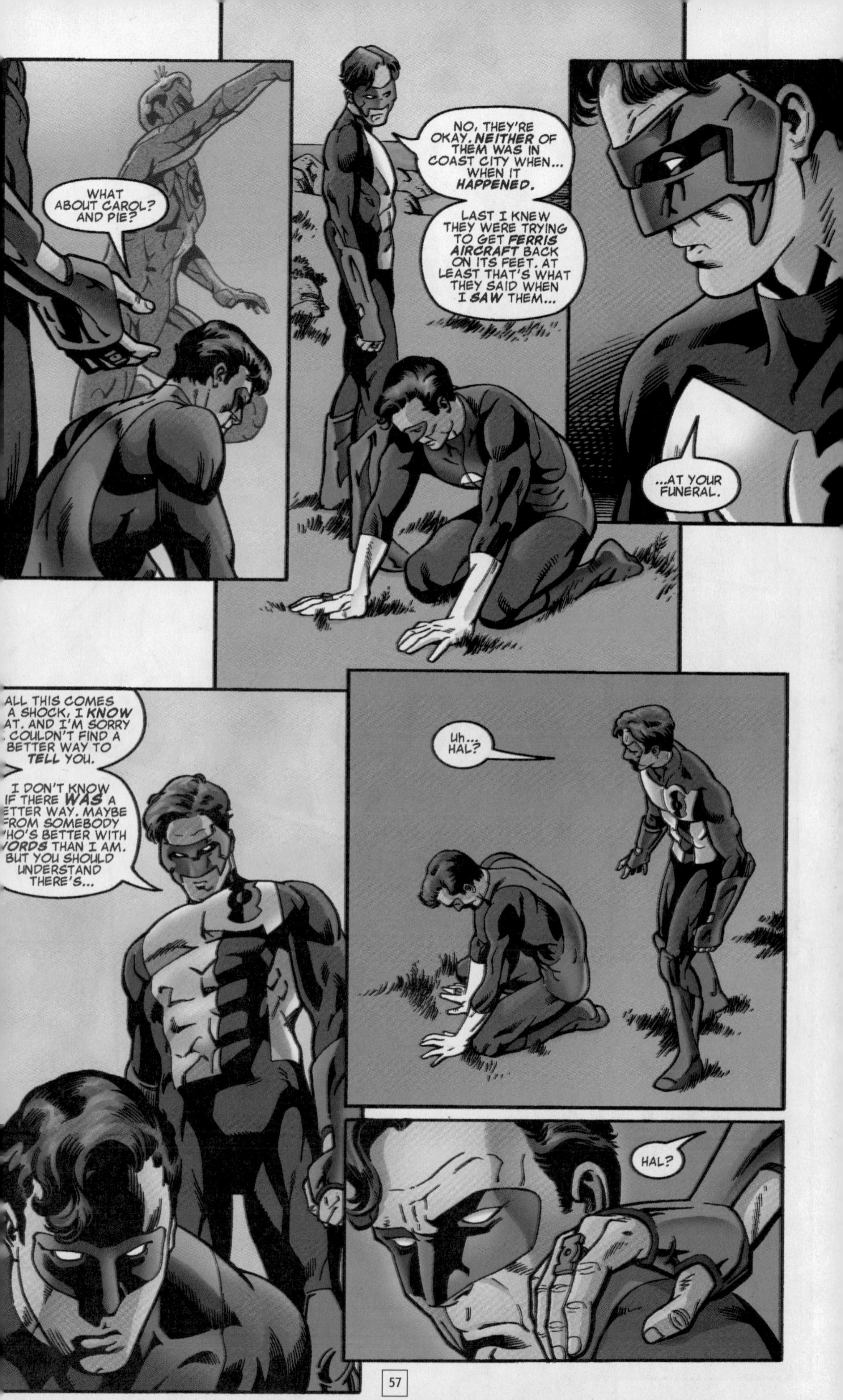
WHAT ABOUT CAROL? AND PIE?
NO, THEY'RE OKAY. NEITHER OF THEM WAS IN COAST CITY WHEN... WHEN IT HAPPENED.
LAST I KNEW THEY WERE TRYING TO GET FERRIS AIRCRAFT BACK ON ITS FEET. AT LEAST THAT'S WHAT THEY SAID WHEN I SAW THEM...
...AT YOUR FUNERAL.
ALL THIS COMES A SHOCK, I KNOW AT. AND I'M SORRY COULDN'T FIND A BETTER WAY TO TELL YOU.
I DON'T KNOW IF THERE WAS A ETTER WAY. MAYBE FROM SOMEBODY HO'S BETTER WITH ORDS THAN I AM. BUT YOU SHOULD UNDERSTAND THERE'S...
UH... HAL?
HAL?

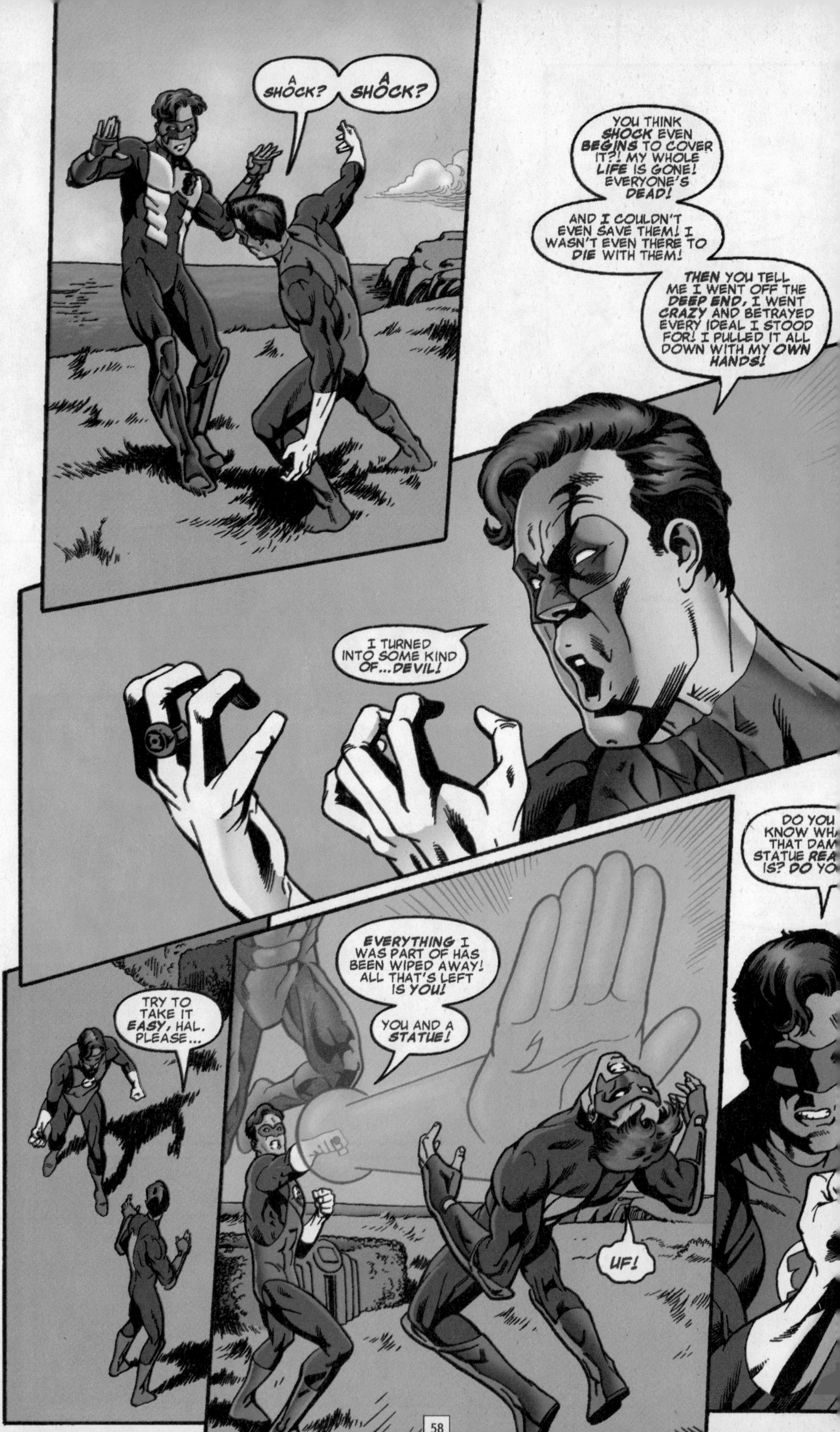

A SHOCK? A SHOCK?
YOU THINK SHOCK EVEN BEGINS TO COVER IT?! MY WHOLE LIFE IS GONE! EVERYONE'S DEAD!
AND I COULDN'T EVEN SAVE THEM! I WASN'T EVEN THERE TO DIE WITH THEM!
THEN YOU TELL ME I WENT OFF THE DEEP END, I WENT CRAZY AND BETRAYED EVERY IDEAL I STOOD FOR! I PULLED IT ALL DOWN WITH MY OWN HANDS!
I TURNED INTO SOME KIND OF...DEVIL!
TRY TO TAKE IT EASY, HAL. PLEASE...
EVERYTHING I WAS PART OF HAS BEEN WIPED AWAY! ALL THAT'S LEFT IS YOU!
YOU AND A STATUE!
UF!
DO YOU KNOW WHA THAT DAM STATUE REA IS? DO YO

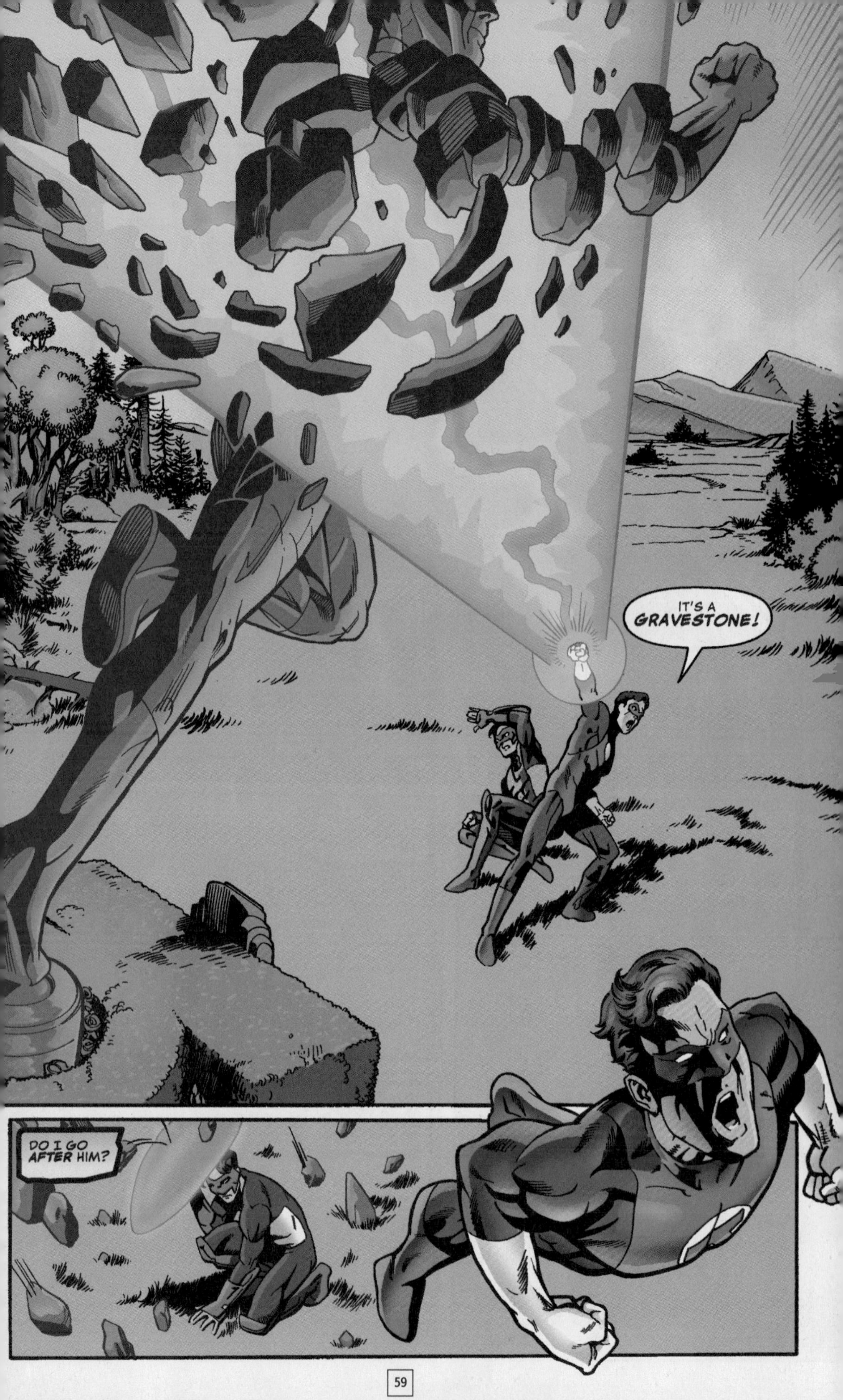
IT'S A GRAVESTONE!
DO I GO AFTER HIM?

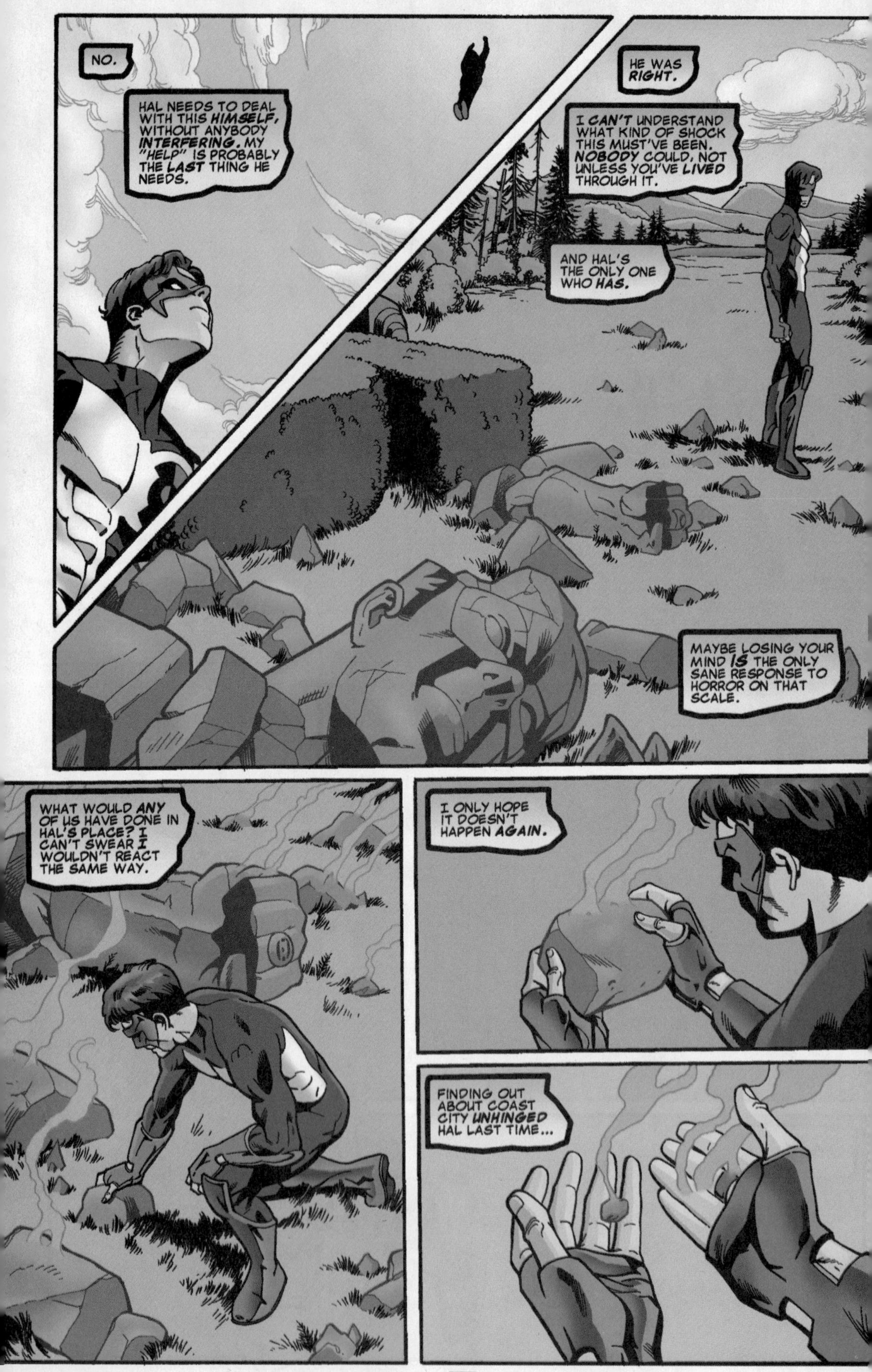
NO.
HAL NEEDS TO DEAL WITH THIS HIMSELF, WITHOUT ANYBODY INTERFERING. MY "HELP" IS PROBABLY THE LAST THING HE NEEDS.
HE WAS RIGHT.
I CAN'T UNDERSTAND WHAT KIND OF SHOCK THIS MUST'VE BEEN. NOBODY COULD, NOT UNLESS YOU'VE LIVED THROUGH IT.
AND HAL'S THE ONLY ONE WHO HAS.
MAYBE LOSING YOUR MIND IS THE ONLY SANE RESPONSE TO HORROR ON THAT SCALE.
WHAT WOULD ANY OF US HAVE DONE IN HAL'S PLACE? I CAN'T SWEAR I WOULDN'T REACT THE SAME WAY.
I ONLY HOPE IT DOESN'T HAPPEN AGAIN.
FINDING OUT ABOUT COAST CITY UNHINGED HAL LAST TIME...

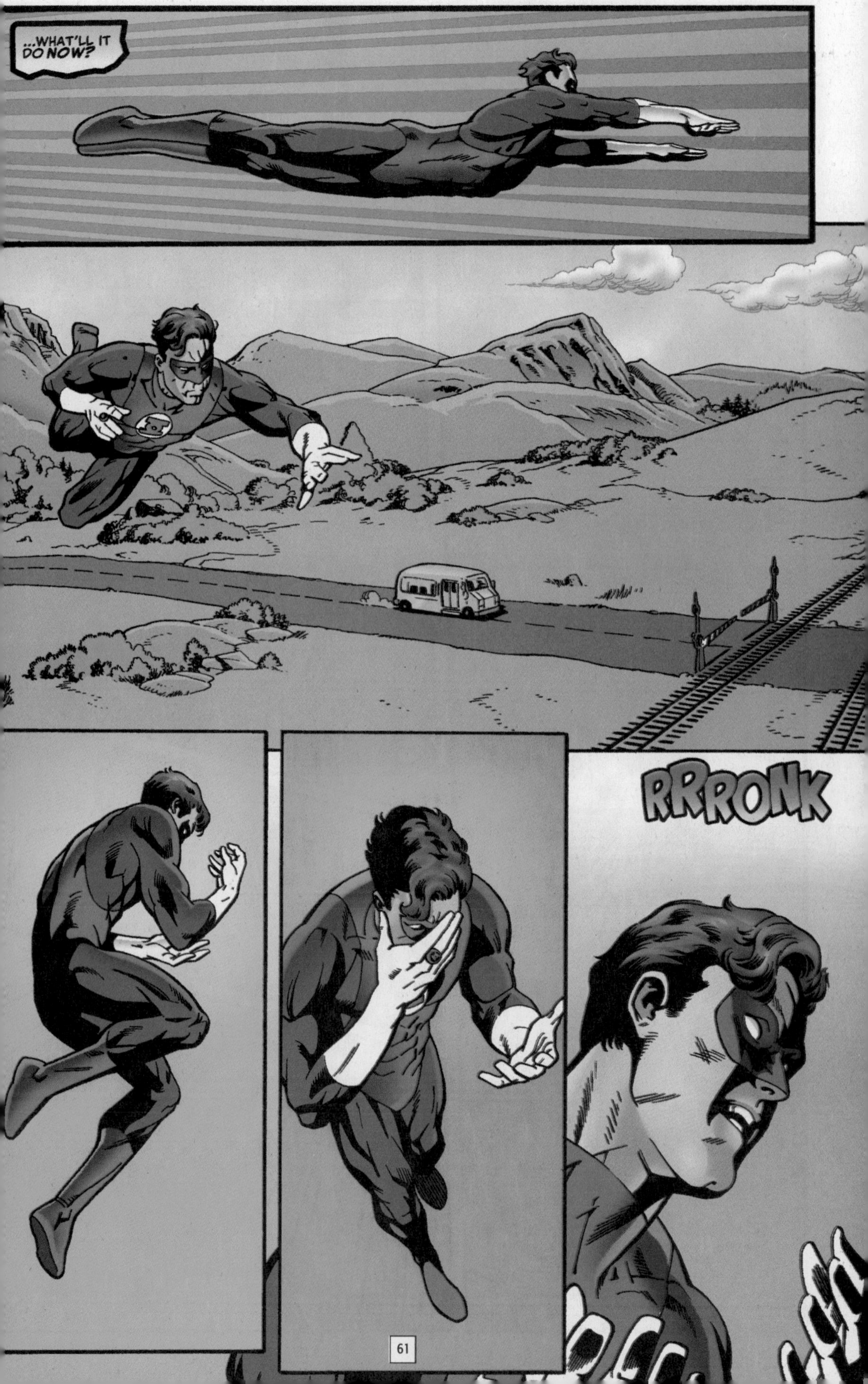
...WHAT'LL IT DO NOW?
RRRONK

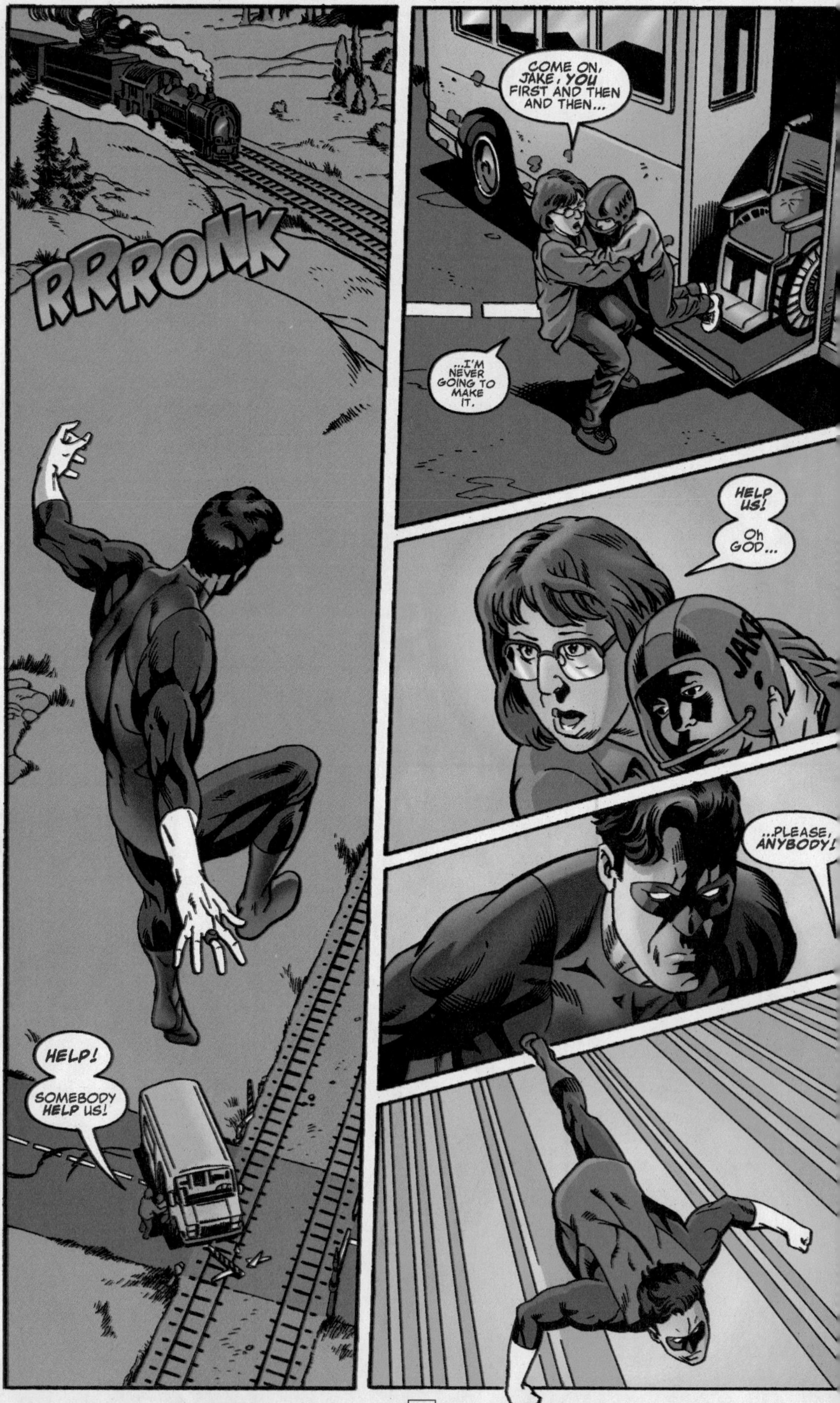
RRRONK
HELP!
SOMEBODY HELP US!
COME ON, JAKE, YOU FIRST AND THEN AND THEN...
...I'M NEVER GOING TO MAKE IT.
HELP US!
Oh GOD...
...PLEASE, ANYBODY!

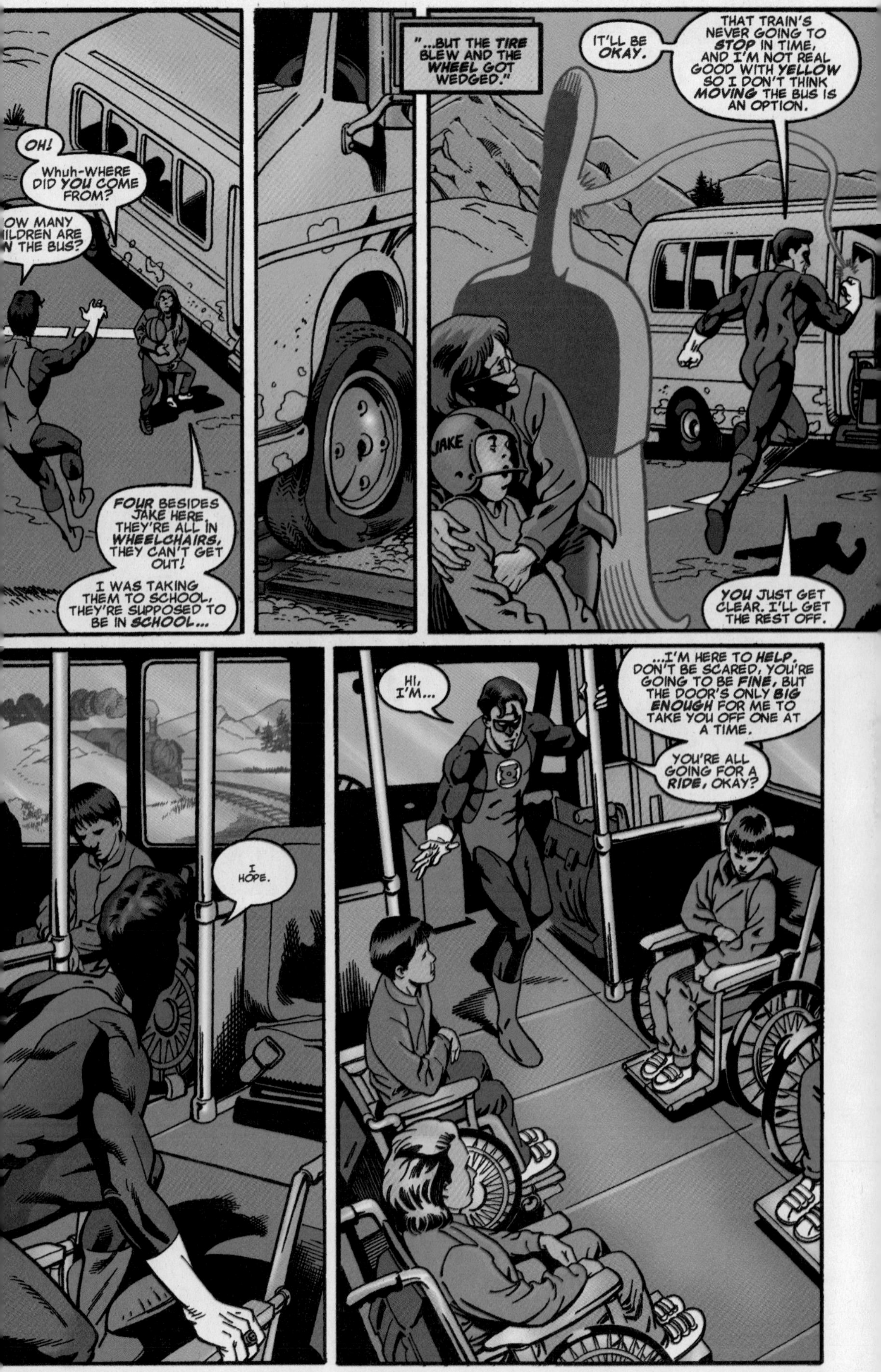
OH!
Whuh-WHERE DID YOU COME FROM?
OW MANY ILDREN ARE N THE BUS?
FOUR BESIDES JAKE HERE. THEY'RE ALL IN WHEELCHAIRS, THEY CAN'T GET OUT!
I WAS TAKING THEM TO SCHOOL, THEY'RE SUPPOSED TO BE IN SCHOOL...
"...BUT THE TIRE BLEW AND THE WHEEL GOT WEDGED."
IT'LL BE OKAY.
THAT TRAIN'S NEVER GOING TO STOP IN TIME, AND I'M NOT REAL GOOD WITH YELLOW SO I DON'T THINK MOVING THE BUS IS AN OPTION.
JAKE
YOU JUST GET CLEAR. I'LL GET THE REST OFF.
I HOPE.
HI, I'M...
...I'M HERE TO HELP. DON'T BE SCARED, YOU'RE GOING TO BE FINE, BUT THE DOOR'S ONLY BIG ENOUGH FOR ME TO TAKE YOU OFF ONE AT A TIME.
YOU'RE ALL GOING FOR A RIDE, OKAY?

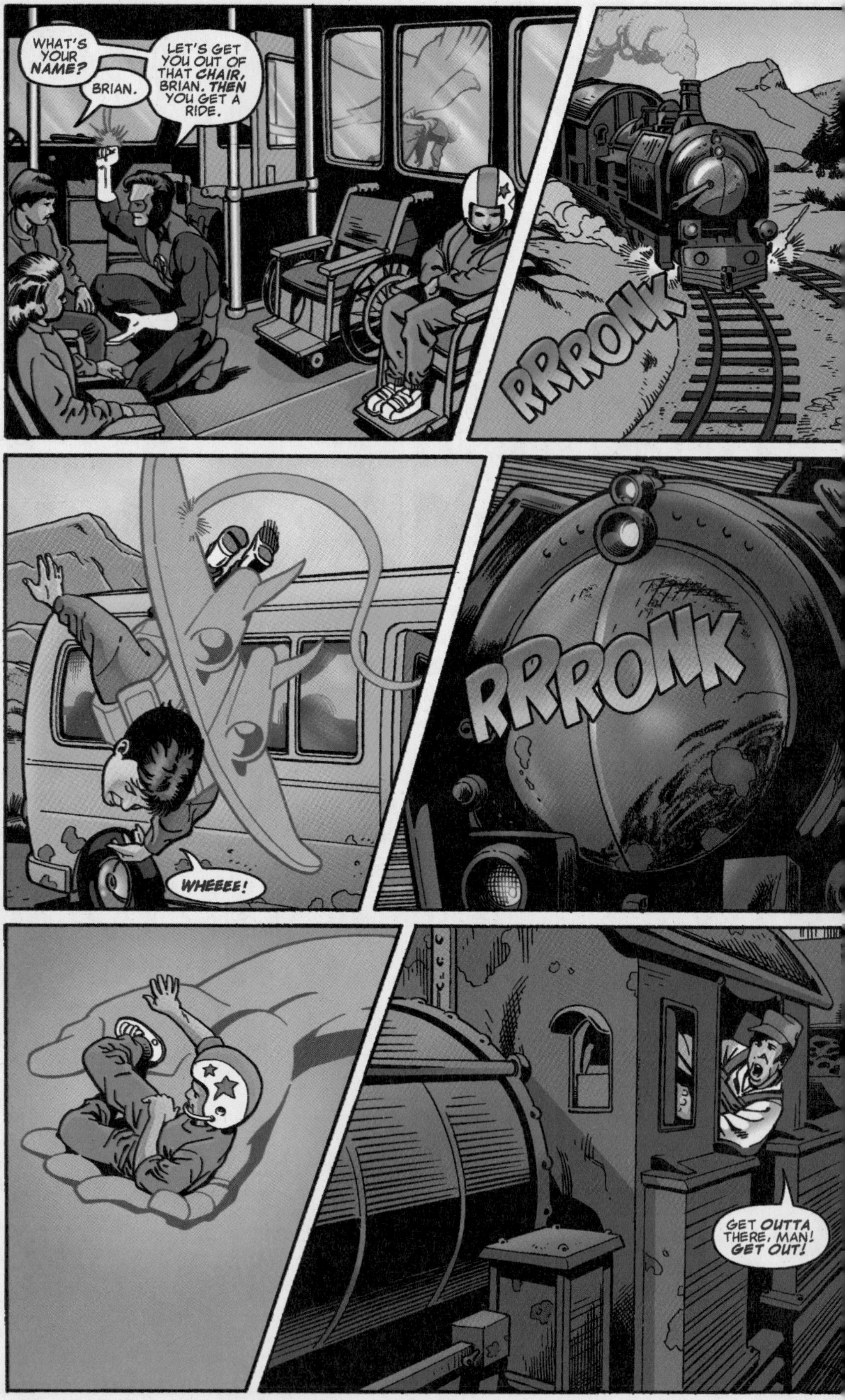
WHAT'S YOUR NAME?
BRIAN.
LET'S GET YOU OUT OF THAT CHAIR, BRIAN. THEN YOU GET A RIDE.
RRRONK
WHEEEE!
RRRONK
GET OUTTA THERE, MAN! GET OUT!

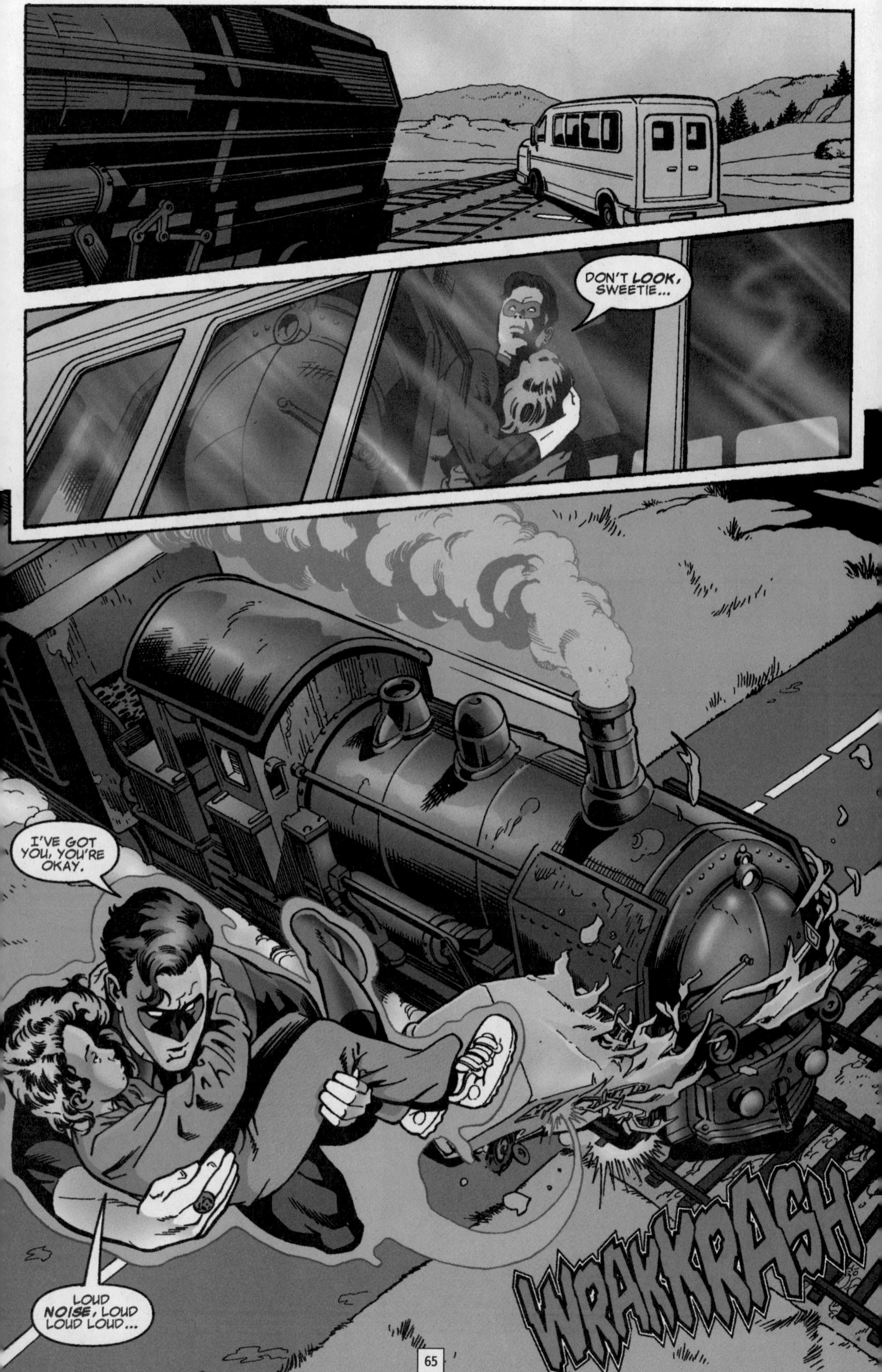

DON'T LOOK, SWEETIE...
I'VE GOT YOU, YOU'RE OKAY.
LOUD NOISE, LOUD LOUD LOUD...
WRAKKRASH

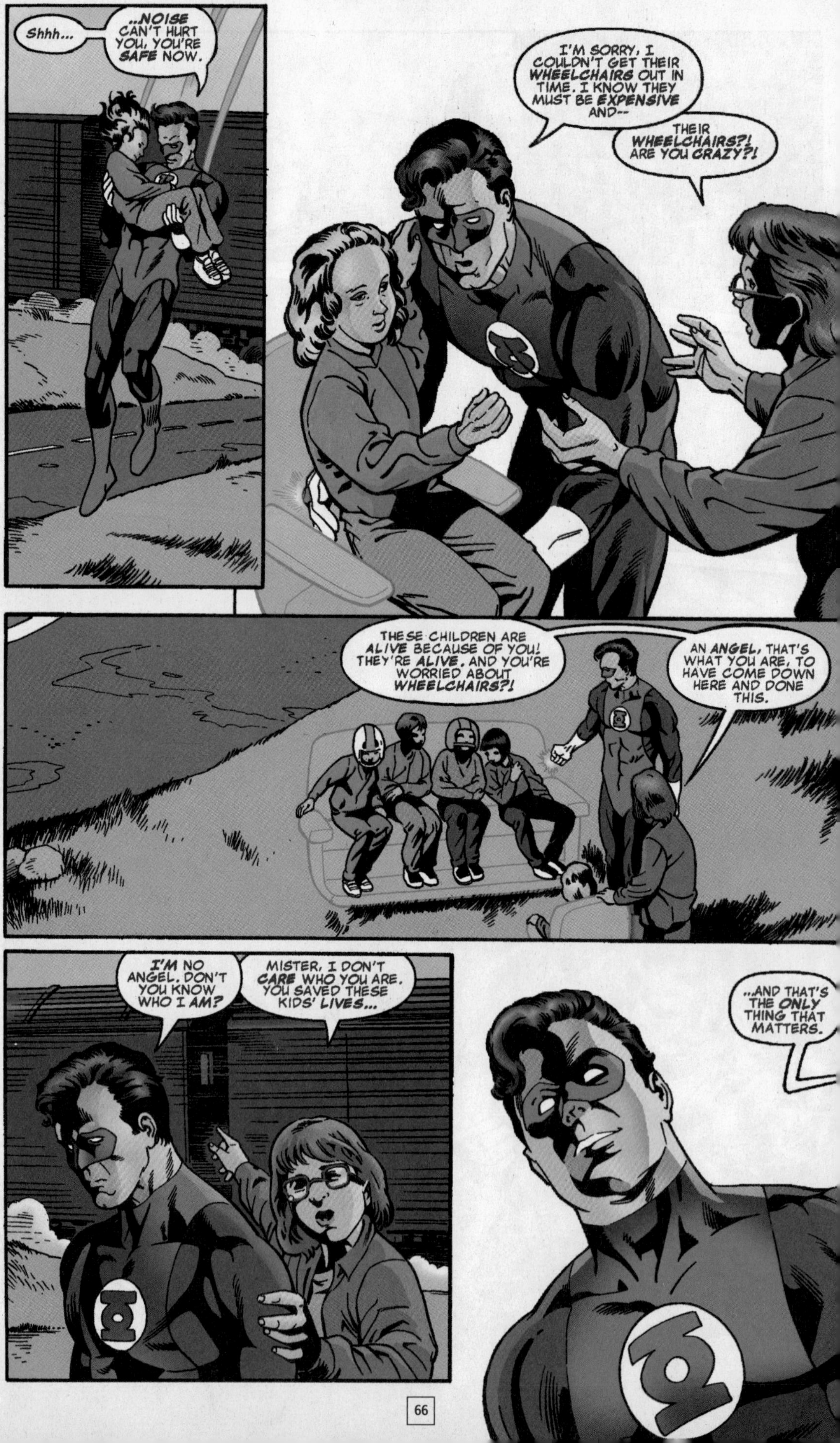

Shhh...
...NOISE CAN'T HURT YOU. YOU'RE SAFE NOW.
I'M SORRY, I COULDN'T GET THEIR WHEELCHAIRS OUT IN TIME. I KNOW THEY MUST BE EXPENSIVE AND--
THEIR WHEELCHAIRS?! ARE YOU CRAZY?!
THESE CHILDREN ARE ALIVE BECAUSE OF YOU! THEY'RE ALIVE. AND YOU'RE WORRIED ABOUT WHEELCHAIRS?!
AN ANGEL, THAT'S WHAT YOU ARE, TO HAVE COME DOWN HERE AND DONE THIS.
I'M NO ANGEL. DON'T YOU KNOW WHO I AM?
MISTER, I DON'T CARE WHO YOU ARE. YOU SAVED THESE KIDS' LIVES...
...AND THAT'S THE ONLY THING THAT MATTERS.

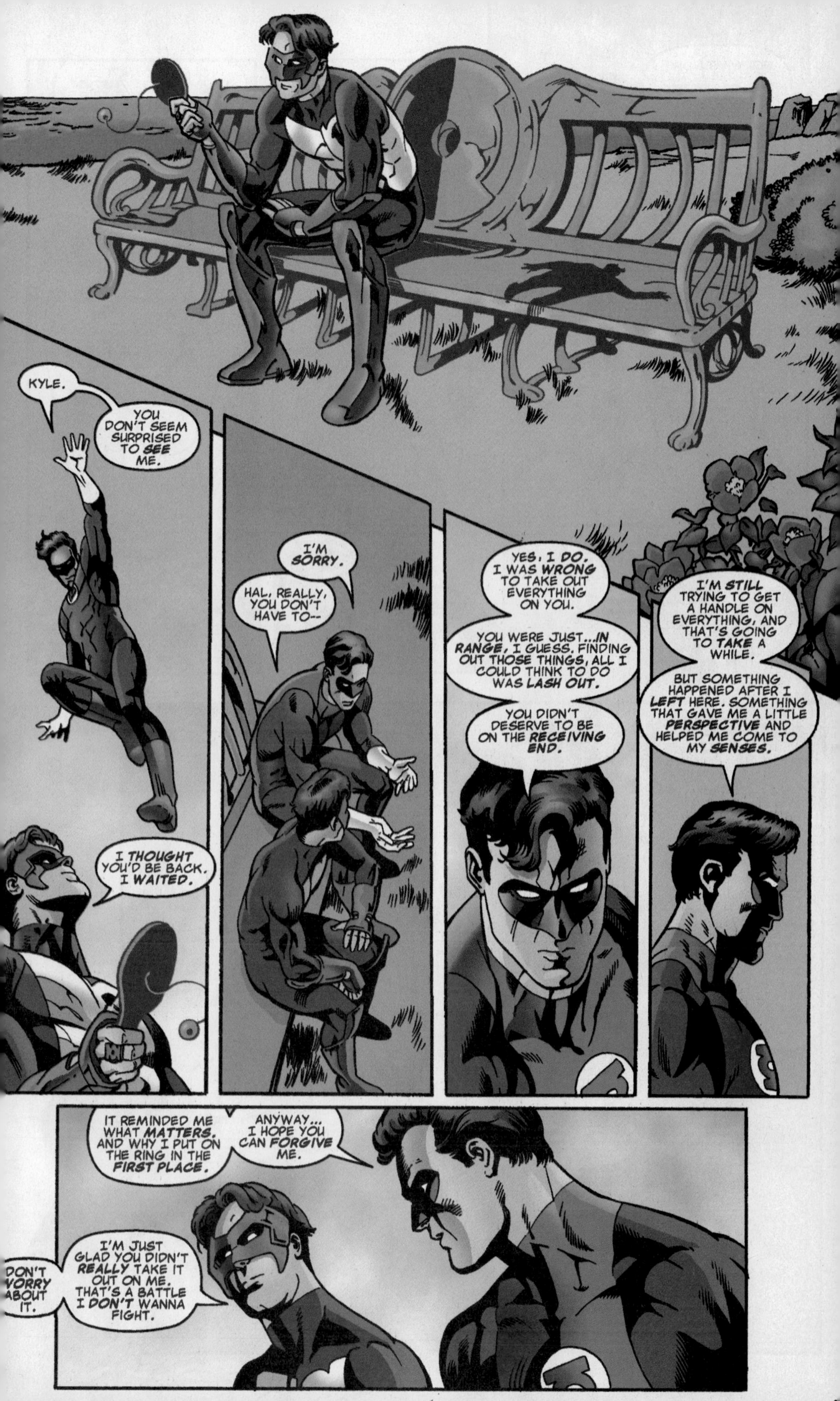
KYLE.
YOU DON'T SEEM SURPRISED TO SEE ME.
I THOUGHT YOU'D BE BACK. I WAITED.
I'M SORRY.
HAL, REALLY, YOU DON'T HAVE TO--
YES, I DO. I WAS WRONG TO TAKE OUT EVERYTHING ON YOU.
YOU WERE JUST...IN RANGE, I GUESS. FINDING OUT THOSE THINGS, ALL I COULD THINK TO DO WAS LASH OUT.
YOU DIDN'T DESERVE TO BE ON THE RECEIVING END.
I'M STILL TRYING TO GET A HANDLE ON EVERYTHING, AND THAT'S GOING TO TAKE A WHILE.
BUT SOMETHING HAPPENED AFTER I LEFT HERE. SOMETHING THAT GAVE ME A LITTLE PERSPECTIVE AND HELPED ME COME TO MY SENSES.
IT REMINDED ME WHAT MATTERS, AND WHY I PUT ON THE RING IN THE FIRST PLACE.
ANYWAY... I HOPE YOU CAN FORGIVE ME.
DON'T WORRY ABOUT IT.
I'M JUST GLAD YOU DIDN'T REALLY TAKE IT OUT ON ME. THAT'S A BATTLE I DON'T WANNA FIGHT.

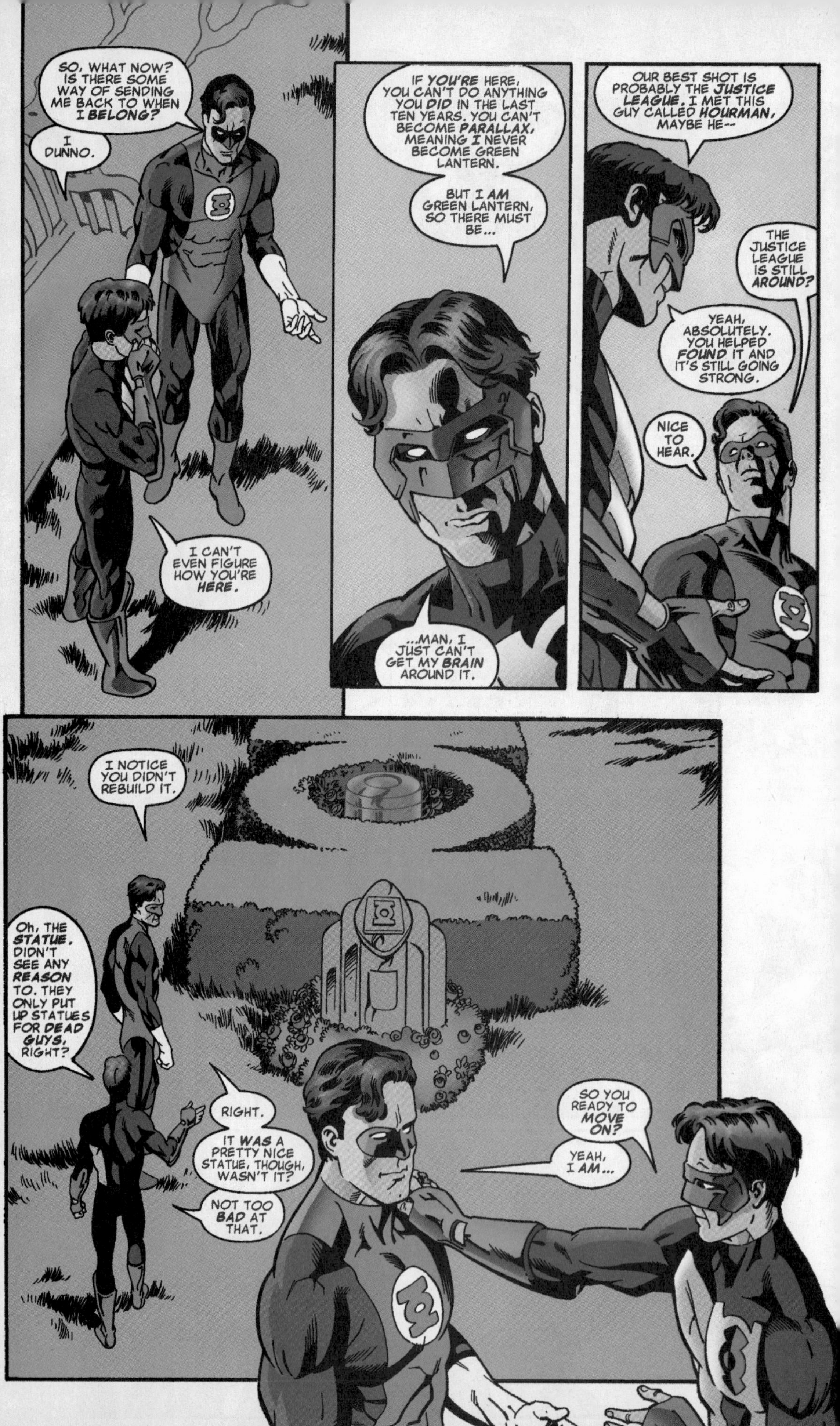
SO, WHAT NOW? IS THERE SOME WAY OF SENDING ME BACK TO WHEN I BELONG?
I DUNNO.
I CAN'T EVEN FIGURE HOW YOU'RE HERE.
IF YOU'RE HERE, YOU CAN'T DO ANYTHING YOU DID IN THE LAST TEN YEARS. YOU CAN'T BECOME PARALLAX, MEANING I NEVER BECOME GREEN LANTERN.
BUT I AM GREEN LANTERN, SO THERE MUST BE...
...MAN, I JUST CAN'T GET MY BRAIN AROUND IT.
OUR BEST SHOT IS PROBABLY THE JUSTICE LEAGUE. I MET THIS GUY CALLED HOURMAN, MAYBE HE--
THE JUSTICE LEAGUE IS STILL AROUND?
YEAH, ABSOLUTELY. YOU HELPED FOUND IT AND IT'S STILL GOING STRONG.
NICE TO HEAR.
I NOTICE YOU DIDN'T REBUILD IT.
Oh, THE STATUE. DIDN'T SEE ANY REASON TO. THEY ONLY PUT UP STATUES FOR DEAD GUYS, RIGHT?
RIGHT.
IT WAS A PRETTY NICE STATUE, THOUGH, WASN'T IT?
NOT TOO BAD AT THAT.
SO YOU READY TO MOVE ON?
YEAH, I AM...

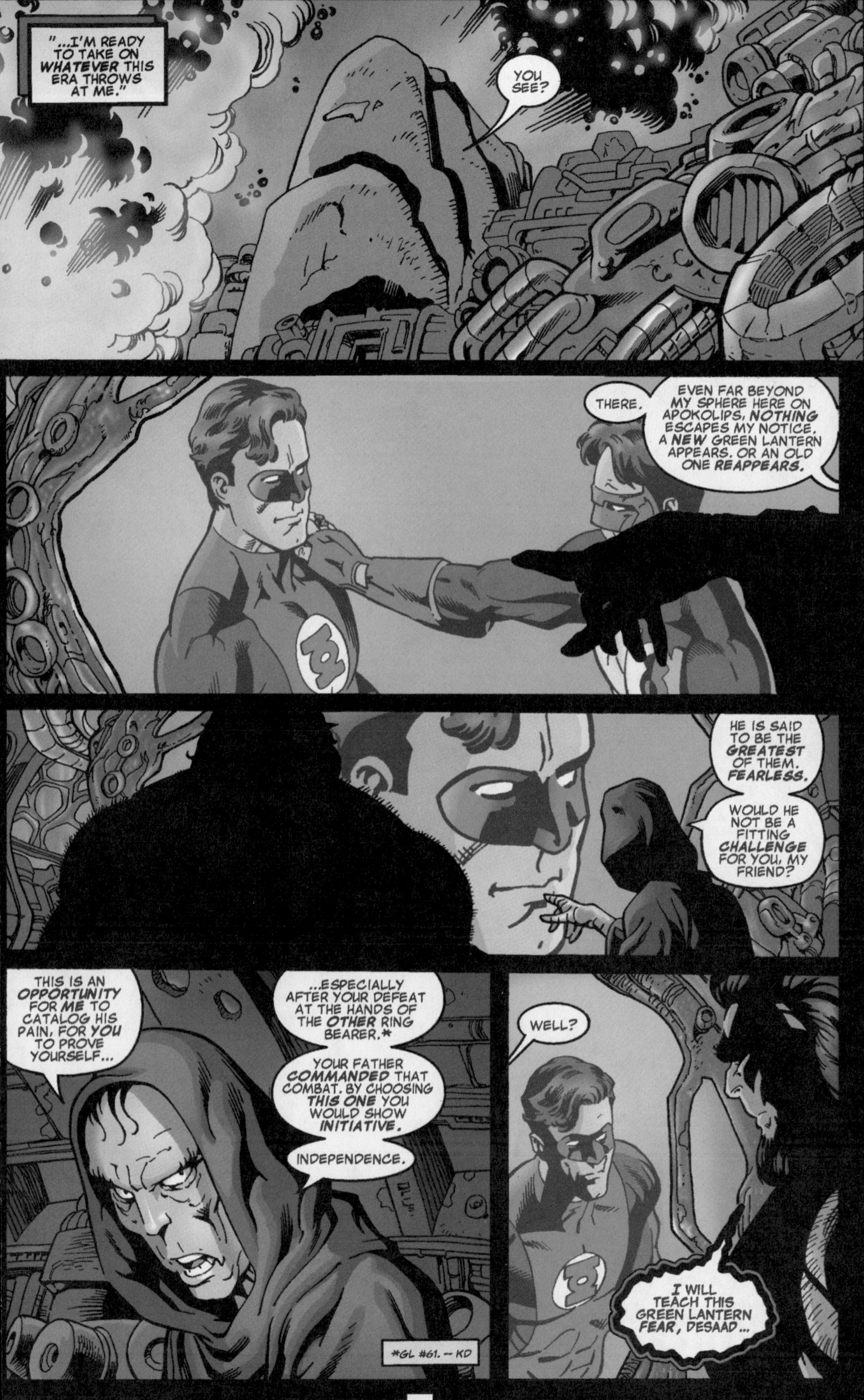
"...I'M READY TO TAKE ON WHATEVER THIS ERA THROWS AT ME."
YOU SEE?
THERE.
EVEN FAR BEYOND MY SPHERE HERE ON APOKOLIPS, NOTHING ESCAPES MY NOTICE. A NEW GREEN LANTERN APPEARS. OR AN OLD ONE REAPPEARS.
HE IS SAID TO BE THE GREATEST OF THEM. FEARLESS.
WOULD HE NOT BE A FITTING CHALLENGE FOR YOU, MY FRIEND?
THIS IS AN OPPORTUNITY FOR ME TO CATALOG HIS PAIN, FOR YOU TO PROVE YOURSELF...
...ESPECIALLY AFTER YOUR DEFEAT AT THE HANDS OF THE OTHER RING BEARER.*
YOUR FATHER COMMANDED THAT COMBAT. BY CHOOSING THIS ONE YOU WOULD SHOW INITIATIVE.
INDEPENDENCE.
*GL #61. -- KD
WELL?
I WILL TEACH THIS GREEN LANTERN FEAR, DESAAD...

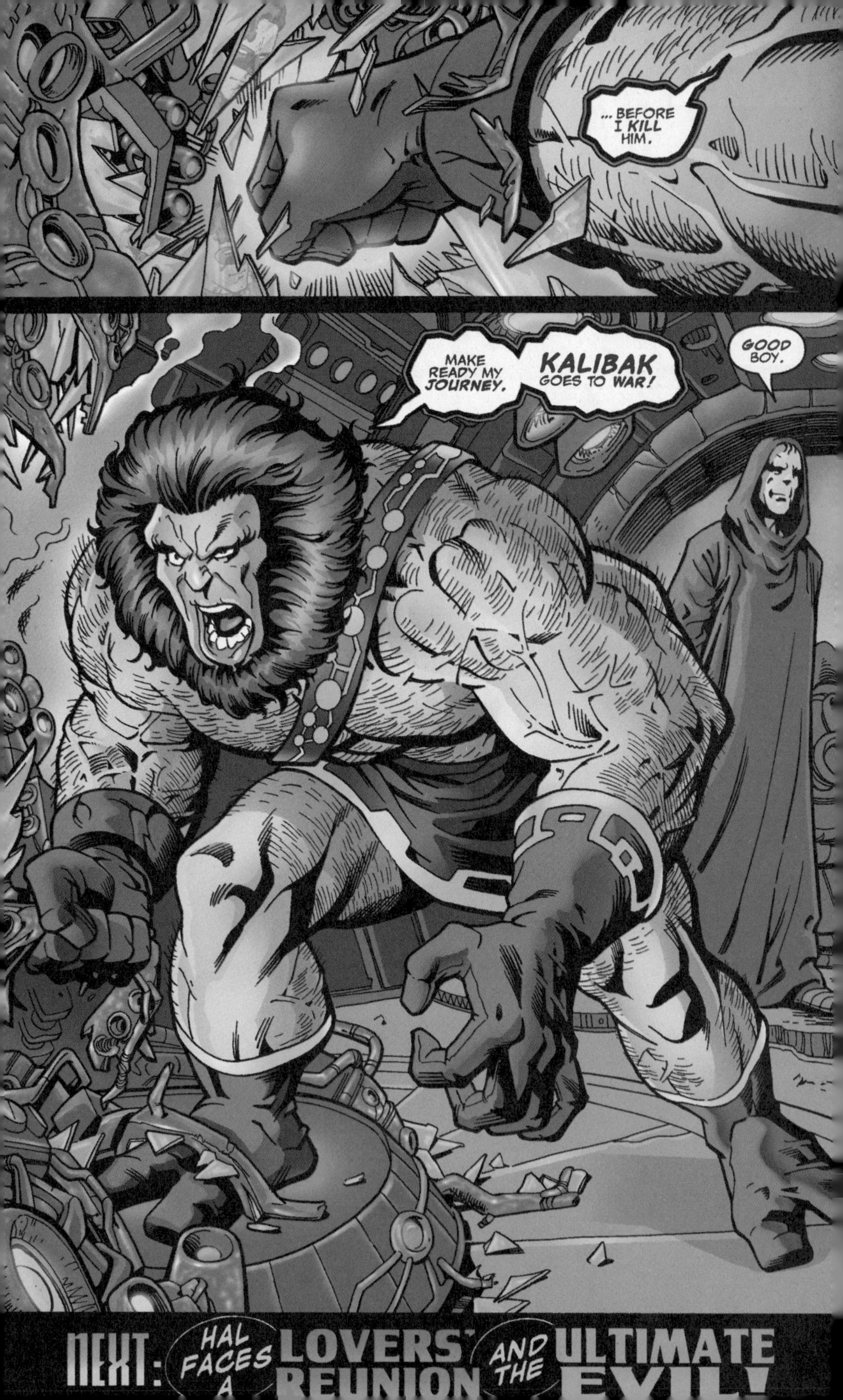
...BEFORE I KILL HIM.
MAKE READY MY JOURNEY.
KALIBAK GOES TO WAR!
GOOD BOY.
NEXT: HAL FACES A LOVERS' REUNION AND THE ULTIMATE EVIL!

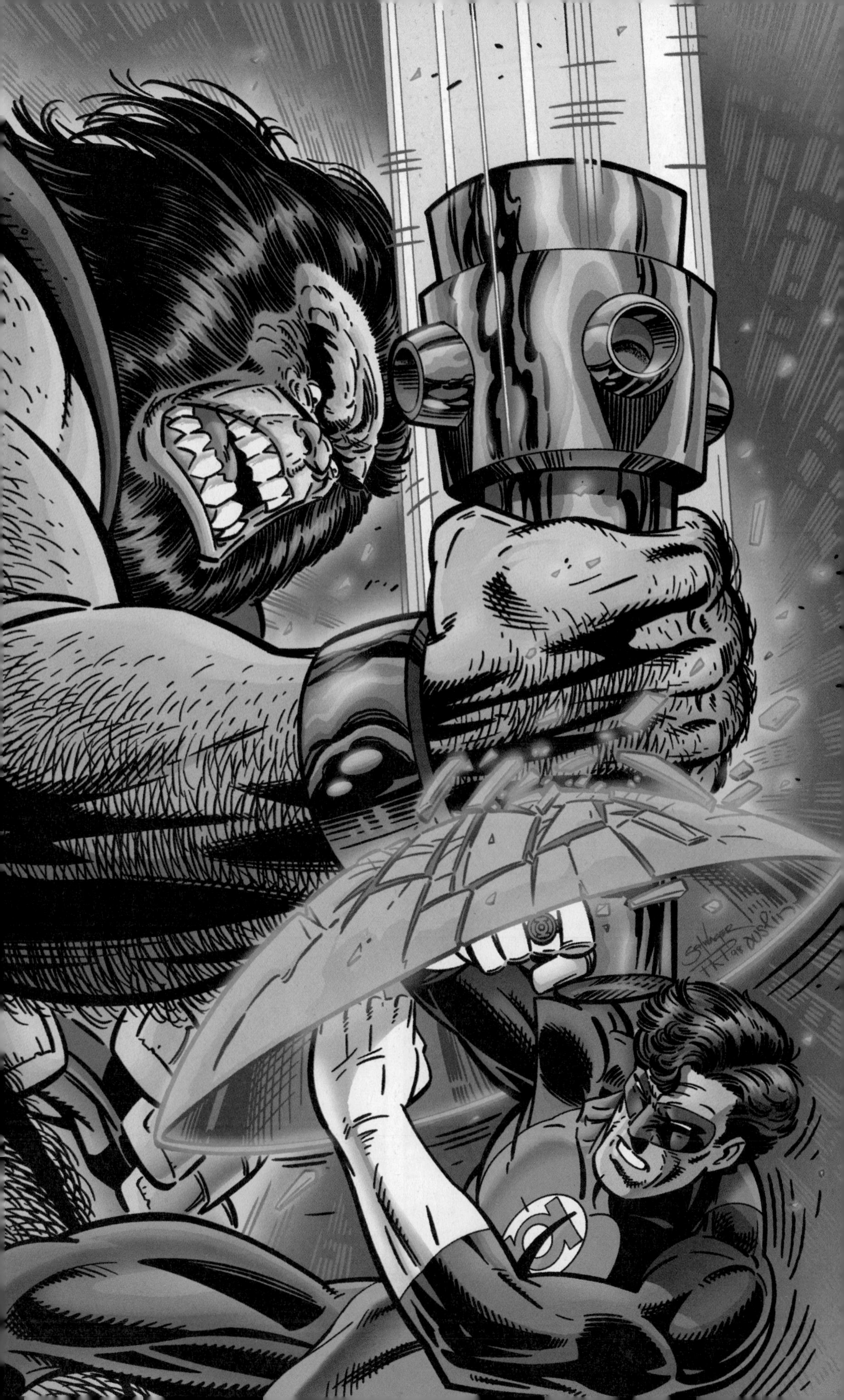

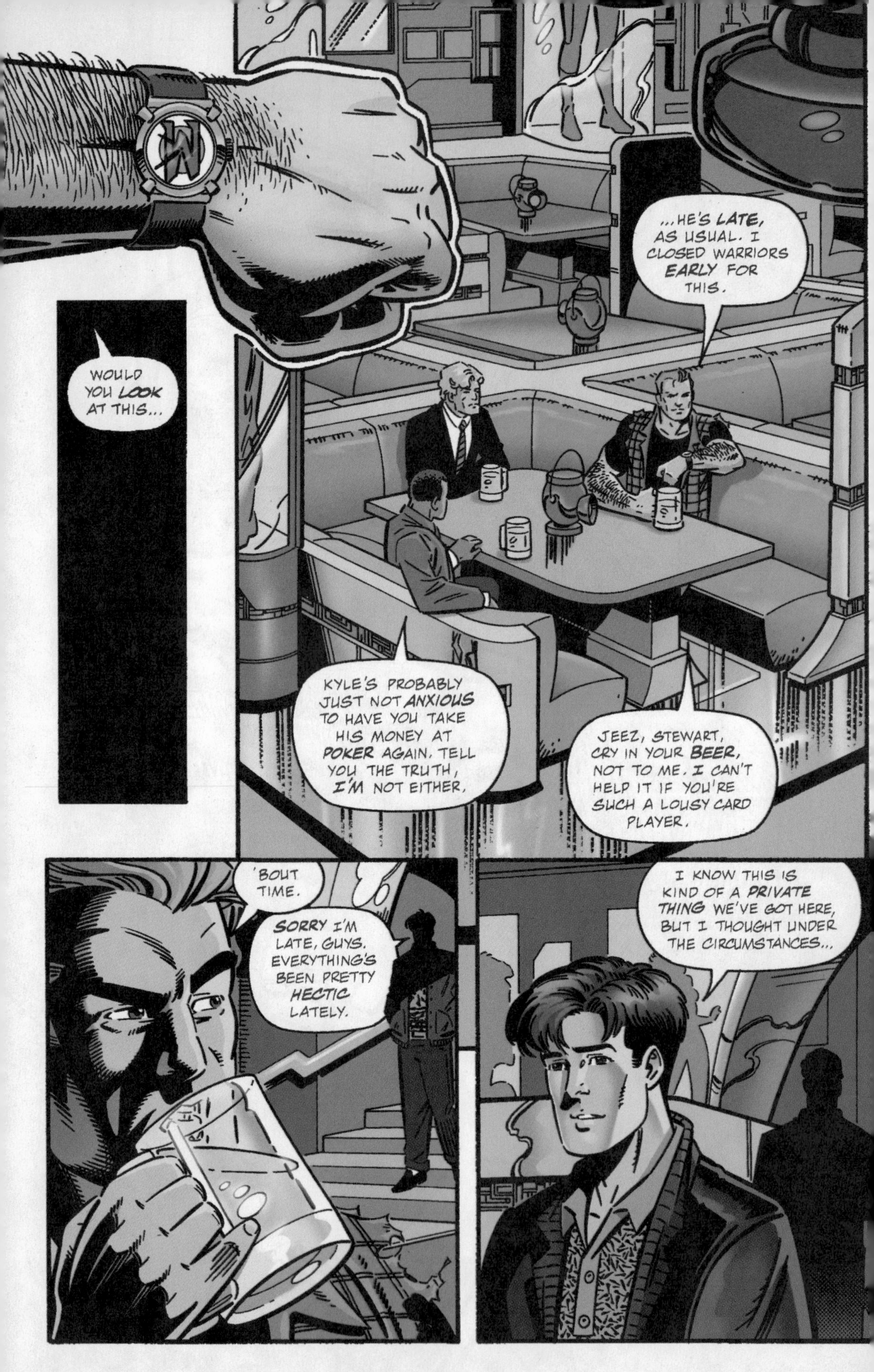

WOULD YOU LOOK AT THIS...
...HE'S LATE, AS USUAL. I CLOSED WARRIORS EARLY FOR THIS.
KYLE'S PROBABLY JUST NOT ANXIOUS TO HAVE YOU TAKE HIS MONEY AT POKER AGAIN. TELL YOU THE TRUTH, I'M NOT EITHER.
JEEZ, STEWART, CRY IN YOUR BEER, NOT TO ME. I CAN'T HELP IT IF YOU'RE SUCH A LOUSY CARD PLAYER.
'BOUT TIME.
SORRY I'M LATE, GUYS. EVERYTHING'S BEEN PRETTY HECTIC LATELY.
I KNOW THIS IS KIND OF A PRIVATE THING WE'VE GOT HERE, BUT I THOUGHT UNDER THE CIRCUMSTANCES...

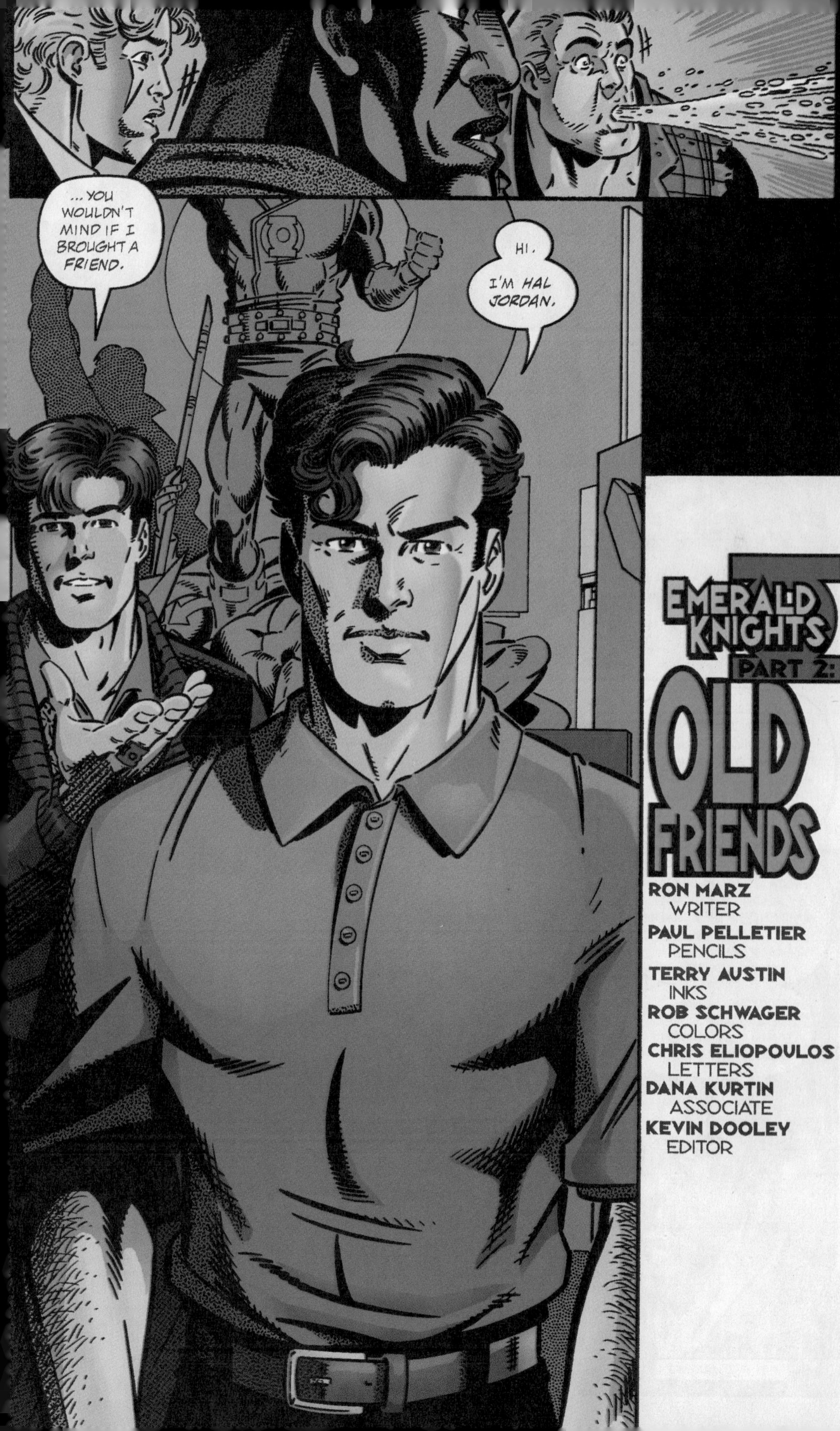
...YOU WOULDN'T MIND IF I BROUGHT A FRIEND.
HI.
I'M HAL JORDAN.
EMERALD KNIGHTS
PART 2:
OLD FRIENDS
RON MARZ
WRITER
PAUL PELLETIER
PENCILS
TERRY AUSTIN
INKS
ROB SCHWAGER
COLORS
CHRIS ELIOPOULOS
LETTERS
DANA KURTIN
ASSOCIATE
KEVIN DOOLEY
EDITOR

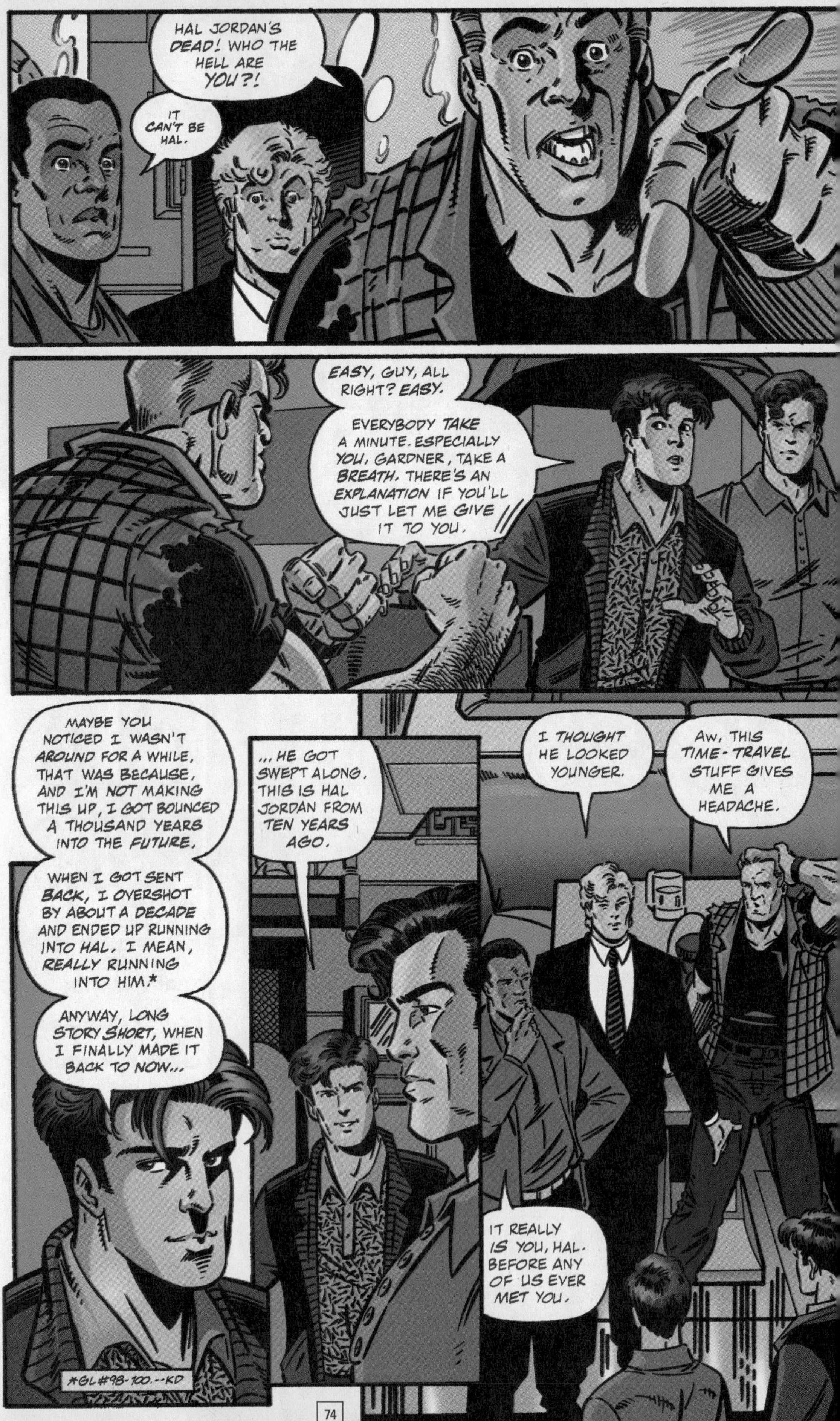
HAL JORDAN'S DEAD! WHO THE HELL ARE YOU?!
IT CAN'T BE HAL.
EASY, GUY, ALL RIGHT? EASY.
EVERYBODY TAKE A MINUTE. ESPECIALLY YOU, GARDNER, TAKE A BREATH. THERE'S AN EXPLANATION IF YOU'LL JUST LET ME GIVE IT TO YOU.
MAYBE YOU NOTICED I WASN'T AROUND FOR A WHILE. THAT WAS BECAUSE, AND I'M NOT MAKING THIS UP, I GOT BOUNCED A THOUSAND YEARS INTO THE FUTURE.
WHEN I GOT SENT BACK, I OVERSHOT BY ABOUT A DECADE AND ENDED UP RUNNING INTO HAL. I MEAN, REALLY RUNNING INTO HIM.*
ANYWAY, LONG STORY SHORT, WHEN I FINALLY MADE IT BACK TO NOW...
*GL #98-100.--KD
...HE GOT SWEPT ALONG. THIS IS HAL JORDAN FROM TEN YEARS AGO.
I THOUGHT HE LOOKED YOUNGER.
AW, THIS TIME-TRAVEL STUFF GIVES ME A HEADACHE.
IT REALLY IS YOU, HAL. BEFORE ANY OF US EVER MET YOU.

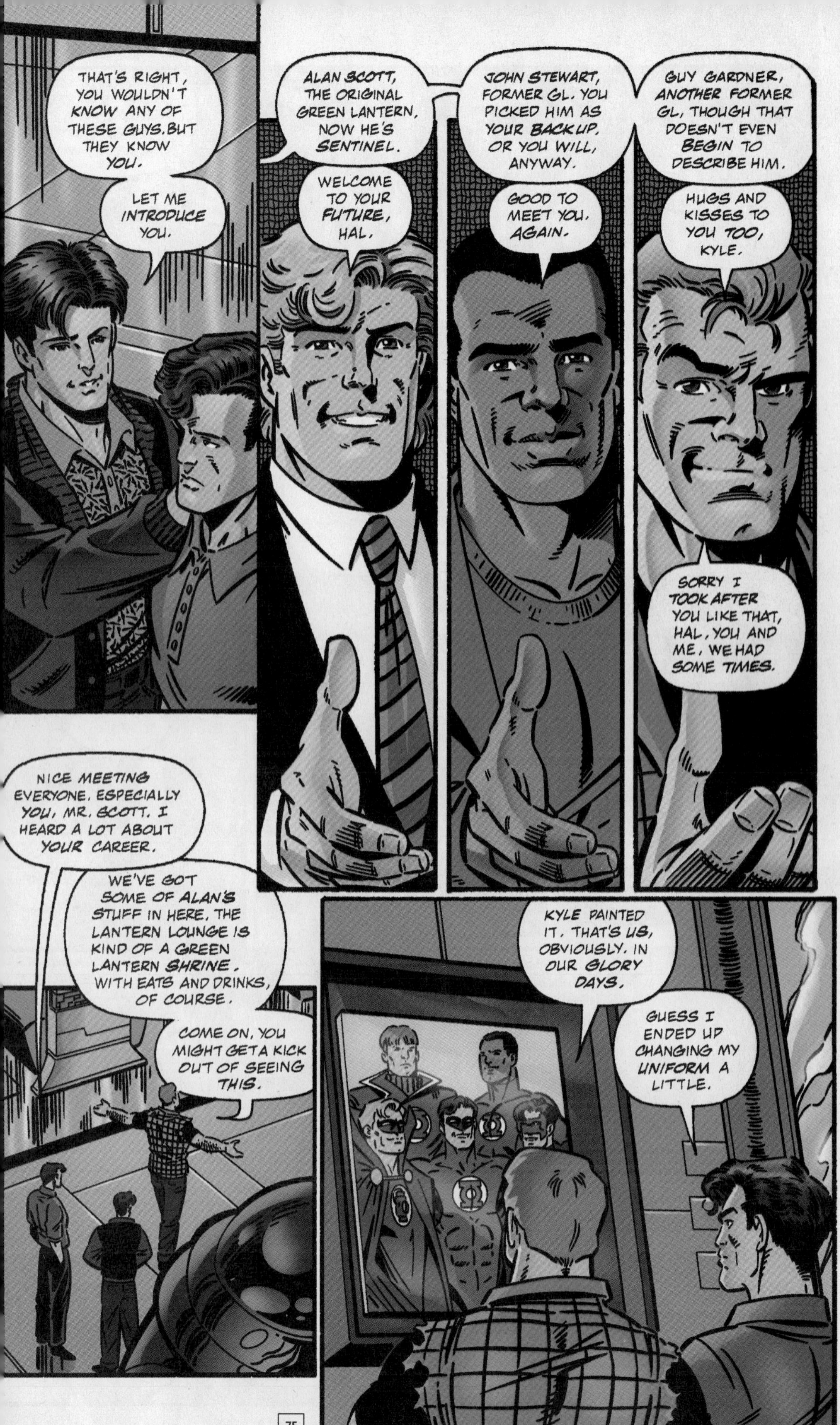

THAT'S RIGHT, YOU WOULDN'T KNOW ANY OF THESE GUYS. BUT THEY KNOW YOU.
LET ME INTRODUCE YOU.
ALAN SCOTT, THE ORIGINAL GREEN LANTERN, NOW HE'S SENTINEL.
WELCOME TO YOUR FUTURE, HAL.
JOHN STEWART, FORMER GL. YOU PICKED HIM AS YOUR BACKUP, OR YOU WILL, ANYWAY.
GOOD TO MEET YOU. AGAIN.
GUY GARDNER, ANOTHER FORMER GL, THOUGH THAT DOESN'T EVEN BEGIN TO DESCRIBE HIM.
HUGS AND KISSES TO YOU TOO, KYLE.
SORRY I TOOK AFTER YOU LIKE THAT, HAL, YOU AND ME, WE HAD SOME TIMES.
NICE MEETING EVERYONE. ESPECIALLY YOU, MR. SCOTT. I HEARD A LOT ABOUT YOUR CAREER.
WE'VE GOT SOME OF ALAN'S STUFF IN HERE. THE LANTERN LOUNGE IS KIND OF A GREEN LANTERN SHRINE. WITH EATS AND DRINKS, OF COURSE.
COME ON, YOU MIGHT GET A KICK OUT OF SEEING THIS.
KYLE PAINTED IT. THAT'S US, OBVIOUSLY. IN OUR GLORY DAYS.
GUESS I ENDED UP CHANGING MY UNIFORM A LITTLE.

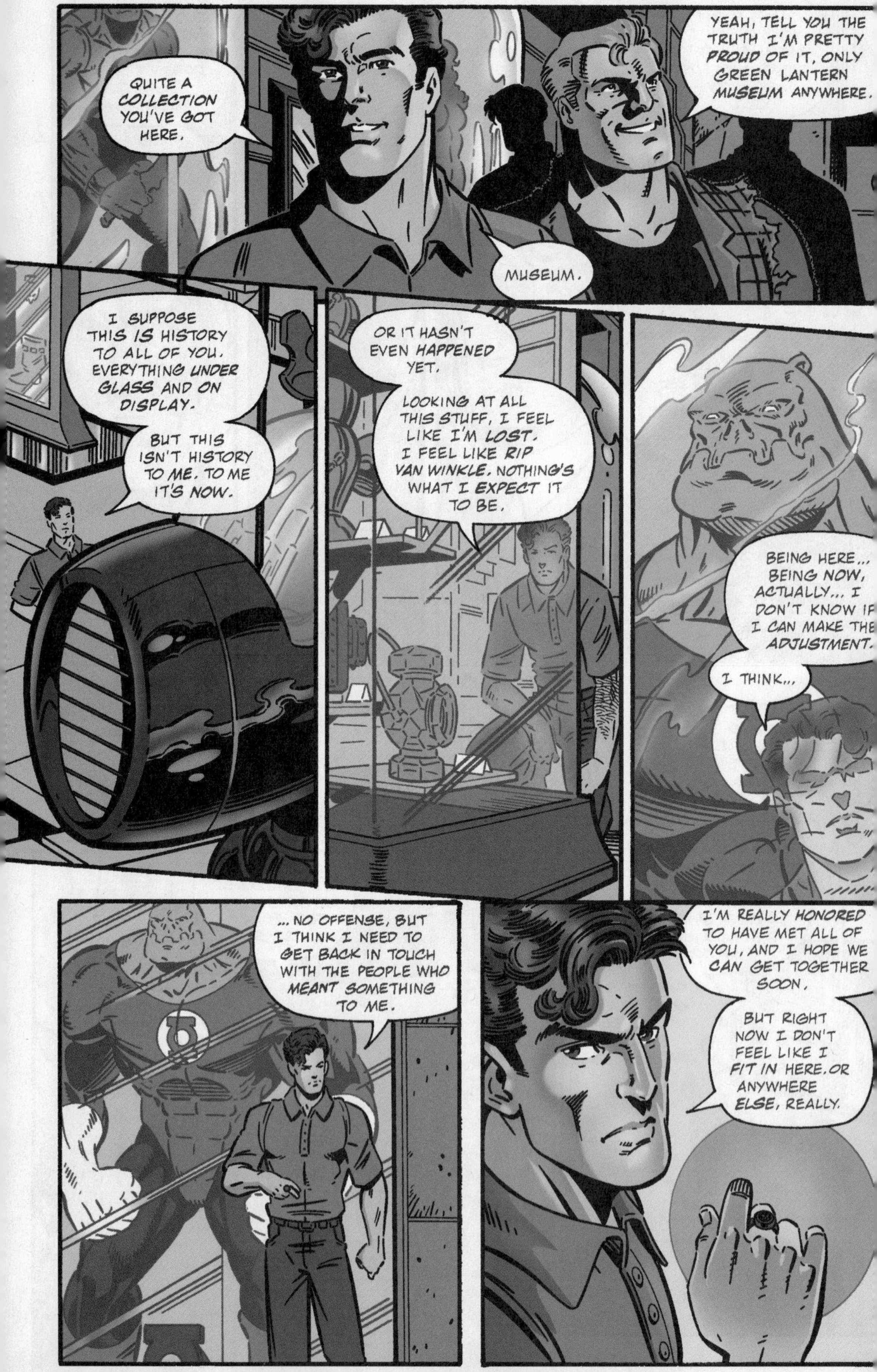
QUITE A COLLECTION YOU'VE GOT HERE.
YEAH, TELL YOU THE TRUTH I'M PRETTY PROUD OF IT. ONLY GREEN LANTERN MUSEUM ANYWHERE.
MUSEUM.
I SUPPOSE THIS IS HISTORY TO ALL OF YOU. EVERYTHING UNDER GLASS AND ON DISPLAY.
BUT THIS ISN'T HISTORY TO ME. TO ME IT'S NOW.
OR IT HASN'T EVEN HAPPENED YET.
LOOKING AT ALL THIS STUFF, I FEEL LIKE I'M LOST. I FEEL LIKE RIP VAN WINKLE. NOTHING'S WHAT I EXPECT IT TO BE.
BEING HERE... BEING NOW, ACTUALLY... I DON'T KNOW IF I CAN MAKE THE ADJUSTMENT.
I THINK...
...NO OFFENSE, BUT I THINK I NEED TO GET BACK IN TOUCH WITH THE PEOPLE WHO MEANT SOMETHING TO ME.
I'M REALLY HONORED TO HAVE MET ALL OF YOU, AND I HOPE WE CAN GET TOGETHER SOON.
BUT RIGHT NOW I DON'T FEEL LIKE I FIT IN HERE. OR ANYWHERE ELSE, REALLY.

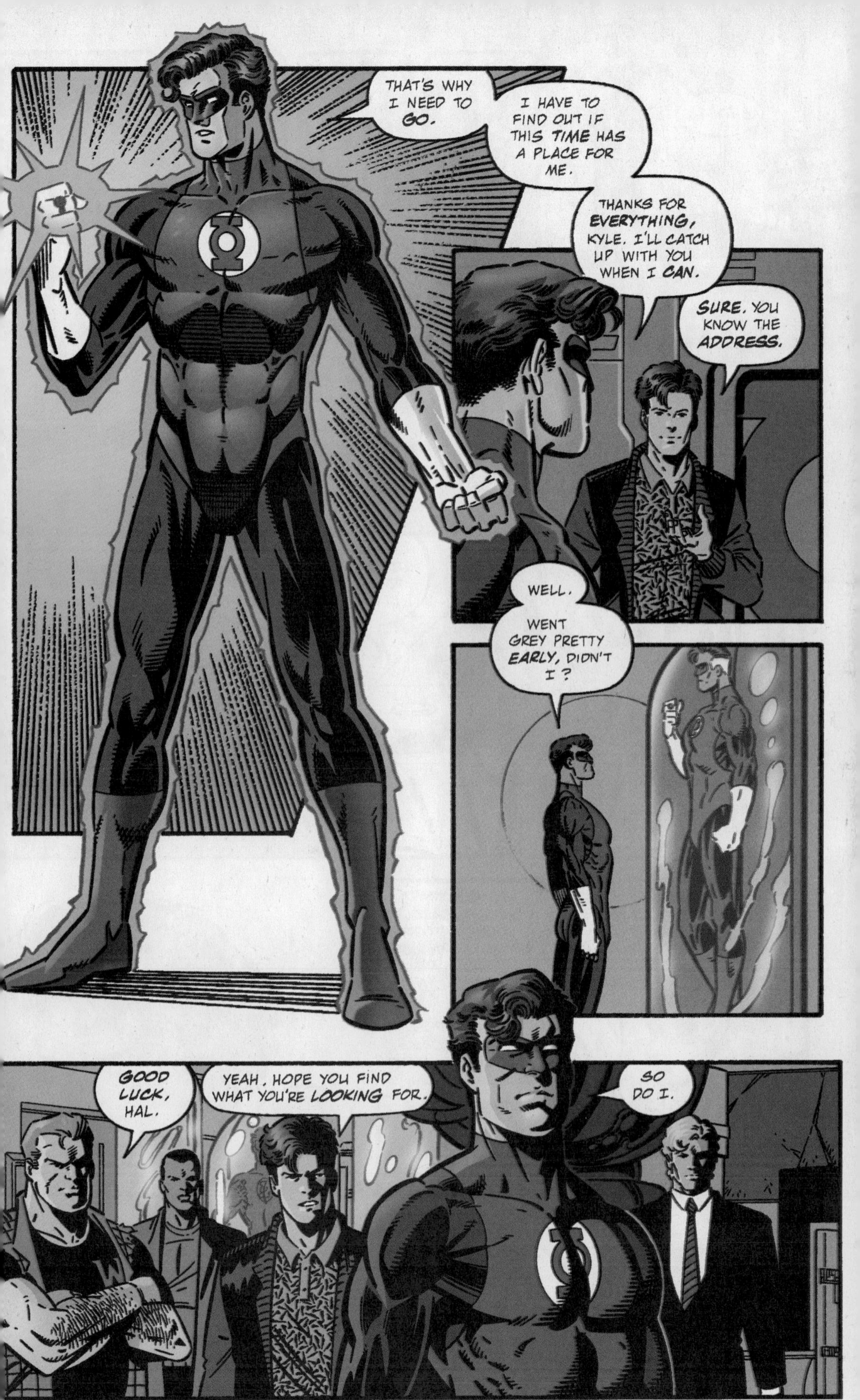

THAT'S WHY I NEED TO GO.
I HAVE TO FIND OUT IF THIS TIME HAS A PLACE FOR ME.
THANKS FOR EVERYTHING, KYLE. I'LL CATCH UP WITH YOU WHEN I CAN.
SURE. YOU KNOW THE ADDRESS.
WELL.
WENT GREY PRETTY EARLY, DIDN'T I?
GOOD LUCK, HAL.
YEAH. HOPE YOU FIND WHAT YOU'RE LOOKING FOR.
SO DO I.

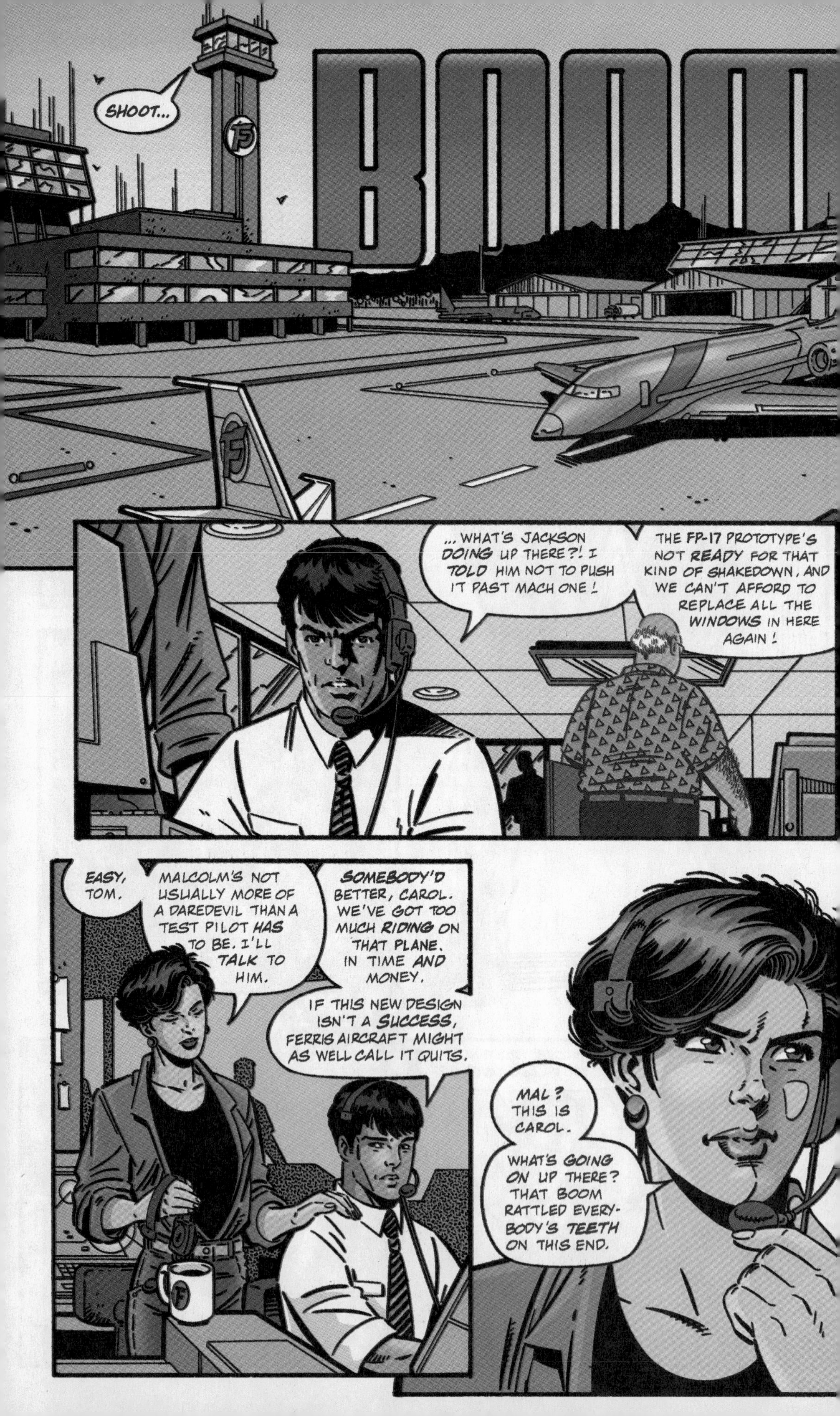
SHOOT...
BOOOM
... WHAT'S JACKSON DOING UP THERE?! I TOLD HIM NOT TO PUSH IT PAST MACH ONE!
THE FP-17 PROTOTYPE'S NOT READY FOR THAT KIND OF SHAKEDOWN, AND WE CAN'T AFFORD TO REPLACE ALL THE WINDOWS IN HERE AGAIN!
EASY, TOM.
MALCOLM'S NOT USUALLY MORE OF A DAREDEVIL THAN A TEST PILOT HAS TO BE. I'LL TALK TO HIM.
SOMEBODY'D BETTER, CAROL. WE'VE GOT TOO MUCH RIDING ON THAT PLANE. IN TIME AND MONEY.
IF THIS NEW DESIGN ISN'T A SUCCESS, FERRIS AIRCRAFT MIGHT AS WELL CALL IT QUITS.
MAL? THIS IS CAROL.
WHAT'S GOING ON UP THERE? THAT BOOM RATTLED EVERY-BODY'S TEETH ON THIS END.

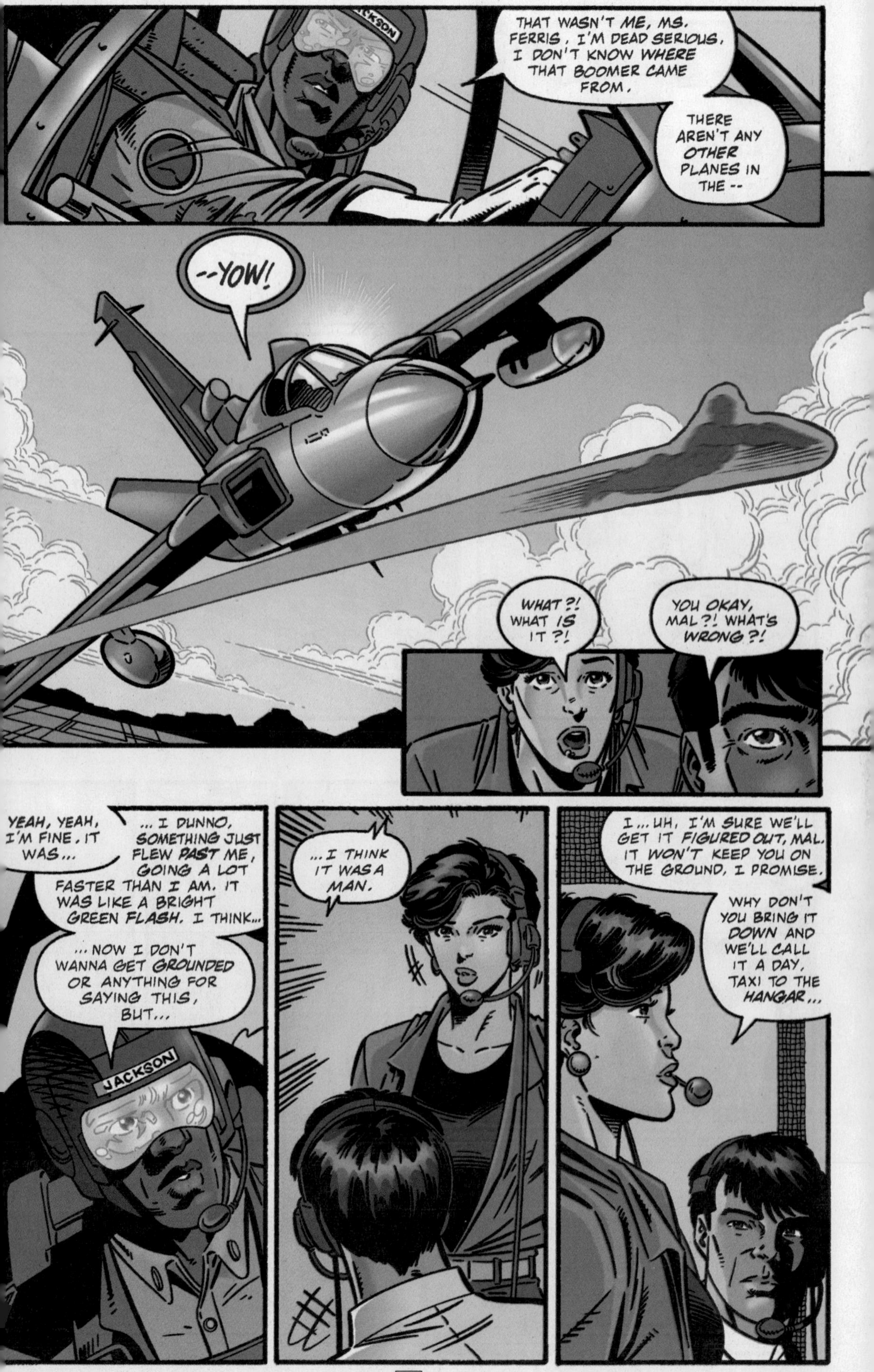
THAT WASN'T ME, MS. FERRIS, I'M DEAD SERIOUS. I DON'T KNOW WHERE THAT BOOMER CAME FROM.
THERE AREN'T ANY OTHER PLANES IN THE --
JACKSON
--YOW!
WHAT?! WHAT IS IT?!
YOU OKAY, MAL?! WHAT'S WRONG?!
YEAH, YEAH, I'M FINE. IT WAS...
... I DUNNO, SOMETHING JUST FLEW PAST ME, GOING A LOT FASTER THAN I AM. IT WAS LIKE A BRIGHT GREEN FLASH. I THINK...
... NOW I DON'T WANNA GET GROUNDED OR ANYTHING FOR SAYING THIS, BUT...
JACKSON
... I THINK IT WAS A MAN.
I ... UH, I'M SURE WE'LL GET IT FIGURED OUT, MAL. IT WON'T KEEP YOU ON THE GROUND, I PROMISE.
WHY DON'T YOU BRING IT DOWN AND WE'LL CALL IT A DAY. TAXI TO THE HANGAR...

"...TOM AND I WILL MEET YOU THERE."

THAT WAS SOMETHING, HUH? MY *HEART* SKIPPED A BEAT WHEN HE... WELL, ALL THAT "FLYING MAN" STUFF.

I KNOW, MINE TOO. SEEMED LIKE THE *OLD DAYS* FOR A MINUTE.

FLYING MEN, YOU BACK AT *FERRIS*.

YOU MADE ME AN OFFER I COULDN'T *REFUSE*.

HELP GET FERRIS AIRCRAFT BACK ON ITS *FEET* AFTER *COAST CITY*? AND THE CHANCE TO BE A *PROJECT MANAGER* INSTEAD OF A *GREASE MONKEY*?

OKAY, SO I HAD TO MOVE TO INDIANA. BUT COME ON, CAROL. I'D BE HERE EVEN IF YOU *WEREN'T* PAYING ME.

THIS IS WHERE I *BELONG*. I DIDN'T REALIZE HOW MUCH I MISSED A JET ENGINE'S ROAR UNTIL I WAS *AWAY* FROM IT FOR THREE MONTHS TO FINISH MY BOOK ON HAL.

STILL NO LUCK FINDING A *PUBLISHER*?

NOT ONE WHO DOESN'T WANT TO PRINT IT AS A "HERO-GOES-INSANE" TELL-ALL LIKE--

PIE?

CAROL?

ah

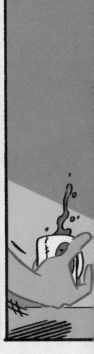

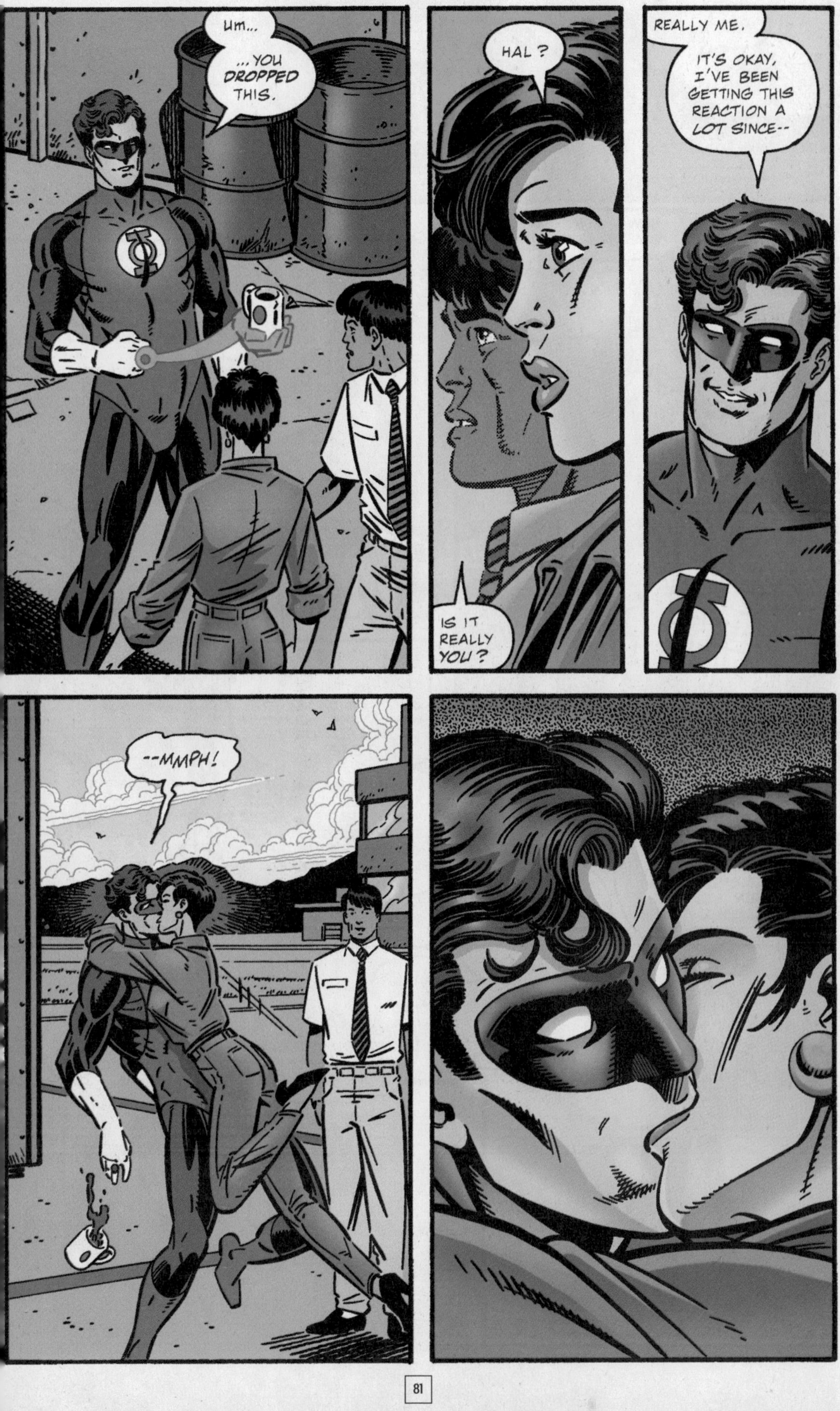
Um...
...YOU DROPPED THIS.
HAL?
IS IT REALLY YOU?
REALLY ME.
IT'S OKAY, I'VE BEEN GETTING THIS REACTION A LOT SINCE--
--MMPH!

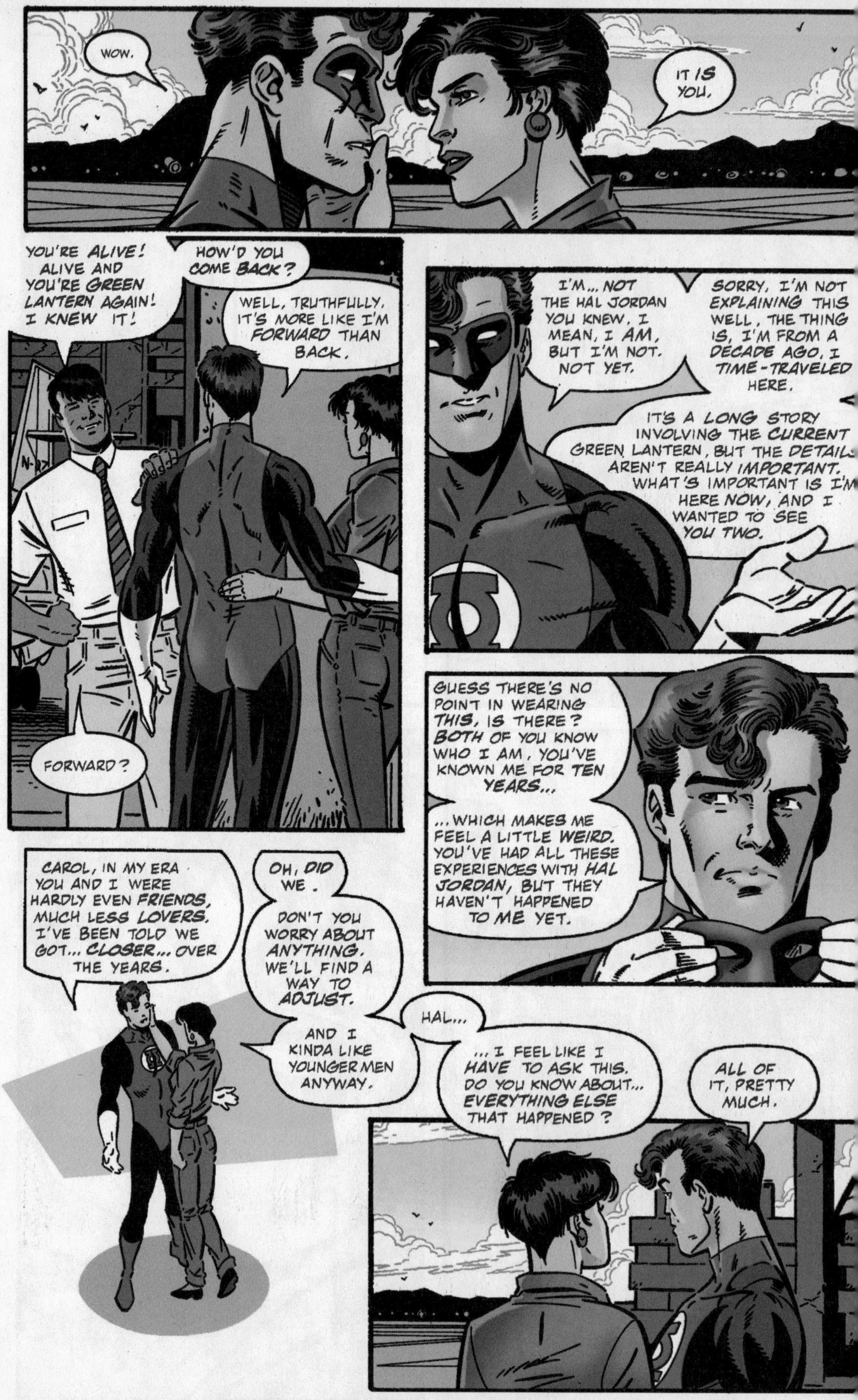

WOW.
IT IS YOU.
YOU'RE ALIVE! ALIVE AND YOU'RE GREEN LANTERN AGAIN! I KNEW IT!
HOW'D YOU COME BACK?
WELL, TRUTHFULLY, IT'S MORE LIKE I'M FORWARD THAN BACK.
FORWARD?
I'M... NOT THE HAL JORDAN YOU KNEW. I MEAN, I AM, BUT I'M NOT. NOT YET.
SORRY, I'M NOT EXPLAINING THIS WELL. THE THING IS, I'M FROM A DECADE AGO. I TIME-TRAVELED HERE.
IT'S A LONG STORY INVOLVING THE CURRENT GREEN LANTERN, BUT THE DETAIL AREN'T REALLY IMPORTANT. WHAT'S IMPORTANT IS I'M HERE NOW, AND I WANTED TO SEE YOU TWO.
GUESS THERE'S NO POINT IN WEARING THIS, IS THERE? BOTH OF YOU KNOW WHO I AM, YOU'VE KNOWN ME FOR TEN YEARS...
...WHICH MAKES ME FEEL A LITTLE WEIRD. YOU'VE HAD ALL THESE EXPERIENCES WITH HAL JORDAN, BUT THEY HAVEN'T HAPPENED TO ME YET.
CAROL, IN MY ERA YOU AND I WERE HARDLY EVEN FRIENDS, MUCH LESS LOVERS. I'VE BEEN TOLD WE GOT... CLOSER... OVER THE YEARS.
OH, DID WE.
DON'T YOU WORRY ABOUT ANYTHING. WE'LL FIND A WAY TO ADJUST.
AND I KINDA LIKE YOUNGER MEN ANYWAY.
HAL...
...I FEEL LIKE I HAVE TO ASK THIS. DO YOU KNOW ABOUT... EVERYTHING ELSE THAT HAPPENED?
ALL OF IT, PRETTY MUCH.

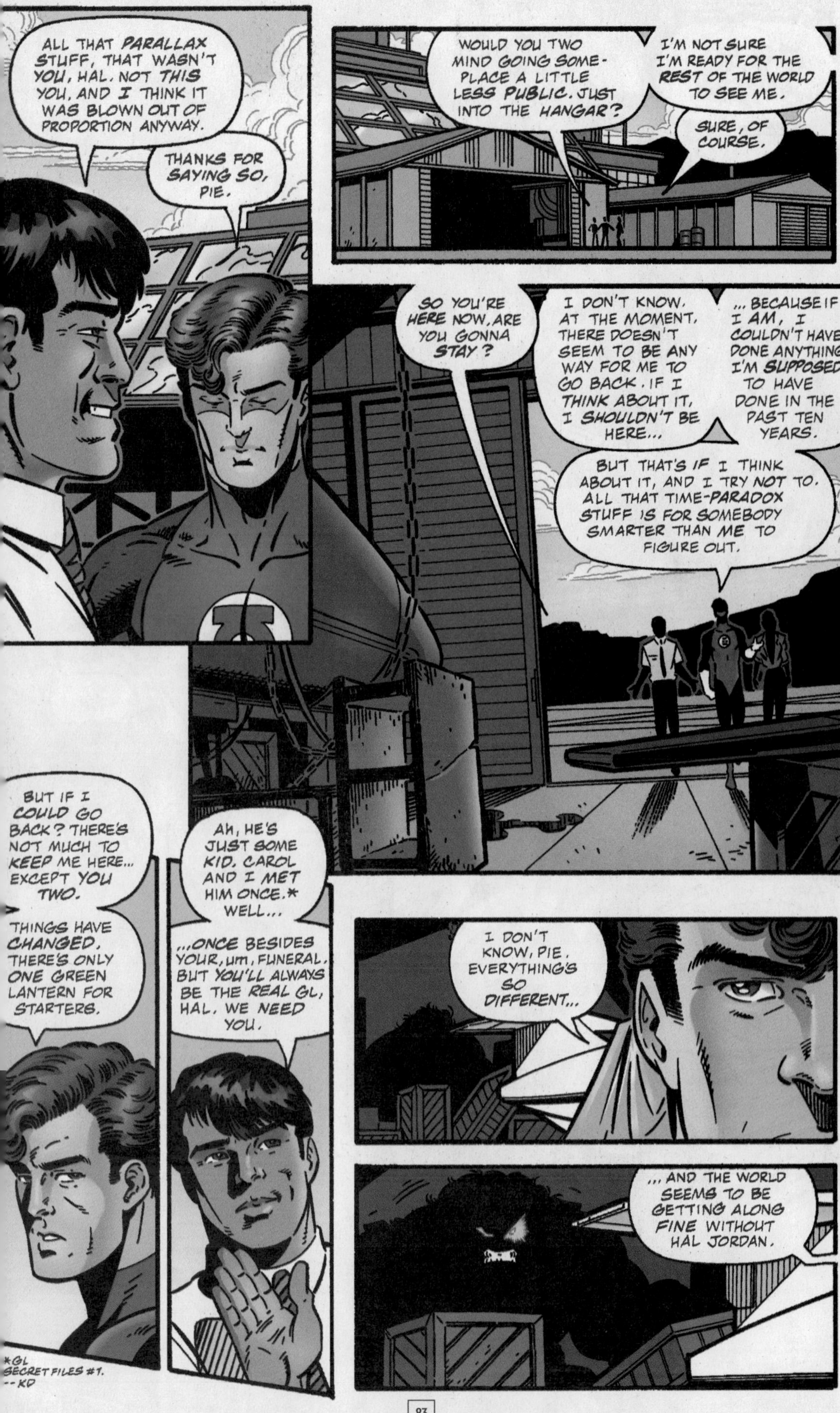
ALL THAT PARALLAX STUFF, THAT WASN'T YOU, HAL. NOT THIS YOU, AND I THINK IT WAS BLOWN OUT OF PROPORTION ANYWAY.
THANKS FOR SAYING SO, PIE.
WOULD YOU TWO MIND GOING SOME-PLACE A LITTLE LESS PUBLIC. JUST INTO THE HANGAR?
I'M NOT SURE I'M READY FOR THE REST OF THE WORLD TO SEE ME.
SURE, OF COURSE.
SO YOU'RE HERE NOW, ARE YOU GONNA STAY?
I DON'T KNOW. AT THE MOMENT, THERE DOESN'T SEEM TO BE ANY WAY FOR ME TO GO BACK. IF I THINK ABOUT IT, I SHOULDN'T BE HERE...
...BECAUSE IF I AM, I COULDN'T HAVE DONE ANYTHING I'M SUPPOSED TO HAVE DONE IN THE PAST TEN YEARS.
BUT THAT'S IF I THINK ABOUT IT, AND I TRY NOT TO. ALL THAT TIME-PARADOX STUFF IS FOR SOMEBODY SMARTER THAN ME TO FIGURE OUT.
BUT IF I COULD GO BACK? THERE'S NOT MUCH TO KEEP ME HERE... EXCEPT YOU TWO.
THINGS HAVE CHANGED. THERE'S ONLY ONE GREEN LANTERN FOR STARTERS.
AH, HE'S JUST SOME KID. CAROL AND I MET HIM ONCE.* WELL...
...ONCE BESIDES YOUR, UM, FUNERAL. BUT YOU'LL ALWAYS BE THE REAL GL, HAL. WE NEED YOU.
*GL SECRET FILES #1. --KD
I DON'T KNOW, PIE. EVERYTHING'S SO DIFFERENT...
...AND THE WORLD SEEMS TO BE GETTING ALONG FINE WITHOUT HAL JORDAN.

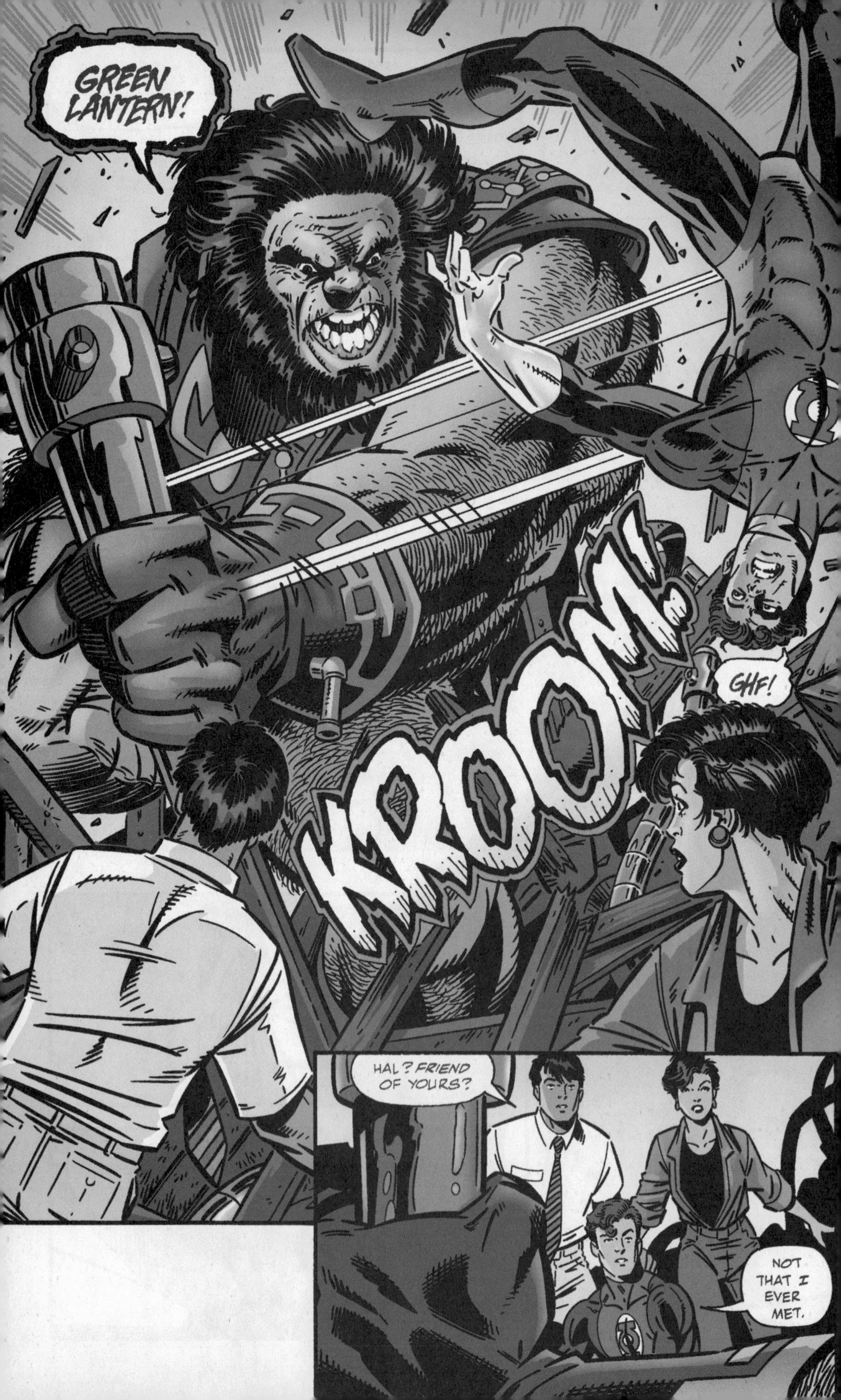
GREEN LANTERN!
GHF!
KROOM!
HAL? FRIEND OF YOURS?
NOT THAT I EVER MET.

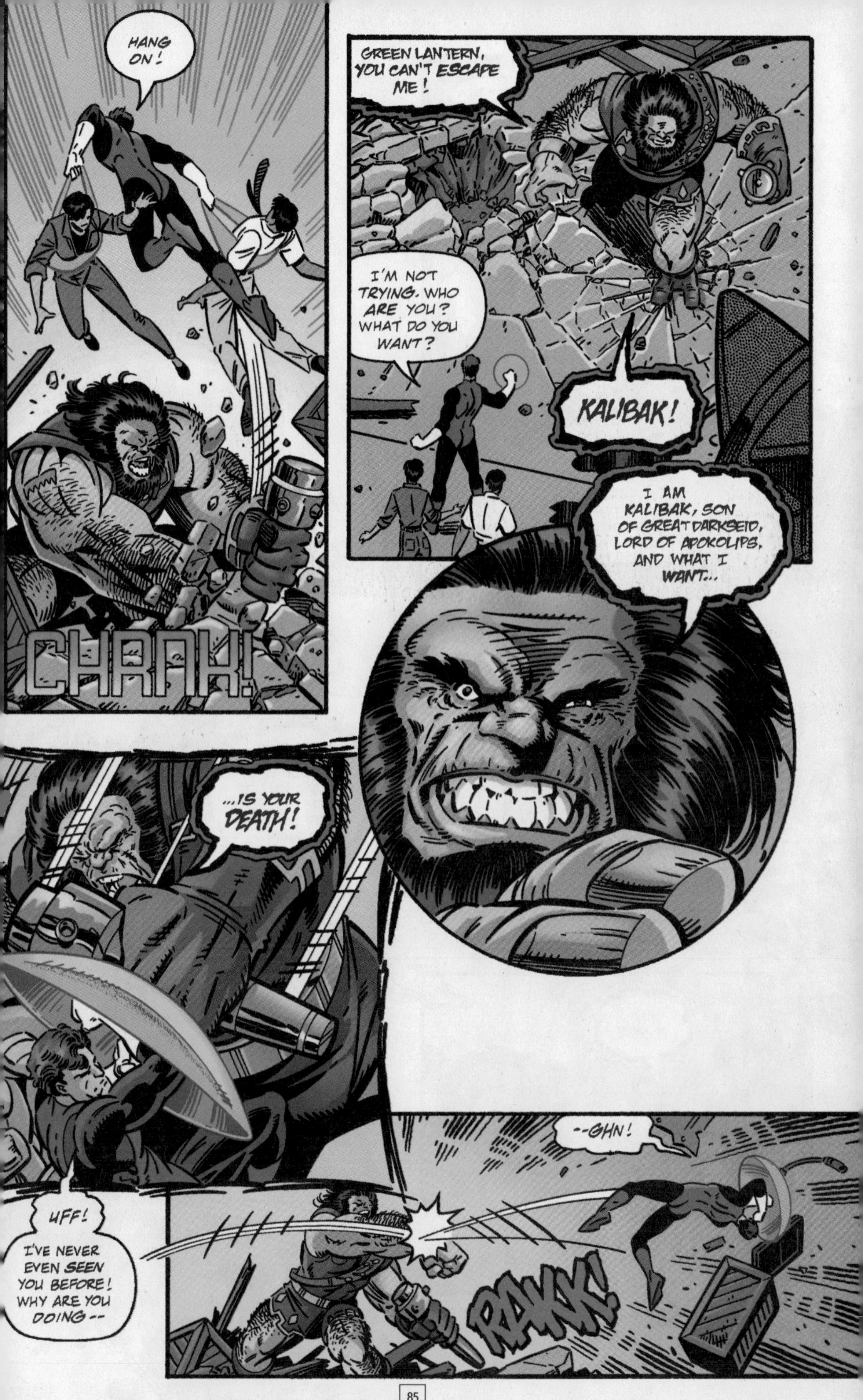

HANG ON!
CHRNK!
GREEN LANTERN, YOU CAN'T ESCAPE ME!
I'M NOT TRYING. WHO ARE YOU? WHAT DO YOU WANT?
KALIBAK!
I AM KALIBAK, SON OF GREAT DARKSEID, LORD OF APOKOLIPS, AND WHAT I WANT...
...IS YOUR DEATH!
UFF!
I'VE NEVER EVEN SEEN YOU BEFORE! WHY ARE YOU DOING --
--GHN!
RAKK!

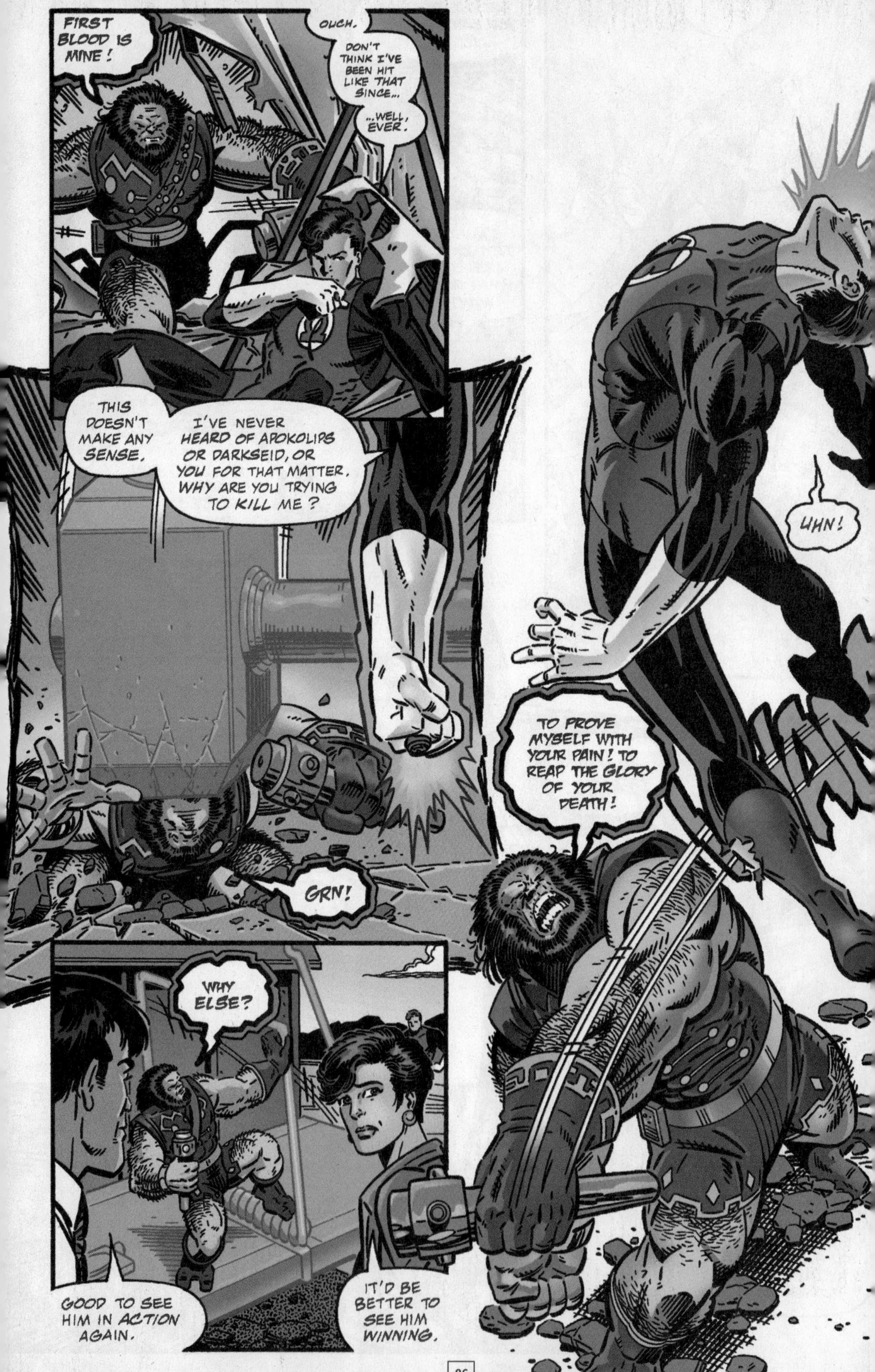

FIRST BLOOD IS MINE!
OUCH.
DON'T THINK I'VE BEEN HIT LIKE THAT SINCE...
...WELL, EVER.
THIS DOESN'T MAKE ANY SENSE.
I'VE NEVER HEARD OF APOKOLIPS OR DARKSEID, OR YOU FOR THAT MATTER. WHY ARE YOU TRYING TO KILL ME?
GRN!
UHN!
TO PROVE MYSELF WITH YOUR PAIN! TO REAP THE GLORY OF YOUR DEATH!
WHY ELSE?
GOOD TO SEE HIM IN ACTION AGAIN.
IT'D BE BETTER TO SEE HIM WINNING.

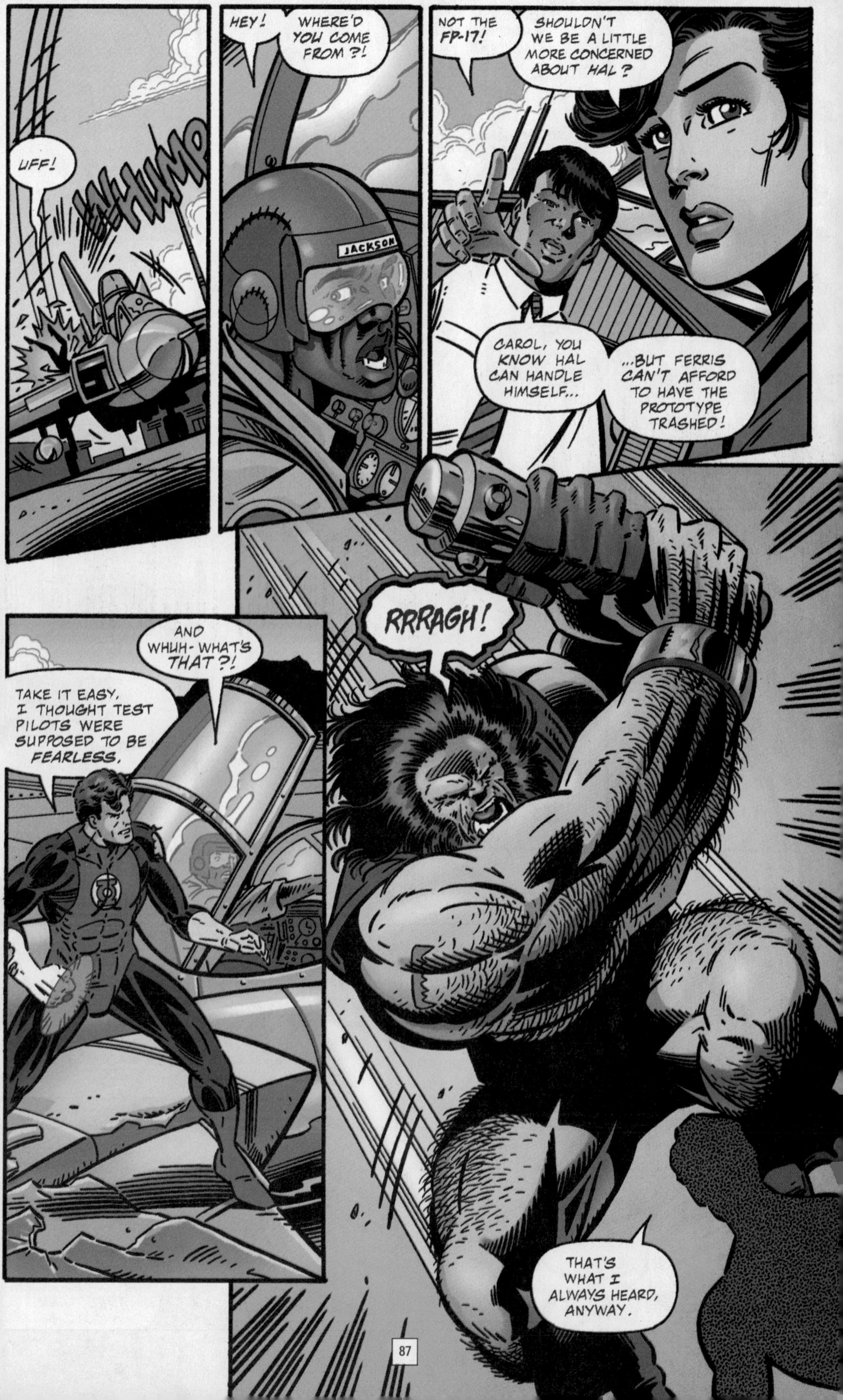
UFF!
WHUMP
HEY!
WHERE'D YOU COME FROM?!
JACKSON
NOT THE FP-17!
SHOULDN'T WE BE A LITTLE MORE CONCERNED ABOUT HAL?
CAROL, YOU KNOW HAL CAN HANDLE HIMSELF...
...BUT FERRIS CAN'T AFFORD TO HAVE THE PROTOTYPE TRASHED!
RRRAGH!
TAKE IT EASY. I THOUGHT TEST PILOTS WERE SUPPOSED TO BE FEARLESS.
AND WHUH-WHAT'S THAT?!
THAT'S WHAT I ALWAYS HEARD, ANYWAY.

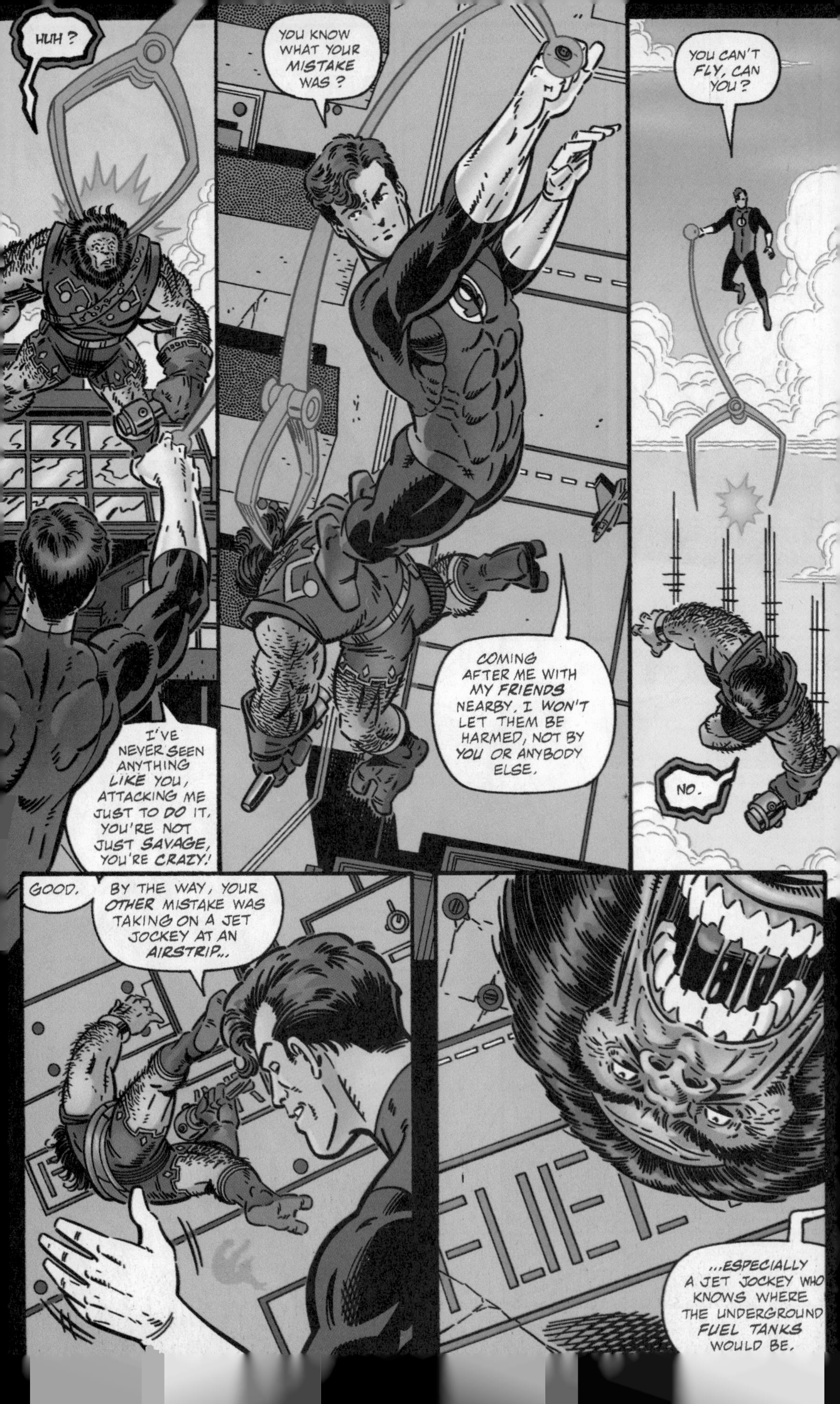
HUH ?
YOU KNOW WHAT YOUR MISTAKE WAS ?
I'VE NEVER SEEN ANYTHING LIKE YOU, ATTACKING ME JUST TO DO IT. YOU'RE NOT JUST SAVAGE, YOU'RE CRAZY!
COMING AFTER ME WITH MY FRIENDS NEARBY. I WON'T LET THEM BE HARMED, NOT BY YOU OR ANYBODY ELSE.
YOU CAN'T FLY, CAN YOU ?
NO.
GOOD.
BY THE WAY, YOUR OTHER MISTAKE WAS TAKING ON A JET JOCKEY AT AN AIRSTRIP...
...ESPECIALLY A JET JOCKEY WHO KNOWS WHERE THE UNDERGROUND FUEL TANKS WOULD BE.

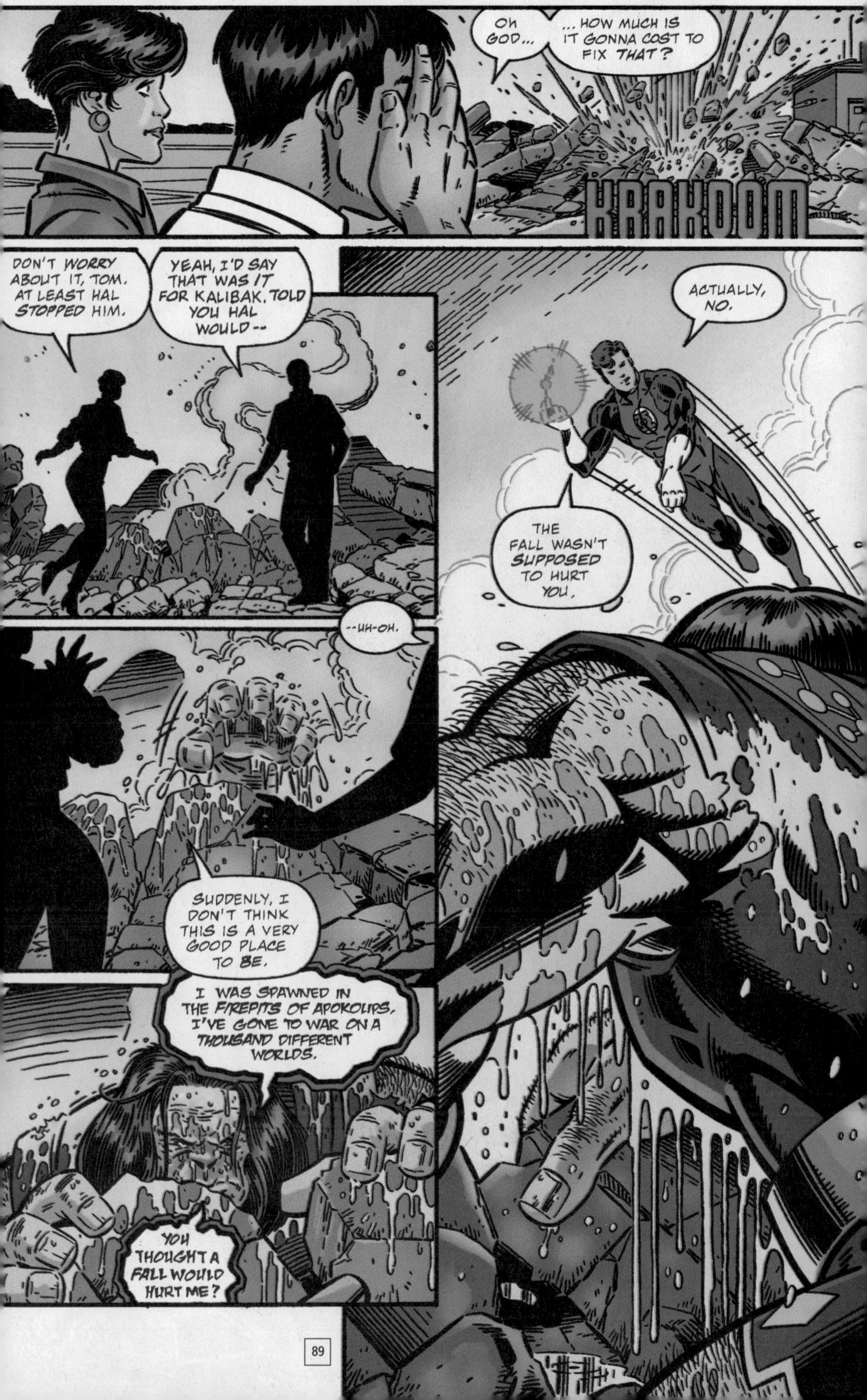

Oh GOD...
... HOW MUCH IS IT GONNA COST TO FIX THAT?
KRAKOOM
DON'T WORRY ABOUT IT, TOM. AT LEAST HAL STOPPED HIM.
YEAH, I'D SAY THAT WAS IT FOR KALIBAK. TOLD YOU HAL WOULD--
ACTUALLY, NO.
THE FALL WASN'T SUPPOSED TO HURT YOU.
--UH-OH.
SUDDENLY, I DON'T THINK THIS IS A VERY GOOD PLACE TO BE.
I WAS SPAWNED IN THE FIREPITS OF APOKOLIPS. I'VE GONE TO WAR ON A THOUSAND DIFFERENT WORLDS.
YOU THOUGHT A FALL WOULD HURT ME?

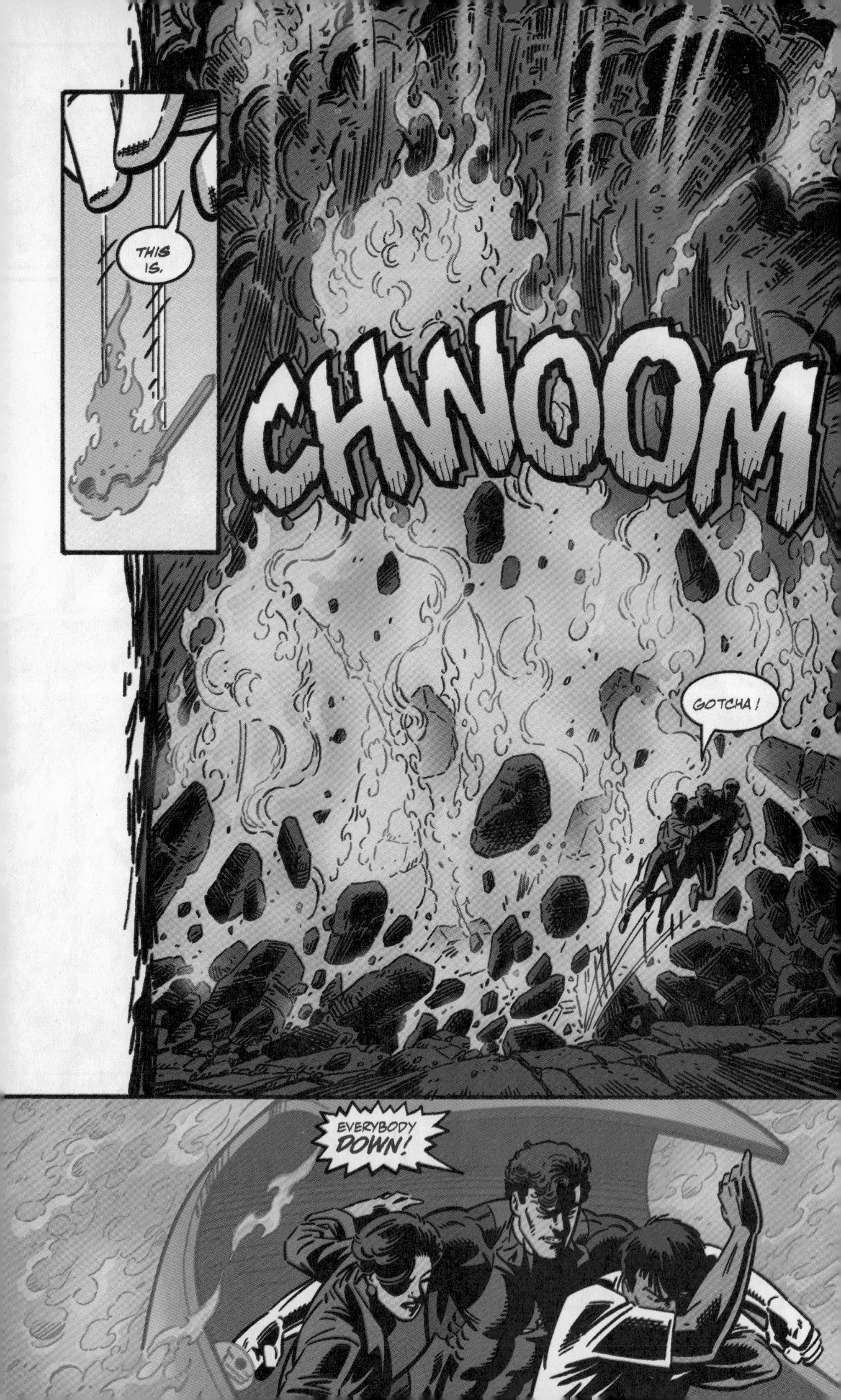
THIS IS.
CHWOOM
GOTCHA!
EVERYBODY DOWN!

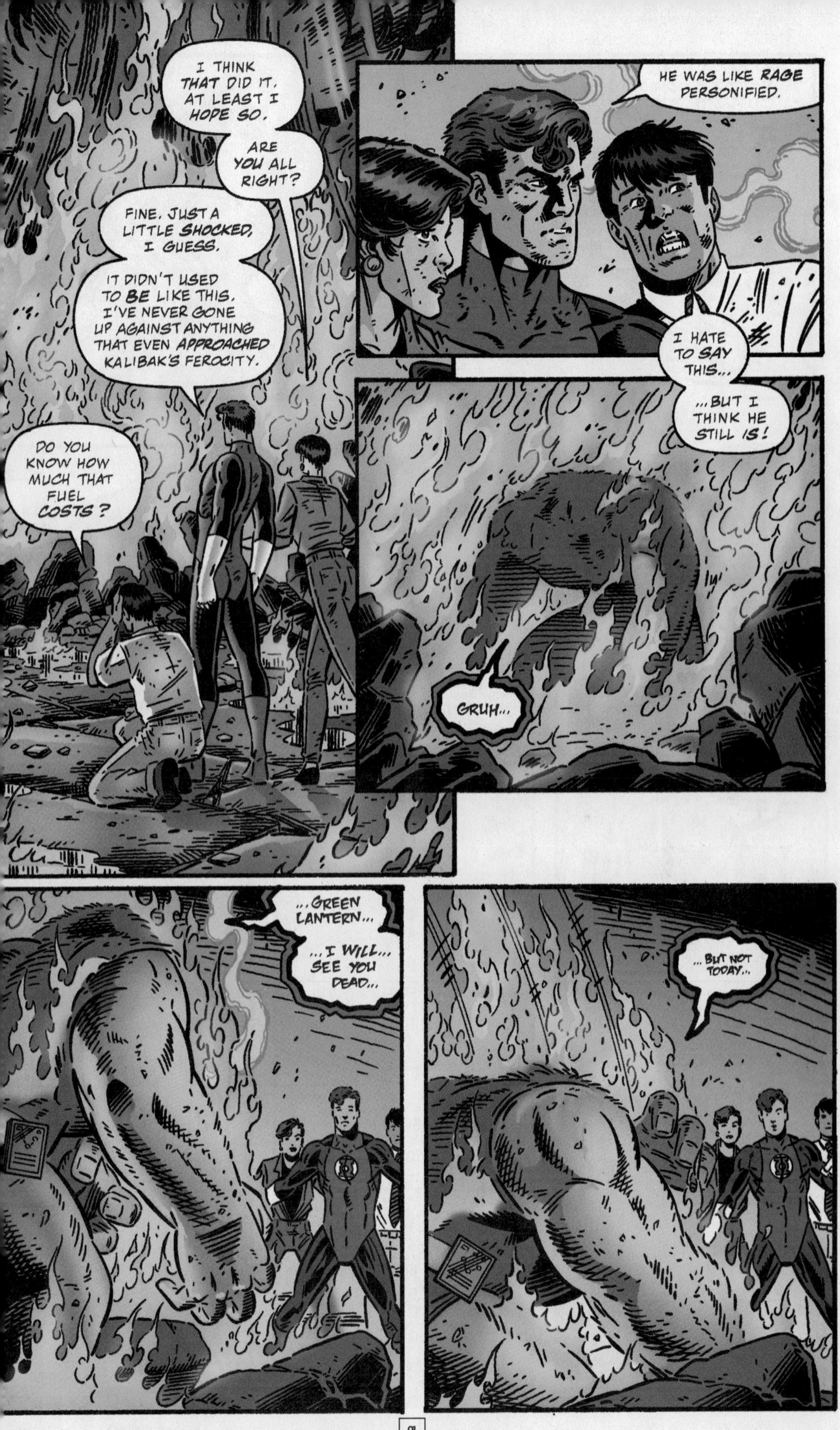
I THINK THAT DID IT. AT LEAST I HOPE SO.
ARE YOU ALL RIGHT?
FINE. JUST A LITTLE SHOCKED, I GUESS.
IT DIDN'T USED TO BE LIKE THIS. I'VE NEVER GONE UP AGAINST ANYTHING THAT EVEN APPROACHED KALIBAK'S FEROCITY.
DO YOU KNOW HOW MUCH THAT FUEL COSTS?
HE WAS LIKE RAGE PERSONIFIED.
I HATE TO SAY THIS...
...BUT I THINK HE STILL IS!
GRUH...
...GREEN LANTERN...
...I WILL... SEE YOU DEAD...
...BUT NOT TODAY...

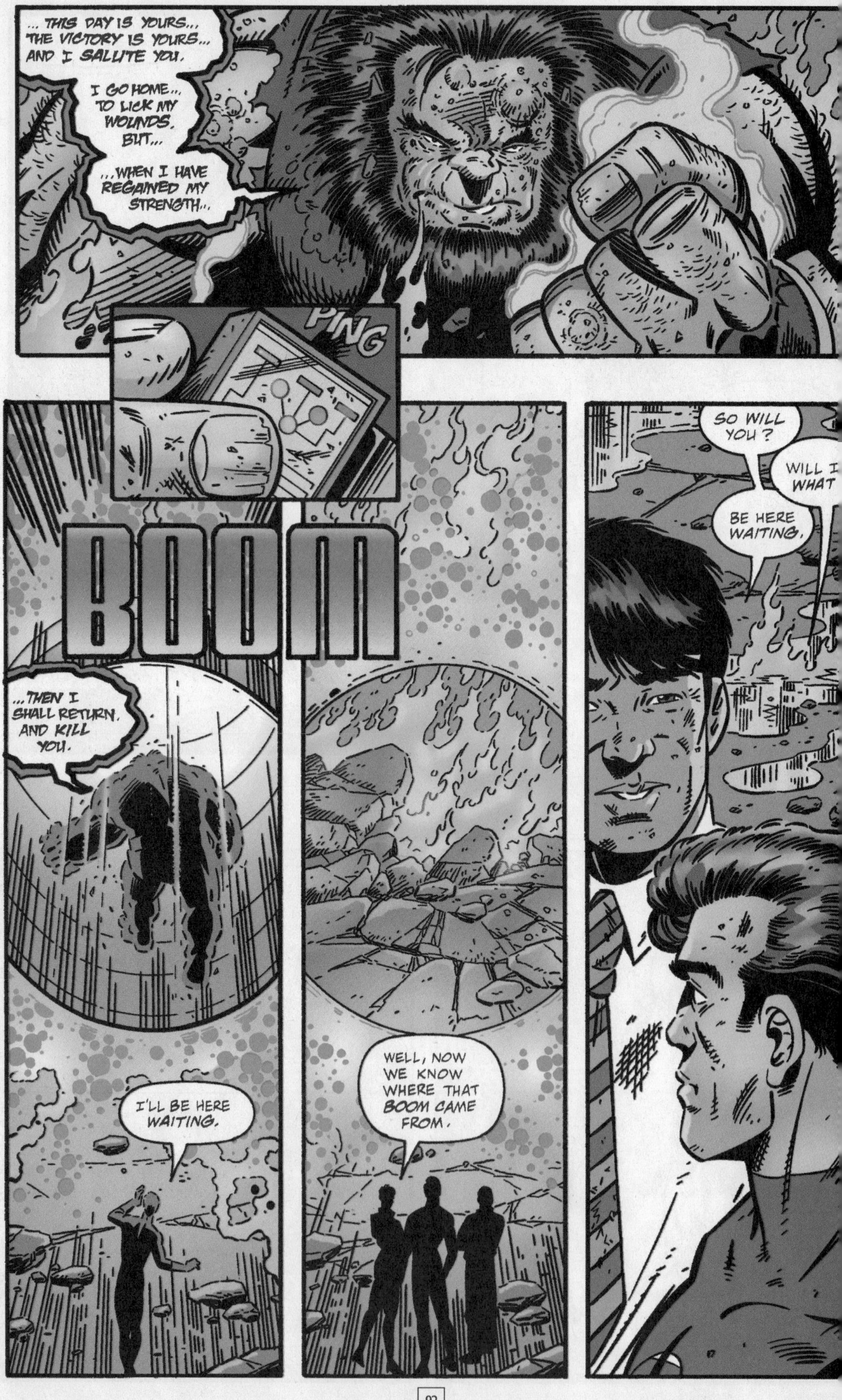
... THIS DAY IS YOURS... THE VICTORY IS YOURS... AND I SALUTE YOU.
I GO HOME... TO LICK MY WOUNDS. BUT...
...WHEN I HAVE REGAINED MY STRENGTH...
PING
BOOM
...THEN I SHALL RETURN. AND KILL YOU.
I'LL BE HERE WAITING.
WELL, NOW WE KNOW WHERE THAT BOOM CAME FROM.
SO WILL YOU?
WILL I WHAT
BE HERE WAITING.

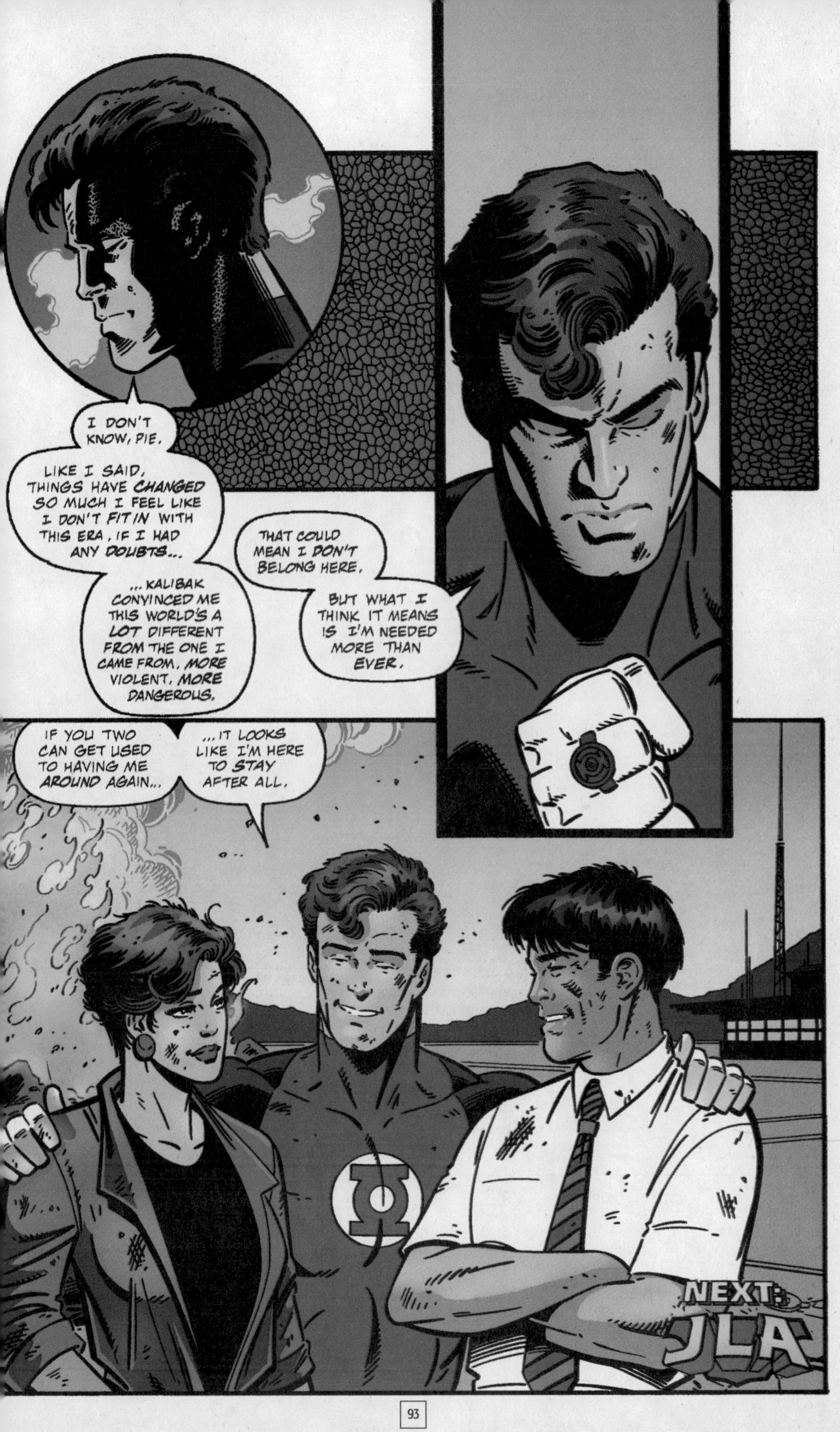
I DON'T KNOW, PIE.
LIKE I SAID, THINGS HAVE CHANGED SO MUCH I FEEL LIKE I DON'T FIT IN WITH THIS ERA. IF I HAD ANY DOUBTS...
...KALIBAK CONVINCED ME THIS WORLD'S A LOT DIFFERENT FROM THE ONE I CAME FROM. MORE VIOLENT. MORE DANGEROUS.
THAT COULD MEAN I DON'T BELONG HERE.
BUT WHAT I THINK IT MEANS IS I'M NEEDED MORE THAN EVER.
IF YOU TWO CAN GET USED TO HAVING ME AROUND AGAIN...
...IT LOOKS LIKE I'M HERE TO STAY AFTER ALL.
NEXT: JLA

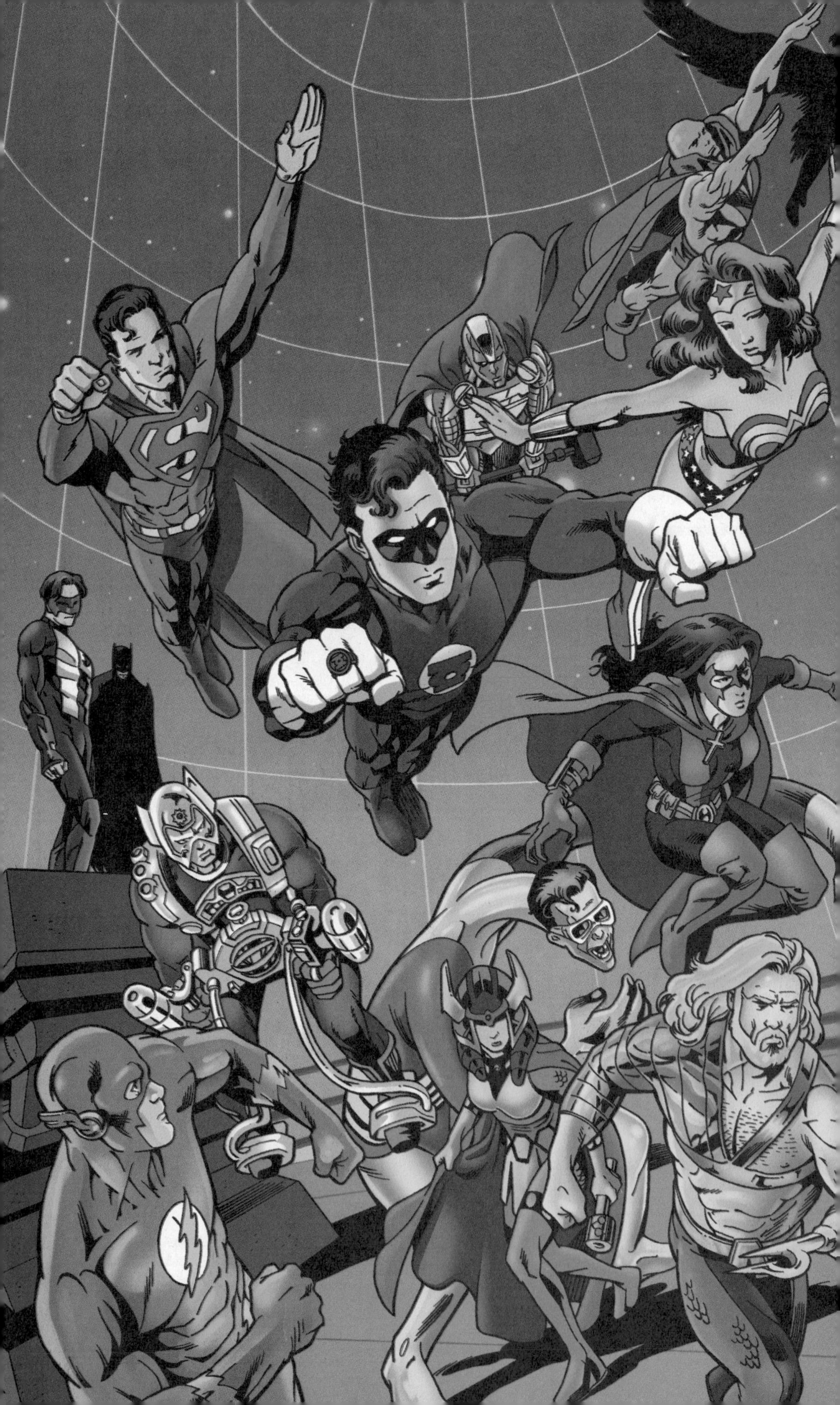

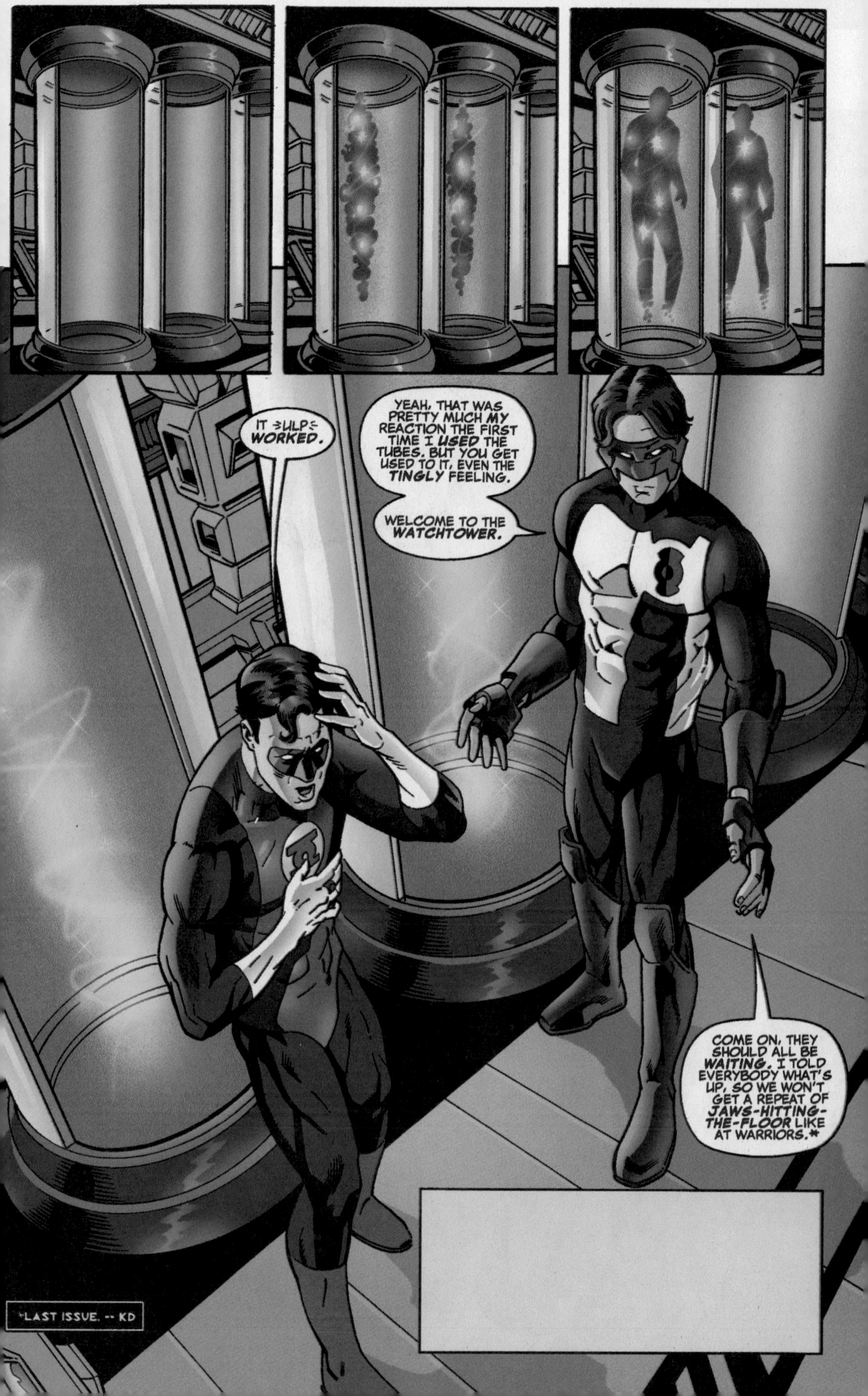
IT ≡ULP≡ WORKED.
YEAH, THAT WAS PRETTY MUCH MY REACTION THE FIRST TIME I USED THE TUBES. BUT YOU GET USED TO IT, EVEN THE TINGLY FEELING.
WELCOME TO THE WATCHTOWER.
COME ON, THEY SHOULD ALL BE WAITING. I TOLD EVERYBODY WHAT'S UP, SO WE WON'T GET A REPEAT OF JAWS-HITTING-THE-FLOOR LIKE AT WARRIORS.*
*LAST ISSUE. -- KD

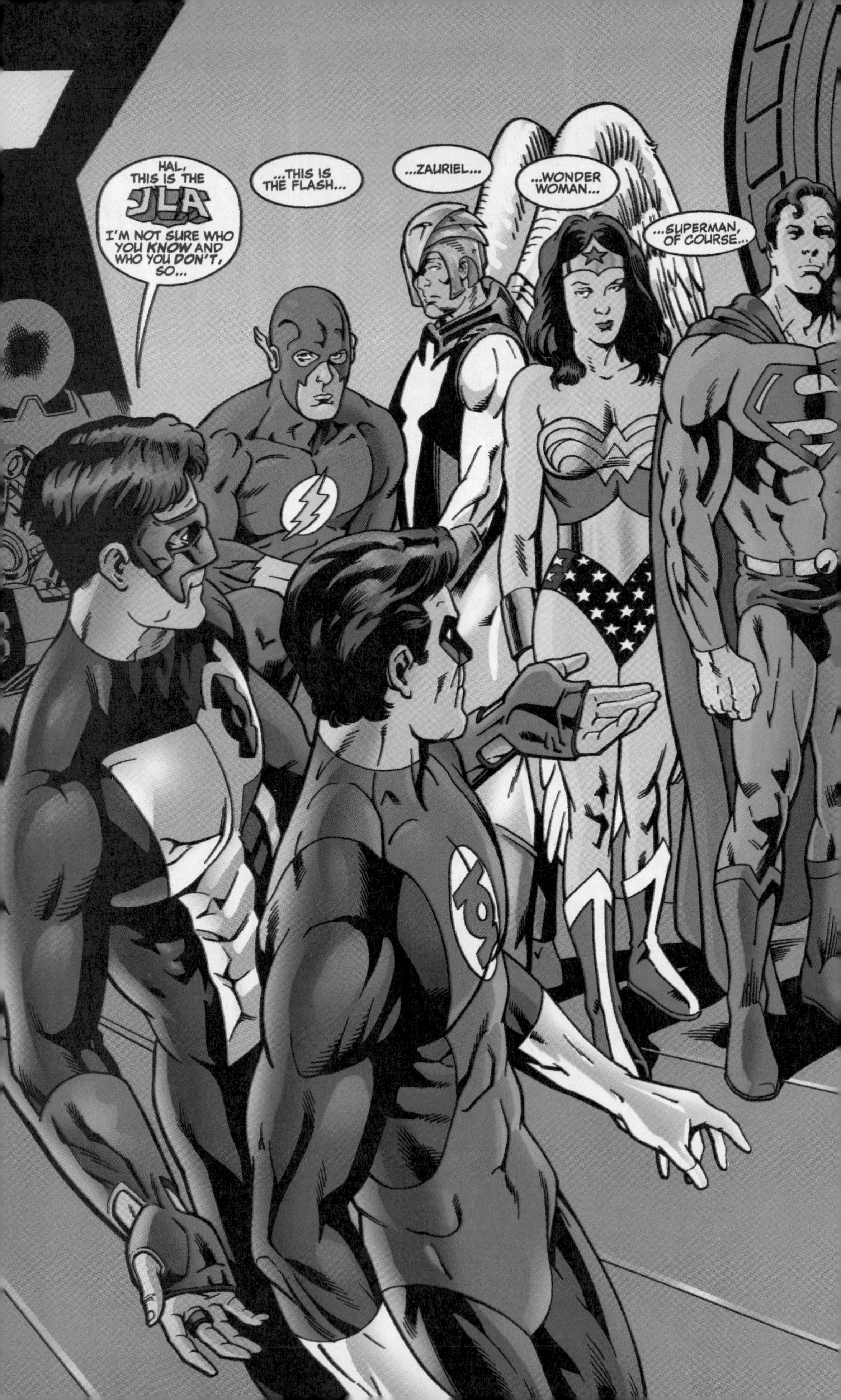
HAL, THIS IS THE JLA I'M NOT SURE WHO YOU KNOW AND WHO YOU DON'T, SO...
...THIS IS THE FLASH...
...ZAURIEL...
...WONDER WOMAN...
...SUPERMAN, OF COURSE...

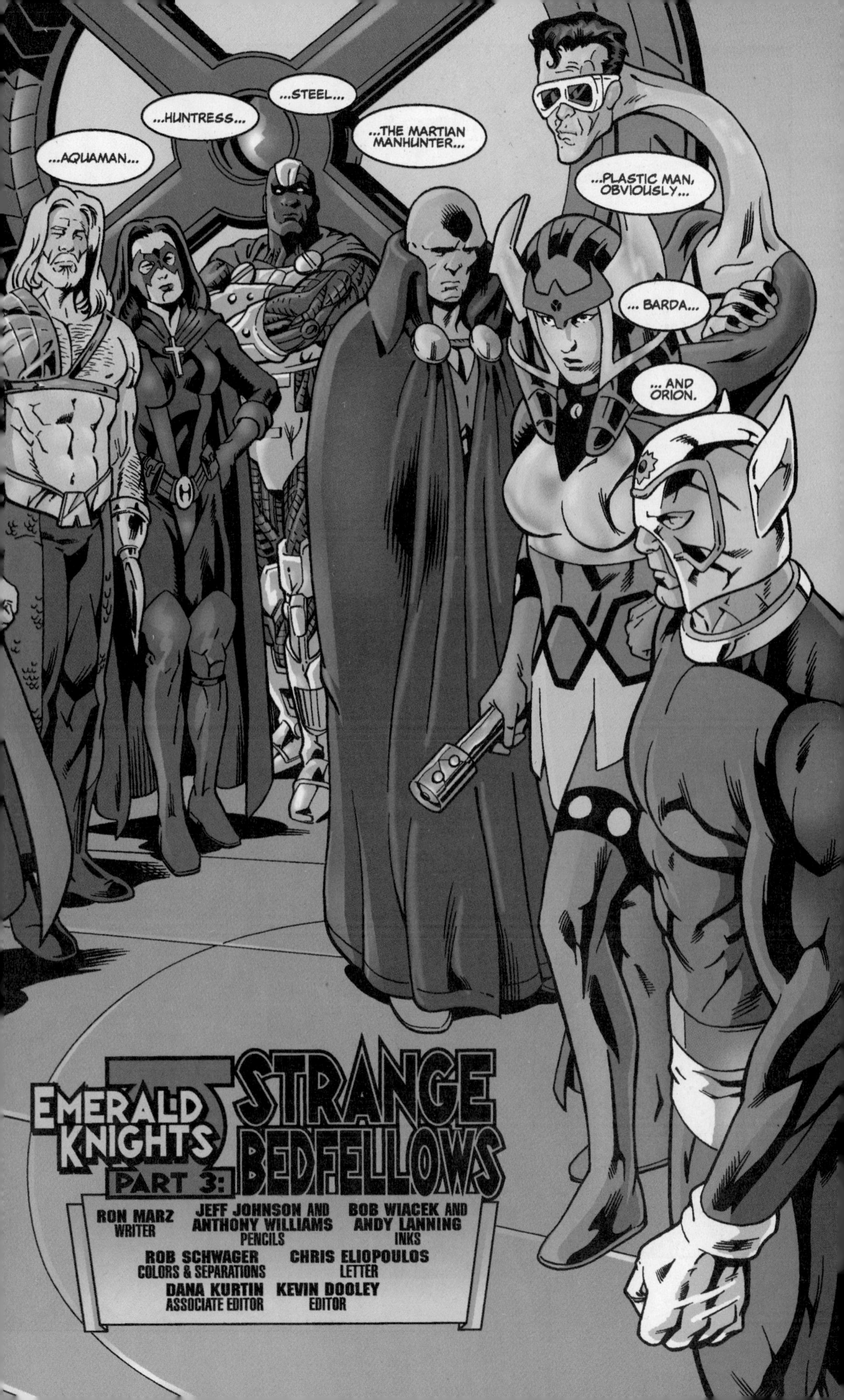

...AQUAMAN...
...HUNTRESS...
...STEEL...
...THE MARTIAN MANHUNTER...
...PLASTIC MAN, OBVIOUSLY...
... BARDA...
... AND ORION.
EMERALD KNIGHTS
PART 3:
STRANGE BEDFELLOWS
RON MARZ WRITER
JEFF JOHNSON AND ANTHONY WILLIAMS PENCILS
BOB WIACEK AND ANDY LANNING INKS
ROB SCHWAGER COLORS & SEPARATIONS
CHRIS ELIOPOULOS LETTER
DANA KURTIN ASSOCIATE EDITOR
KEVIN DOOLEY EDITOR

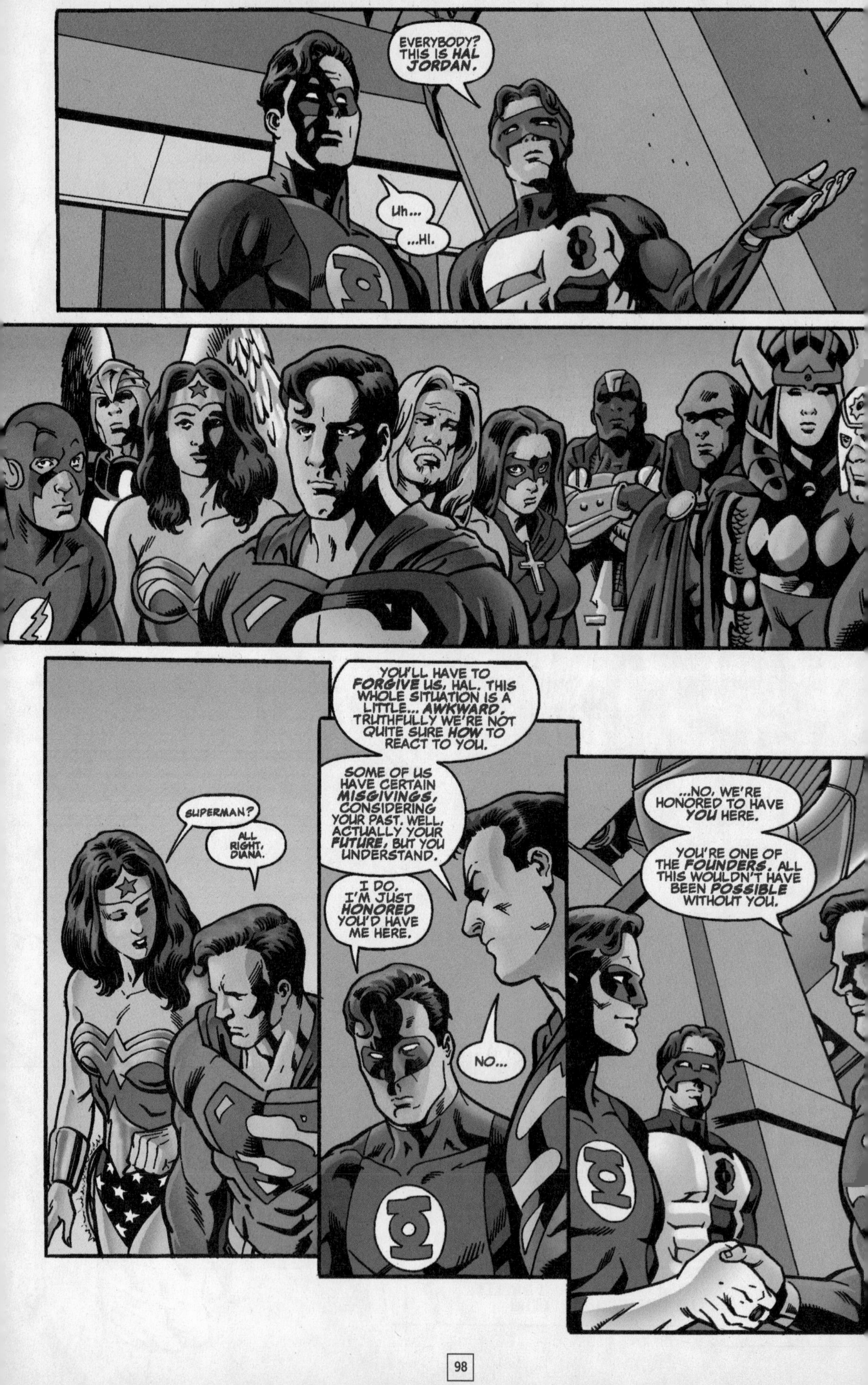
EVERYBODY? THIS IS HAL JORDAN.
Uh... ...HI.
SUPERMAN?
ALL RIGHT, DIANA.
YOU'LL HAVE TO FORGIVE US, HAL. THIS WHOLE SITUATION IS A LITTLE... AWKWARD. TRUTHFULLY WE'RE NOT QUITE SURE HOW TO REACT TO YOU.
SOME OF US HAVE CERTAIN MISGIVINGS, CONSIDERING YOUR PAST. WELL, ACTUALLY YOUR FUTURE, BUT YOU UNDERSTAND.
I DO. I'M JUST HONORED YOU'D HAVE ME HERE.
NO...
...NO, WE'RE HONORED TO HAVE YOU HERE.
YOU'RE ONE OF THE FOUNDERS. ALL THIS WOULDN'T HAVE BEEN POSSIBLE WITHOUT YOU.

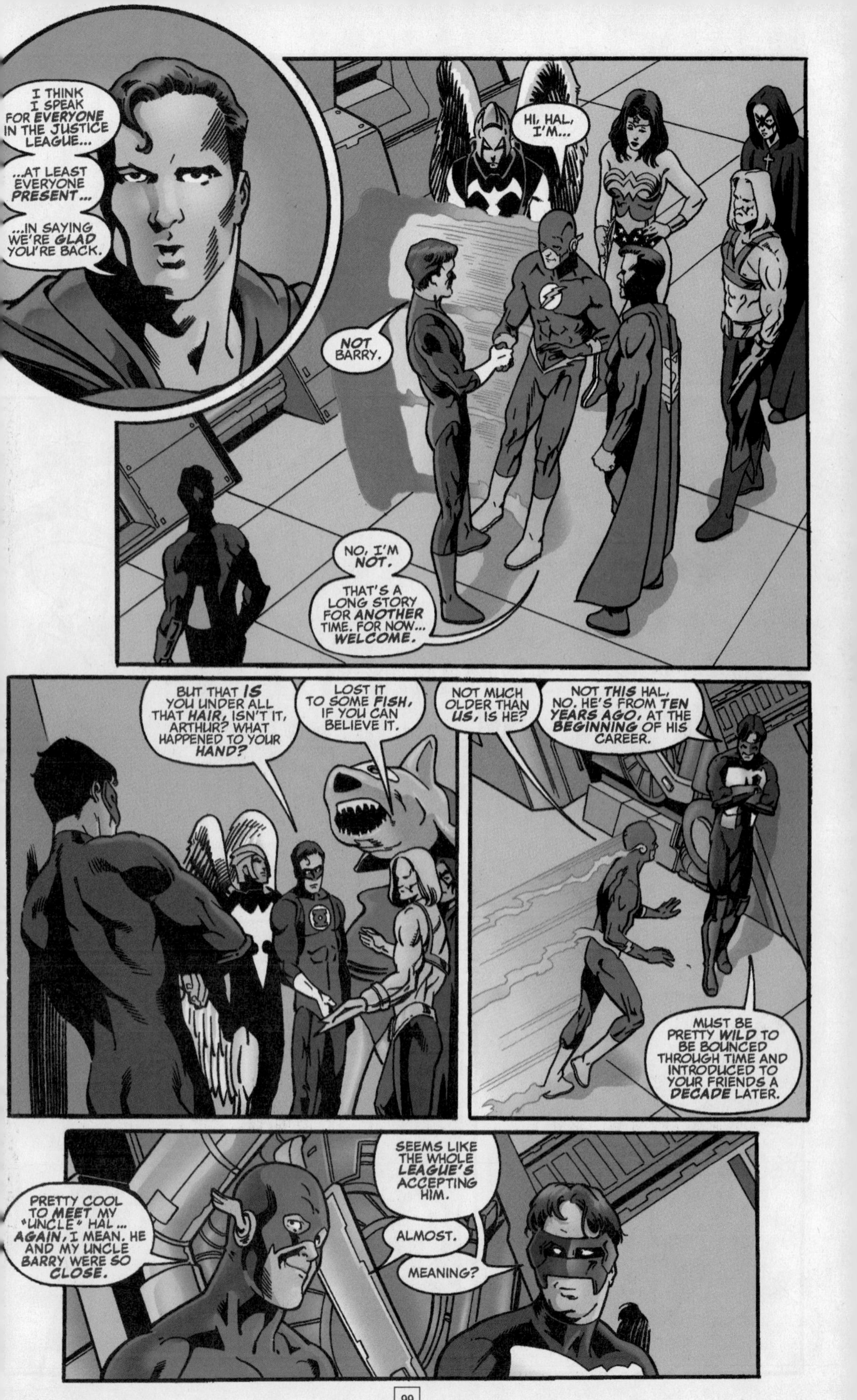
I THINK I SPEAK FOR EVERYONE IN THE JUSTICE LEAGUE...
...AT LEAST EVERYONE PRESENT...
...IN SAYING WE'RE GLAD YOU'RE BACK.
HI, HAL, I'M...
NOT BARRY.
NO, I'M NOT.
THAT'S A LONG STORY FOR ANOTHER TIME. FOR NOW... WELCOME.
BUT THAT IS YOU UNDER ALL THAT HAIR, ISN'T IT, ARTHUR? WHAT HAPPENED TO YOUR HAND?
LOST IT TO SOME FISH, IF YOU CAN BELIEVE IT.
NOT MUCH OLDER THAN US, IS HE?
NOT THIS HAL, NO. HE'S FROM TEN YEARS AGO, AT THE BEGINNING OF HIS CAREER.
MUST BE PRETTY WILD TO BE BOUNCED THROUGH TIME AND INTRODUCED TO YOUR FRIENDS A DECADE LATER.
PRETTY COOL TO MEET MY "UNCLE" HAL... AGAIN, I MEAN. HE AND MY UNCLE BARRY WERE SO CLOSE.
SEEMS LIKE THE WHOLE LEAGUE'S ACCEPTING HIM.
ALMOST.
MEANING?

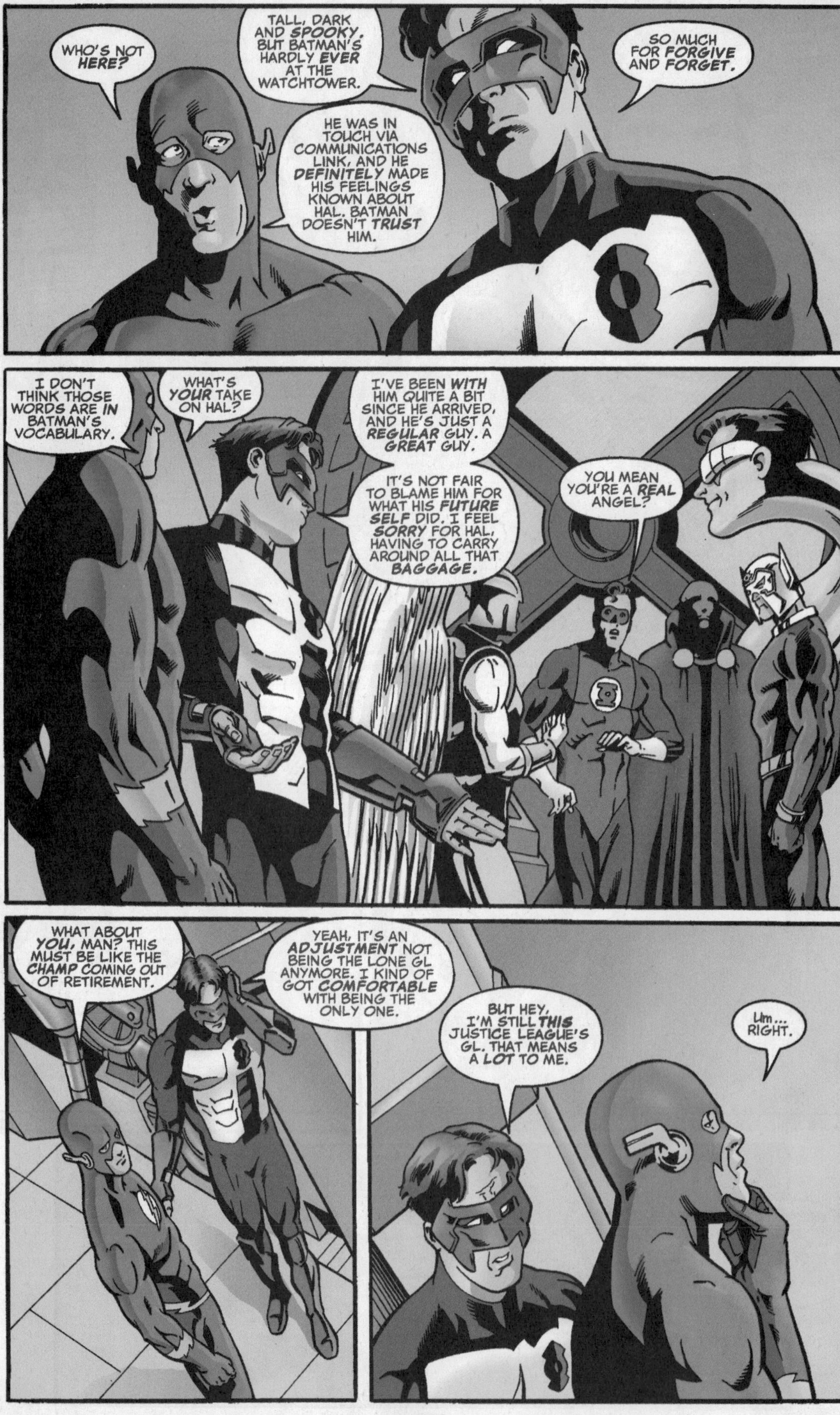
WHO'S NOT HERE?
TALL, DARK AND SPOOKY. BUT BATMAN'S HARDLY EVER AT THE WATCHTOWER.
HE WAS IN TOUCH VIA COMMUNICATIONS LINK, AND HE DEFINITELY MADE HIS FEELINGS KNOWN ABOUT HAL. BATMAN DOESN'T TRUST HIM.
SO MUCH FOR FORGIVE AND FORGET.
I DON'T THINK THOSE WORDS ARE IN BATMAN'S VOCABULARY.
WHAT'S YOUR TAKE ON HAL?
I'VE BEEN WITH HIM QUITE A BIT SINCE HE ARRIVED, AND HE'S JUST A REGULAR GUY. A GREAT GUY.
IT'S NOT FAIR TO BLAME HIM FOR WHAT HIS FUTURE SELF DID. I FEEL SORRY FOR HAL, HAVING TO CARRY AROUND ALL THAT BAGGAGE.
YOU MEAN YOU'RE A REAL ANGEL?
WHAT ABOUT YOU, MAN? THIS MUST BE LIKE THE CHAMP COMING OUT OF RETIREMENT.
YEAH, IT'S AN ADJUSTMENT NOT BEING THE LONE GL ANYMORE. I KIND OF GOT COMFORTABLE WITH BEING THE ONLY ONE.
BUT HEY, I'M STILL THIS JUSTICE LEAGUE'S GL. THAT MEANS A LOT TO ME.
UM... RIGHT.

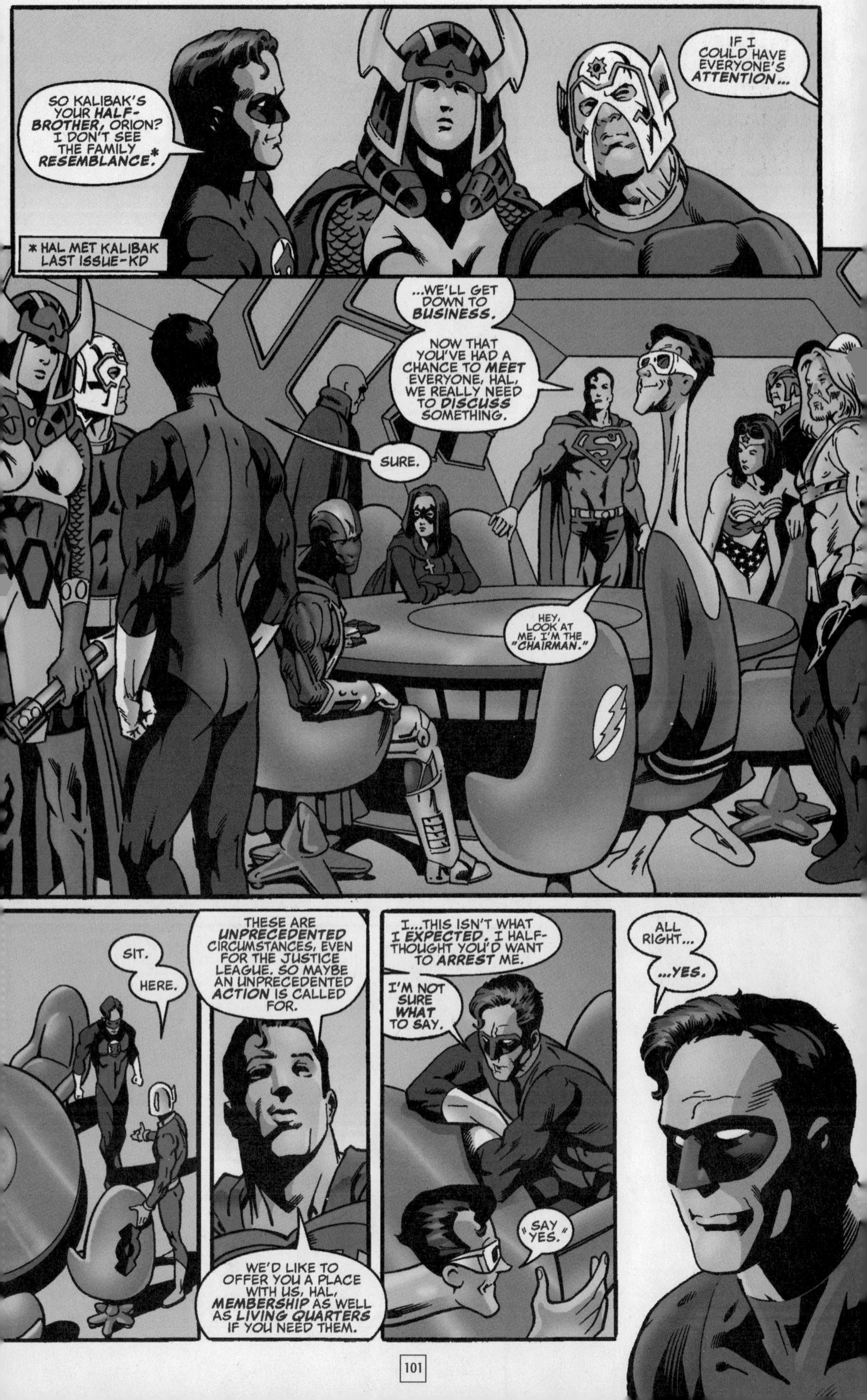
SO KALIBAK'S YOUR HALF-BROTHER, ORION? I DON'T SEE THE FAMILY RESEMBLANCE.*
IF I COULD HAVE EVERYONE'S ATTENTION...
* HAL MET KALIBAK LAST ISSUE-KD
...WE'LL GET DOWN TO BUSINESS.
NOW THAT YOU'VE HAD A CHANCE TO MEET EVERYONE, HAL, WE REALLY NEED TO DISCUSS SOMETHING.
SURE.
HEY, LOOK AT ME, I'M THE "CHAIRMAN."
SIT.
HERE.
THESE ARE UNPRECEDENTED CIRCUMSTANCES, EVEN FOR THE JUSTICE LEAGUE. SO MAYBE AN UNPRECEDENTED ACTION IS CALLED FOR.
WE'D LIKE TO OFFER YOU A PLACE WITH US, HAL, MEMBERSHIP AS WELL AS LIVING QUARTERS IF YOU NEED THEM.
I...THIS ISN'T WHAT I EXPECTED. I HALF-THOUGHT YOU'D WANT TO ARREST ME.
I'M NOT SURE WHAT TO SAY.
"SAY YES."
ALL RIGHT...
...YES.

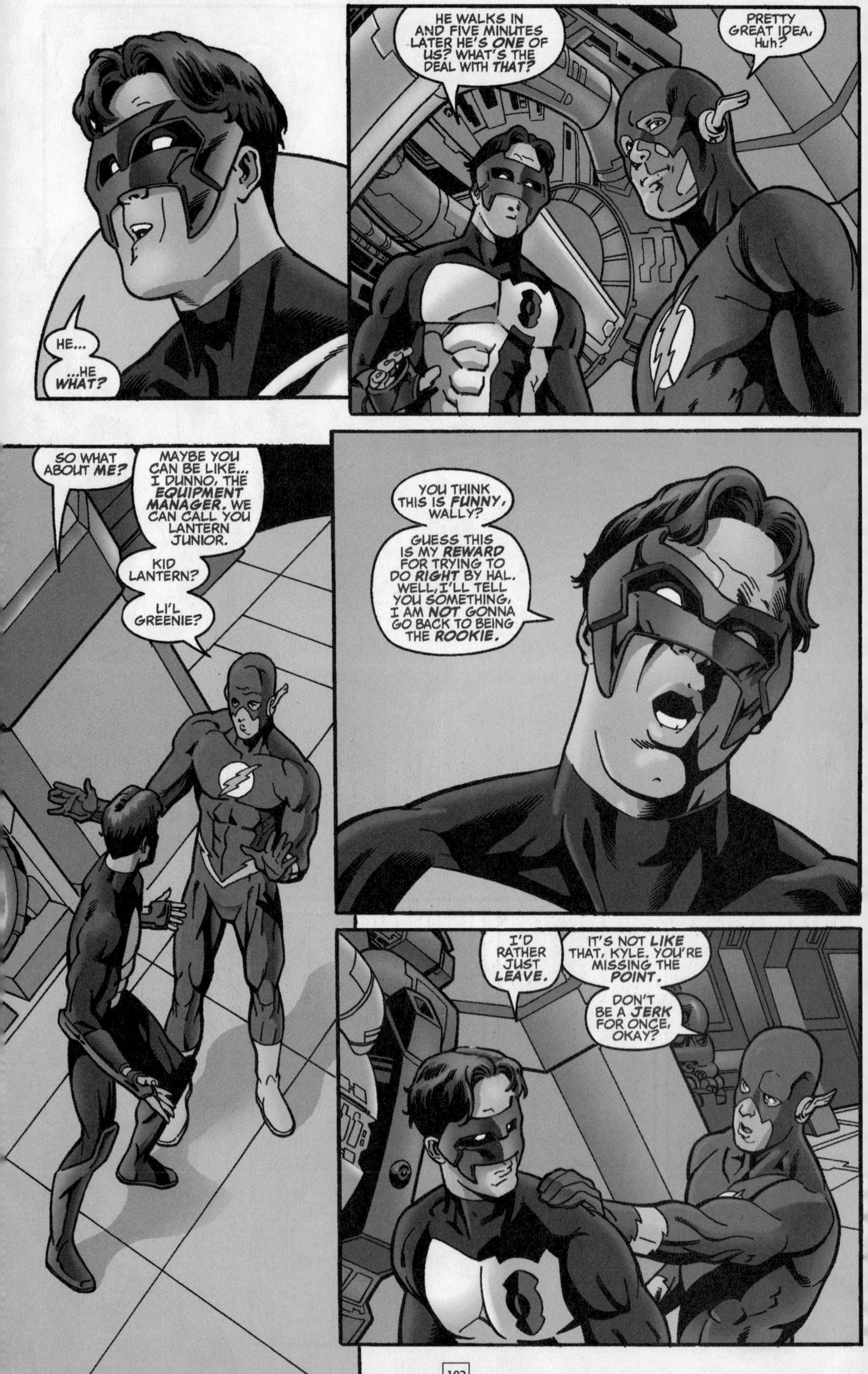
HE...
...HE WHAT?
HE WALKS IN AND FIVE MINUTES LATER HE'S ONE OF US? WHAT'S THE DEAL WITH THAT?
PRETTY GREAT IDEA, Huh?
SO WHAT ABOUT ME?
MAYBE YOU CAN BE LIKE... I DUNNO, THE EQUIPMENT MANAGER. WE CAN CALL YOU LANTERN JUNIOR.
KID LANTERN?
LI'L GREENIE?
YOU THINK THIS IS FUNNY, WALLY?
GUESS THIS IS MY REWARD FOR TRYING TO DO RIGHT BY HAL. WELL, I'LL TELL YOU SOMETHING, I AM NOT GONNA GO BACK TO BEING THE ROOKIE.
I'D RATHER JUST LEAVE.
IT'S NOT LIKE THAT, KYLE. YOU'RE MISSING THE POINT.
DON'T BE A JERK FOR ONCE, OKAY?

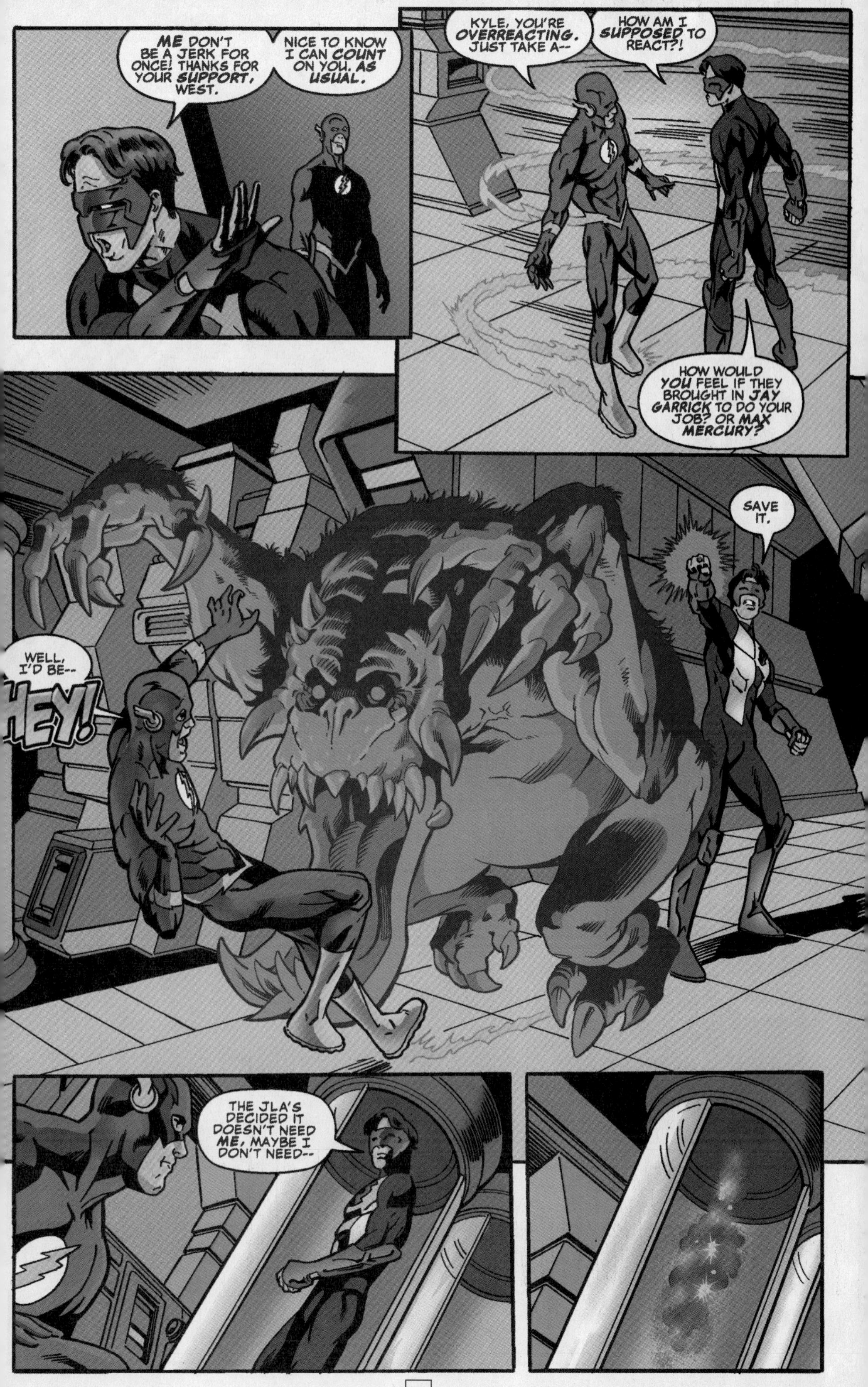
ME DON'T BE A JERK FOR ONCE! THANKS FOR YOUR SUPPORT, WEST.
NICE TO KNOW I CAN COUNT ON YOU. AS USUAL.
KYLE, YOU'RE OVERREACTING. JUST TAKE A--
HOW AM I SUPPOSED TO REACT?!
HOW WOULD YOU FEEL IF THEY BROUGHT IN JAY GARRICK TO DO YOUR JOB? OR MAX MERCURY?
SAVE IT.
WELL, I'D BE--
HEY!
THE JLA'S DECIDED IT DOESN'T NEED ME, MAYBE I DON'T NEED--

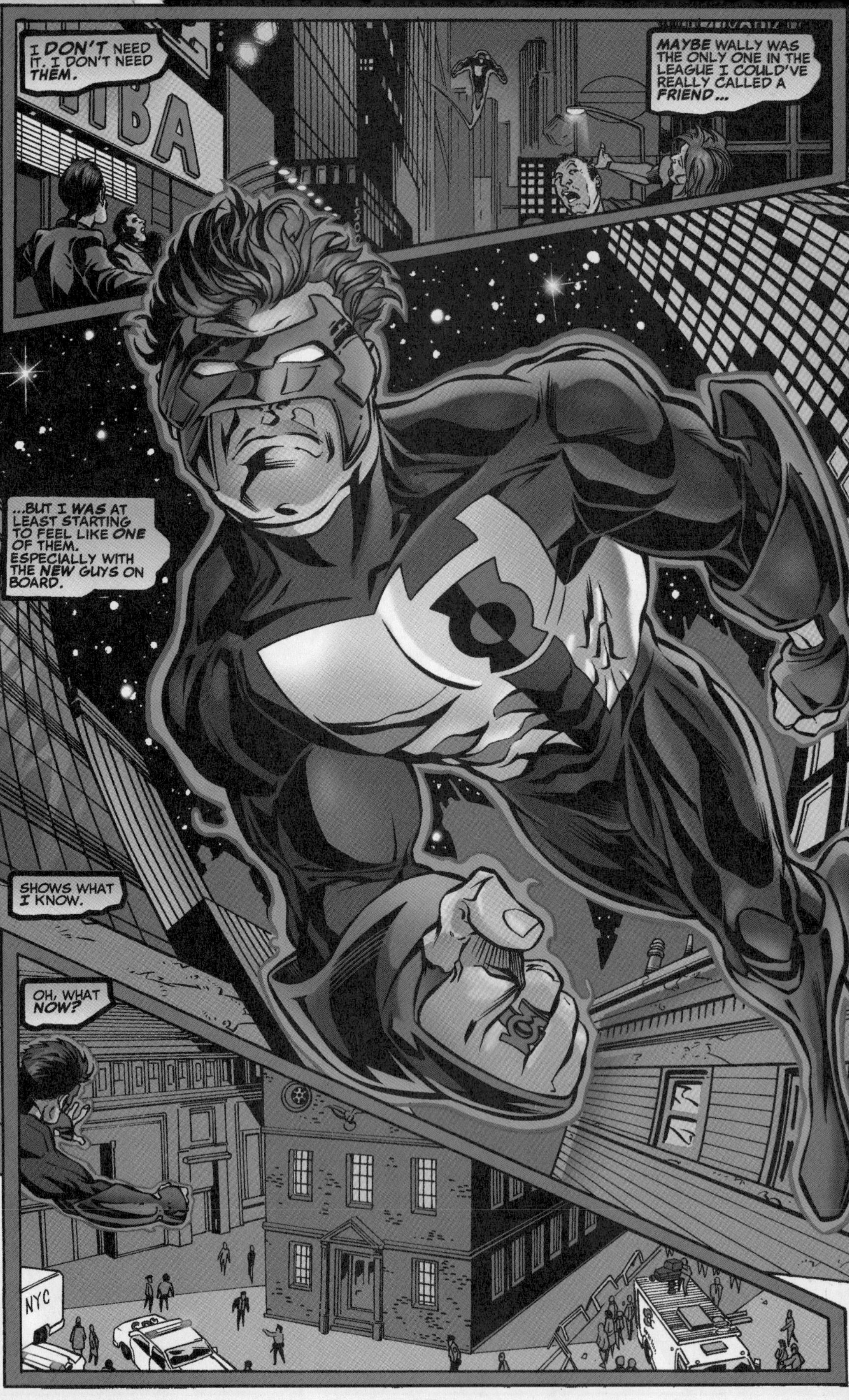
I DON'T NEED IT. I DON'T NEED THEM.
MAYBE WALLY WAS THE ONLY ONE IN THE LEAGUE I COULD'VE REALLY CALLED A FRIEND...
...BUT I WAS AT LEAST STARTING TO FEEL LIKE ONE OF THEM. ESPECIALLY WITH THE NEW GUYS ON BOARD.
SHOWS WHAT I KNOW.
OH, WHAT NOW?
NYC

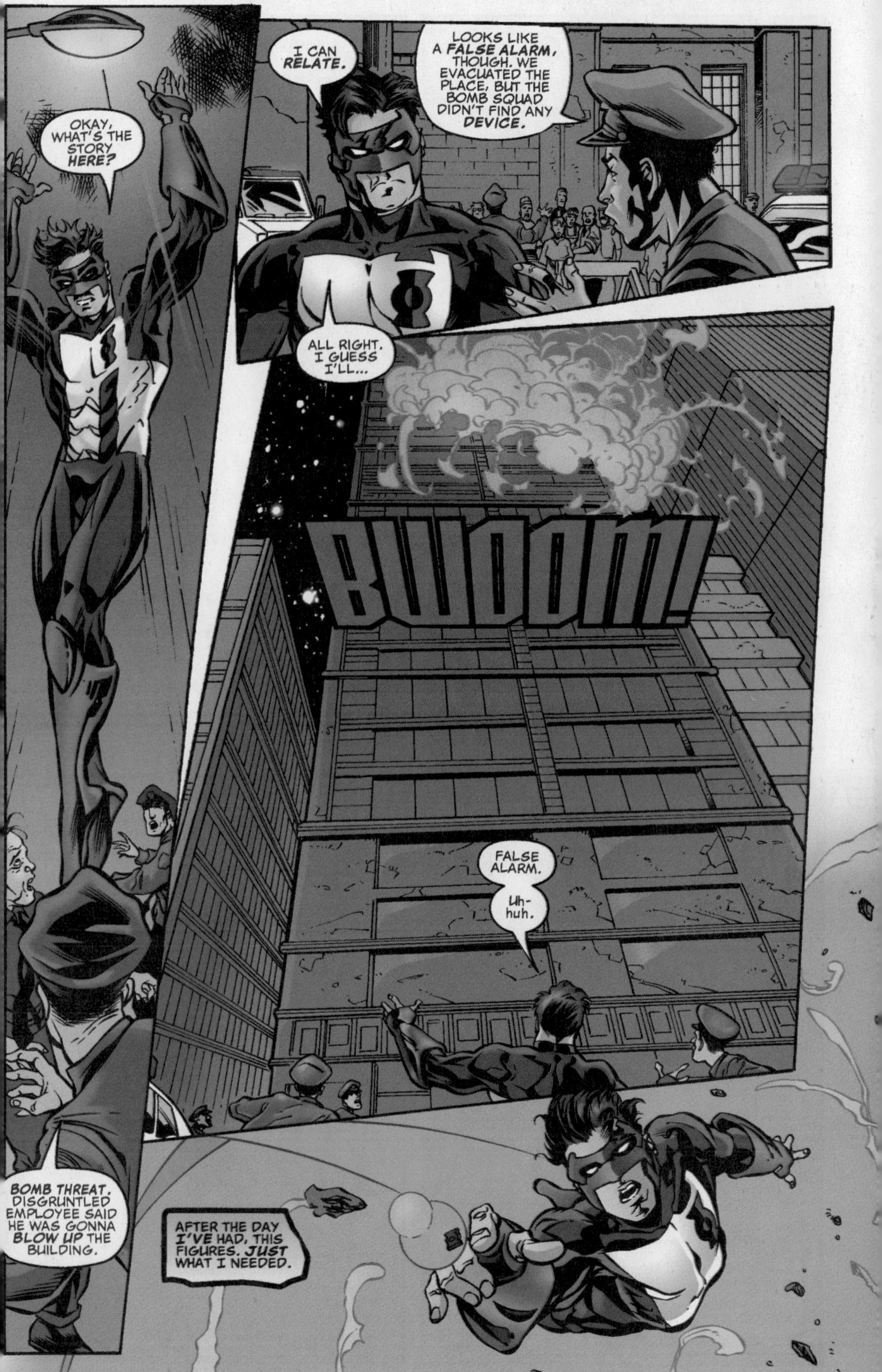

OKAY, WHAT'S THE STORY HERE?
BOMB THREAT. DISGRUNTLED EMPLOYEE SAID HE WAS GONNA BLOW UP THE BUILDING.
AFTER THE DAY I'VE HAD, THIS FIGURES. JUST WHAT I NEEDED.
I CAN RELATE.
LOOKS LIKE A FALSE ALARM, THOUGH. WE EVACUATED THE PLACE, BUT THE BOMB SQUAD DIDN'T FIND ANY DEVICE.
ALL RIGHT. I GUESS I'LL...
BWOOM!
FALSE ALARM.
Uh-huh.

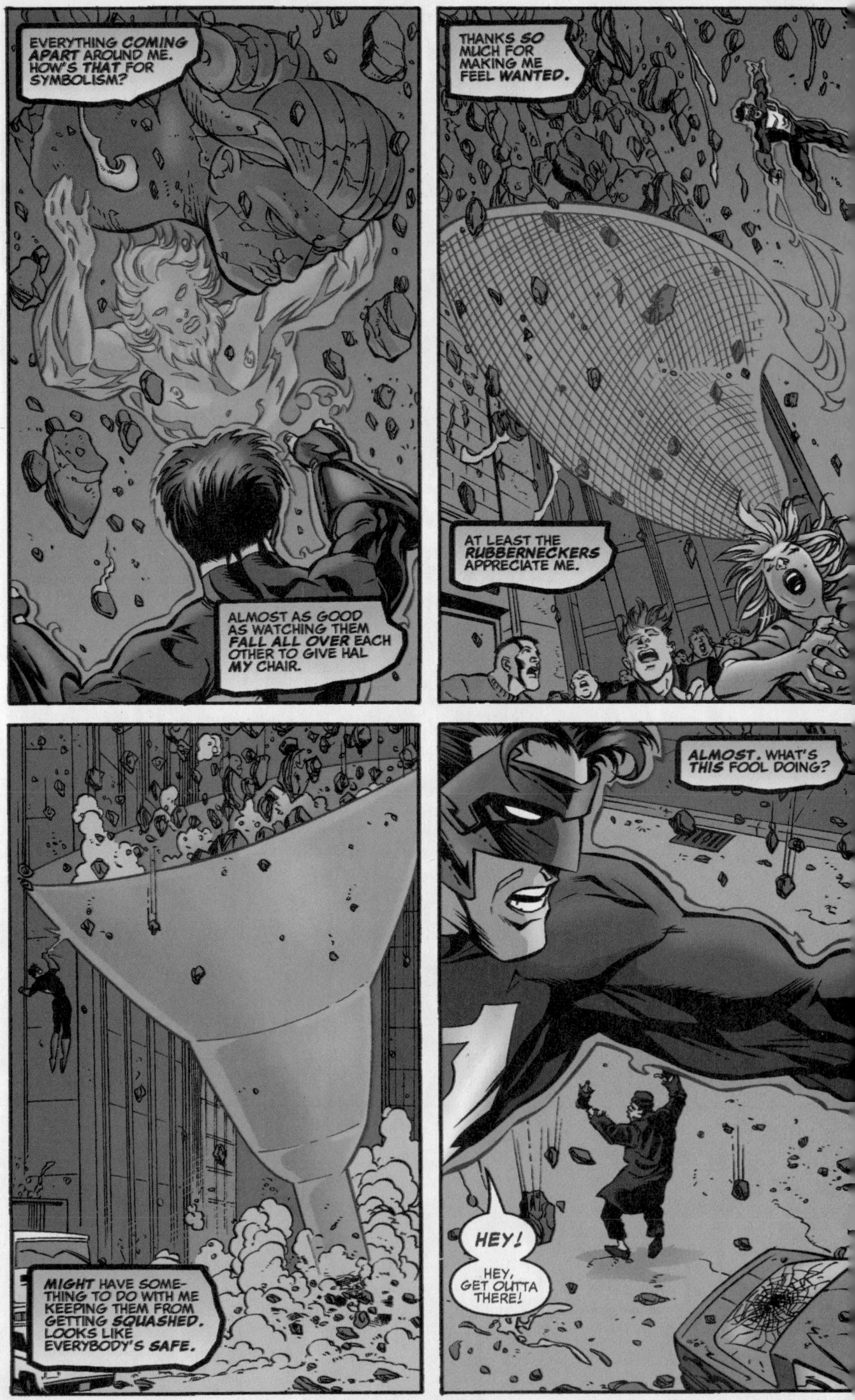
EVERYTHING COMING APART AROUND ME. HOW'S THAT FOR SYMBOLISM?
ALMOST AS GOOD AS WATCHING THEM FALL ALL OVER EACH OTHER TO GIVE HAL MY CHAIR.
THANKS SO MUCH FOR MAKING ME FEEL WANTED.
AT LEAST THE RUBBERNECKERS APPRECIATE ME.
MIGHT HAVE SOMETHING TO DO WITH ME KEEPING THEM FROM GETTING SQUASHED. LOOKS LIKE EVERYBODY'S SAFE.
ALMOST. WHAT'S THIS FOOL DOING?
HEY!
HEY, GET OUTTA THERE!

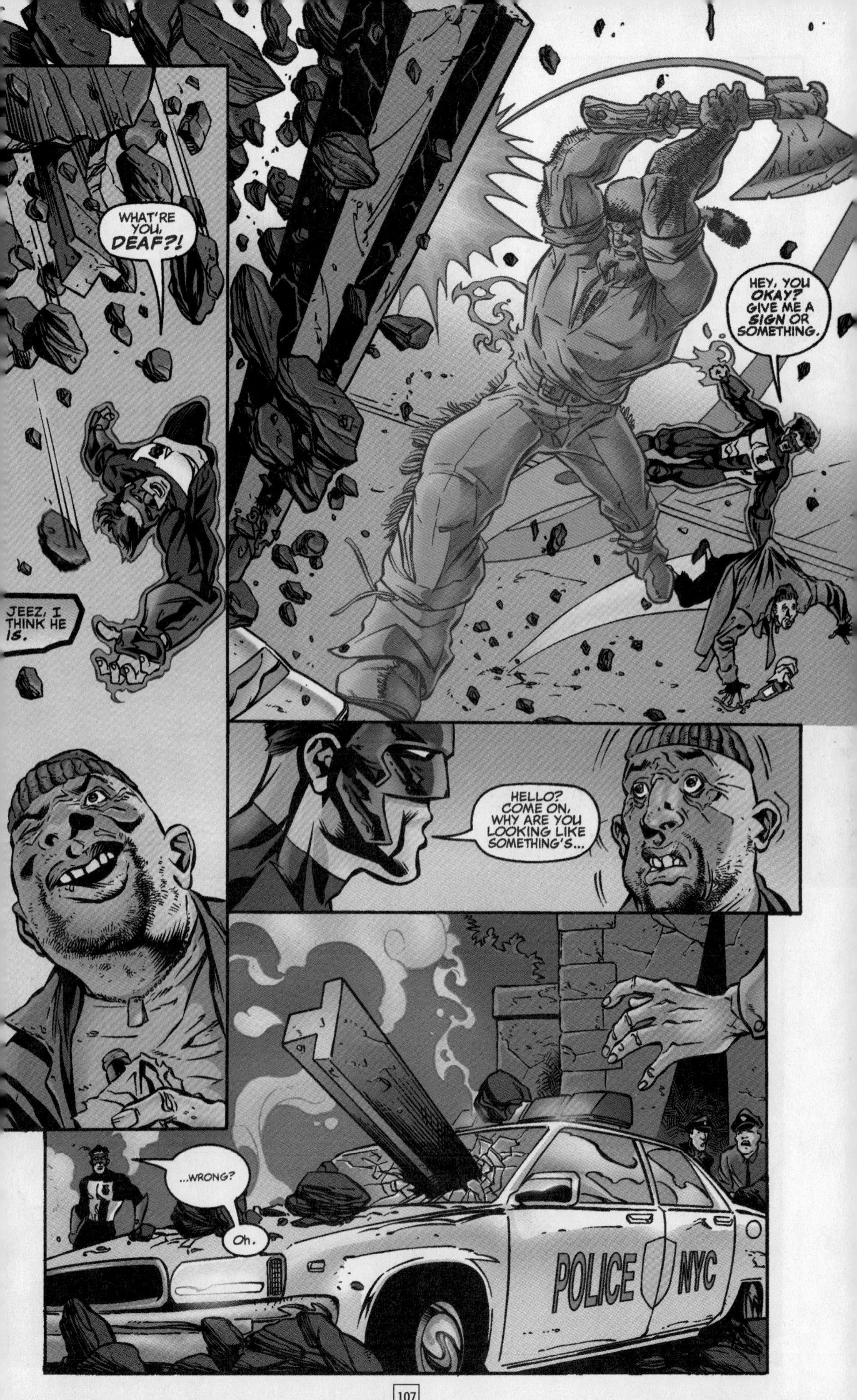
WHAT'RE YOU, DEAF?!
JEEZ, I THINK HE IS.
HEY, YOU OKAY? GIVE ME A SIGN OR SOMETHING.
HELLO? COME ON, WHY ARE YOU LOOKING LIKE SOMETHING'S...
...WRONG?
Oh.
POLICE NYC

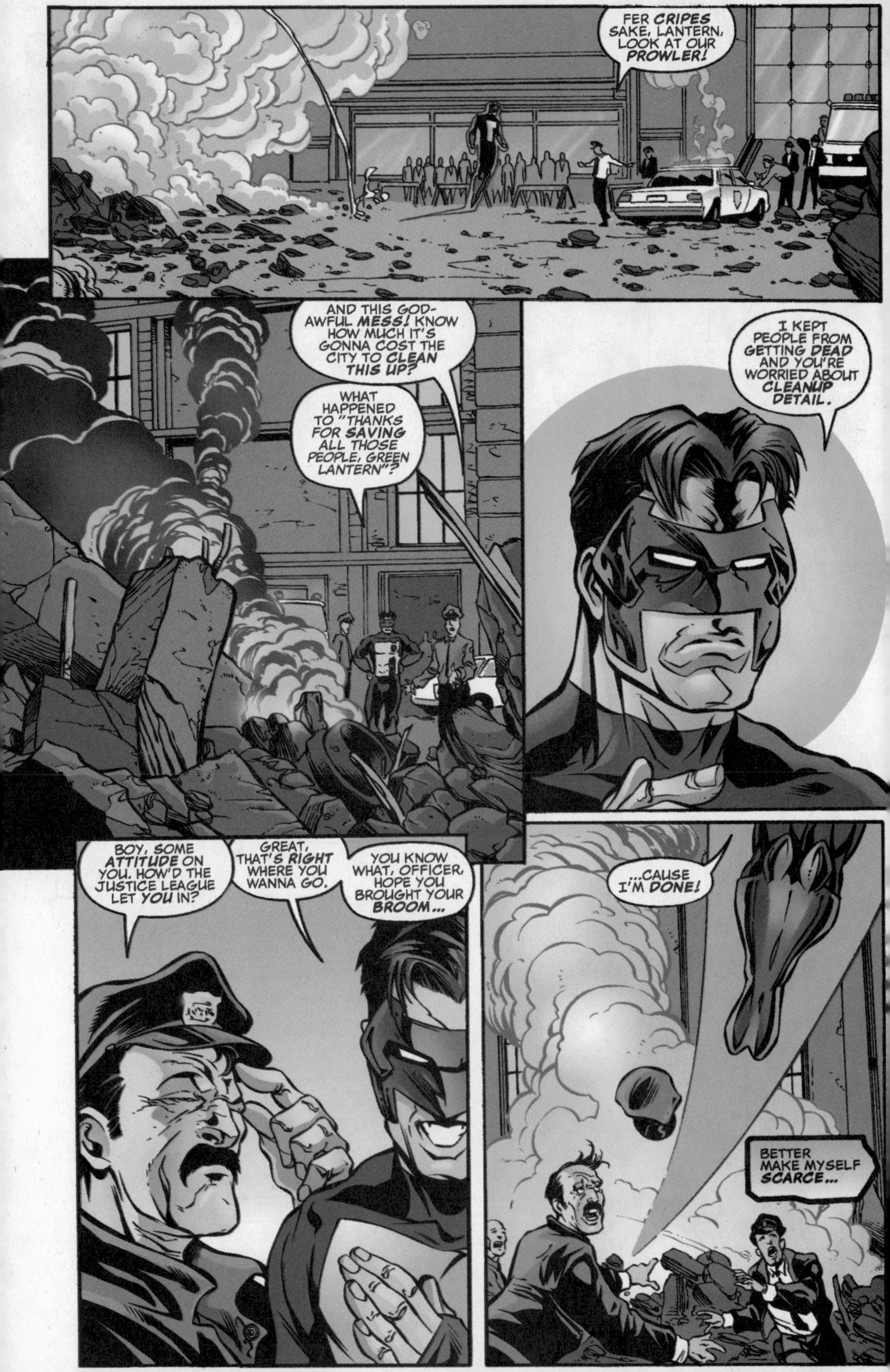

FER CRIPES SAKE, LANTERN, LOOK AT OUR PROWLER!
AND THIS GOD-AWFUL MESS! KNOW HOW MUCH IT'S GONNA COST THE CITY TO CLEAN THIS UP?
WHAT HAPPENED TO "THANKS FOR SAVING ALL THOSE PEOPLE, GREEN LANTERN"?
I KEPT PEOPLE FROM GETTING DEAD AND YOU'RE WORRIED ABOUT CLEANUP DETAIL.
BOY, SOME ATTITUDE ON YOU. HOW'D THE JUSTICE LEAGUE LET YOU IN?
GREAT, THAT'S RIGHT WHERE YOU WANNA GO.
YOU KNOW WHAT, OFFICER, HOPE YOU BROUGHT YOUR BROOM...
...CAUSE I'M DONE!
BETTER MAKE MYSELF SCARCE...

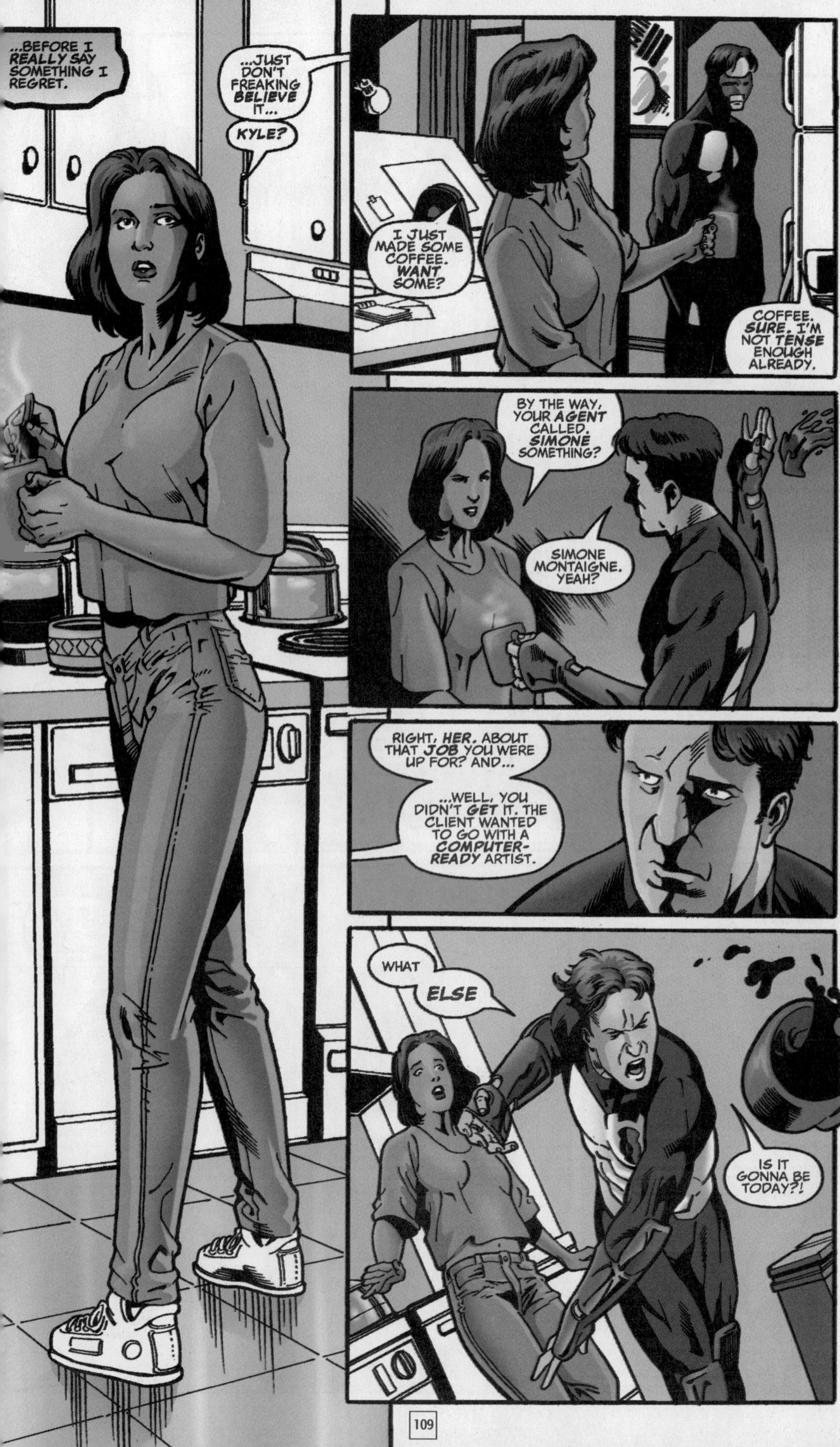
...BEFORE I REALLY SAY SOMETHING I REGRET.
...JUST DON'T FREAKING BELIEVE IT...
KYLE?
I JUST MADE SOME COFFEE. WANT SOME?
COFFEE. SURE. I'M NOT TENSE ENOUGH ALREADY.
BY THE WAY, YOUR AGENT CALLED. SIMONE SOMETHING?
SIMONE MONTAIGNE. YEAH?
RIGHT, HER. ABOUT THAT JOB YOU WERE UP FOR? AND...
...WELL, YOU DIDN'T GET IT. THE CLIENT WANTED TO GO WITH A COMPUTER-READY ARTIST.
WHAT ELSE
IS IT GONNA BE TODAY?!

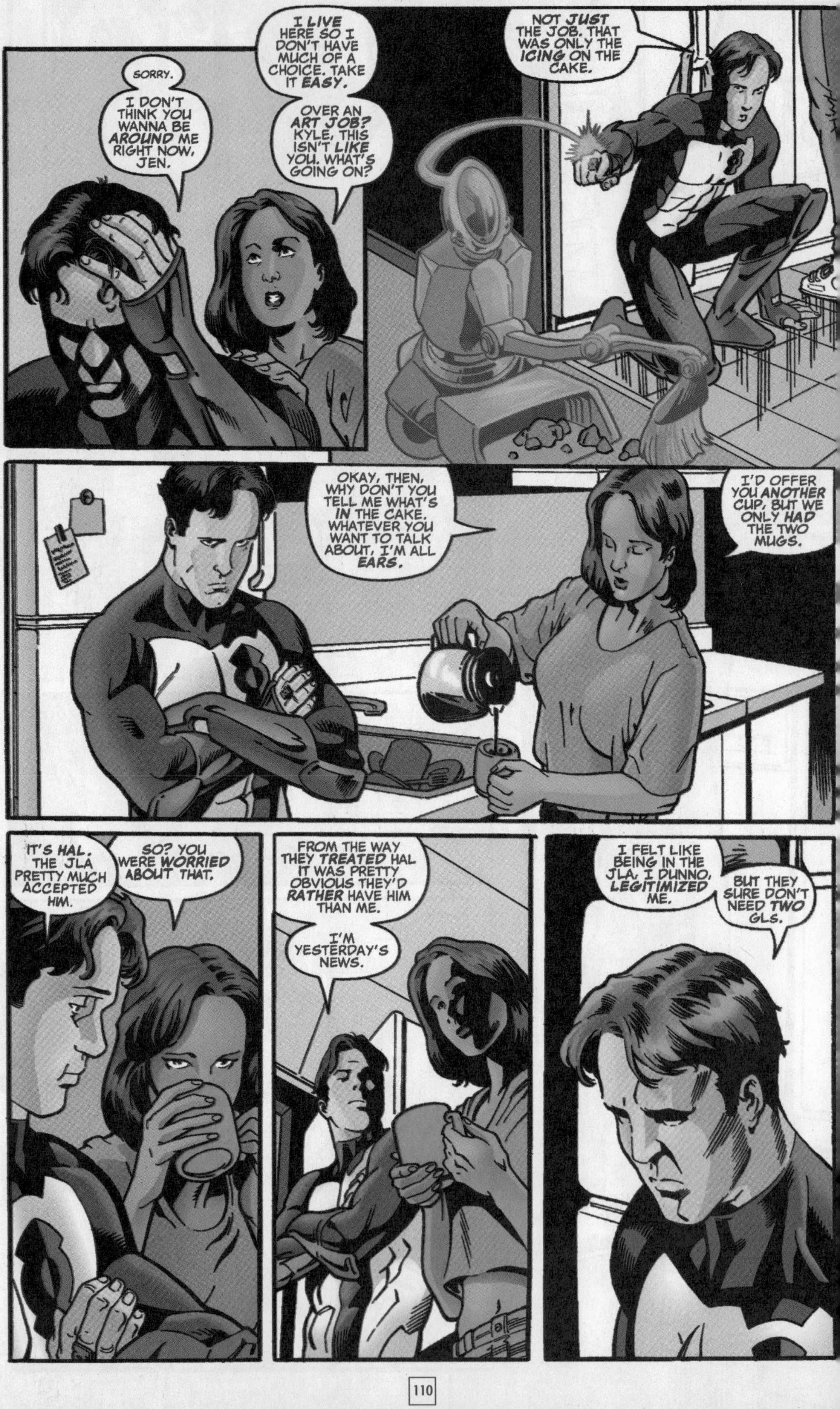
SORRY.
I DON'T THINK YOU WANNA BE AROUND ME RIGHT NOW, JEN.
I LIVE HERE SO I DON'T HAVE MUCH OF A CHOICE. TAKE IT EASY.
OVER AN ART JOB? KYLE, THIS ISN'T LIKE YOU. WHAT'S GOING ON?
NOT JUST THE JOB. THAT WAS ONLY THE ICING ON THE CAKE.
OKAY, THEN, WHY DON'T YOU TELL ME WHAT'S IN THE CAKE. WHATEVER YOU WANT TO TALK ABOUT, I'M ALL EARS.
I'D OFFER YOU ANOTHER CUP, BUT WE ONLY HAD THE TWO MUGS.
IT'S HAL. THE JLA PRETTY MUCH ACCEPTED HIM.
SO? YOU WERE WORRIED ABOUT THAT.
FROM THE WAY THEY TREATED HAL IT WAS PRETTY OBVIOUS THEY'D RATHER HAVE HIM THAN ME.
I'M YESTERDAY'S NEWS.
I FELT LIKE BEING IN THE JLA, I DUNNO, LEGITIMIZED ME.
BUT THEY SURE DON'T NEED TWO GLS.

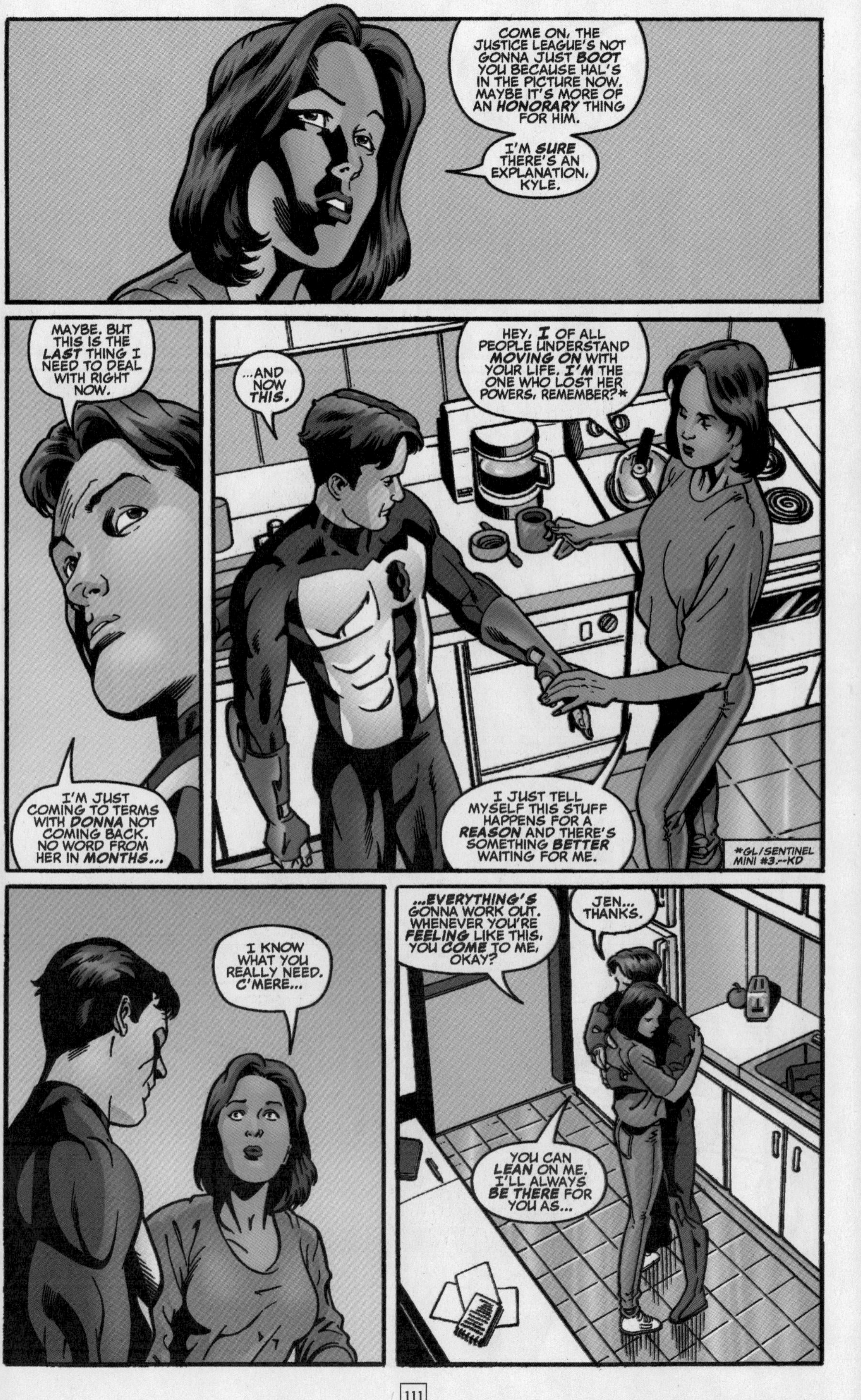
COME ON, THE JUSTICE LEAGUE'S NOT GONNA JUST BOOT YOU BECAUSE HAL'S IN THE PICTURE NOW. MAYBE IT'S MORE OF AN HONORARY THING FOR HIM.
I'M SURE THERE'S AN EXPLANATION, KYLE.
MAYBE. BUT THIS IS THE LAST THING I NEED TO DEAL WITH RIGHT NOW.
I'M JUST COMING TO TERMS WITH DONNA NOT COMING BACK. NO WORD FROM HER IN MONTHS...
...AND NOW THIS.
HEY, I OF ALL PEOPLE UNDERSTAND MOVING ON WITH YOUR LIFE. I'M THE ONE WHO LOST HER POWERS, REMEMBER?*
I JUST TELL MYSELF THIS STUFF HAPPENS FOR A REASON AND THERE'S SOMETHING BETTER WAITING FOR ME.
*GL/SENTINEL MINI #3.--KD
I KNOW WHAT YOU REALLY NEED. C'MERE...
...EVERYTHING'S GONNA WORK OUT. WHENEVER YOU'RE FEELING LIKE THIS, YOU COME TO ME, OKAY?
JEN... THANKS.
YOU CAN LEAN ON ME. I'LL ALWAYS BE THERE FOR YOU AS...

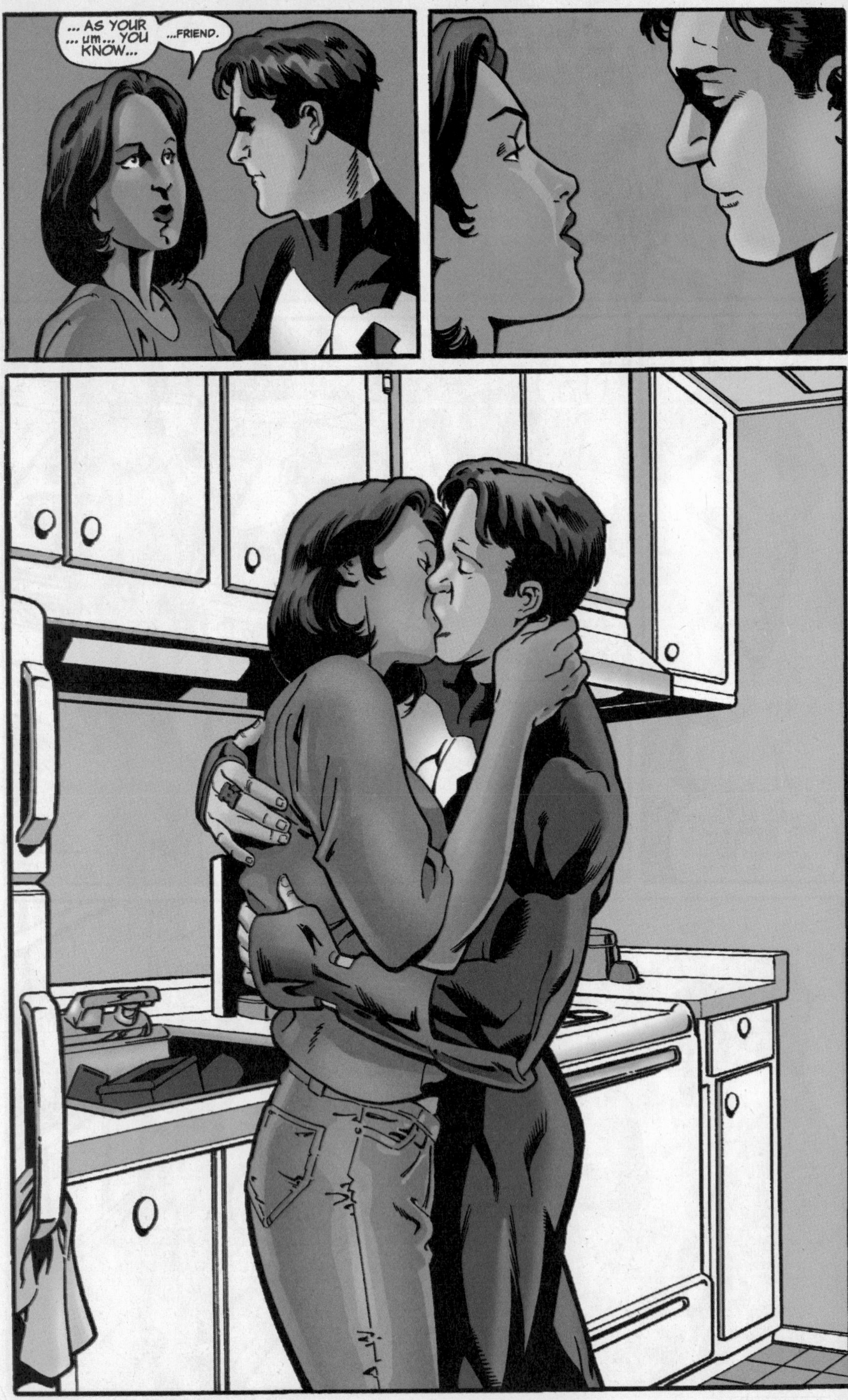
... AS YOUR ... um... YOU KNOW...
...FRIEND.

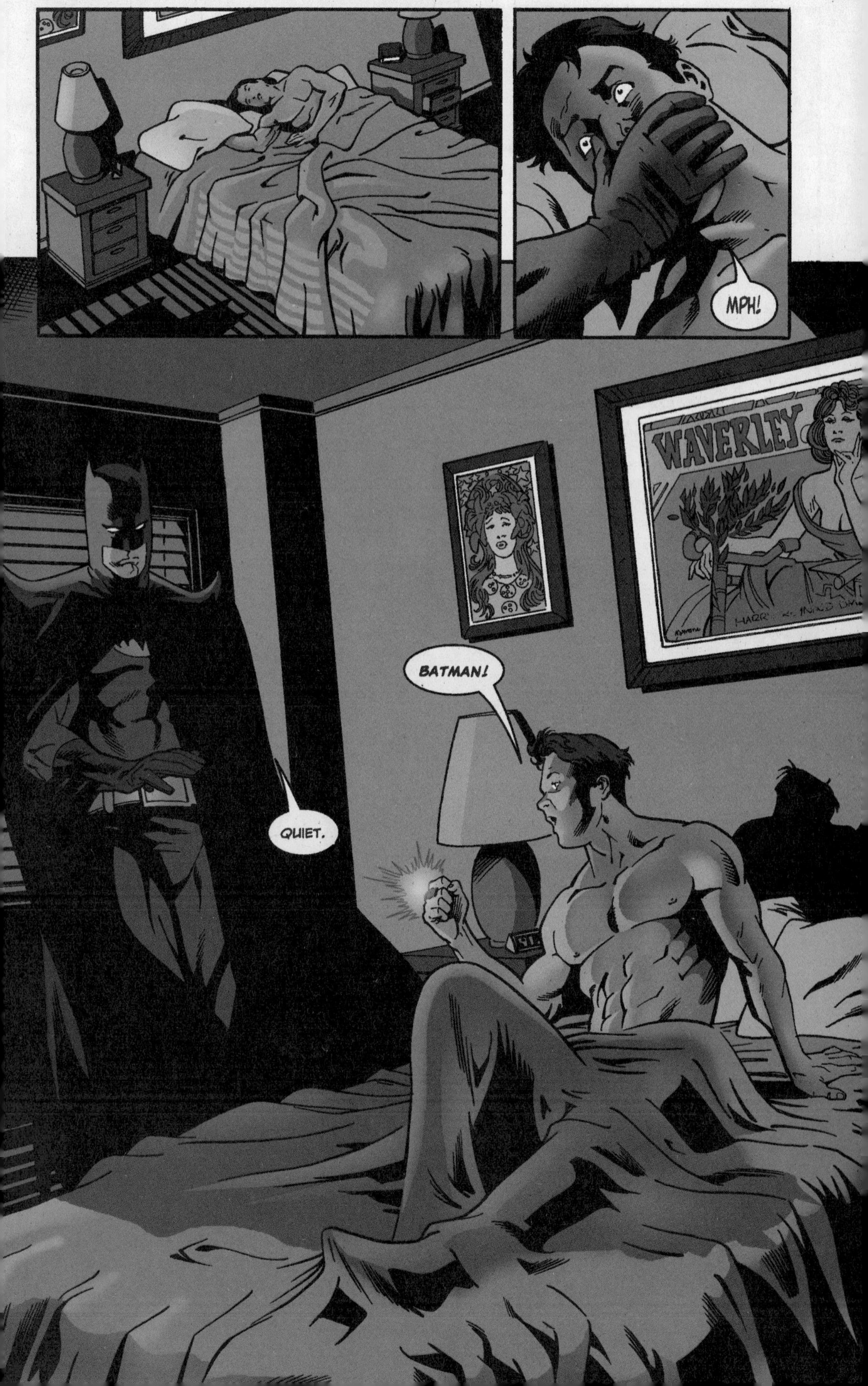
MPH!
BATMAN!
QUIET.
WAVERLEY

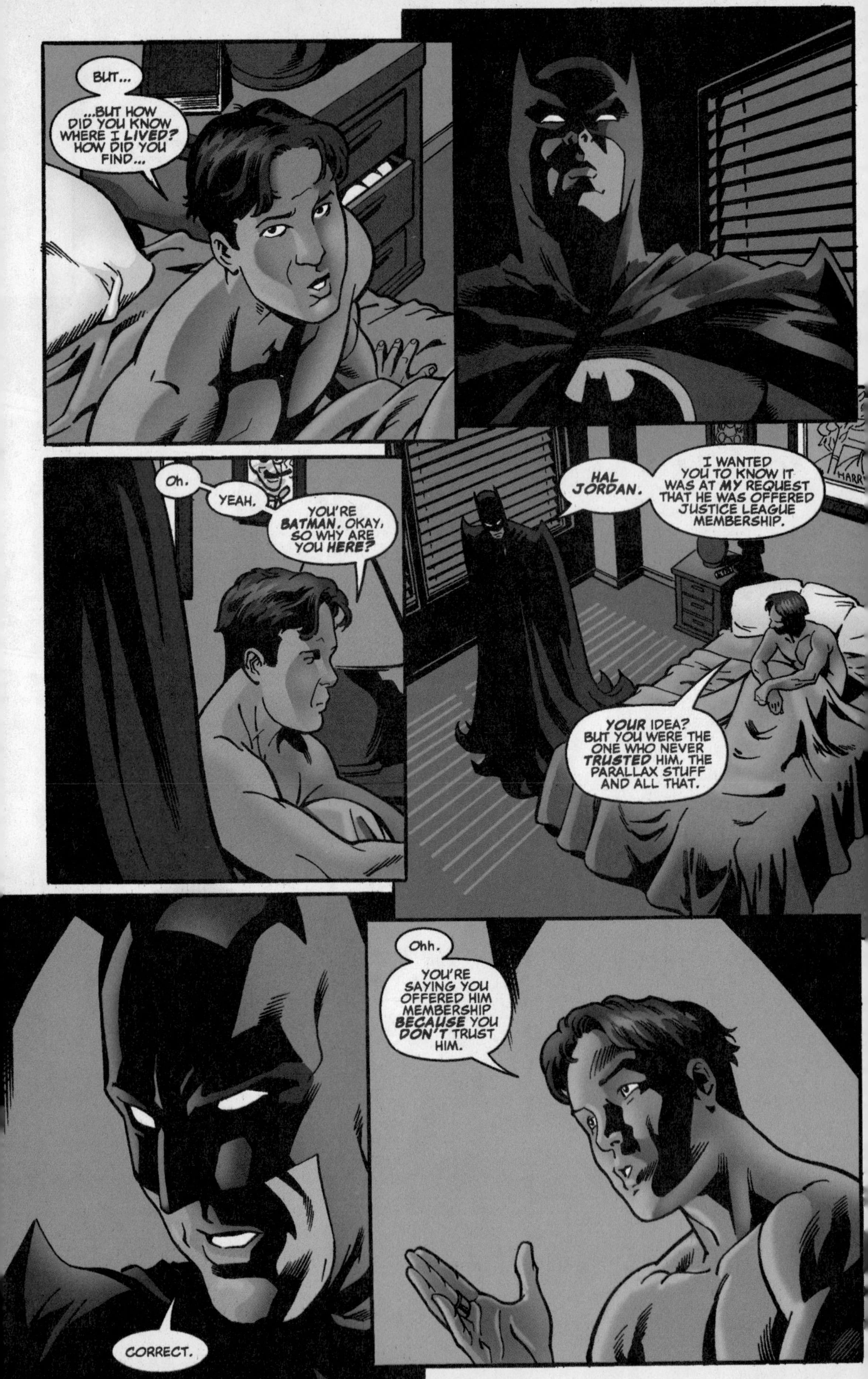

BUT...
...BUT HOW DID YOU KNOW WHERE I LIVED? HOW DID YOU FIND...
Oh.
YEAH.
YOU'RE BATMAN. OKAY, SO WHY ARE YOU HERE?
HAL JORDAN.
I WANTED YOU TO KNOW IT WAS AT MY REQUEST THAT HE WAS OFFERED JUSTICE LEAGUE MEMBERSHIP.
YOUR IDEA? BUT YOU WERE THE ONE WHO NEVER TRUSTED HIM, THE PARALLAX STUFF AND ALL THAT.
Ohh.
YOU'RE SAYING YOU OFFERED HIM MEMBERSHIP BECAUSE YOU DON'T TRUST HIM.
CORRECT.

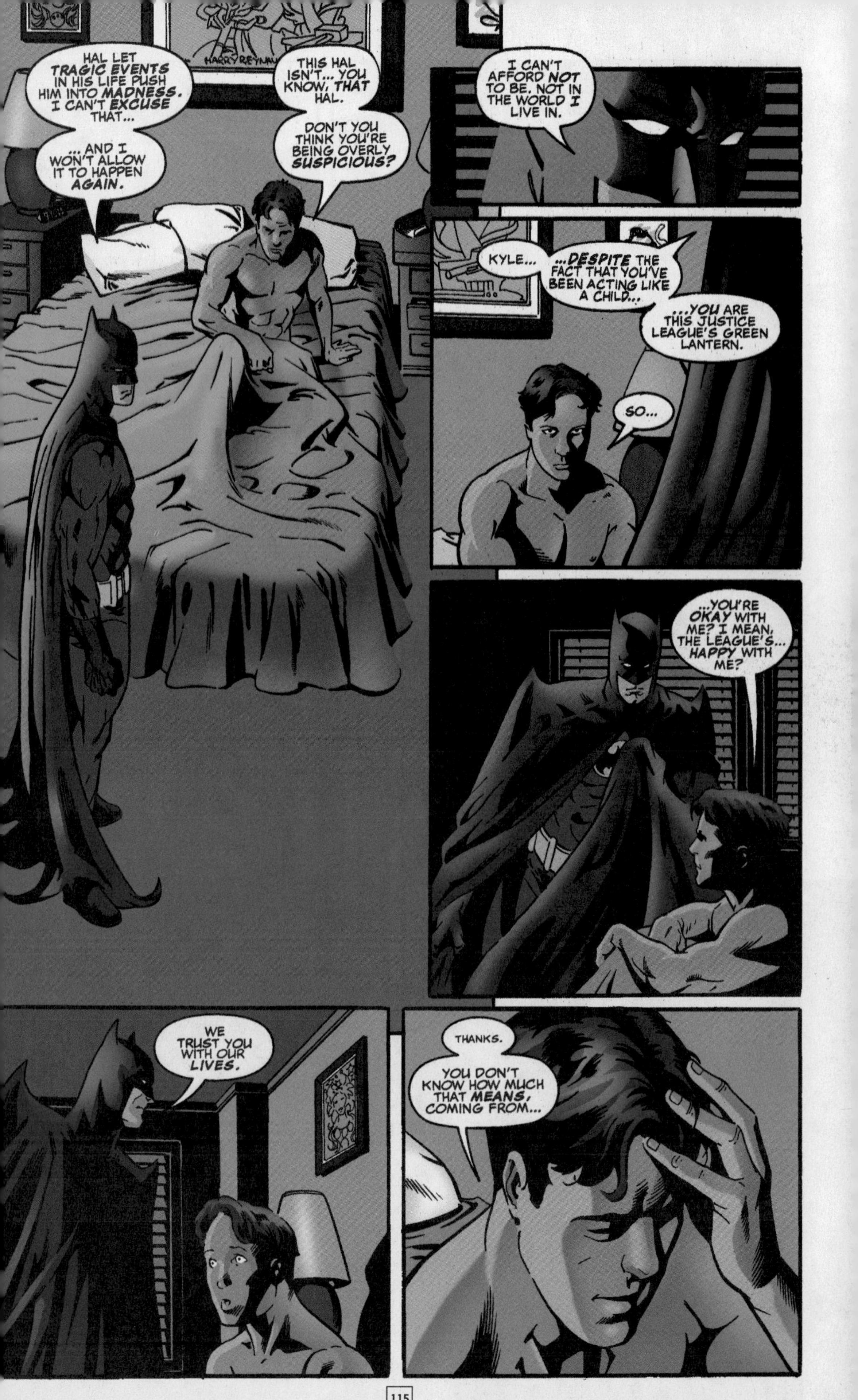
HAL LET TRAGIC EVENTS IN HIS LIFE PUSH HIM INTO MADNESS. I CAN'T EXCUSE THAT...
...AND I WON'T ALLOW IT TO HAPPEN AGAIN.
THIS HAL ISN'T... YOU KNOW, THAT HAL.
DON'T YOU THINK YOU'RE BEING OVERLY SUSPICIOUS?
I CAN'T AFFORD NOT TO BE. NOT IN THE WORLD I LIVE IN.
KYLE...
...DESPITE THE FACT THAT YOU'VE BEEN ACTING LIKE A CHILD...
...YOU ARE THIS JUSTICE LEAGUE'S GREEN LANTERN.
SO...
...YOU'RE OKAY WITH ME? I MEAN, THE LEAGUE'S... HAPPY WITH ME?
WE TRUST YOU WITH OUR LIVES.
THANKS.
YOU DON'T KNOW HOW MUCH THAT MEANS, COMING FROM...

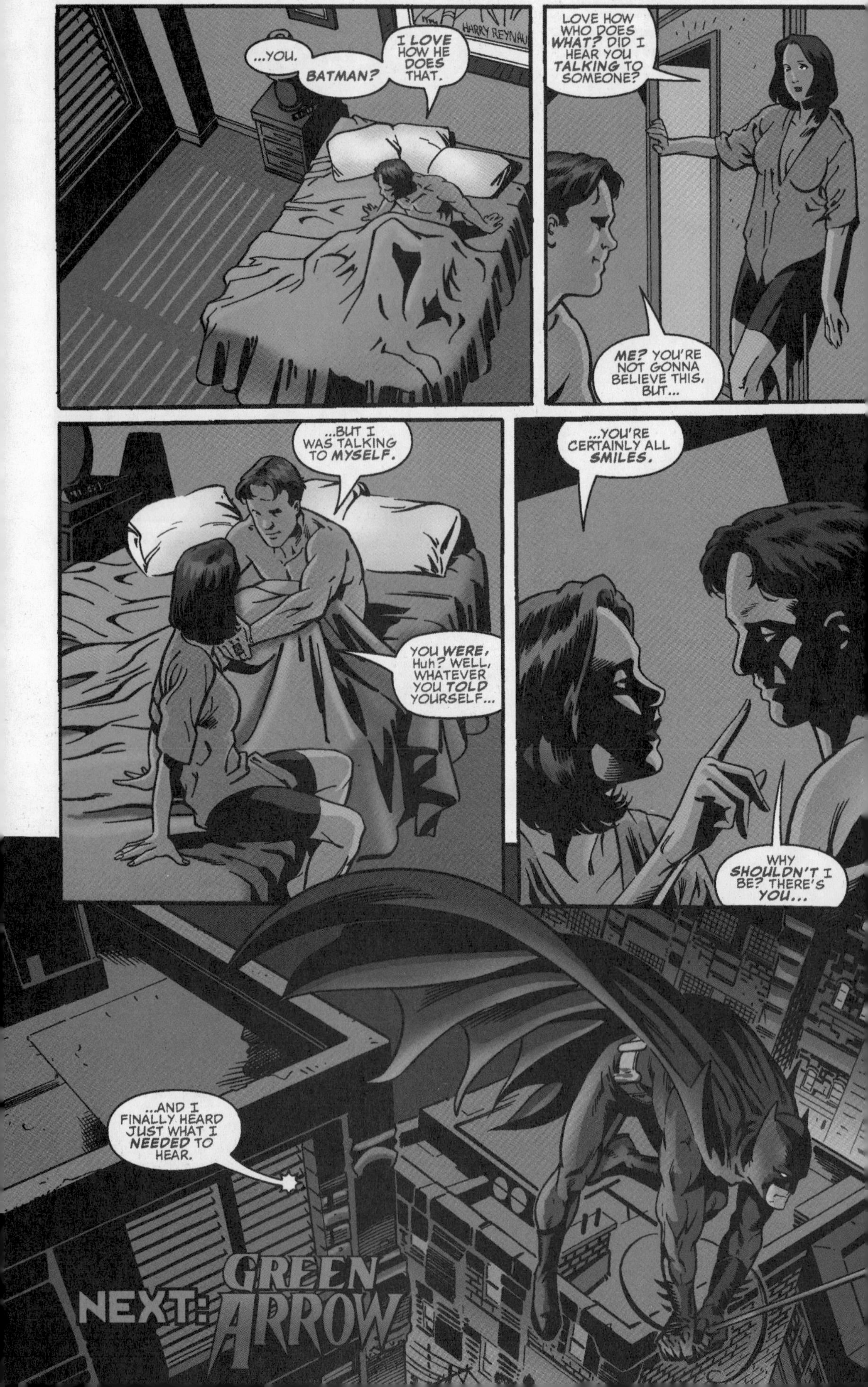
HARRY REYNAU
...YOU.
BATMAN?
I LOVE HOW HE DOES THAT.
LOVE HOW WHO DOES WHAT? DID I HEAR YOU TALKING TO SOMEONE?
ME? YOU'RE NOT GONNA BELIEVE THIS, BUT...
...BUT I WAS TALKING TO MYSELF.
YOU WERE, Huh? WELL, WHATEVER YOU TOLD YOURSELF...
...YOU'RE CERTAINLY ALL SMILES.
WHY SHOULDN'T I BE? THERE'S YOU...
...AND I FINALLY HEARD JUST WHAT I NEEDED TO HEAR.
NEXT: GREEN ARROW

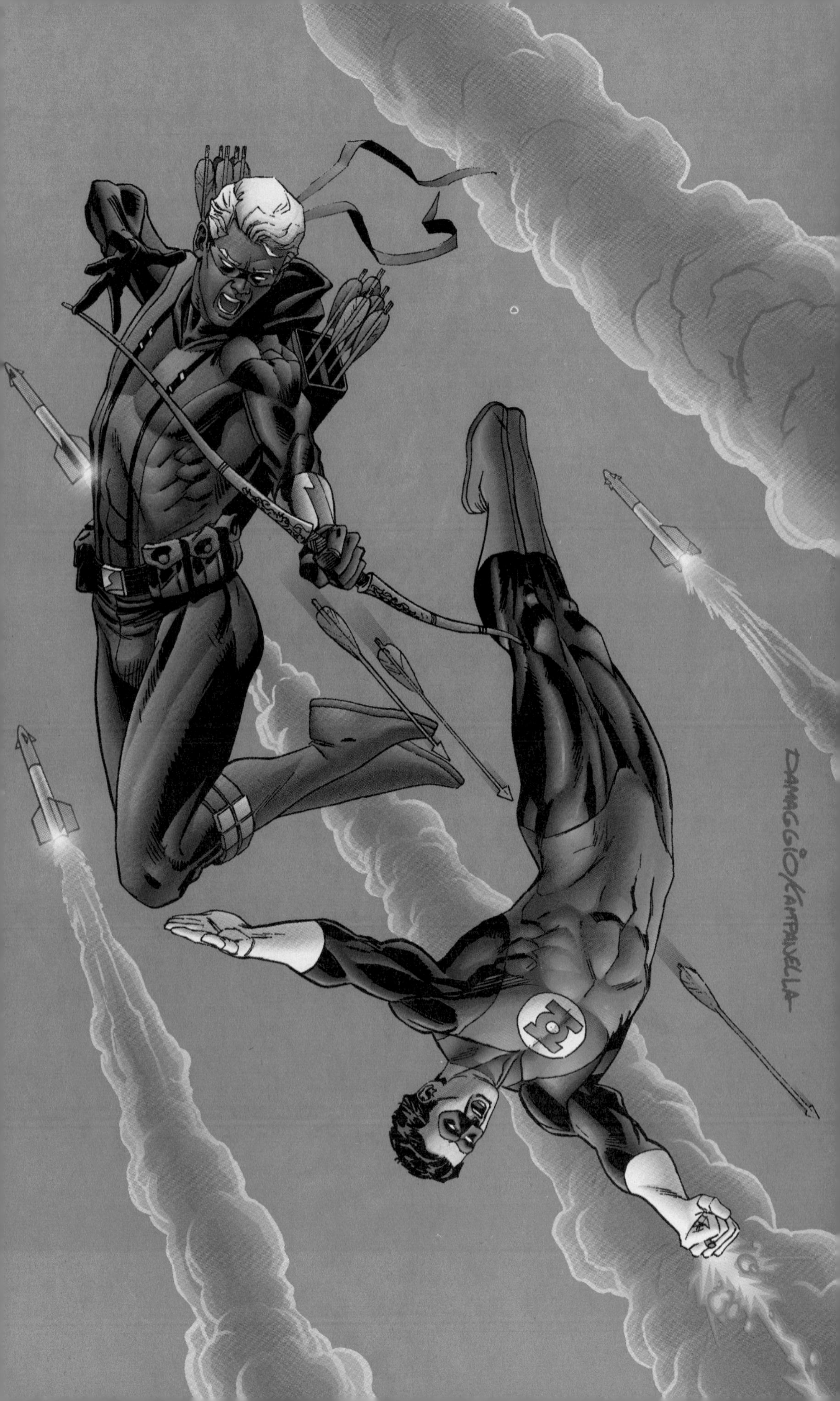
DAMAGGIO/CAMPANELLA

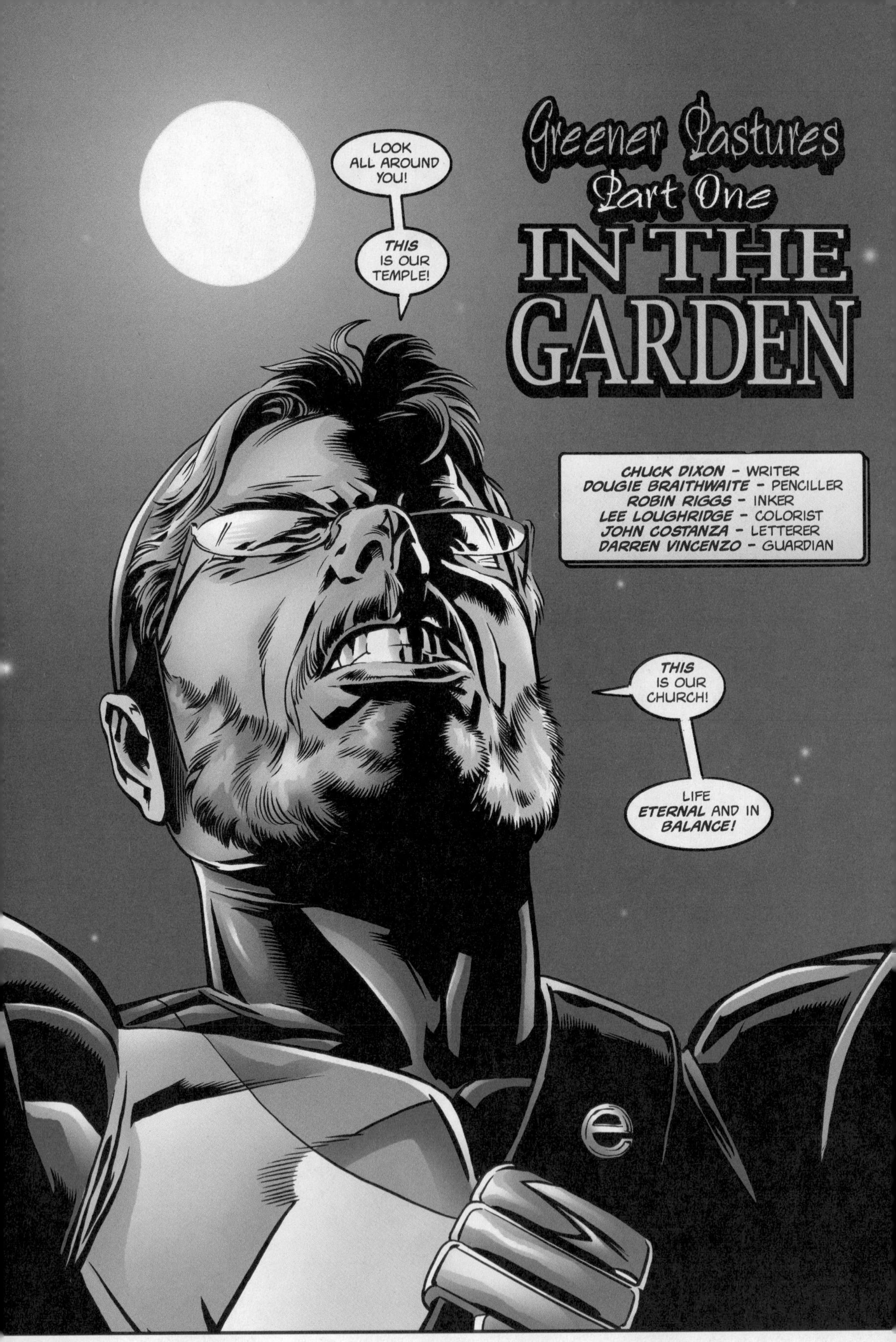
Greener Pastures
Part One
IN THE GARDEN
LOOK ALL AROUND YOU!
THIS IS OUR TEMPLE!
CHUCK DIXON - WRITER
DOUGIE BRAITHWAITE - PENCILLER
ROBIN RIGGS - INKER
LEE LOUGHRIDGE - COLORIST
JOHN COSTANZA - LETTERER
DARREN VINCENZO - GUARDIAN
THIS IS OUR CHURCH!
LIFE ETERNAL AND IN BALANCE!

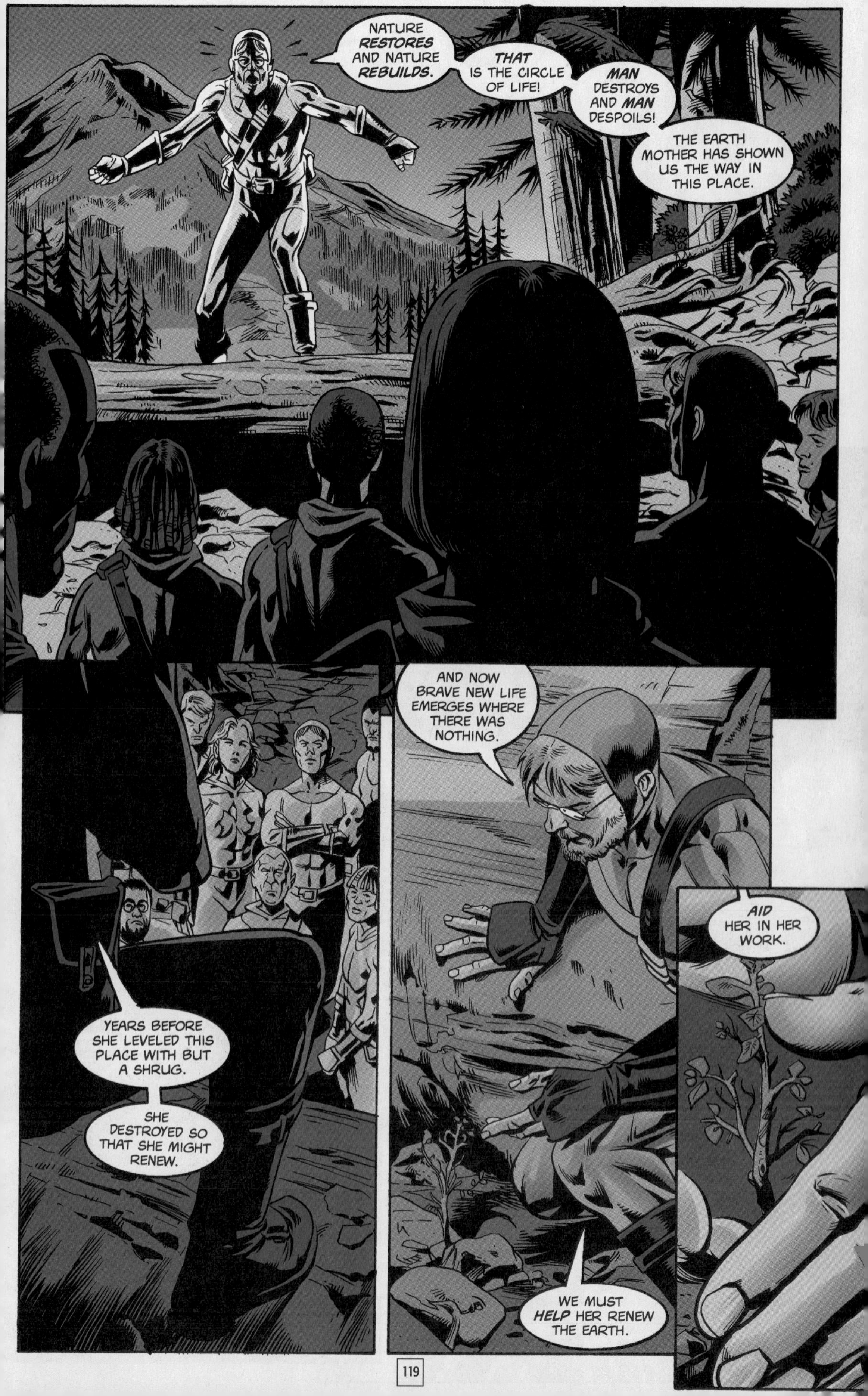

NATURE RESTORES AND NATURE REBUILDS.
THAT IS THE CIRCLE OF LIFE!
MAN DESTROYS AND MAN DESPOILS!
THE EARTH MOTHER HAS SHOWN US THE WAY IN THIS PLACE.
YEARS BEFORE SHE LEVELED THIS PLACE WITH BUT A SHRUG.
SHE DESTROYED SO THAT SHE MIGHT RENEW.
AND NOW BRAVE NEW LIFE EMERGES WHERE THERE WAS NOTHING.
WE MUST HELP HER RENEW THE EARTH.
AID HER IN HER WORK.

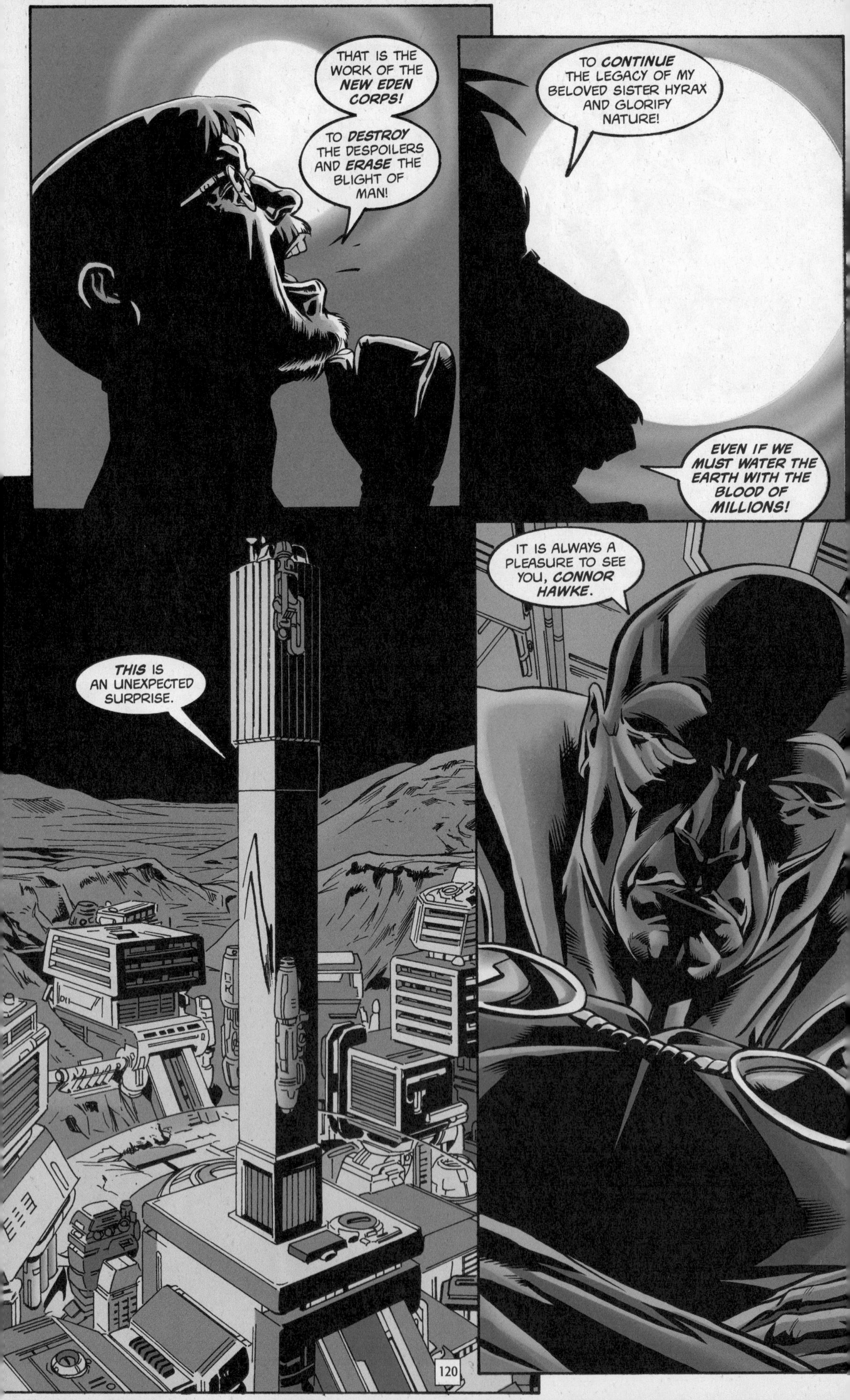
THAT IS THE WORK OF THE NEW EDEN CORPS!
TO DESTROY THE DESPOILERS AND ERASE THE BLIGHT OF MAN!
TO CONTINUE THE LEGACY OF MY BELOVED SISTER HYRAX AND GLORIFY NATURE!
EVEN IF WE MUST WATER THE EARTH WITH THE BLOOD OF MILLIONS!
THIS IS AN UNEXPECTED SURPRISE.
IT IS ALWAYS A PLEASURE TO SEE YOU, CONNOR HAWKE.

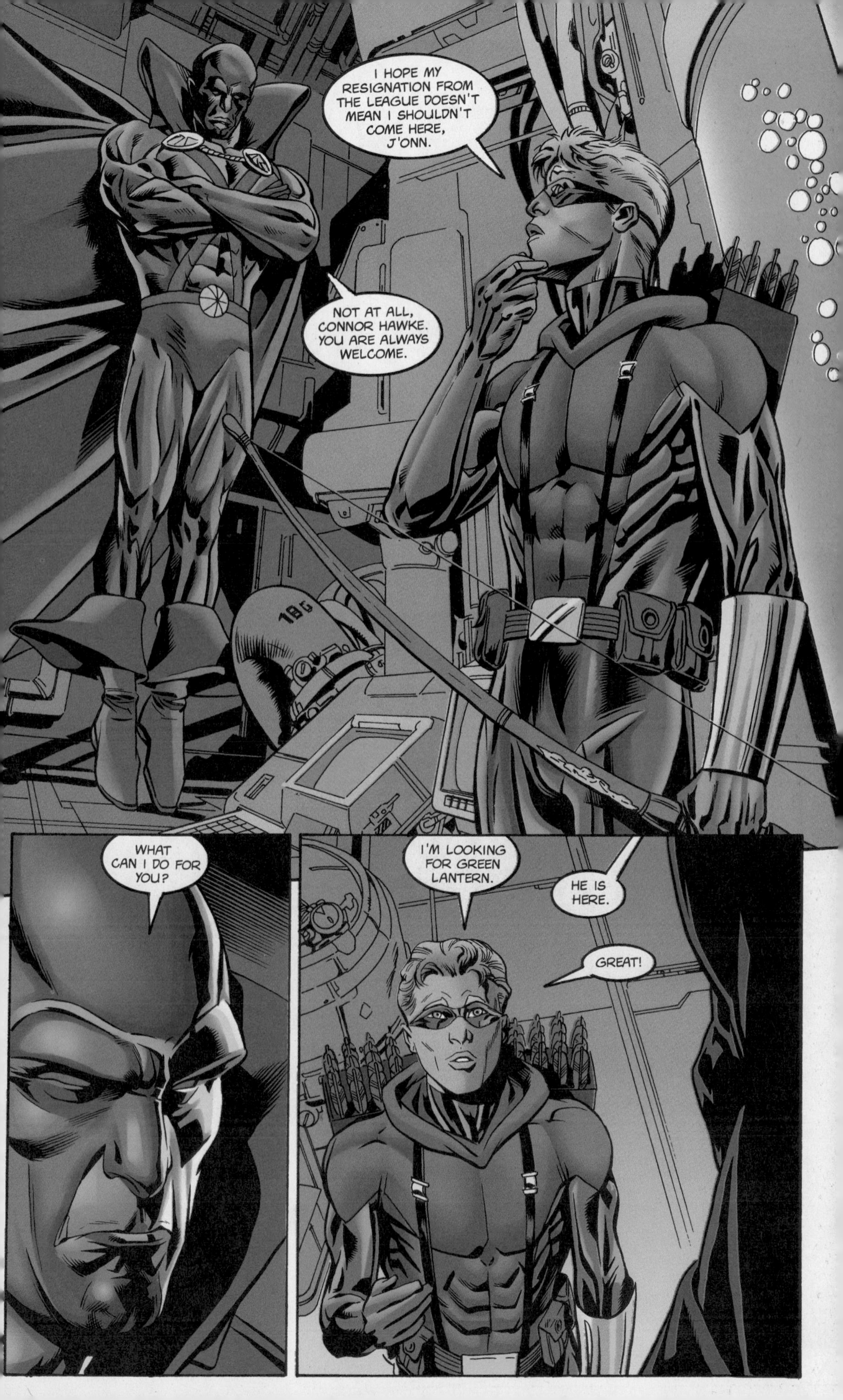
I HOPE MY RESIGNATION FROM THE LEAGUE DOESN'T MEAN I SHOULDN'T COME HERE, J'ONN.
NOT AT ALL, CONNOR HAWKE. YOU ARE ALWAYS WELCOME.
18G
WHAT CAN I DO FOR YOU?
I'M LOOKING FOR GREEN LANTERN.
HE IS HERE.
GREAT!

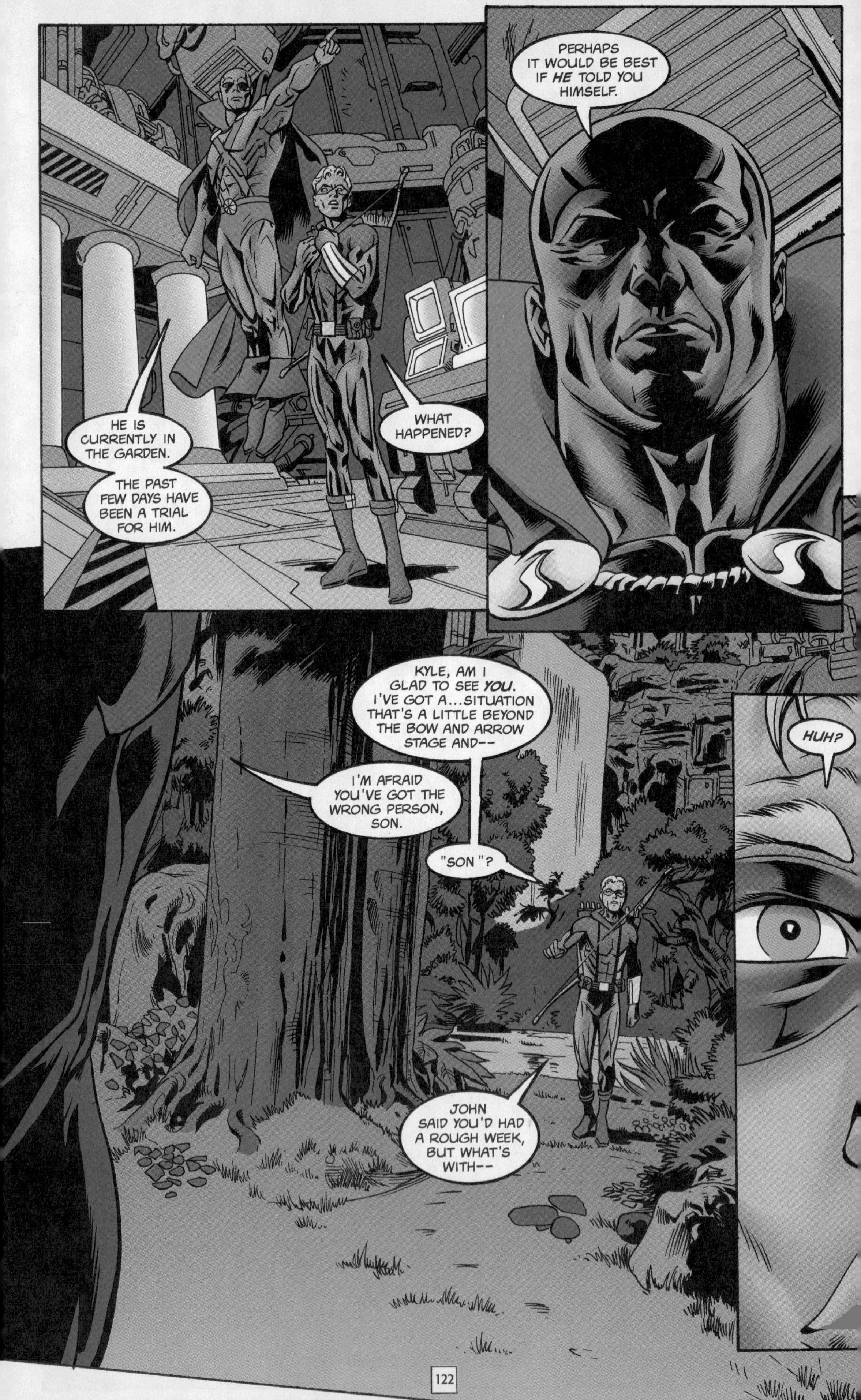
HE IS CURRENTLY IN THE GARDEN.
THE PAST FEW DAYS HAVE BEEN A TRIAL FOR HIM.
WHAT HAPPENED?
PERHAPS IT WOULD BE BEST IF HE TOLD YOU HIMSELF.
KYLE, AM I GLAD TO SEE YOU. I'VE GOT A...SITUATION THAT'S A LITTLE BEYOND THE BOW AND ARROW STAGE AND--
I'M AFRAID YOU'VE GOT THE WRONG PERSON, SON.
"SON"?
JOHN SAID YOU'D HAD A ROUGH WEEK, BUT WHAT'S WITH--
HUH?

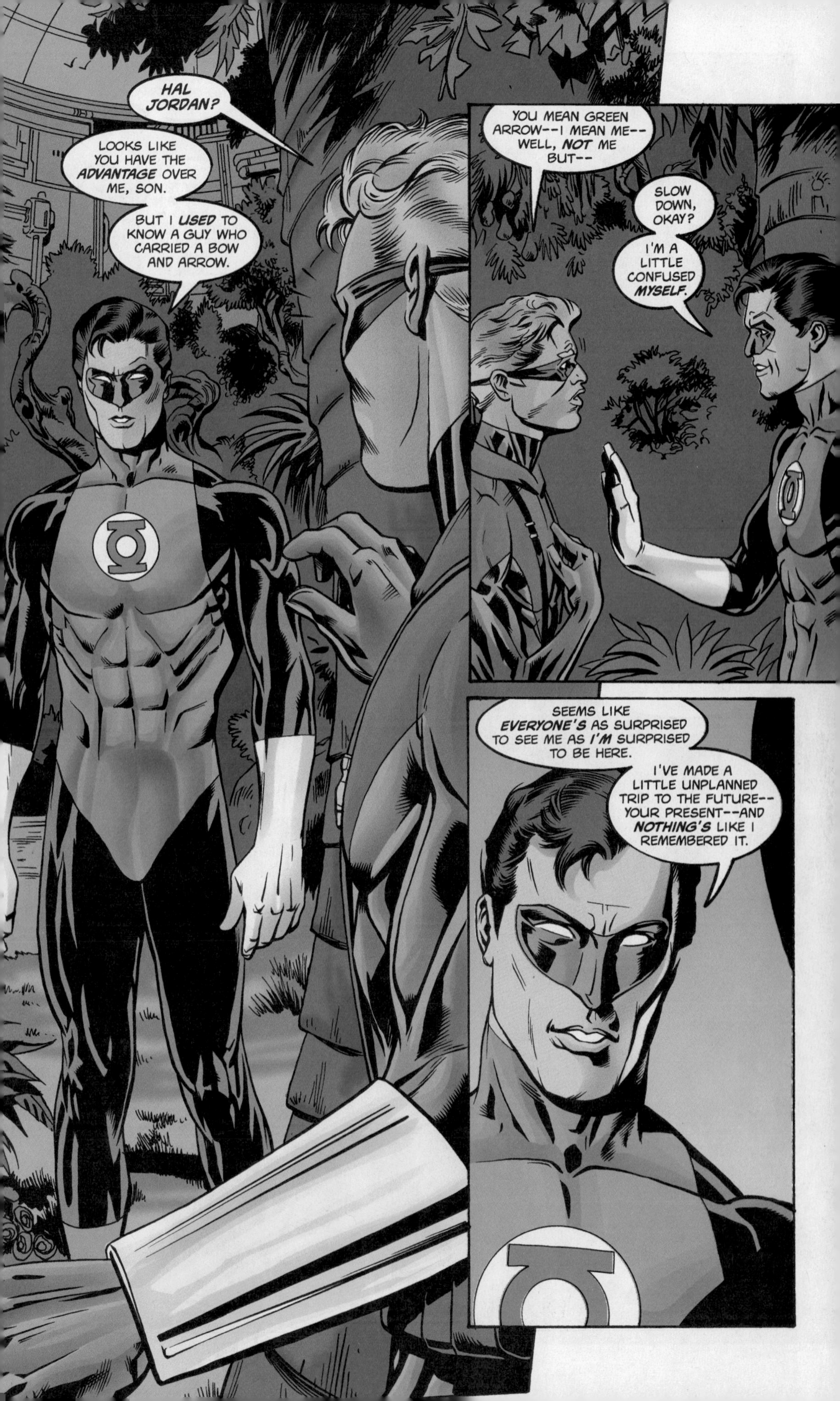
HAL JORDAN?
LOOKS LIKE YOU HAVE THE ADVANTAGE OVER ME, SON.
BUT I USED TO KNOW A GUY WHO CARRIED A BOW AND ARROW.
YOU MEAN GREEN ARROW--I MEAN ME--WELL, NOT ME BUT--
SLOW DOWN, OKAY?
I'M A LITTLE CONFUSED MYSELF.
SEEMS LIKE EVERYONE'S AS SURPRISED TO SEE ME AS I'M SURPRISED TO BE HERE.
I'VE MADE A LITTLE UNPLANNED TRIP TO THE FUTURE--YOUR PRESENT--AND NOTHING'S LIKE I REMEMBERED IT.

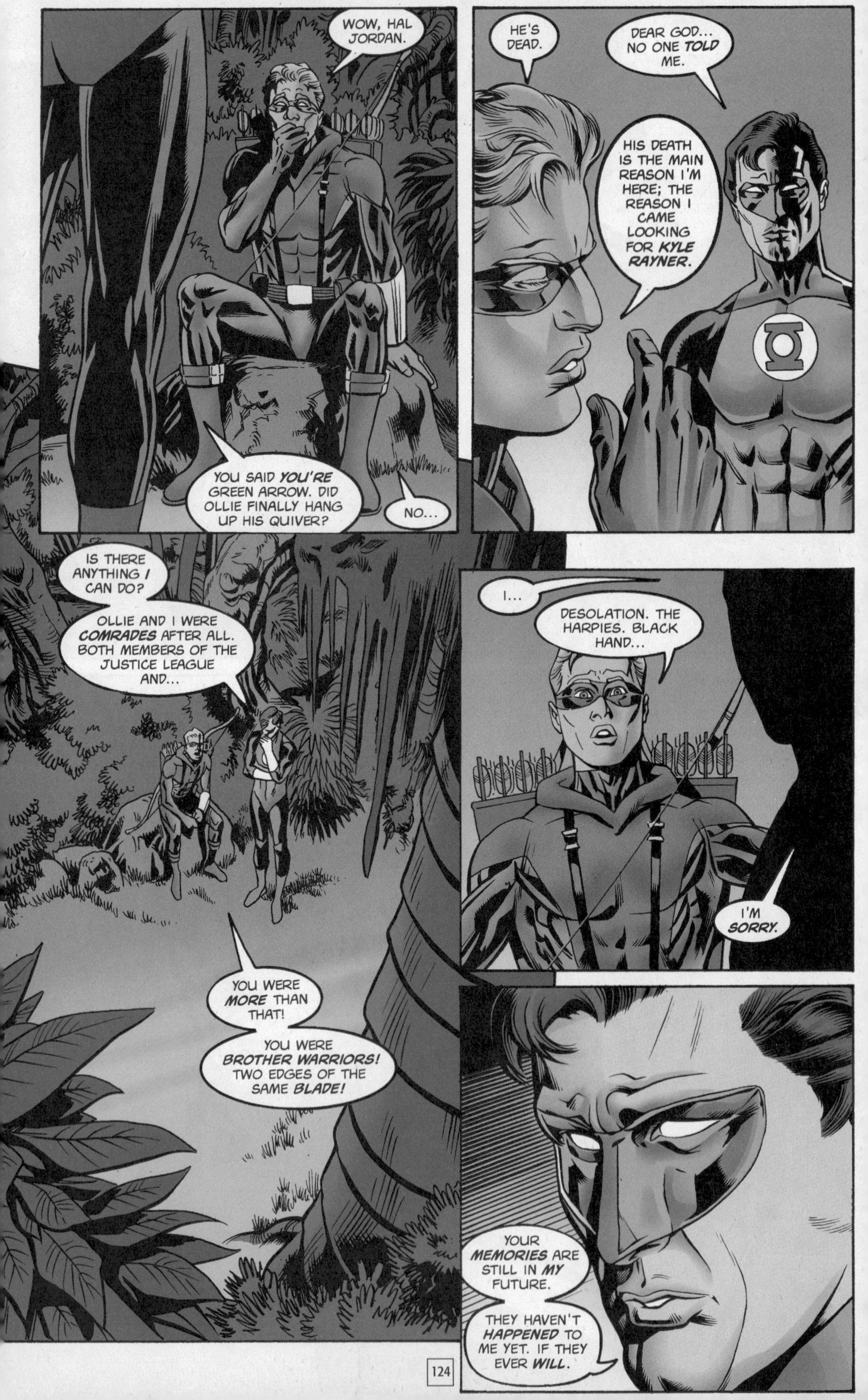
WOW, HAL JORDAN.
YOU SAID YOU'RE GREEN ARROW. DID OLLIE FINALLY HANG UP HIS QUIVER?
NO...
HE'S DEAD.
DEAR GOD... NO ONE TOLD ME.
HIS DEATH IS THE MAIN REASON I'M HERE; THE REASON I CAME LOOKING FOR KYLE RAYNER.
IS THERE ANYTHING I CAN DO?
OLLIE AND I WERE COMRADES AFTER ALL. BOTH MEMBERS OF THE JUSTICE LEAGUE AND...
YOU WERE MORE THAN THAT!
YOU WERE BROTHER WARRIORS! TWO EDGES OF THE SAME BLADE!
I...
DESOLATION. THE HARPIES. BLACK HAND...
I'M SORRY.
YOUR MEMORIES ARE STILL IN MY FUTURE.
THEY HAVEN'T HAPPENED TO ME YET. IF THEY EVER WILL.

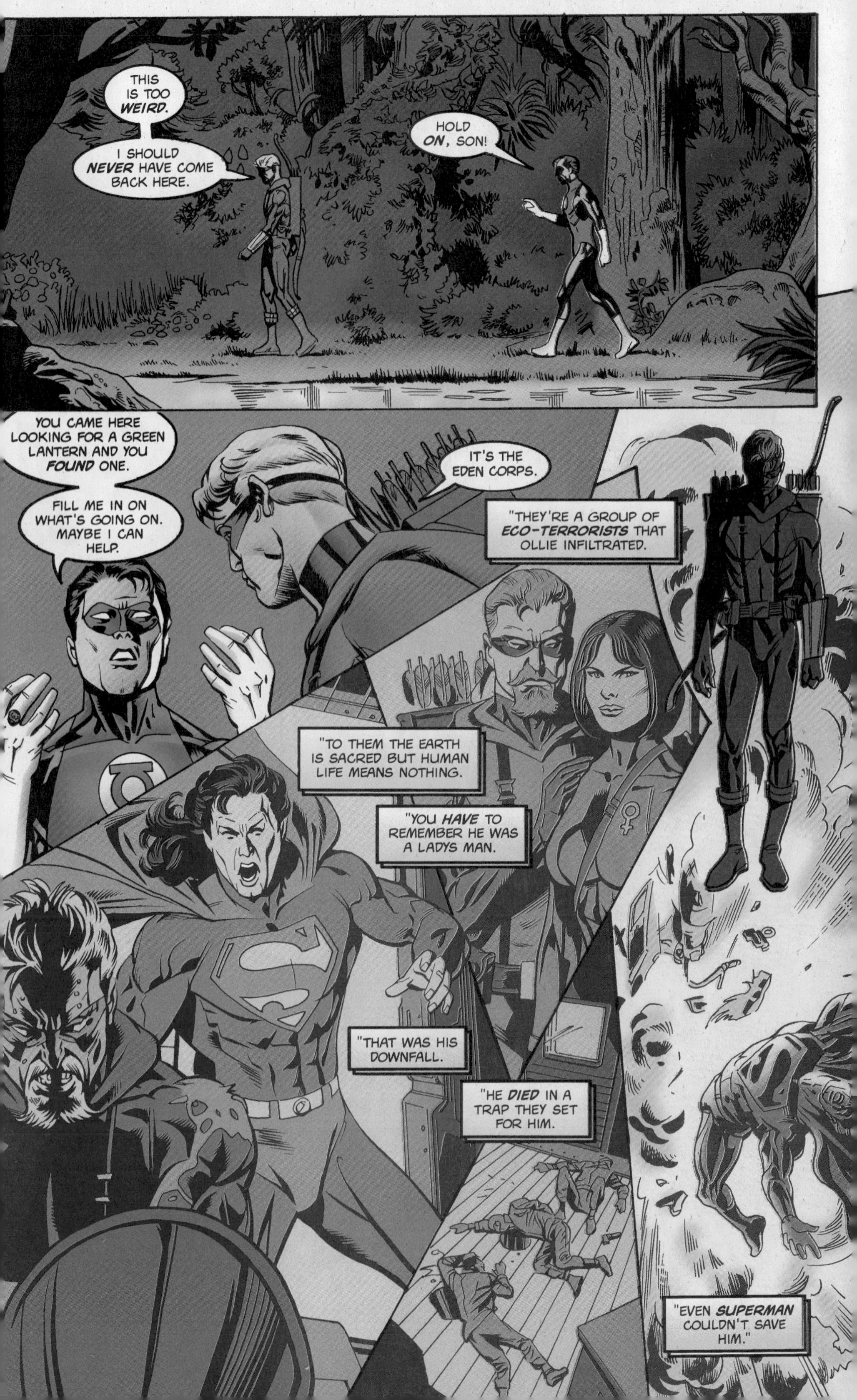
THIS IS TOO WEIRD.
I SHOULD NEVER HAVE COME BACK HERE.
HOLD ON, SON!
YOU CAME HERE LOOKING FOR A GREEN LANTERN AND YOU FOUND ONE.
FILL ME IN ON WHAT'S GOING ON. MAYBE I CAN HELP.
IT'S THE EDEN CORPS.
"THEY'RE A GROUP OF ECO-TERRORISTS THAT OLLIE INFILTRATED.
"TO THEM THE EARTH IS SACRED BUT HUMAN LIFE MEANS NOTHING.
"YOU HAVE TO REMEMBER HE WAS A LADYS MAN.
"THAT WAS HIS DOWNFALL.
"HE DIED IN A TRAP THEY SET FOR HIM.
"EVEN SUPERMAN COULDN'T SAVE HIM."

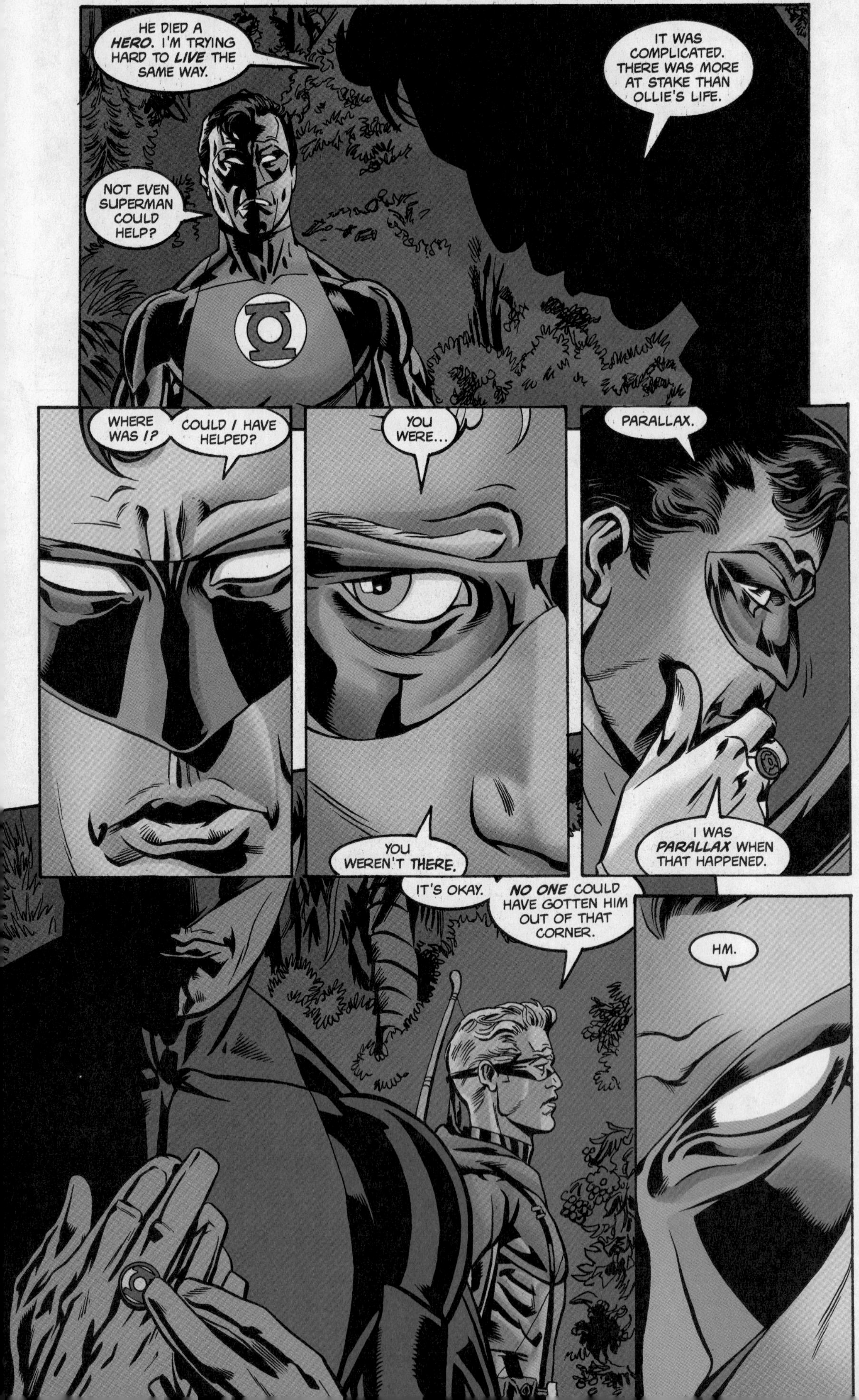
HE DIED A HERO. I'M TRYING HARD TO LIVE THE SAME WAY.
IT WAS COMPLICATED. THERE WAS MORE AT STAKE THAN OLLIE'S LIFE.
NOT EVEN SUPERMAN COULD HELP?
WHERE WAS I?
COULD I HAVE HELPED?
YOU WERE...
YOU WEREN'T THERE.
PARALLAX.
I WAS PARALLAX WHEN THAT HAPPENED.
IT'S OKAY.
NO ONE COULD HAVE GOTTEN HIM OUT OF THAT CORNER.
HM.

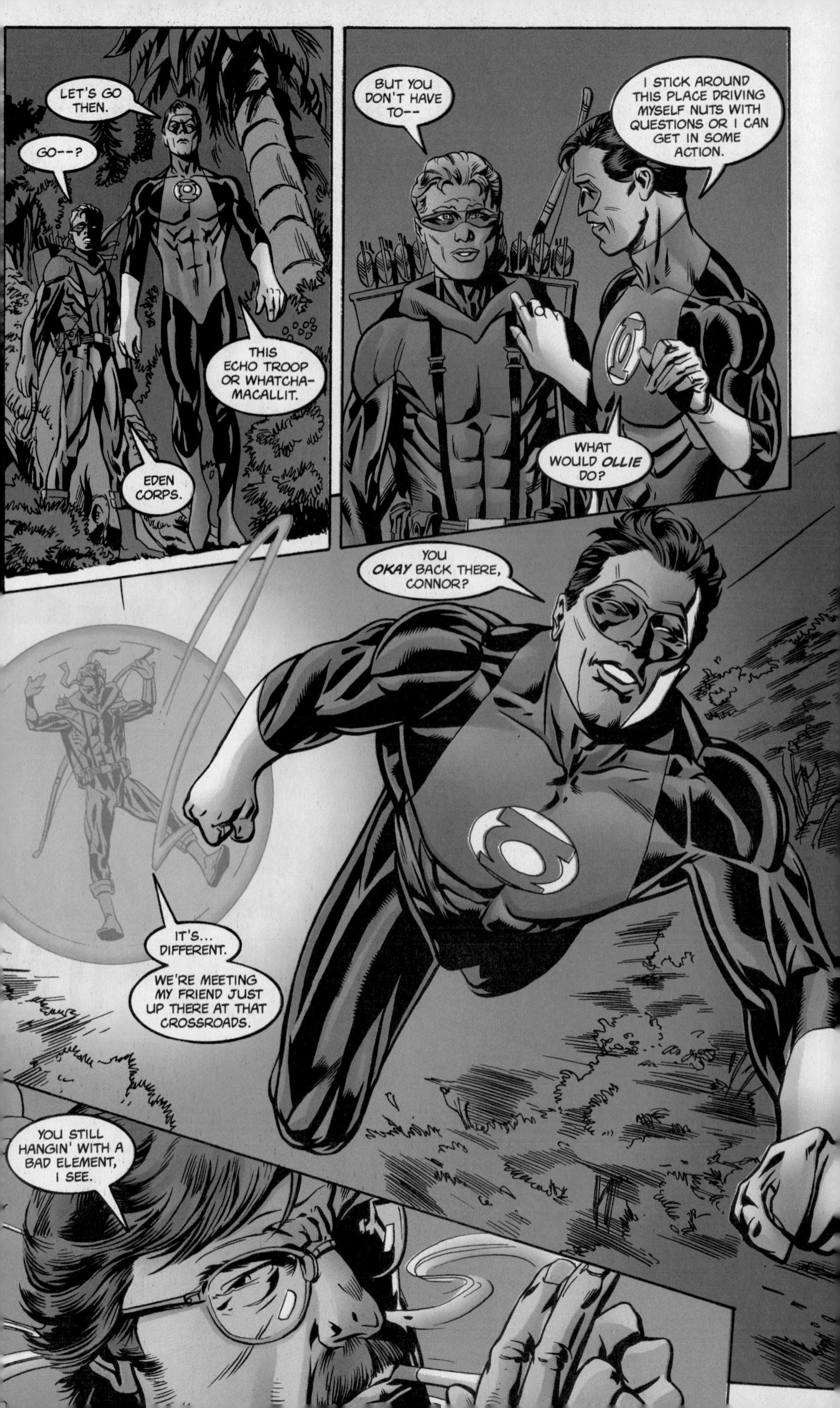
LET'S GO THEN.
GO--?
THIS ECHO TROOP OR WHATCHA-MACALLIT.
EDEN CORPS.
BUT YOU DON'T HAVE TO--
I STICK AROUND THIS PLACE DRIVING MYSELF NUTS WITH QUESTIONS OR I CAN GET IN SOME ACTION.
WHAT WOULD OLLIE DO?
YOU OKAY BACK THERE, CONNOR?
IT'S... DIFFERENT.
WE'RE MEETING MY FRIEND JUST UP THERE AT THAT CROSSROADS.
YOU STILL HANGIN' WITH A BAD ELEMENT, I SEE.

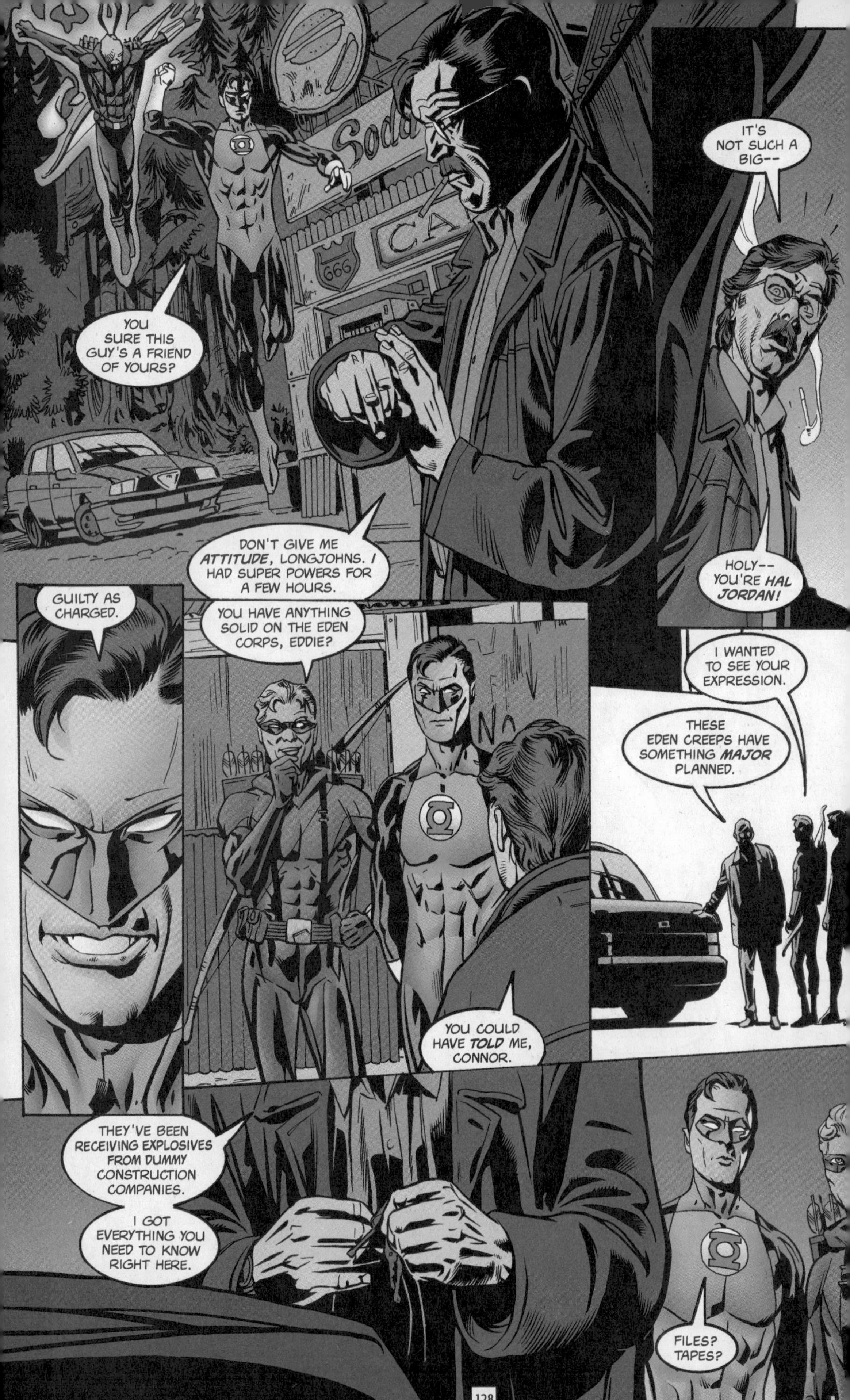

Soda
CA
666
YOU SURE THIS GUY'S A FRIEND OF YOURS?
DON'T GIVE ME *ATTITUDE*, LONGJOHNS. *I* HAD SUPER POWERS FOR A FEW HOURS.
IT'S NOT SUCH A BIG--
HOLY-- YOU'RE *HAL JORDAN!*
GUILTY AS CHARGED.
YOU HAVE ANYTHING SOLID ON THE EDEN CORPS, EDDIE?
YOU COULD HAVE *TOLD* ME, CONNOR.
I WANTED TO SEE YOUR EXPRESSION.
THESE EDEN CREEPS HAVE SOMETHING *MAJOR* PLANNED.
THEY'VE BEEN RECEIVING EXPLOSIVES FROM DUMMY CONSTRUCTION COMPANIES.
I GOT EVERYTHING YOU NEED TO KNOW RIGHT HERE.
FILES? TAPES?

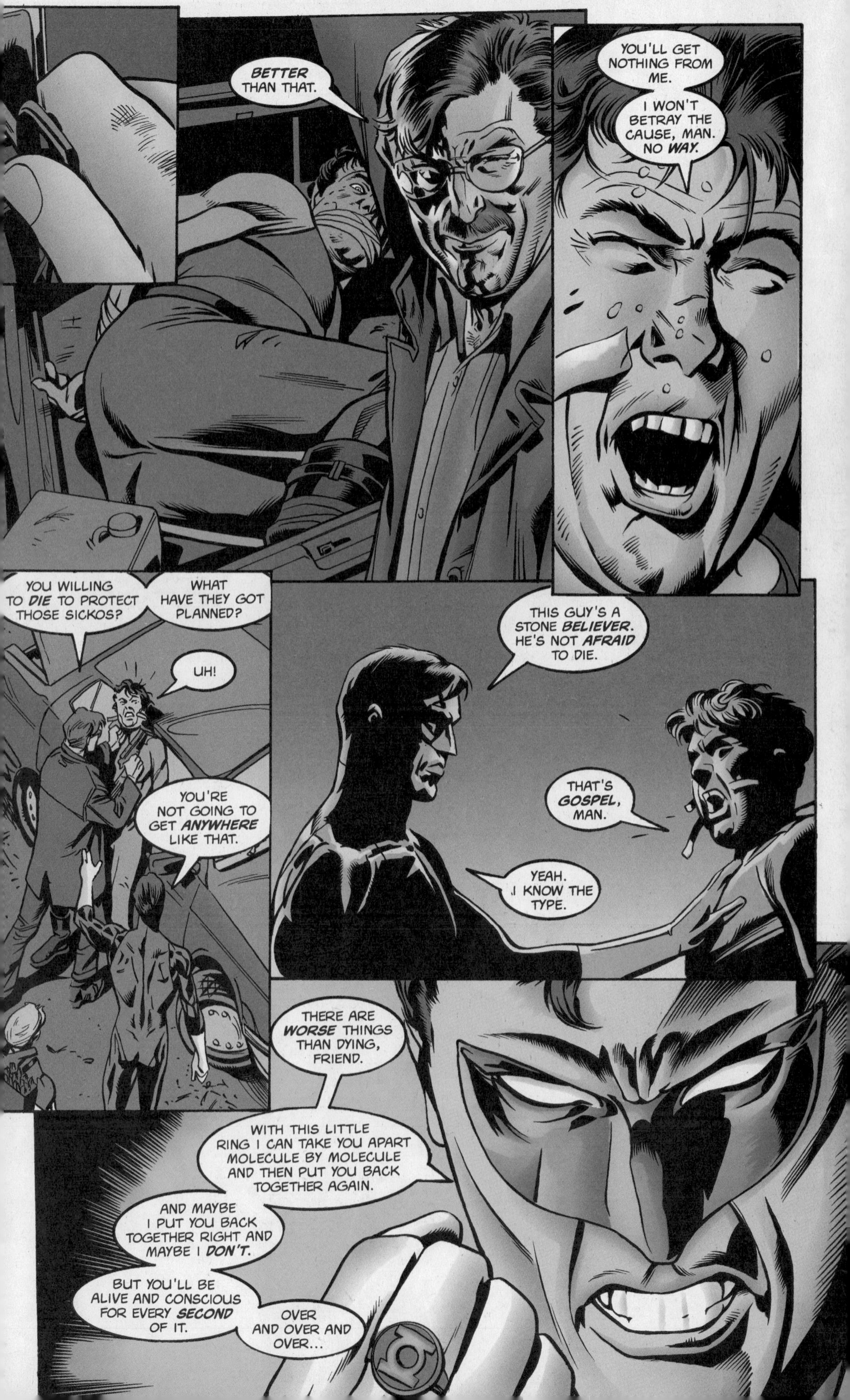

BETTER THAN THAT.
YOU'LL GET NOTHING FROM ME.
I WON'T BETRAY THE CAUSE, MAN. NO WAY.
YOU WILLING TO DIE TO PROTECT THOSE SICKOS?
WHAT HAVE THEY GOT PLANNED?
UH!
YOU'RE NOT GOING TO GET ANYWHERE LIKE THAT.
THIS GUY'S A STONE BELIEVER. HE'S NOT AFRAID TO DIE.
THAT'S GOSPEL, MAN.
YEAH. I KNOW THE TYPE.
THERE ARE WORSE THINGS THAN DYING, FRIEND.
WITH THIS LITTLE RING I CAN TAKE YOU APART MOLECULE BY MOLECULE AND THEN PUT YOU BACK TOGETHER AGAIN.
AND MAYBE I PUT YOU BACK TOGETHER RIGHT AND MAYBE I DON'T.
BUT YOU'LL BE ALIVE AND CONSCIOUS FOR EVERY SECOND OF IT.
OVER AND OVER AND OVER...

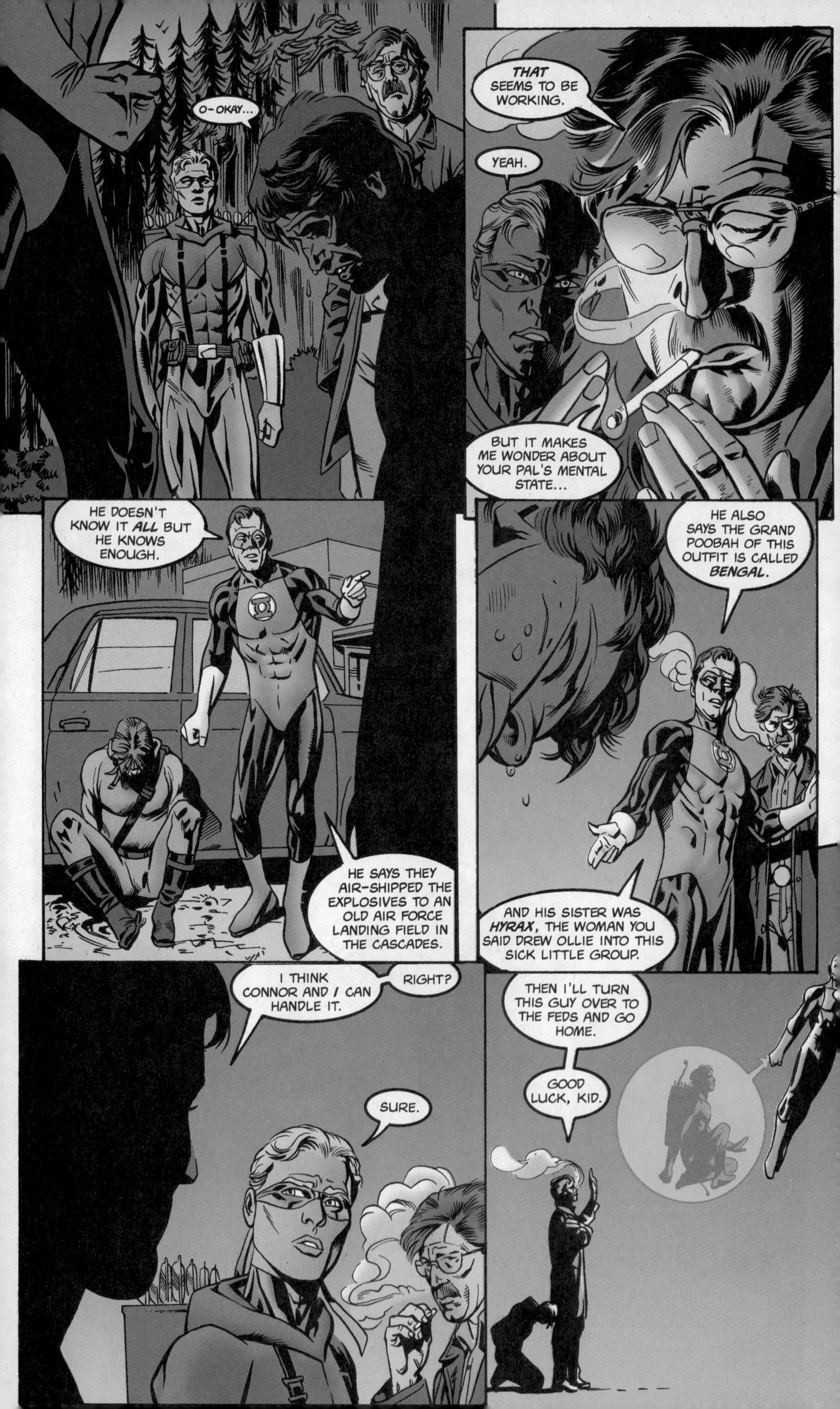
O-OKAY...
THAT SEEMS TO BE WORKING.
YEAH.
BUT IT MAKES ME WONDER ABOUT YOUR PAL'S MENTAL STATE...
HE DOESN'T KNOW IT ALL BUT HE KNOWS ENOUGH.
HE SAYS THEY AIR-SHIPPED THE EXPLOSIVES TO AN OLD AIR FORCE LANDING FIELD IN THE CASCADES.
HE ALSO SAYS THE GRAND POOBAH OF THIS OUTFIT IS CALLED BENGAL.
AND HIS SISTER WAS HYRAX, THE WOMAN YOU SAID DREW OLLIE INTO THIS SICK LITTLE GROUP.
I THINK CONNOR AND I CAN HANDLE IT.
RIGHT?
SURE.
THEN I'LL TURN THIS GUY OVER TO THE FEDS AND GO HOME.
GOOD LUCK, KID.

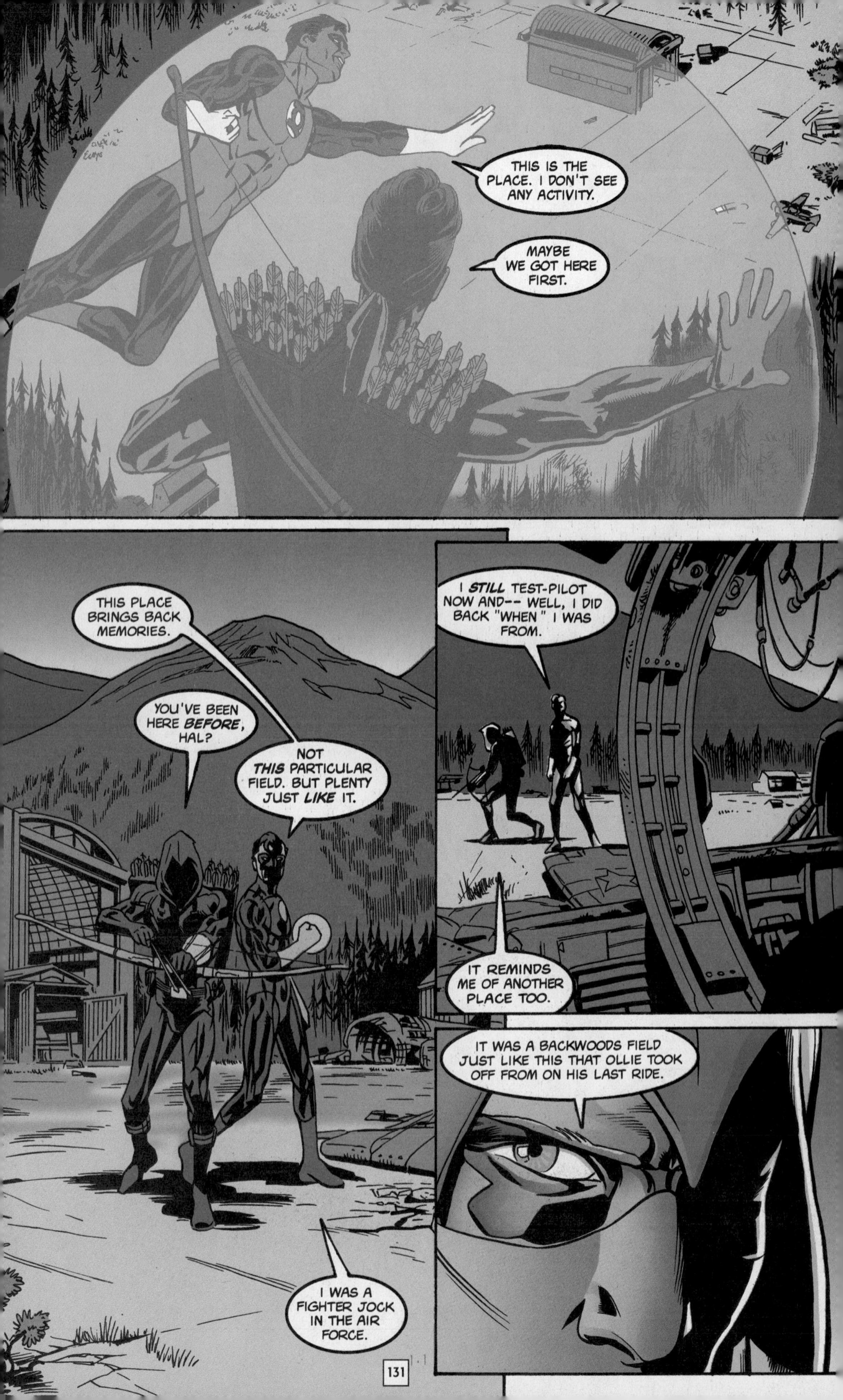
THIS IS THE PLACE. I DON'T SEE ANY ACTIVITY.
MAYBE WE GOT HERE FIRST.
THIS PLACE BRINGS BACK MEMORIES.
YOU'VE BEEN HERE *BEFORE*, HAL?
NOT *THIS* PARTICULAR FIELD. BUT PLENTY JUST *LIKE* IT.
I WAS A FIGHTER JOCK IN THE AIR FORCE.
I *STILL* TEST-PILOT NOW AND-- WELL, I DID BACK "WHEN" I WAS FROM.
IT REMINDS ME OF ANOTHER PLACE TOO.
IT WAS A BACKWOODS FIELD JUST LIKE THIS THAT OLLIE TOOK OFF FROM ON HIS LAST RIDE.

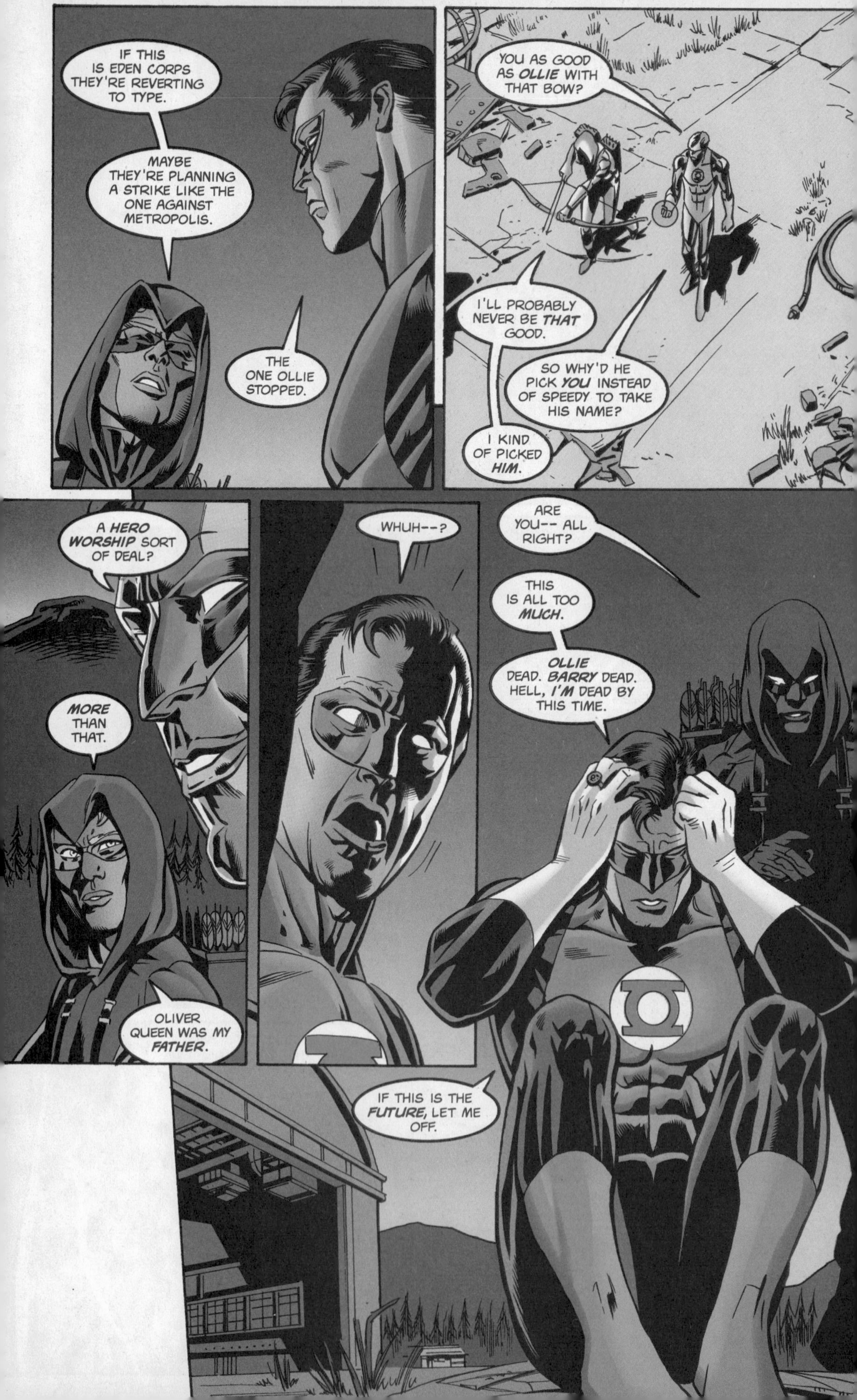
IF THIS IS EDEN CORPS THEY'RE REVERTING TO TYPE.
MAYBE THEY'RE PLANNING A STRIKE LIKE THE ONE AGAINST METROPOLIS.
THE ONE OLLIE STOPPED.
YOU AS GOOD AS OLLIE WITH THAT BOW?
I'LL PROBABLY NEVER BE THAT GOOD.
SO WHY'D HE PICK YOU INSTEAD OF SPEEDY TO TAKE HIS NAME?
I KIND OF PICKED HIM.
A HERO WORSHIP SORT OF DEAL?
MORE THAN THAT.
OLIVER QUEEN WAS MY FATHER.
WHUH--?
ARE YOU-- ALL RIGHT?
THIS IS ALL TOO MUCH.
OLLIE DEAD. BARRY DEAD. HELL, I'M DEAD BY THIS TIME.
IF THIS IS THE FUTURE, LET ME OFF.

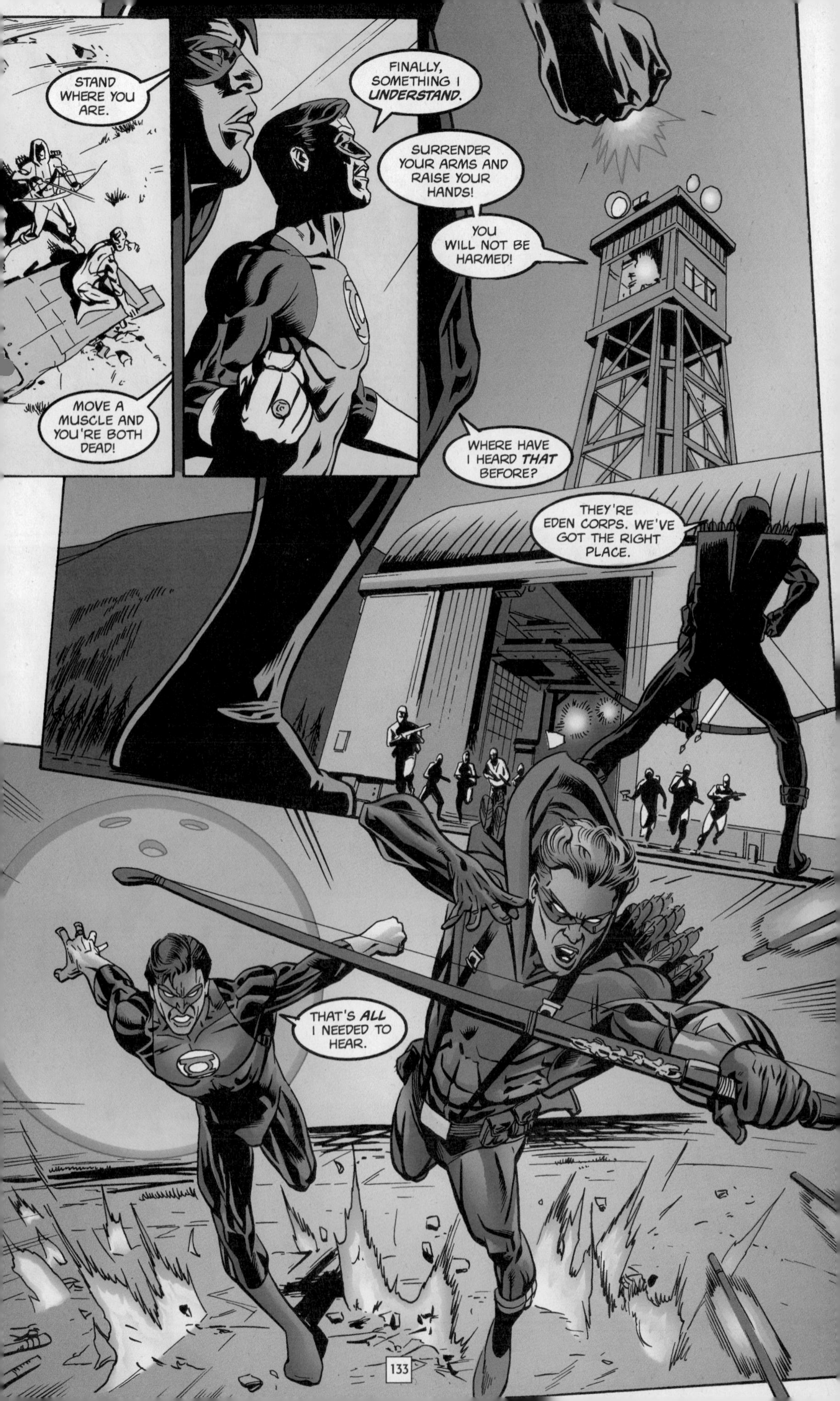
STAND WHERE YOU ARE.
MOVE A MUSCLE AND YOU'RE BOTH DEAD!
FINALLY, SOMETHING I UNDERSTAND.
SURRENDER YOUR ARMS AND RAISE YOUR HANDS!
YOU WILL NOT BE HARMED!
WHERE HAVE I HEARD THAT BEFORE?
THEY'RE EDEN CORPS. WE'VE GOT THE RIGHT PLACE.
THAT'S ALL I NEEDED TO HEAR.

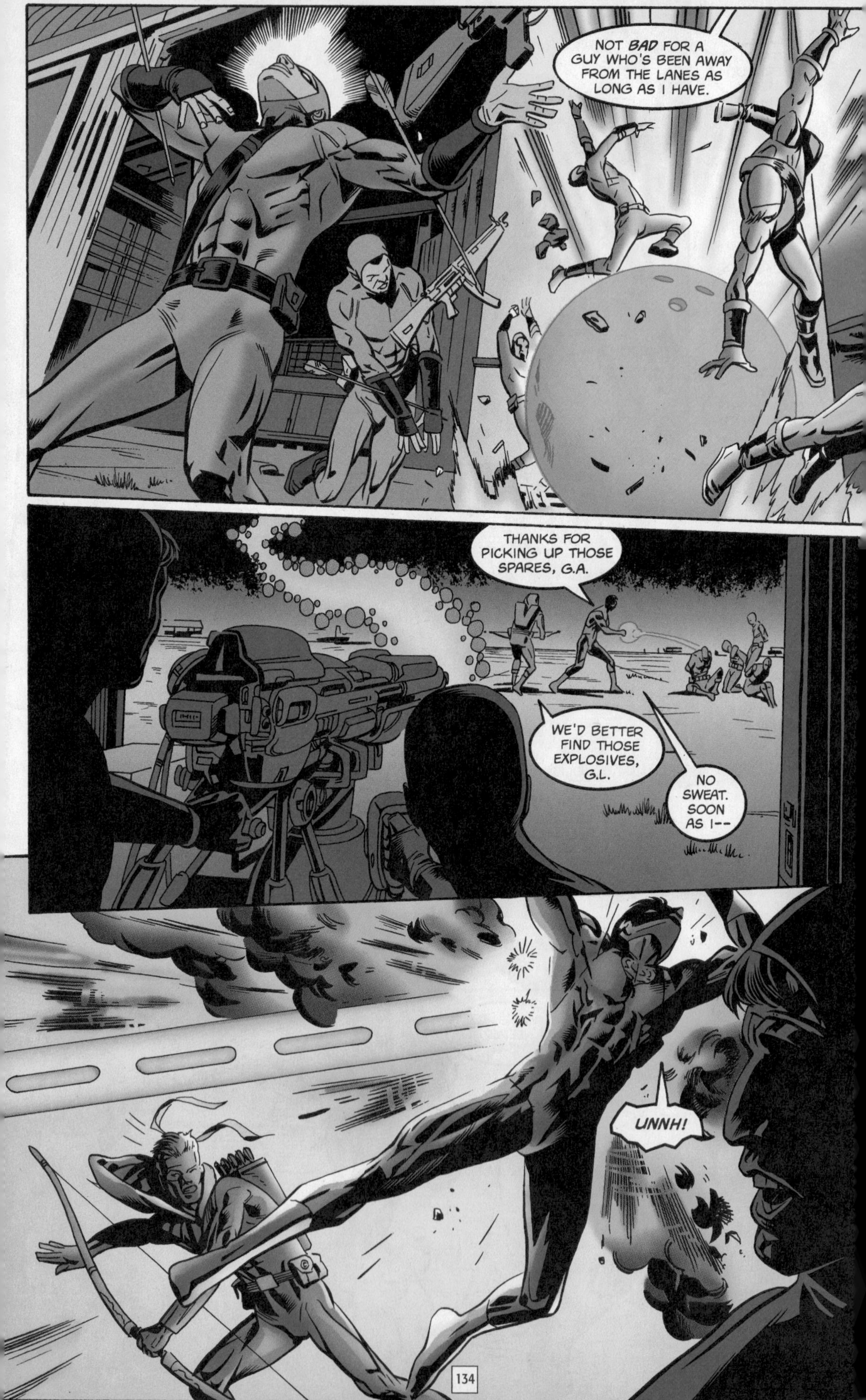
NOT BAD FOR A GUY WHO'S BEEN AWAY FROM THE LANES AS LONG AS I HAVE.
THANKS FOR PICKING UP THOSE SPARES, G.A.
WE'D BETTER FIND THOSE EXPLOSIVES, G.L.
NO SWEAT. SOON AS I--
UNNH!

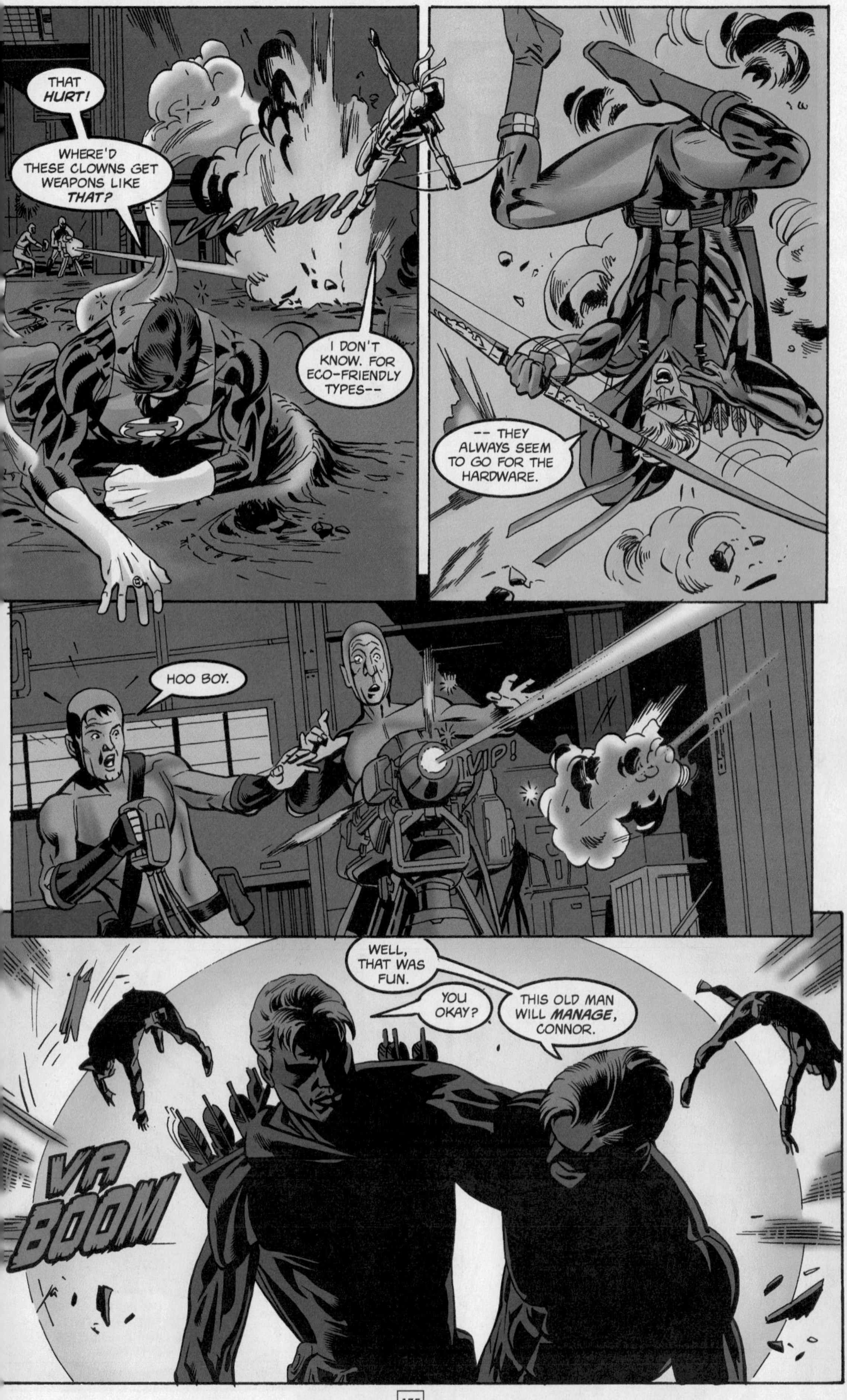

THAT *HURT!*
WHERE'D THESE CLOWNS GET WEAPONS LIKE *THAT?*
VVVAM!
I DON'T KNOW. FOR ECO-FRIENDLY TYPES--
-- THEY ALWAYS SEEM TO GO FOR THE HARDWARE.
HOO BOY.
VIP!
WELL, THAT WAS FUN.
YOU OKAY?
THIS OLD MAN WILL *MANAGE*, CONNOR.
VA BOOM

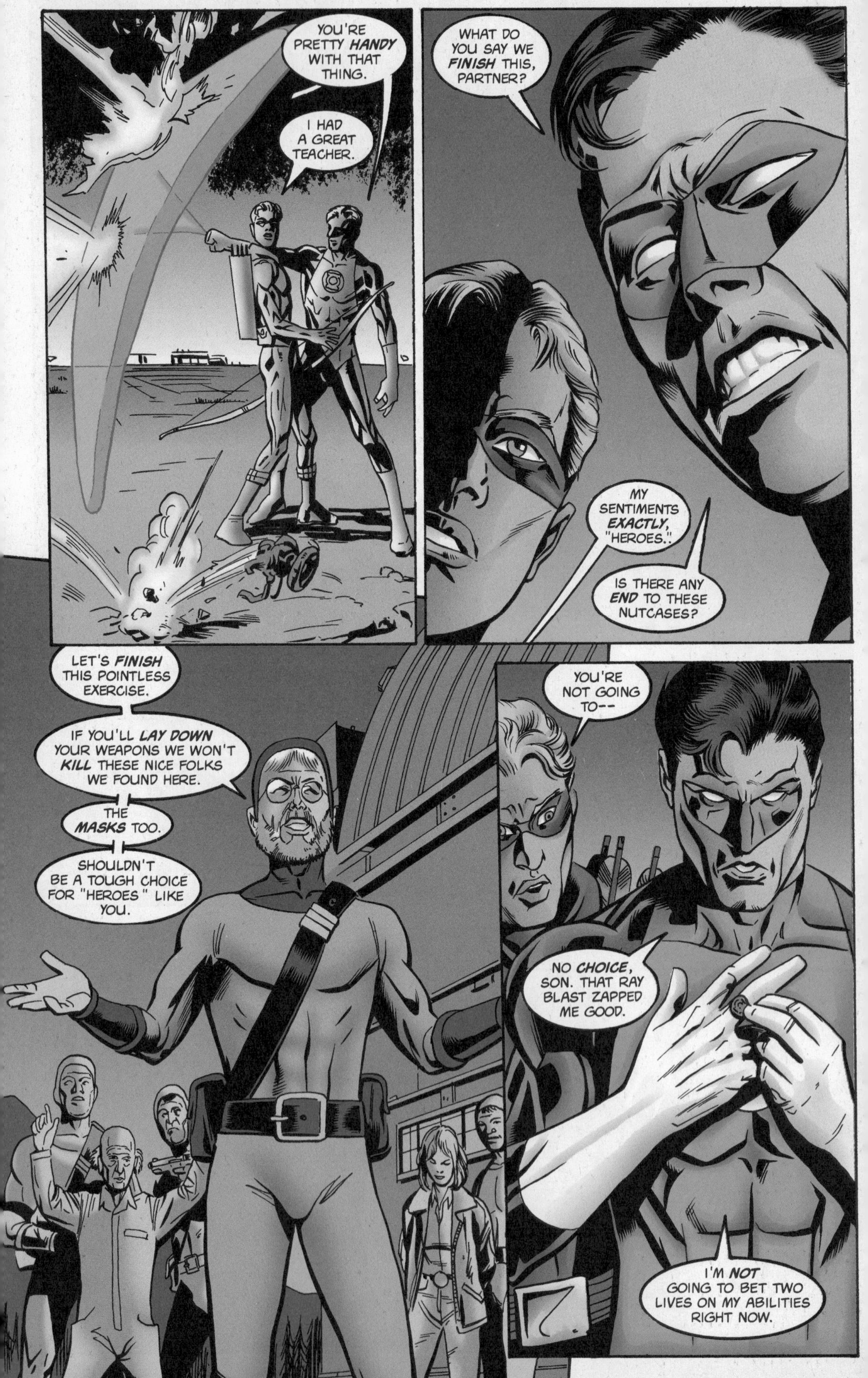

YOU'RE PRETTY HANDY WITH THAT THING.
I HAD A GREAT TEACHER.
WHAT DO YOU SAY WE FINISH THIS, PARTNER?
MY SENTIMENTS EXACTLY, "HEROES."
IS THERE ANY END TO THESE NUTCASES?
LET'S FINISH THIS POINTLESS EXERCISE.
IF YOU'LL LAY DOWN YOUR WEAPONS WE WON'T KILL THESE NICE FOLKS WE FOUND HERE.
THE MASKS TOO.
SHOULDN'T BE A TOUGH CHOICE FOR "HEROES" LIKE YOU.
YOU'RE NOT GOING TO--
NO CHOICE, SON. THAT RAY BLAST ZAPPED ME GOOD.
I'M NOT GOING TO BET TWO LIVES ON MY ABILITIES RIGHT NOW.

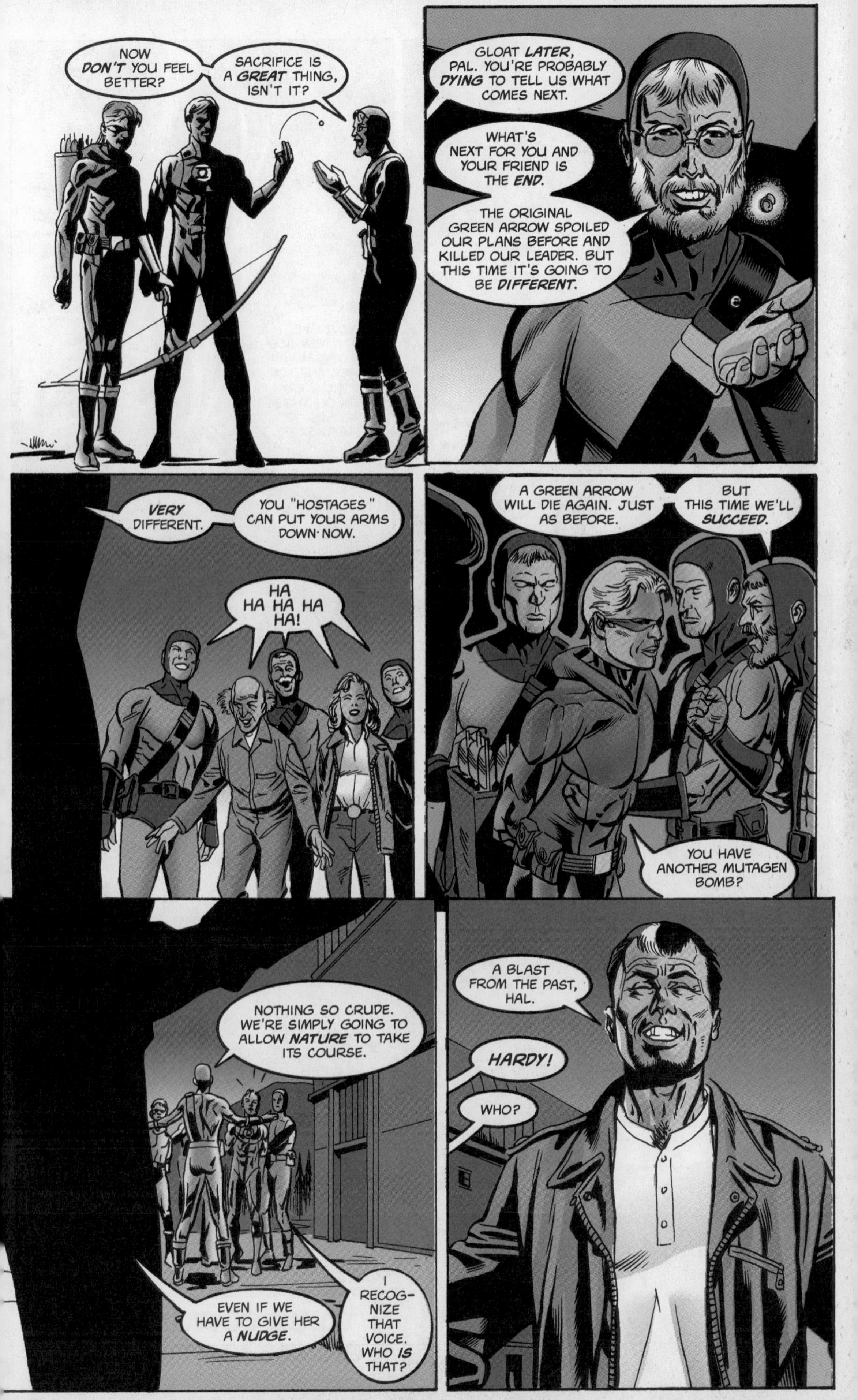
NOW DON'T YOU FEEL BETTER?
SACRIFICE IS A GREAT THING, ISN'T IT?
GLOAT LATER, PAL. YOU'RE PROBABLY DYING TO TELL US WHAT COMES NEXT.
WHAT'S NEXT FOR YOU AND YOUR FRIEND IS THE END.
THE ORIGINAL GREEN ARROW SPOILED OUR PLANS BEFORE AND KILLED OUR LEADER. BUT THIS TIME IT'S GOING TO BE DIFFERENT.
VERY DIFFERENT.
YOU "HOSTAGES" CAN PUT YOUR ARMS DOWN NOW.
HA HA HA HA HA!
A GREEN ARROW WILL DIE AGAIN. JUST AS BEFORE.
BUT THIS TIME WE'LL SUCCEED.
YOU HAVE ANOTHER MUTAGEN BOMB?
NOTHING SO CRUDE. WE'RE SIMPLY GOING TO ALLOW NATURE TO TAKE ITS COURSE.
EVEN IF WE HAVE TO GIVE HER A NUDGE.
I RECOG-NIZE THAT VOICE. WHO IS THAT?
A BLAST FROM THE PAST, HAL.
HARDY!
WHO?

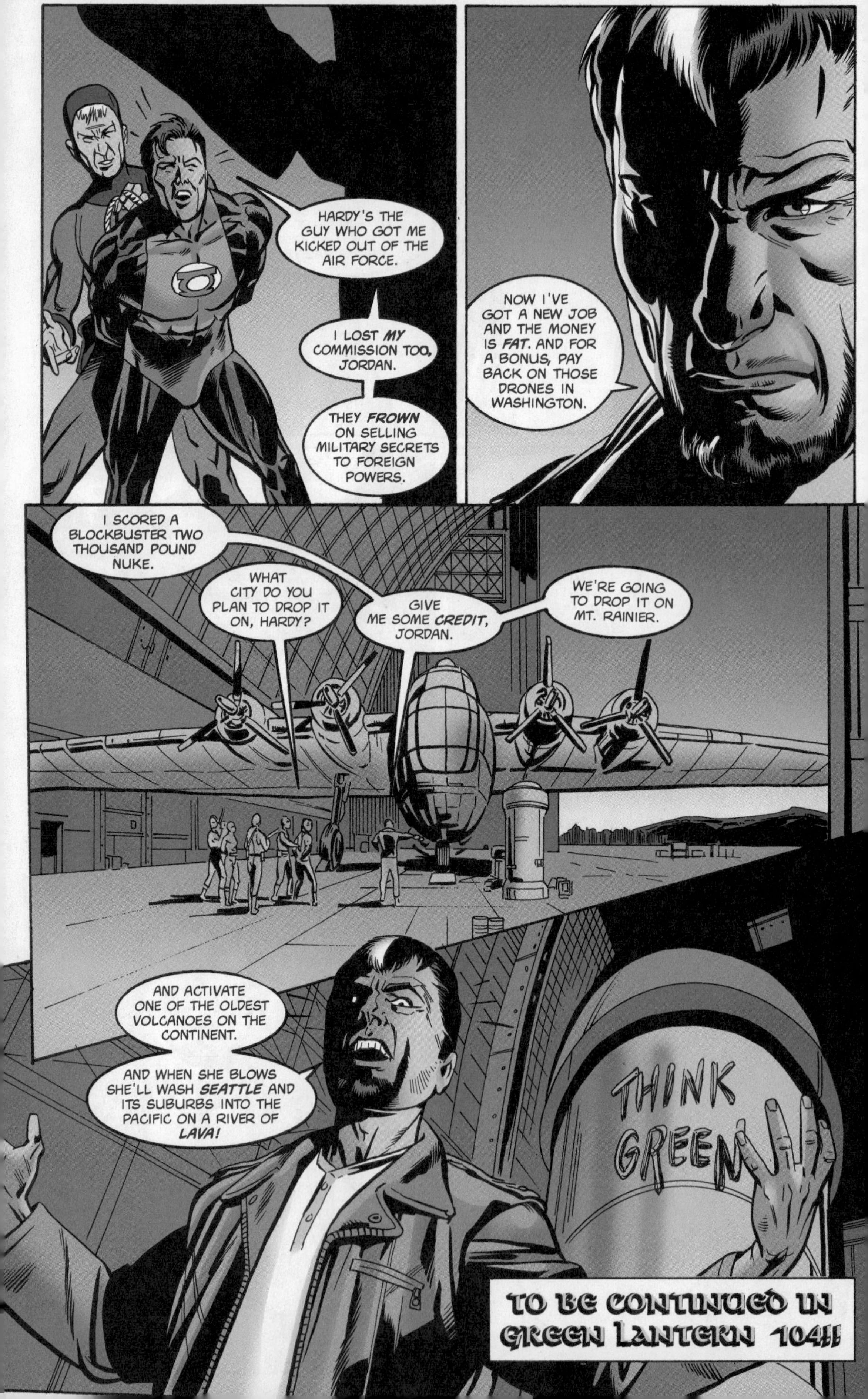
HARDY'S THE GUY WHO GOT ME KICKED OUT OF THE AIR FORCE.
I LOST *MY* COMMISSION TOO, JORDAN.
THEY *FROWN* ON SELLING MILITARY SECRETS TO FOREIGN POWERS.
NOW I'VE GOT A NEW JOB AND THE MONEY IS *FAT*. AND FOR A BONUS, PAY BACK ON THOSE DRONES IN WASHINGTON.
I SCORED A BLOCKBUSTER TWO THOUSAND POUND NUKE.
WHAT CITY DO YOU PLAN TO DROP IT ON, HARDY?
GIVE ME SOME *CREDIT*, JORDAN.
WE'RE GOING TO DROP IT ON MT. RAINIER.
AND ACTIVATE ONE OF THE OLDEST VOLCANOES ON THE CONTINENT.
AND WHEN SHE BLOWS SHE'LL WASH *SEATTLE* AND ITS SUBURBS INTO THE PACIFIC ON A RIVER OF *LAVA!*
THINK GREEN
TO BE CONTINUED IN GREEN LANTERN 104!!

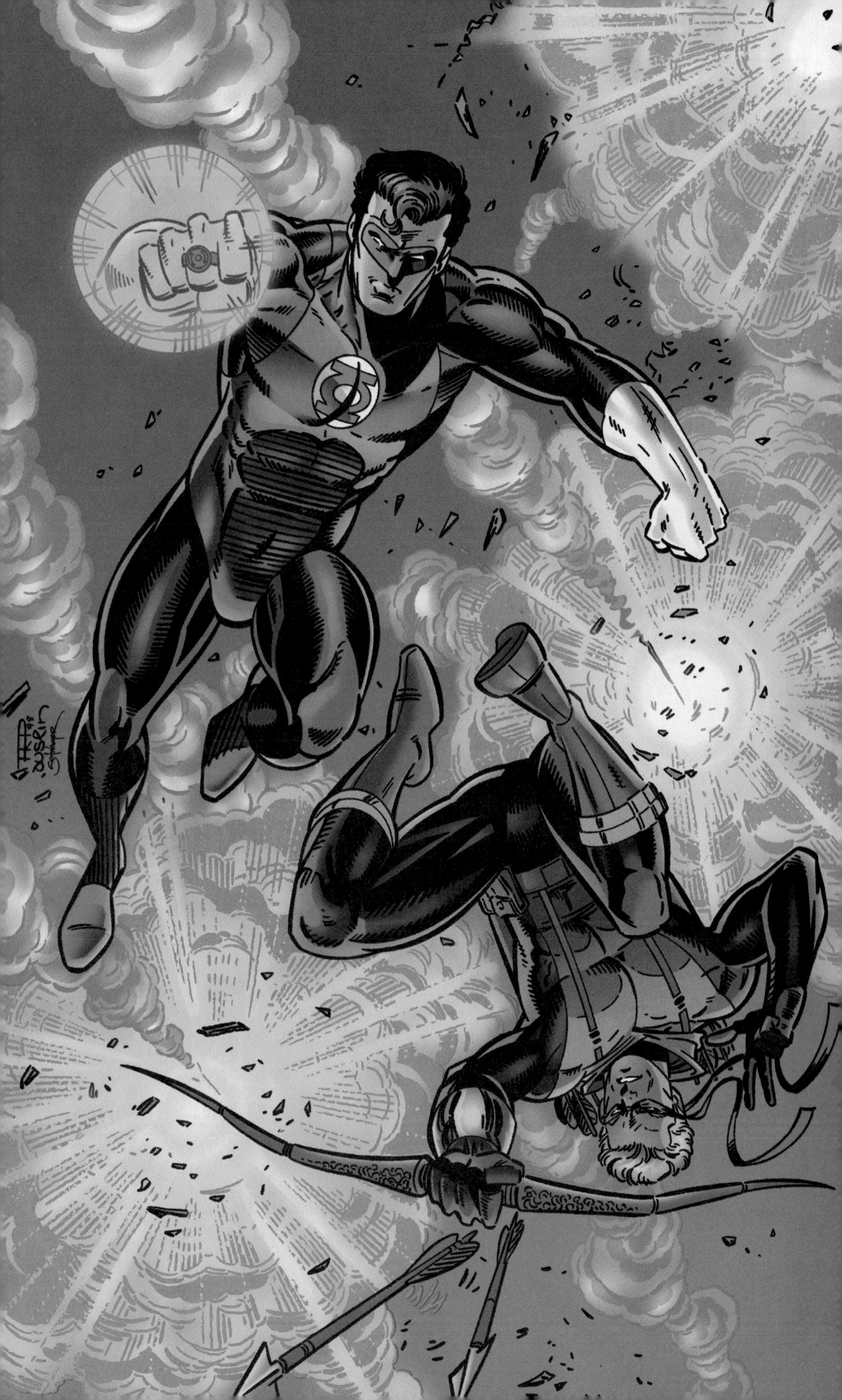

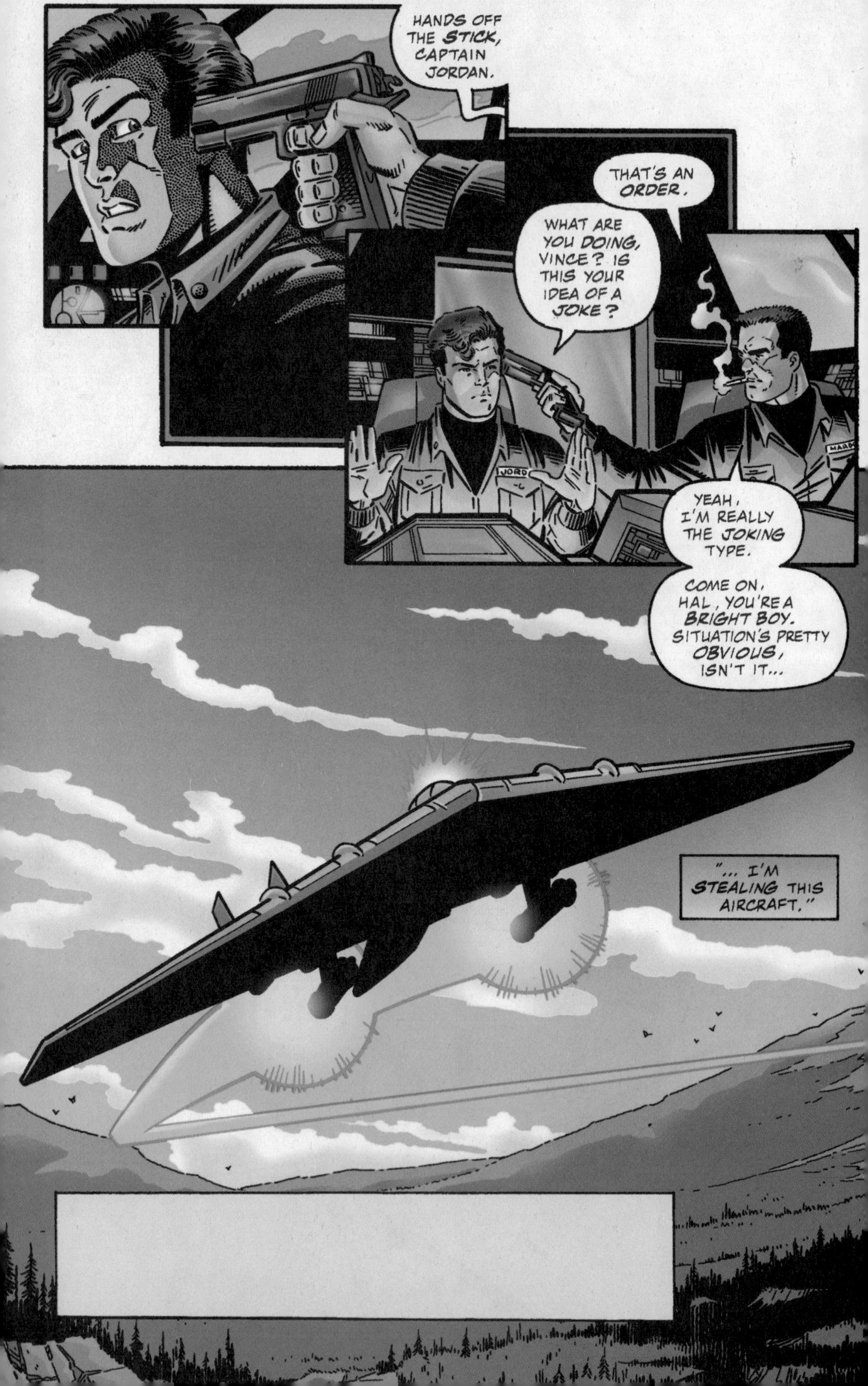
HANDS OFF THE STICK, CAPTAIN JORDAN.
THAT'S AN ORDER.
WHAT ARE YOU DOING, VINCE? IS THIS YOUR IDEA OF A JOKE?
YEAH, I'M REALLY THE JOKING TYPE.
COME ON, HAL, YOU'RE A BRIGHT BOY. SITUATION'S PRETTY OBVIOUS, ISN'T IT...
"... I'M STEALING THIS AIRCRAFT."

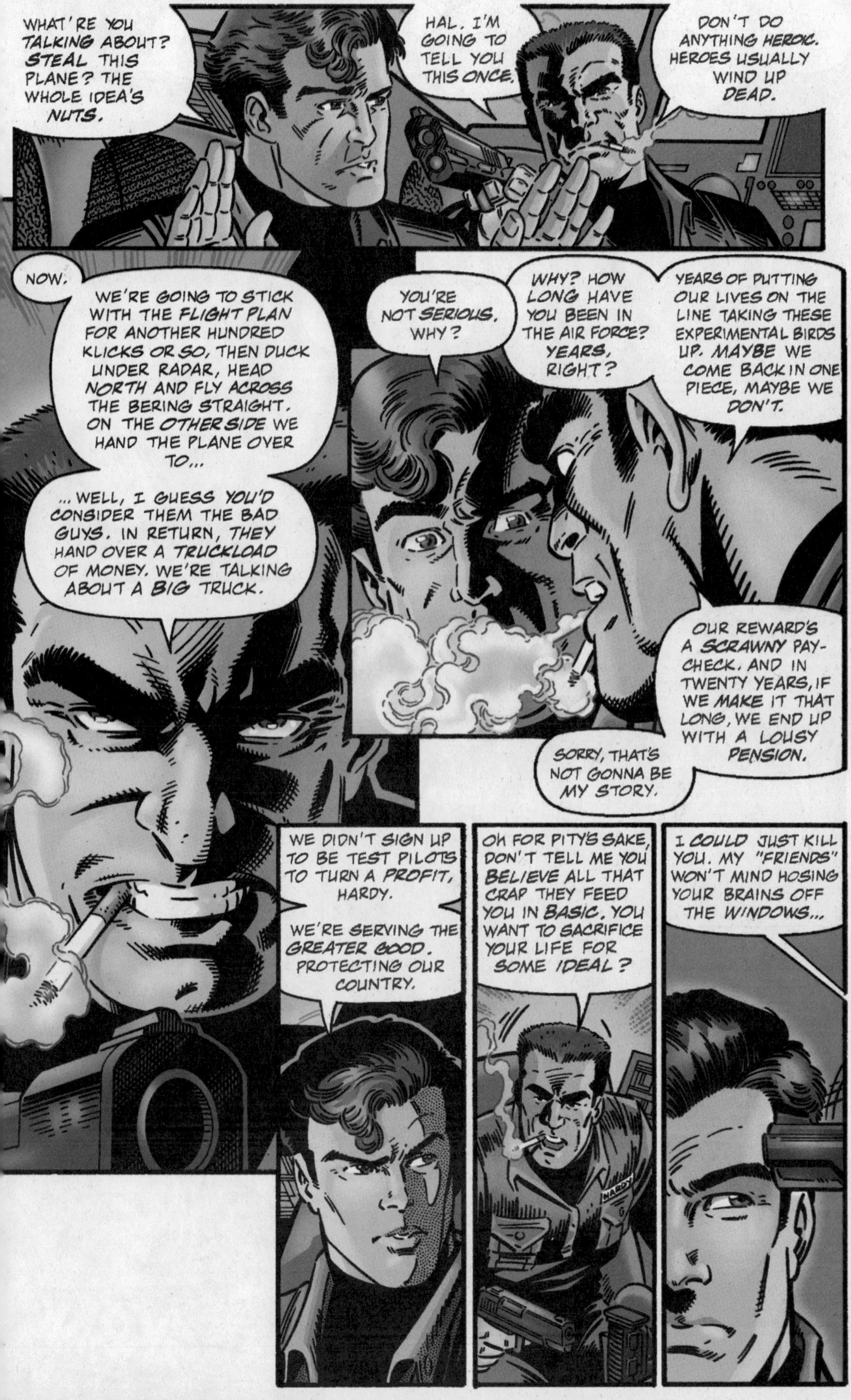
WHAT'RE YOU TALKING ABOUT? STEAL THIS PLANE? THE WHOLE IDEA'S NUTS.
HAL, I'M GOING TO TELL YOU THIS ONCE.
DON'T DO ANYTHING HEROIC. HEROES USUALLY WIND UP DEAD.
NOW.
WE'RE GOING TO STICK WITH THE FLIGHT PLAN FOR ANOTHER HUNDRED KLICKS OR SO, THEN DUCK UNDER RADAR, HEAD NORTH AND FLY ACROSS THE BERING STRAIGHT. ON THE OTHER SIDE WE HAND THE PLANE OVER TO...
...WELL, I GUESS YOU'D CONSIDER THEM THE BAD GUYS. IN RETURN, THEY HAND OVER A TRUCKLOAD OF MONEY. WE'RE TALKING ABOUT A BIG TRUCK.
YOU'RE NOT SERIOUS. WHY?
WHY? HOW LONG HAVE YOU BEEN IN THE AIR FORCE? YEARS, RIGHT?
YEARS OF PUTTING OUR LIVES ON THE LINE TAKING THESE EXPERIMENTAL BIRDS UP. MAYBE WE COME BACK IN ONE PIECE, MAYBE WE DON'T.
OUR REWARD'S A SCRAWNY PAY-CHECK. AND IN TWENTY YEARS, IF WE MAKE IT THAT LONG, WE END UP WITH A LOUSY PENSION.
SORRY, THAT'S NOT GONNA BE MY STORY.
WE DIDN'T SIGN UP TO BE TEST PILOTS TO TURN A PROFIT, HARDY.
WE'RE SERVING THE GREATER GOOD. PROTECTING OUR COUNTRY.
Oh FOR PITY'S SAKE, DON'T TELL ME YOU BELIEVE ALL THAT CRAP THEY FEED YOU IN BASIC. YOU WANT TO SACRIFICE YOUR LIFE FOR SOME IDEAL?
HARDY
I COULD JUST KILL YOU. MY "FRIENDS" WON'T MIND HOSING YOUR BRAINS OFF THE WINDOWS...

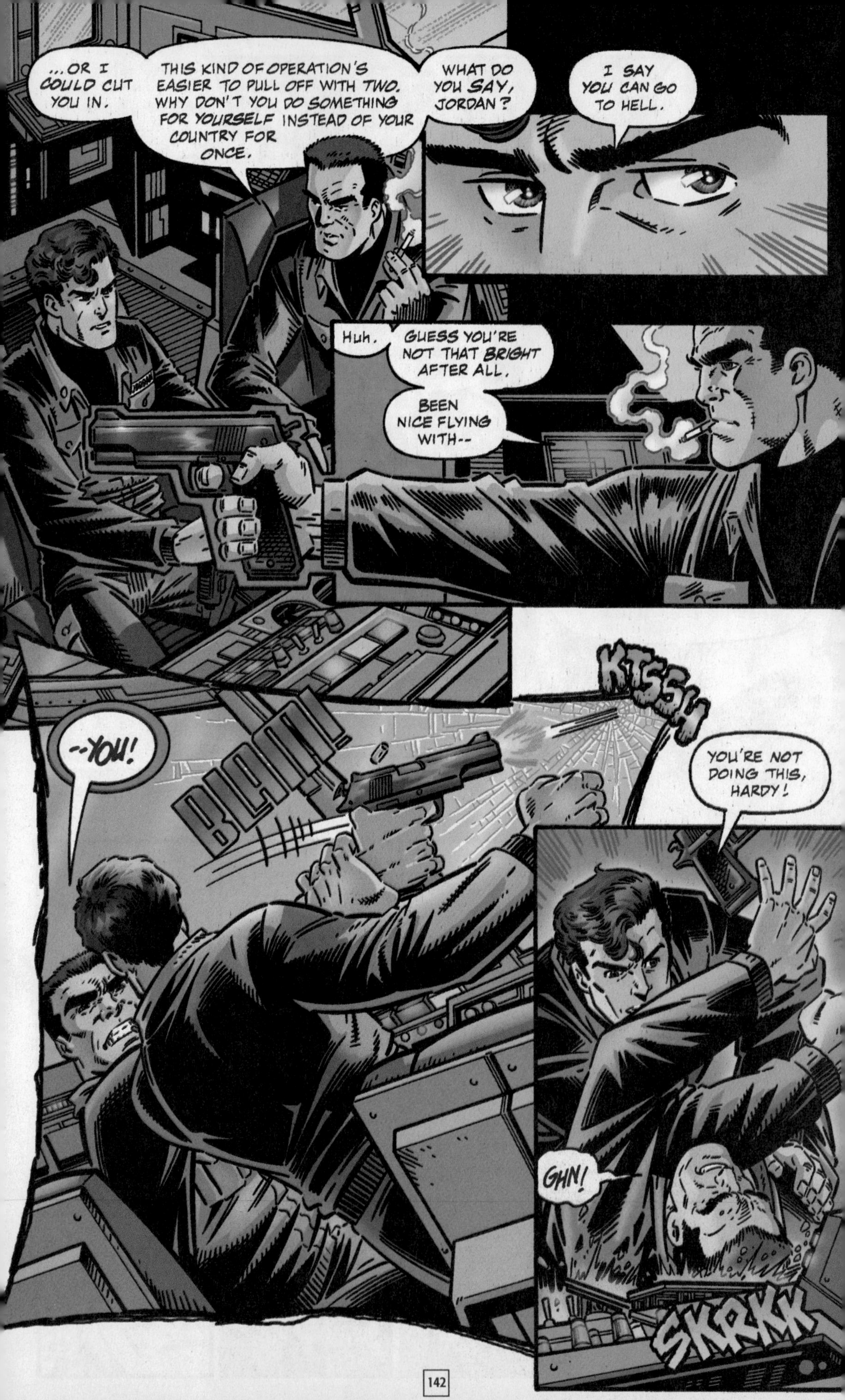

...OR I COULD CUT YOU IN.
THIS KIND OF OPERATION'S EASIER TO PULL OFF WITH TWO. WHY DON'T YOU DO SOMETHING FOR YOURSELF INSTEAD OF YOUR COUNTRY FOR ONCE.
WHAT DO YOU SAY, JORDAN?
I SAY YOU CAN GO TO HELL.
Huh.
GUESS YOU'RE NOT THAT BRIGHT AFTER ALL.
BEEN NICE FLYING WITH--
--YOU!
BLAM
KTSSH
YOU'RE NOT DOING THIS, HARDY!
GHN!
SKRKK

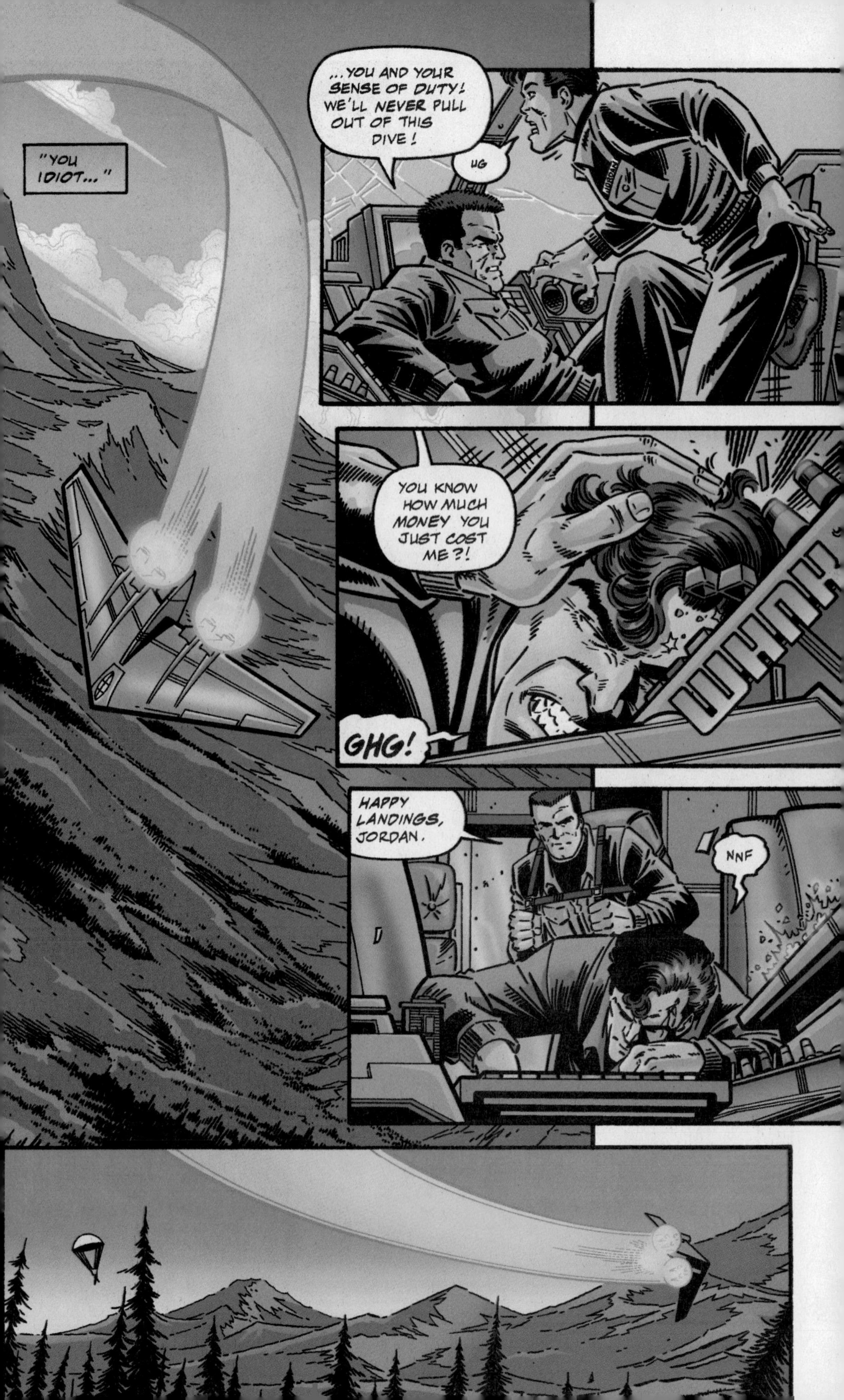
"YOU IDIOT..."
...YOU AND YOUR SENSE OF DUTY! WE'LL NEVER PULL OUT OF THIS DIVE!
UG
YOU KNOW HOW MUCH MONEY YOU JUST COST ME?!
WHAK!
GHG!
HAPPY LANDINGS, JORDAN.
NNF

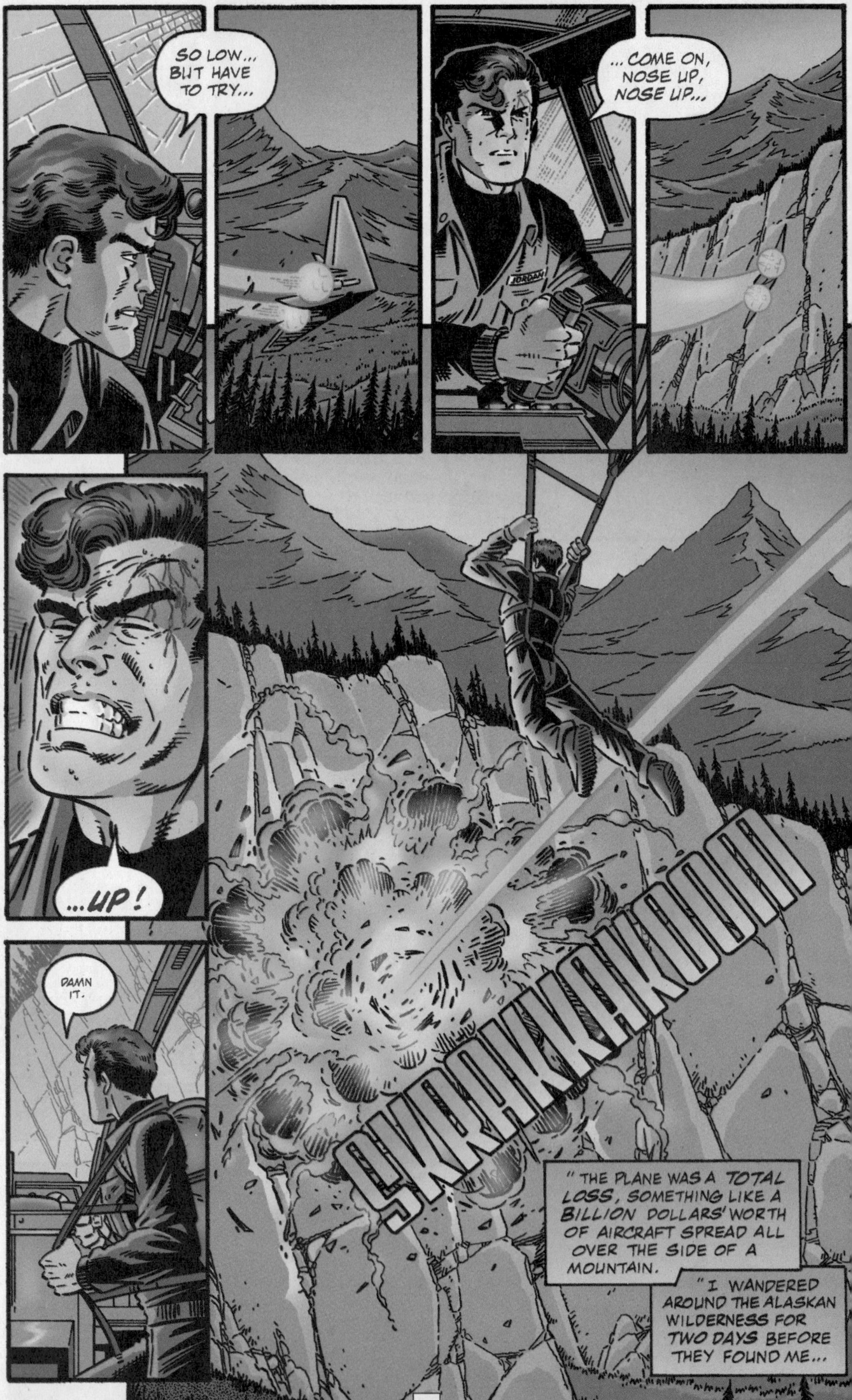
SO LOW... BUT HAVE TO TRY...
...COME ON, NOSE UP, NOSE UP...
JORDAN
...UP!
DAMN IT.
SKRAKKAKOOM
"THE PLANE WAS A TOTAL LOSS, SOMETHING LIKE A BILLION DOLLARS' WORTH OF AIRCRAFT SPREAD ALL OVER THE SIDE OF A MOUNTAIN.
"I WANDERED AROUND THE ALASKAN WILDERNESS FOR TWO DAYS BEFORE THEY FOUND ME...

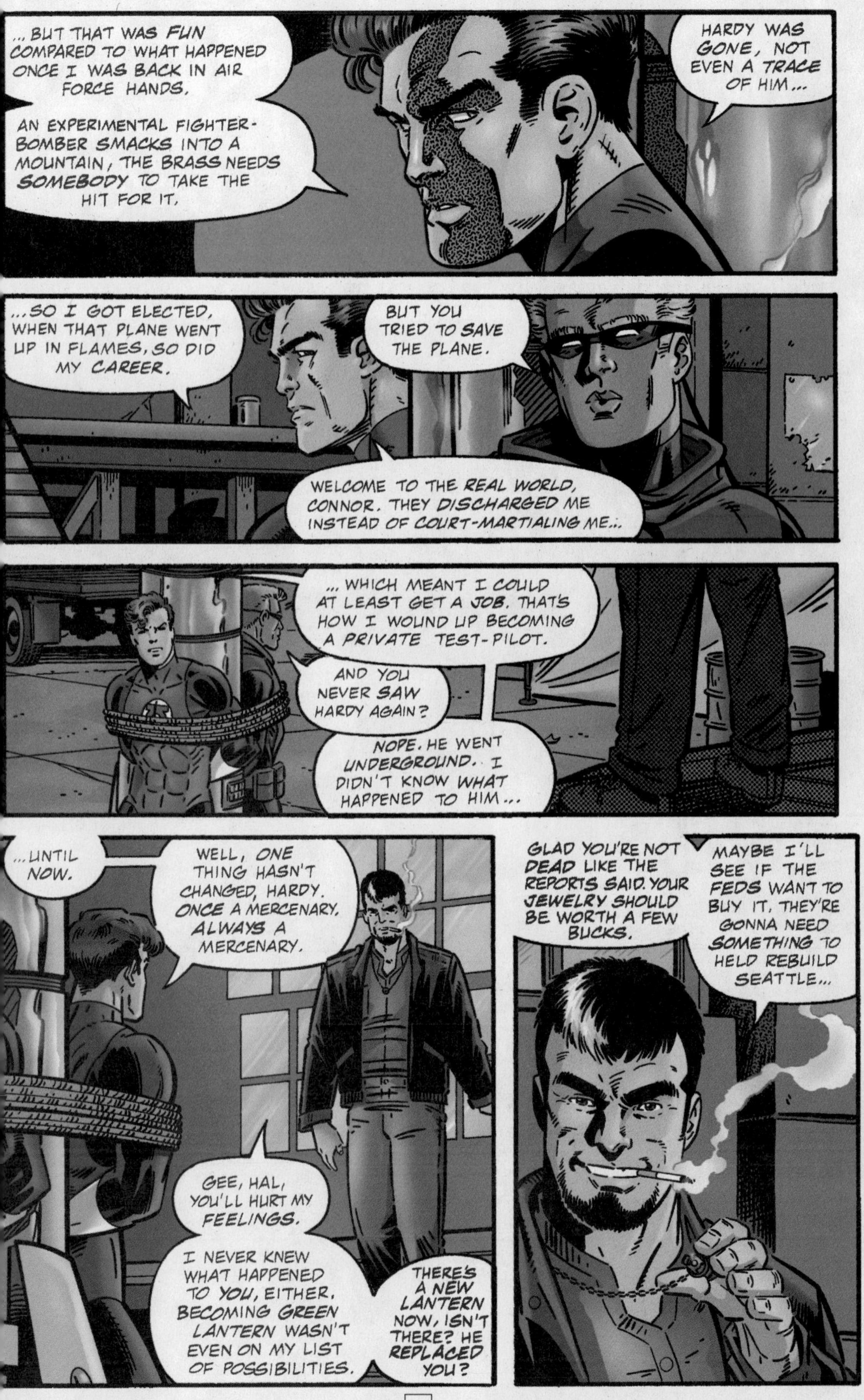

... BUT THAT WAS FUN COMPARED TO WHAT HAPPENED ONCE I WAS BACK IN AIR FORCE HANDS.
AN EXPERIMENTAL FIGHTER-BOMBER SMACKS INTO A MOUNTAIN, THE BRASS NEEDS SOMEBODY TO TAKE THE HIT FOR IT.
HARDY WAS GONE, NOT EVEN A TRACE OF HIM...
...SO I GOT ELECTED. WHEN THAT PLANE WENT UP IN FLAMES, SO DID MY CAREER.
BUT YOU TRIED TO SAVE THE PLANE.
WELCOME TO THE REAL WORLD, CONNOR. THEY DISCHARGED ME INSTEAD OF COURT-MARTIALING ME...
... WHICH MEANT I COULD AT LEAST GET A JOB. THAT'S HOW I WOUND UP BECOMING A PRIVATE TEST-PILOT.
AND YOU NEVER SAW HARDY AGAIN?
NOPE. HE WENT UNDERGROUND. I DIDN'T KNOW WHAT HAPPENED TO HIM...
...UNTIL NOW.
WELL, ONE THING HASN'T CHANGED, HARDY. ONCE A MERCENARY, ALWAYS A MERCENARY.
GEE, HAL, YOU'LL HURT MY FEELINGS.
I NEVER KNEW WHAT HAPPENED TO YOU, EITHER. BECOMING GREEN LANTERN WASN'T EVEN ON MY LIST OF POSSIBILITIES.
THERE'S A NEW LANTERN NOW, ISN'T THERE? HE REPLACED YOU?
GLAD YOU'RE NOT DEAD LIKE THE REPORTS SAID. YOUR JEWELRY SHOULD BE WORTH A FEW BUCKS.
MAYBE I'LL SEE IF THE FEDS WANT TO BUY IT. THEY'RE GONNA NEED SOMETHING TO HELP REBUILD SEATTLE...

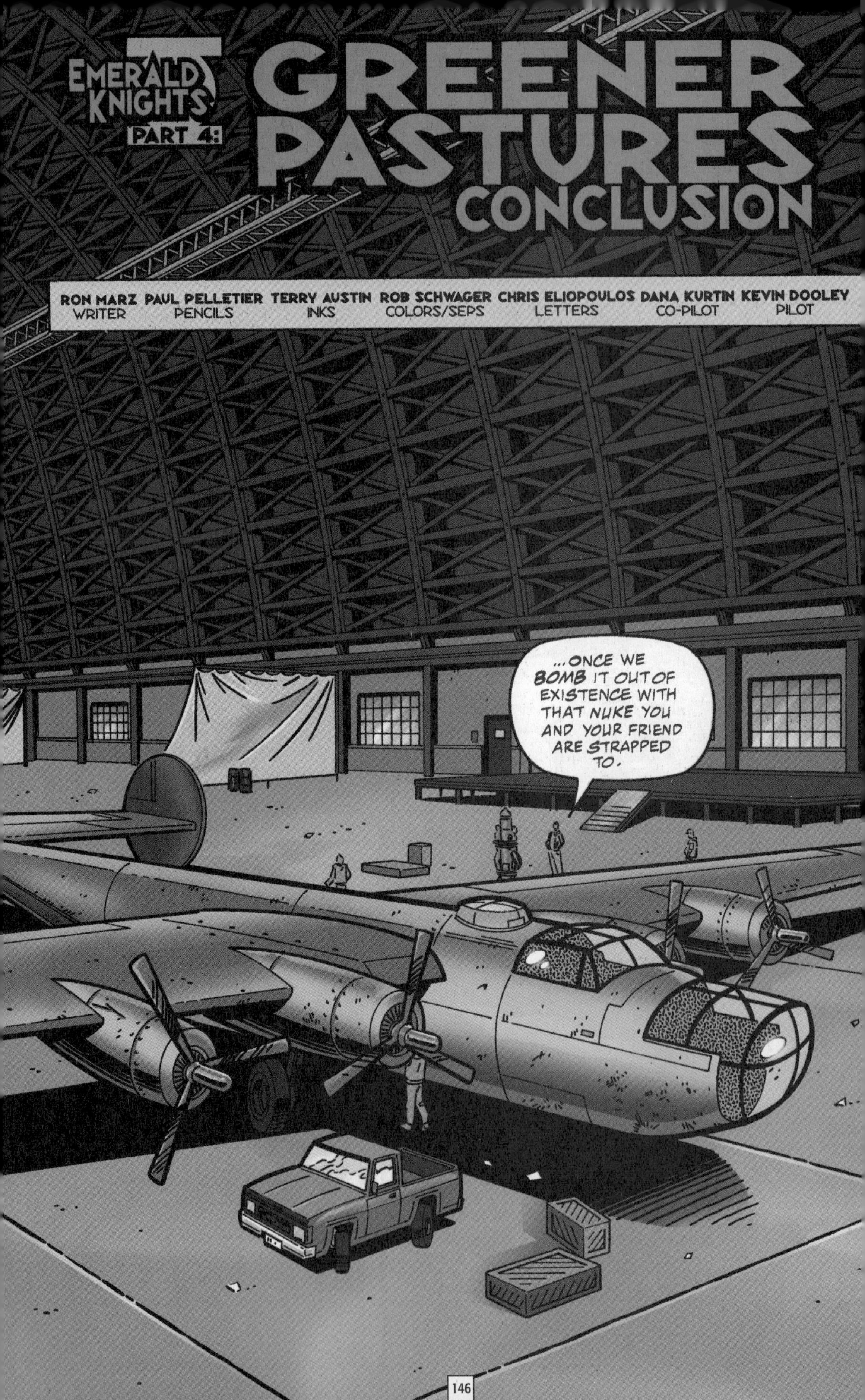
EMERALD KNIGHTS PART 4:
GREENER PASTURES CONCLUSION
RON MARZ WRITER PAUL PELLETIER PENCILS TERRY AUSTIN INKS ROB SCHWAGER COLORS/SEPS CHRIS ELIOPOULOS LETTERS DANA KURTIN CO-PILOT KEVIN DOOLEY PILOT
...ONCE WE BOMB IT OUT OF EXISTENCE WITH THAT NUKE YOU AND YOUR FRIEND ARE STRAPPED TO.

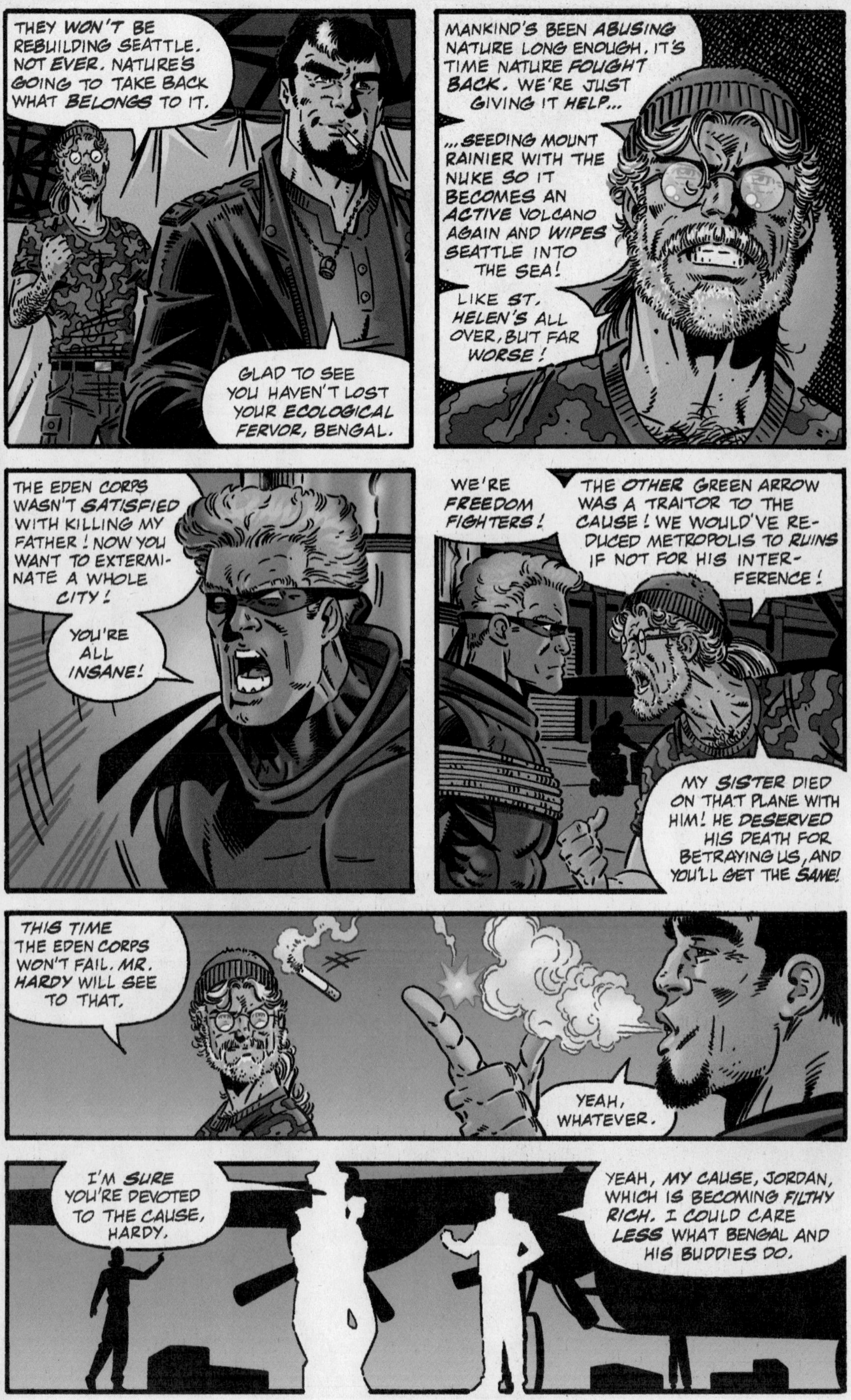
THEY WON'T BE REBUILDING SEATTLE. NOT EVER. NATURE'S GOING TO TAKE BACK WHAT BELONGS TO IT.
GLAD TO SEE YOU HAVEN'T LOST YOUR ECOLOGICAL FERVOR, BENGAL.
MANKIND'S BEEN ABUSING NATURE LONG ENOUGH. IT'S TIME NATURE FOUGHT BACK. WE'RE JUST GIVING IT HELP...
...SEEDING MOUNT RAINIER WITH THE NUKE SO IT BECOMES AN ACTIVE VOLCANO AGAIN AND WIPES SEATTLE INTO THE SEA!
LIKE ST. HELEN'S ALL OVER, BUT FAR WORSE!
THE EDEN CORPS WASN'T SATISFIED WITH KILLING MY FATHER! NOW YOU WANT TO EXTERMINATE A WHOLE CITY!
YOU'RE ALL INSANE!
WE'RE FREEDOM FIGHTERS!
THE OTHER GREEN ARROW WAS A TRAITOR TO THE CAUSE! WE WOULD'VE REDUCED METROPOLIS TO RUINS IF NOT FOR HIS INTERFERENCE!
MY SISTER DIED ON THAT PLANE WITH HIM! HE DESERVED HIS DEATH FOR BETRAYING US, AND YOU'LL GET THE SAME!
THIS TIME THE EDEN CORPS WON'T FAIL. MR. HARDY WILL SEE TO THAT.
YEAH, WHATEVER.
I'M SURE YOU'RE DEVOTED TO THE CAUSE, HARDY.
YEAH, MY CAUSE, JORDAN, WHICH IS BECOMING FILTHY RICH. I COULD CARE LESS WHAT BENGAL AND HIS BUDDIES DO.

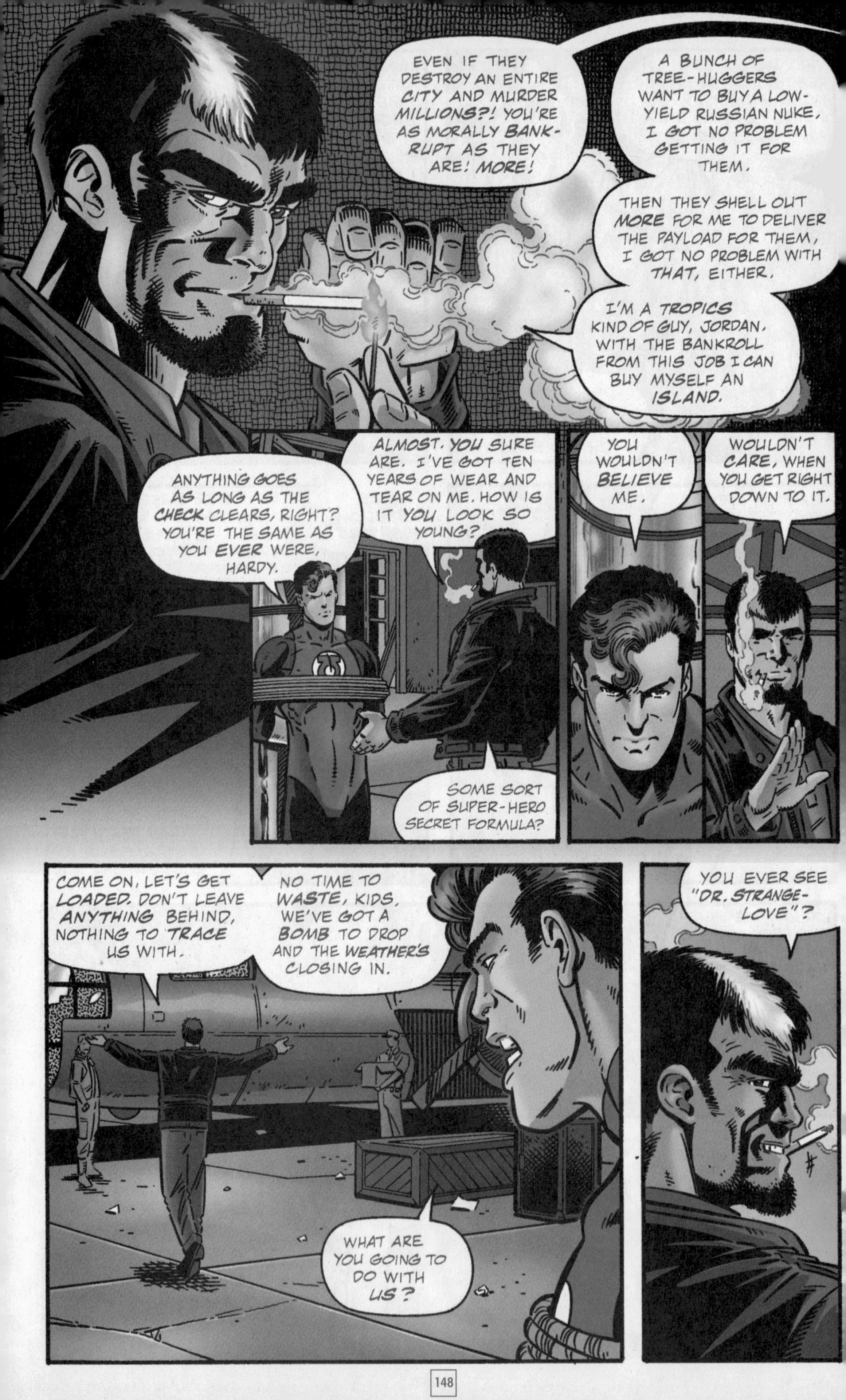
EVEN IF THEY DESTROY AN ENTIRE CITY AND MURDER MILLIONS?! YOU'RE AS MORALLY BANKRUPT AS THEY ARE! MORE!
A BUNCH OF TREE-HUGGERS WANT TO BUY A LOW-YIELD RUSSIAN NUKE, I GOT NO PROBLEM GETTING IT FOR THEM.
THEN THEY SHELL OUT MORE FOR ME TO DELIVER THE PAYLOAD FOR THEM, I GOT NO PROBLEM WITH THAT, EITHER.
I'M A TROPICS KIND OF GUY, JORDAN. WITH THE BANKROLL FROM THIS JOB I CAN BUY MYSELF AN ISLAND.
ANYTHING GOES AS LONG AS THE CHECK CLEARS, RIGHT? YOU'RE THE SAME AS YOU EVER WERE, HARDY.
ALMOST. YOU SURE ARE. I'VE GOT TEN YEARS OF WEAR AND TEAR ON ME. HOW IS IT YOU LOOK SO YOUNG?
SOME SORT OF SUPER-HERO SECRET FORMULA?
YOU WOULDN'T BELIEVE ME.
WOULDN'T CARE, WHEN YOU GET RIGHT DOWN TO IT.
COME ON, LET'S GET LOADED. DON'T LEAVE ANYTHING BEHIND, NOTHING TO TRACE US WITH.
NO TIME TO WASTE, KIDS. WE'VE GOT A BOMB TO DROP AND THE WEATHER'S CLOSING IN.
WHAT ARE YOU GOING TO DO WITH US?
YOU EVER SEE "DR. STRANGELOVE"?

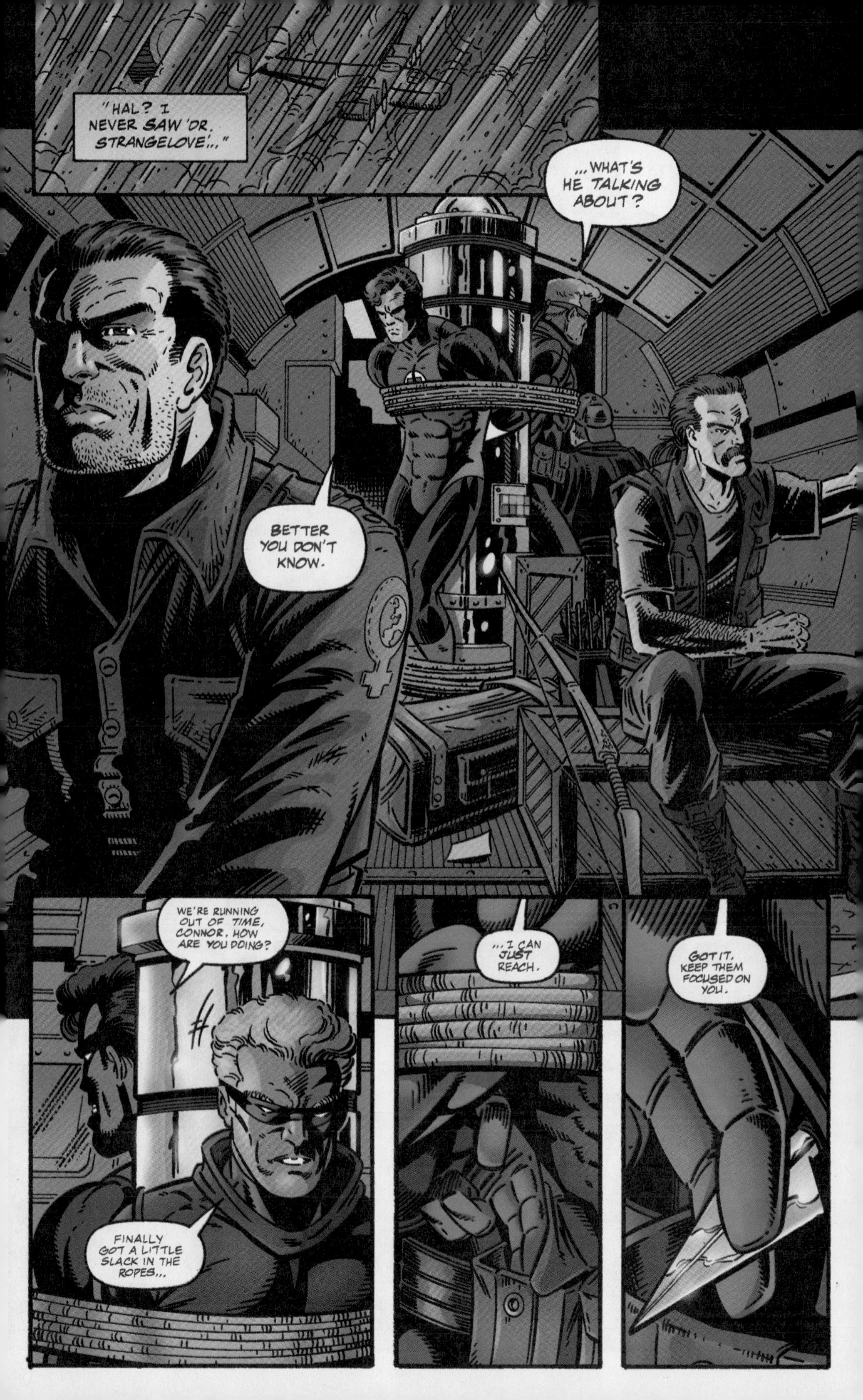
"HAL? I NEVER SAW 'DR. STRANGELOVE'..."
...WHAT'S HE TALKING ABOUT?
BETTER YOU DON'T KNOW.
WE'RE RUNNING OUT OF TIME, CONNOR. HOW ARE YOU DOING?
FINALLY GOT A LITTLE SLACK IN THE ROPES...
...I CAN JUST REACH.
GOT IT. KEEP THEM FOCUSED ON YOU.

HEY, HARDY!

YOU KNOW, MAYBE I SHOULD BE *THANKING* YOU. IF YOU HADN'T GOTTEN ME *BOOTED* FROM THE AIR FORCE...

...MAYBE I WOULDN'T HAVE BEEN WHERE I NEEDED TO BE TO GET THE *RING*.

GLAD I COULD HELP...

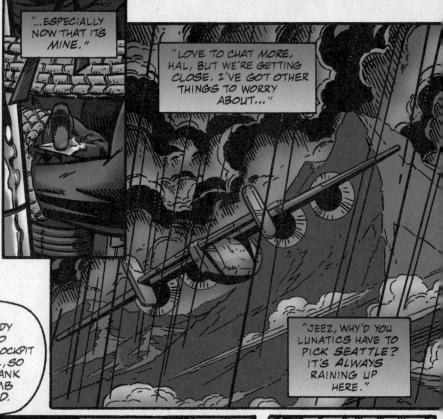

"...ESPECIALLY NOW THAT IT'S *MINE*."

"LOVE TO CHAT MORE, *HAL*, BUT WE'RE GETTING *CLOSE*. I'VE GOT OTHER THINGS TO WORRY ABOUT..."

THREE MINUTES TO TARGET. HARDY SAID THE *AUTO* SWITCH IN THE COCKPIT *DOESN'T WORK*, SO WE HAVE TO CRANK OPEN THE BOMB BAY BY HAND.

"*JEEZ*, WHY'D YOU LUNATICS HAVE TO PICK *SEATTLE*? IT'S *ALWAYS* RAINING UP HERE."

ALREADY DOING IT, SEE? CALM YOURSELF, BENGAL...

"...I'M ALMOST THERE."

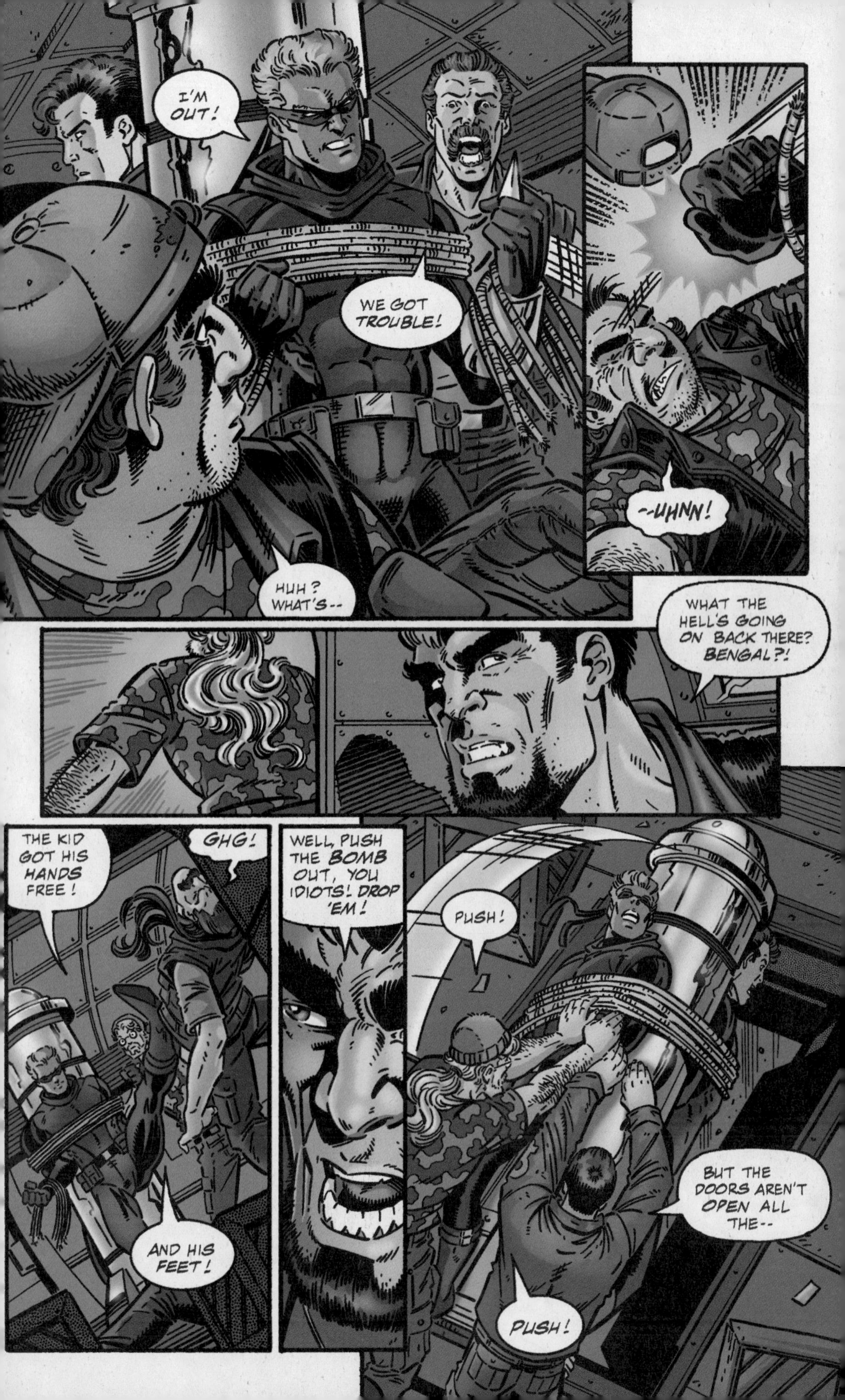
I'M OUT!
WE GOT TROUBLE!
HUH? WHAT'S--
--UHNN!
WHAT THE HELL'S GOING ON BACK THERE? BENGAL?!
THE KID GOT HIS HANDS FREE!
GHG!
AND HIS FEET!
WELL, PUSH THE BOMB OUT, YOU IDIOTS! DROP 'EM!
PUSH!
BUT THE DOORS AREN'T OPEN ALL THE--
PUSH!

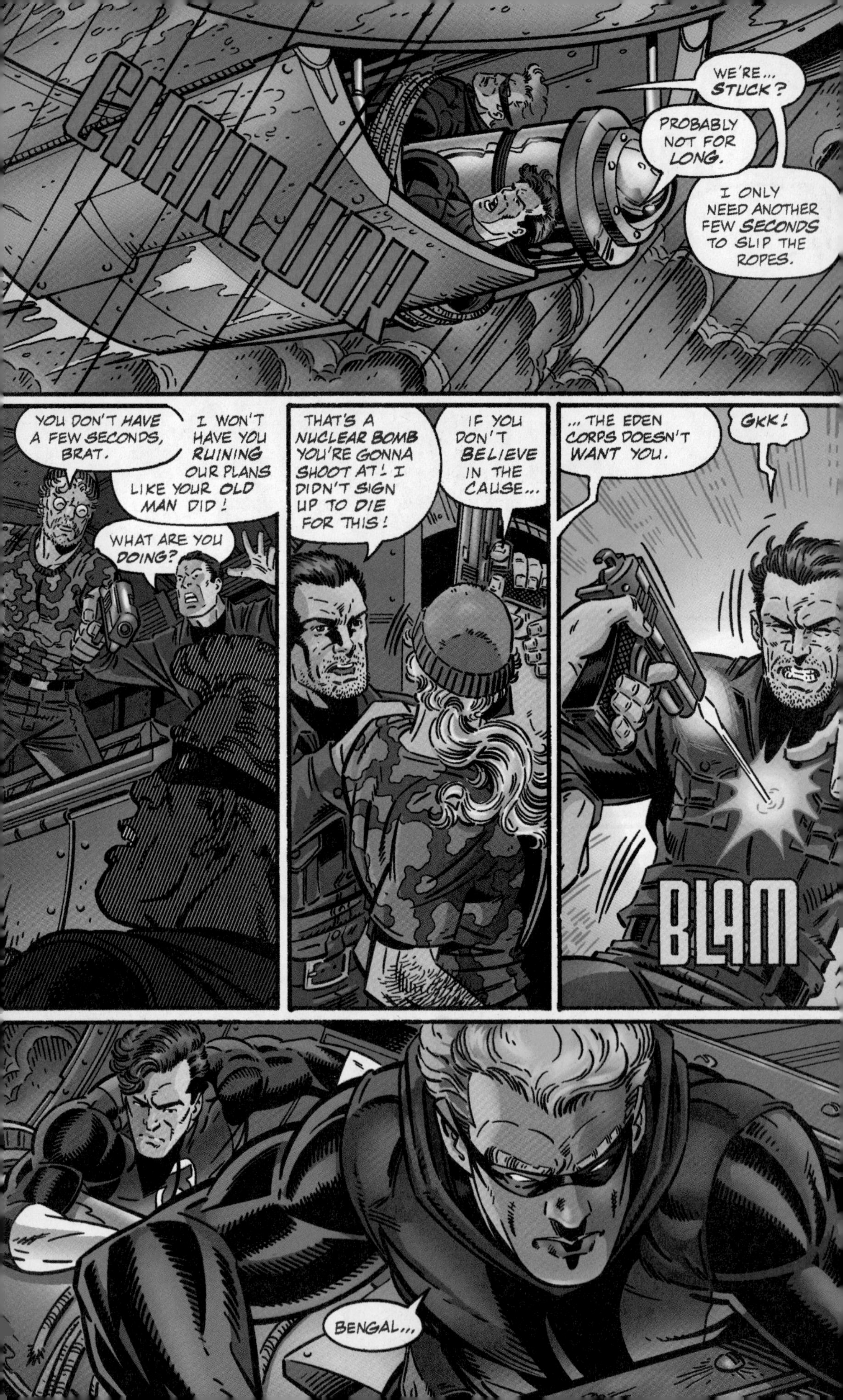
CHARLUNK
WE'RE... STUCK?
PROBABLY NOT FOR LONG.
I ONLY NEED ANOTHER FEW SECONDS TO SLIP THE ROPES.
YOU DON'T HAVE A FEW SECONDS, BRAT.
I WON'T HAVE YOU RUINING OUR PLANS LIKE YOUR OLD MAN DID!
WHAT ARE YOU DOING?
THAT'S A NUCLEAR BOMB YOU'RE GONNA SHOOT AT! I DIDN'T SIGN UP TO DIE FOR THIS!
IF YOU DON'T BELIEVE IN THE CAUSE...
...THE EDEN CORPS DOESN'T WANT YOU.
GKK!
BLAM
BENGAL...

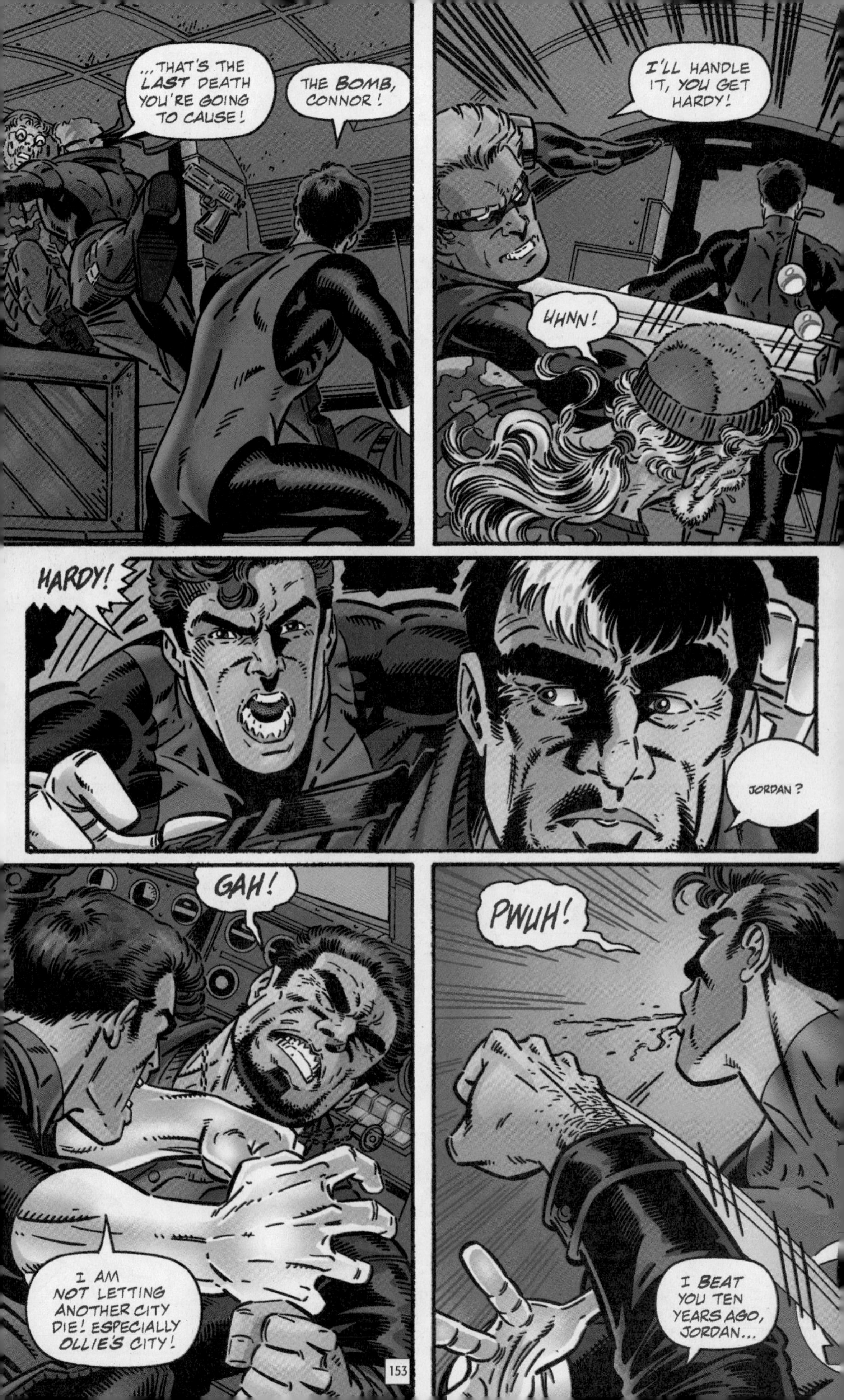
...THAT'S THE LAST DEATH YOU'RE GOING TO CAUSE!
THE BOMB, CONNOR!
I'LL HANDLE IT, YOU GET HARDY!
UHNN!
HARDY!
JORDAN?
GAH!
I AM NOT LETTING ANOTHER CITY DIE! ESPECIALLY OLLIE'S CITY!
PWUH!
I BEAT YOU TEN YEARS AGO, JORDAN...

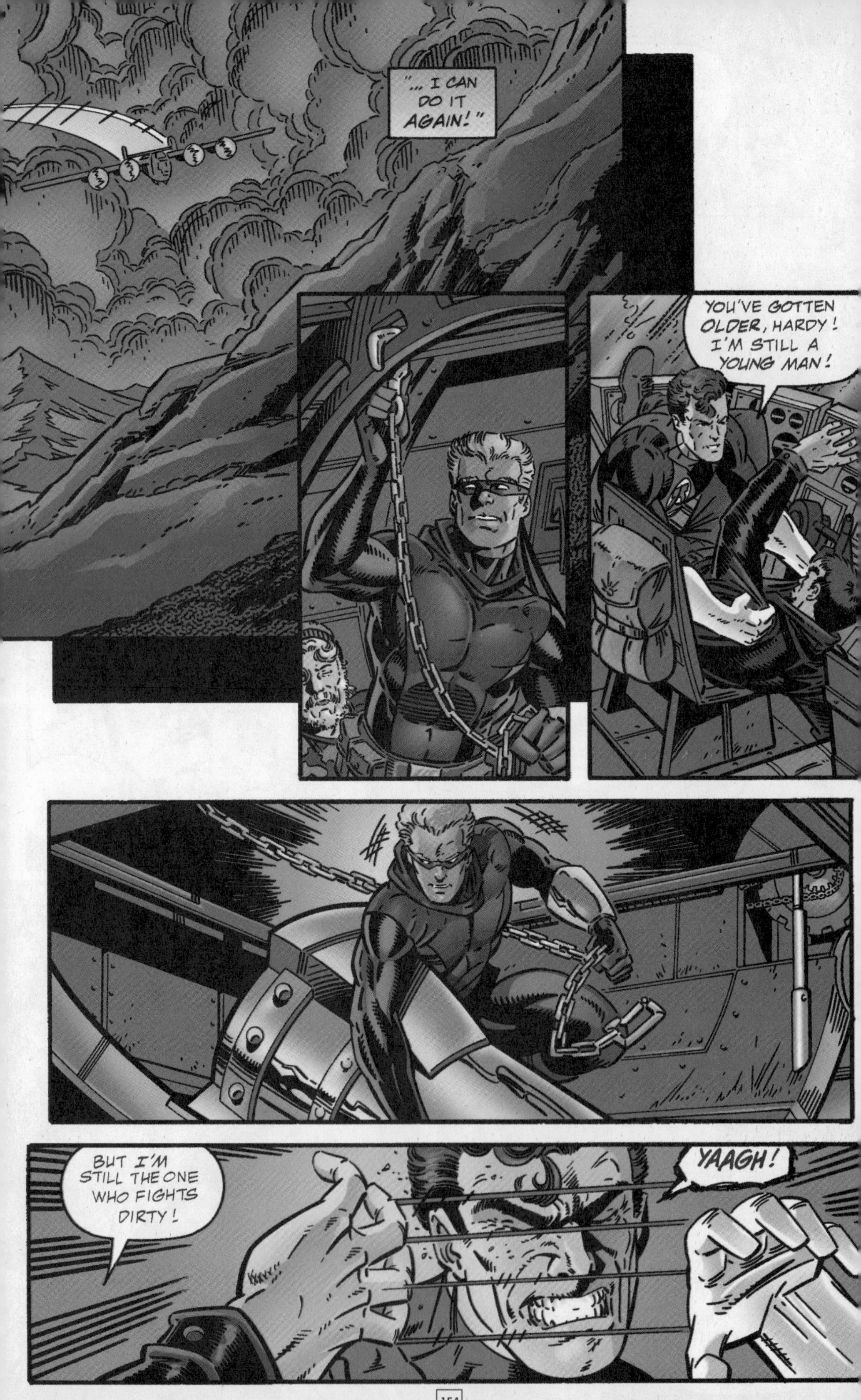
"... I CAN DO IT AGAIN!"
YOU'VE GOTTEN OLDER, HARDY! I'M STILL A YOUNG MAN!
BUT I'M STILL THE ONE WHO FIGHTS DIRTY!
YAAGH!

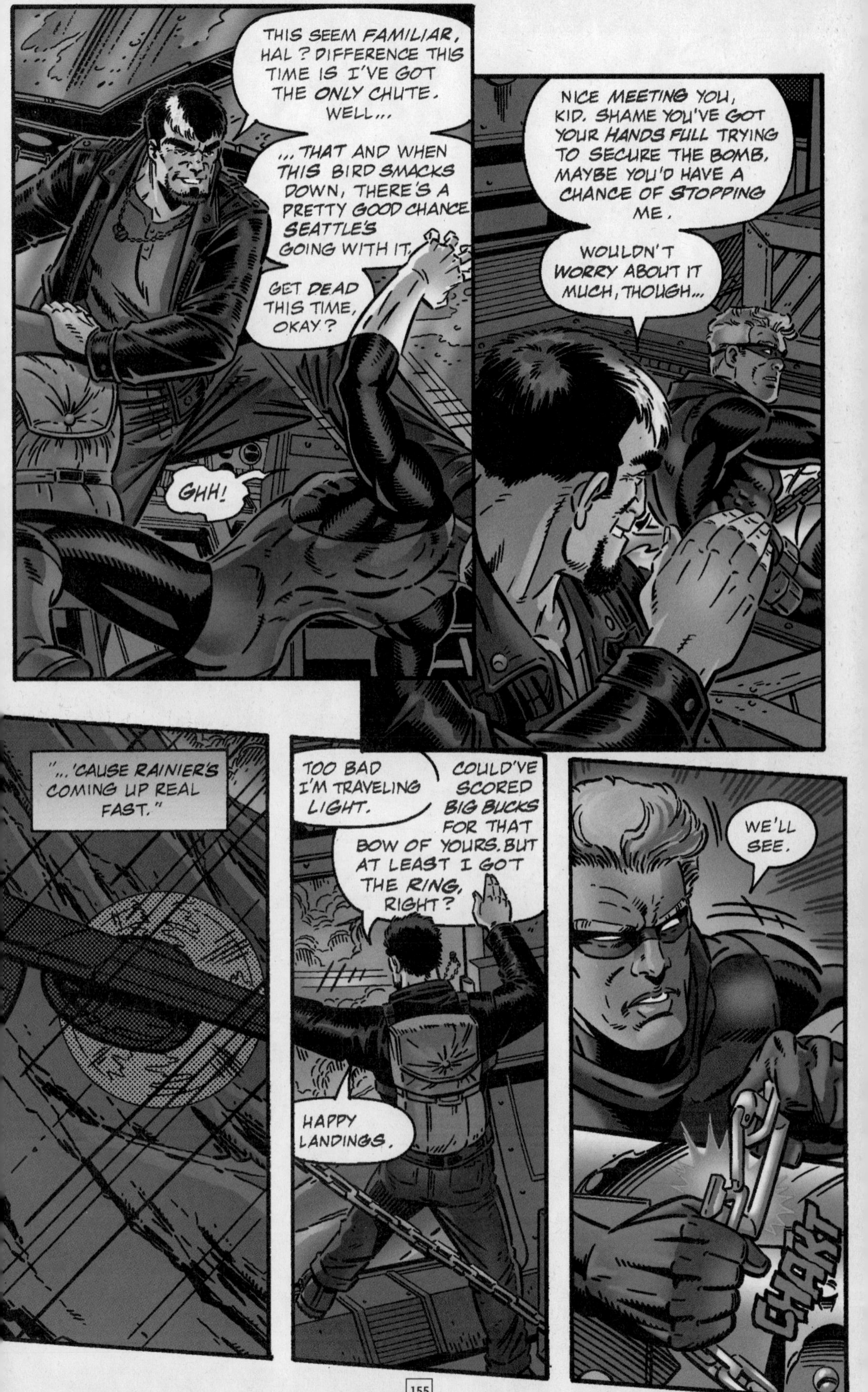
THIS SEEM FAMILIAR, HAL? DIFFERENCE THIS TIME IS I'VE GOT THE ONLY CHUTE. WELL...
...THAT AND WHEN THIS BIRD SMACKS DOWN, THERE'S A PRETTY GOOD CHANCE SEATTLE'S GOING WITH IT.
GET DEAD THIS TIME, OKAY?
GHH!
NICE MEETING YOU, KID. SHAME YOU'VE GOT YOUR HANDS FULL TRYING TO SECURE THE BOMB. MAYBE YOU'D HAVE A CHANCE OF STOPPING ME.
WOULDN'T WORRY ABOUT IT MUCH, THOUGH...
"...'CAUSE RAINIER'S COMING UP REAL FAST."
TOO BAD I'M TRAVELING LIGHT.
COULD'VE SCORED BIG BUCKS FOR THAT BOW OF YOURS. BUT AT LEAST I GOT THE RING, RIGHT?
HAPPY LANDINGS.
WE'LL SEE.
CHAKT

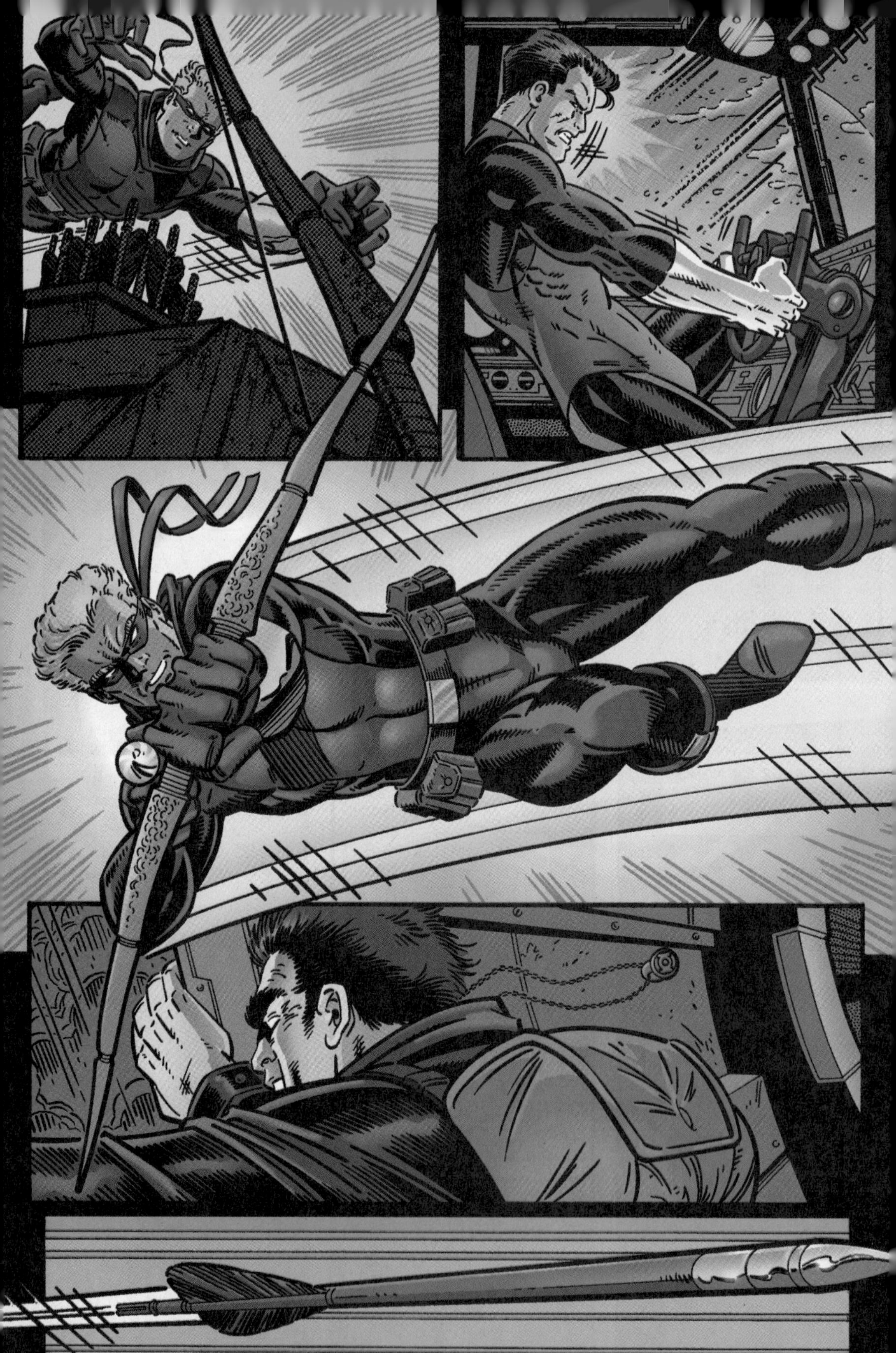

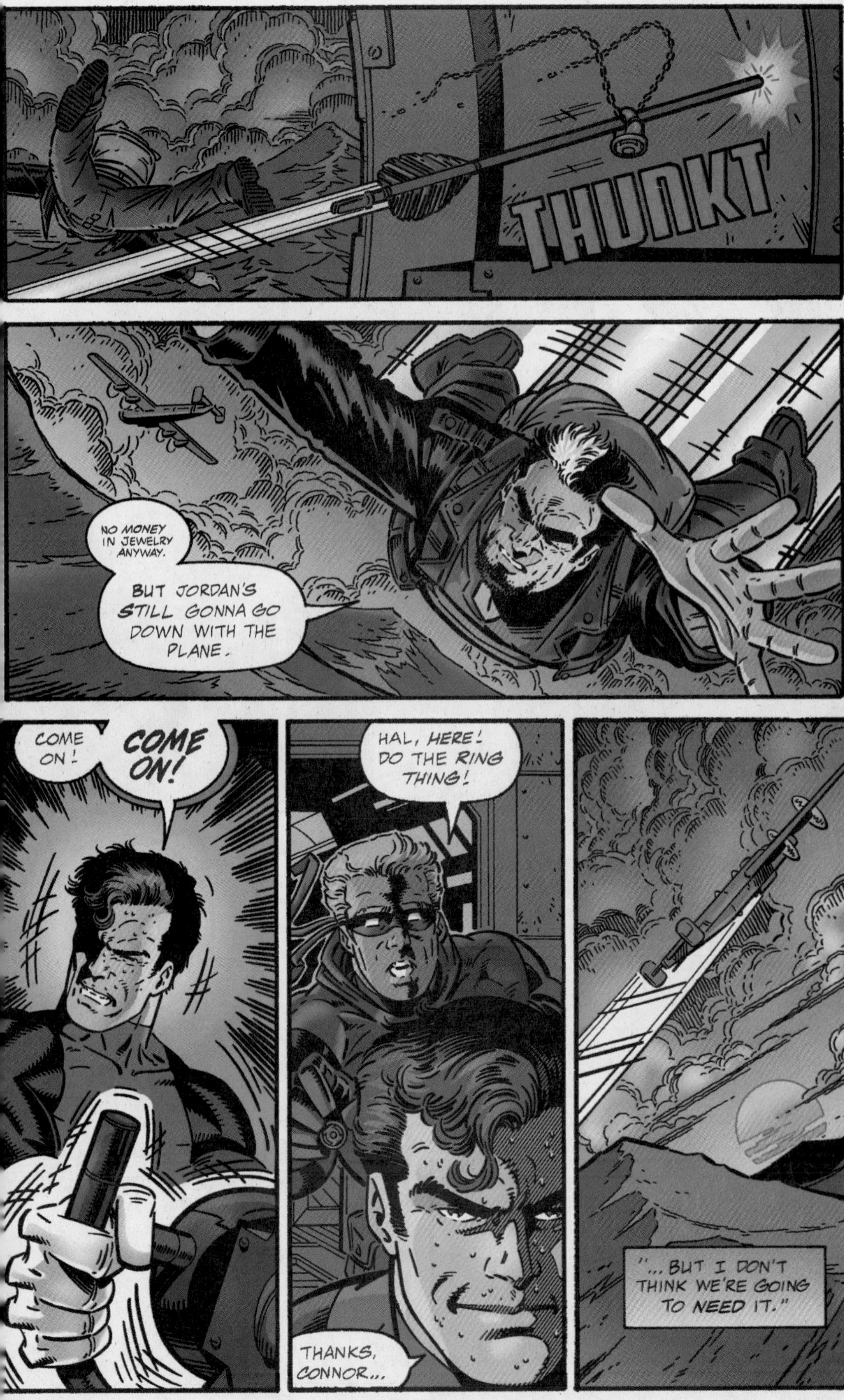
THUNKT
NO MONEY IN JEWELRY ANYWAY.
BUT JORDAN'S STILL GONNA GO DOWN WITH THE PLANE.
COME ON!
COME ON!
HAL, HERE! DO THE RING THING!
THANKS, CONNOR...
"...BUT I DON'T THINK WE'RE GOING TO NEED IT."

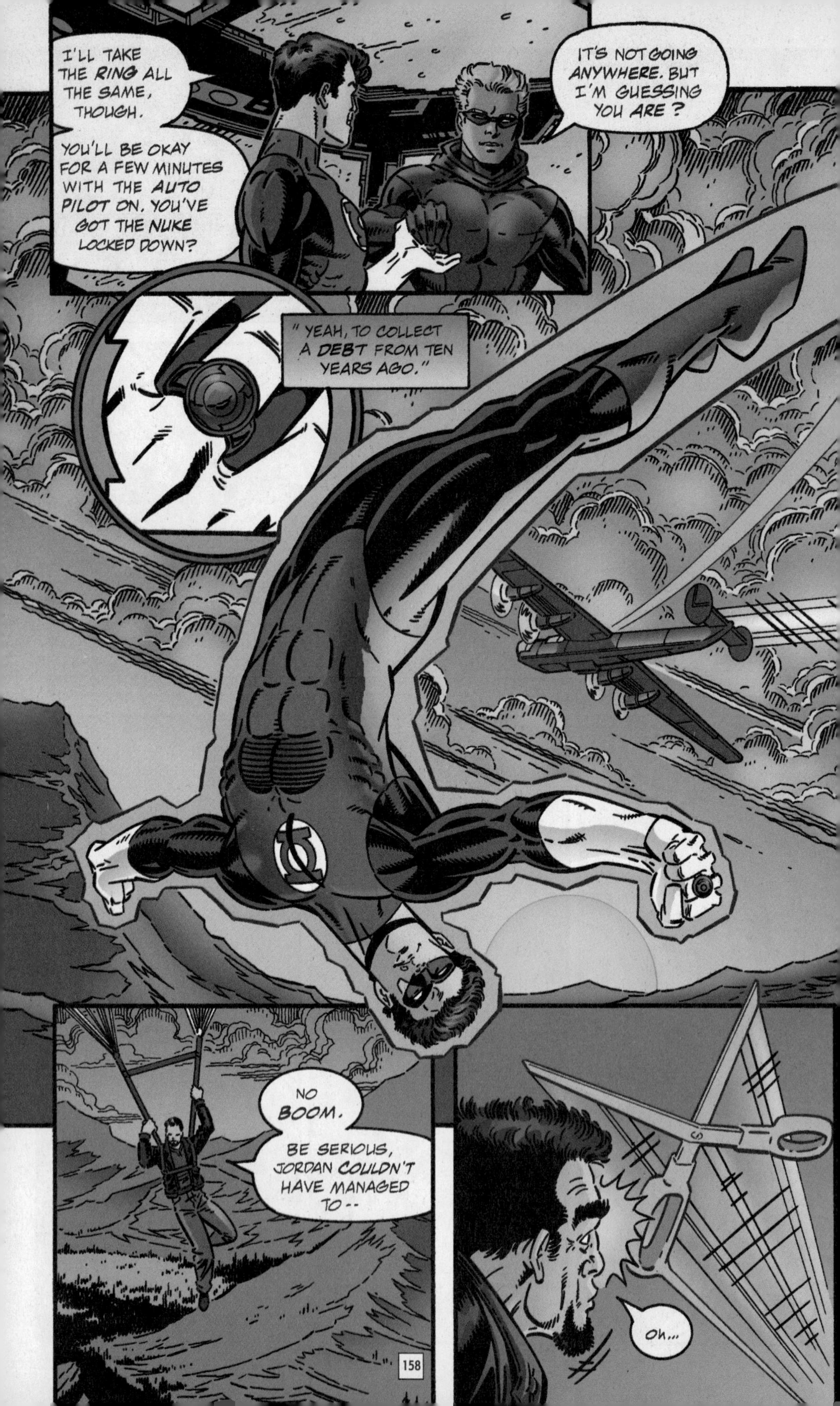

I'LL TAKE THE RING ALL THE SAME, THOUGH.
YOU'LL BE OKAY FOR A FEW MINUTES WITH THE AUTO PILOT ON. YOU'VE GOT THE NUKE LOCKED DOWN?
IT'S NOT GOING ANYWHERE. BUT I'M GUESSING YOU ARE?
"YEAH, TO COLLECT A DEBT FROM TEN YEARS AGO."
NO BOOM.
BE SERIOUS, JORDAN COULDN'T HAVE MANAGED TO--
Oh...

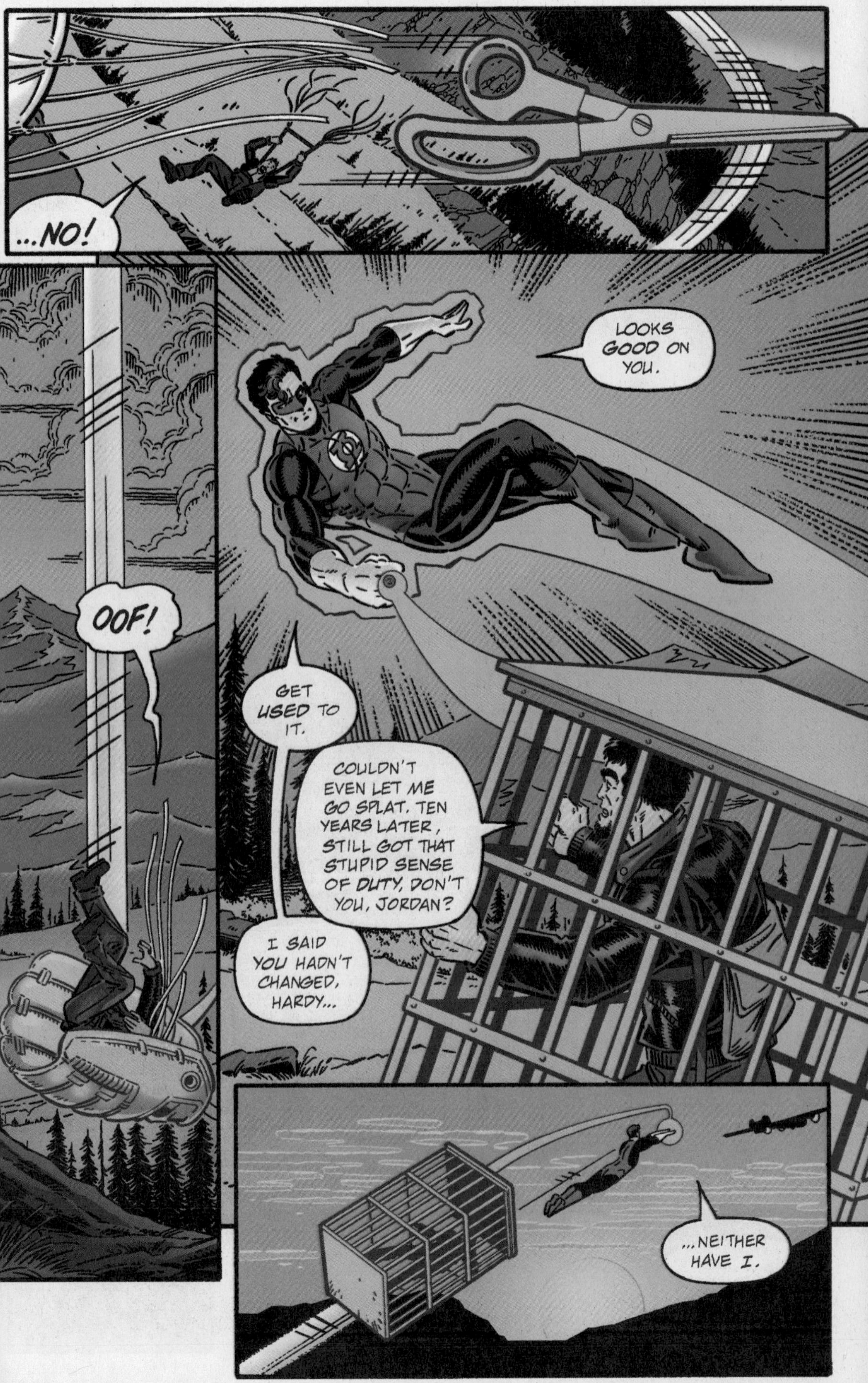
...NO!
OOF!
LOOKS GOOD ON YOU.
GET USED TO IT.
COULDN'T EVEN LET ME GO SPLAT. TEN YEARS LATER, STILL GOT THAT STUPID SENSE OF DUTY, DON'T YOU, JORDAN?
I SAID YOU HADN'T CHANGED, HARDY...
...NEITHER HAVE I.

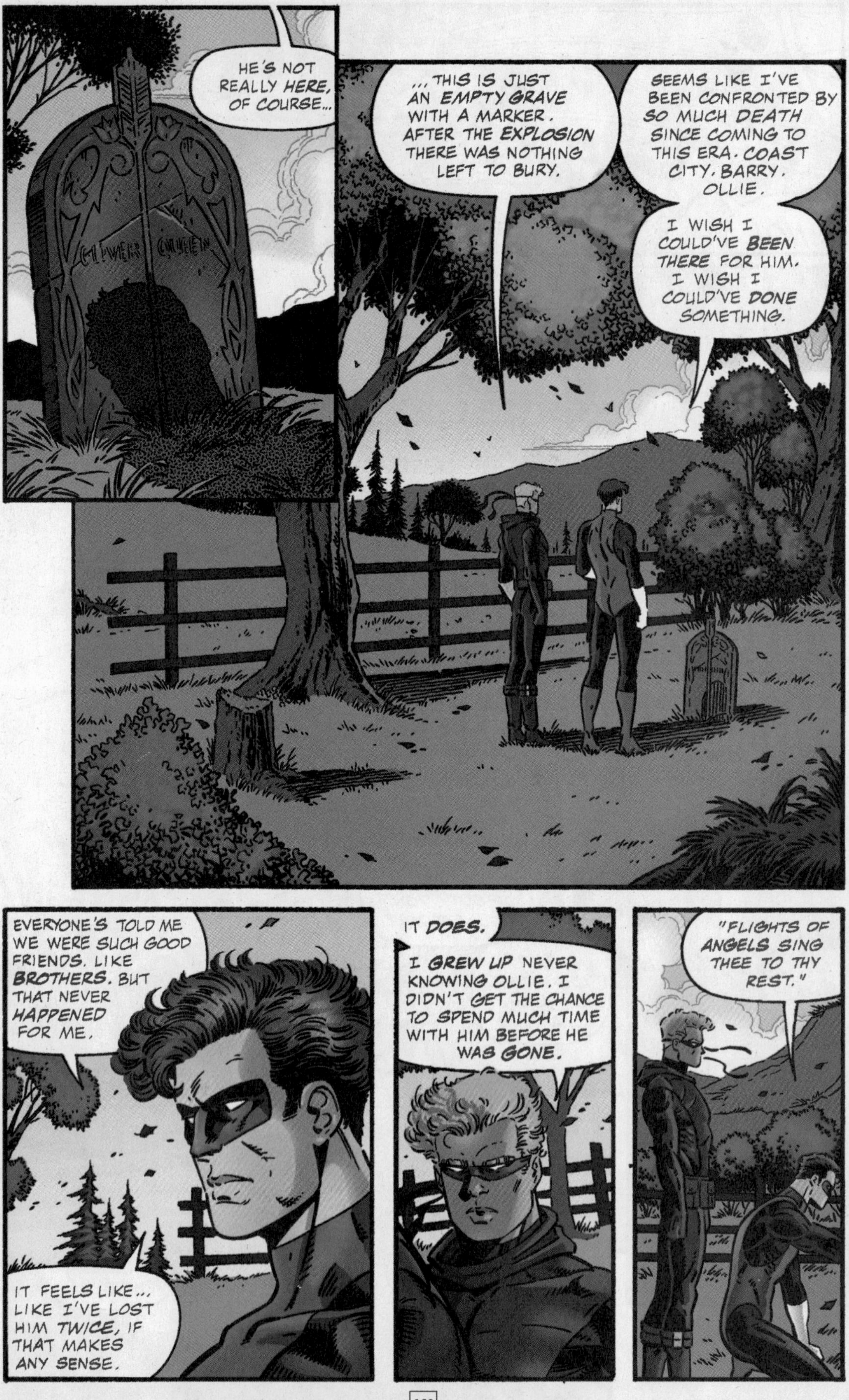
HE'S NOT REALLY HERE, OF COURSE...
...THIS IS JUST AN EMPTY GRAVE WITH A MARKER. AFTER THE EXPLOSION THERE WAS NOTHING LEFT TO BURY.
SEEMS LIKE I'VE BEEN CONFRONTED BY SO MUCH DEATH SINCE COMING TO THIS ERA. COAST CITY. BARRY. OLLIE.
I WISH I COULD'VE BEEN THERE FOR HIM. I WISH I COULD'VE DONE SOMETHING.
EVERYONE'S TOLD ME WE WERE SUCH GOOD FRIENDS. LIKE BROTHERS. BUT THAT NEVER HAPPENED FOR ME.
IT FEELS LIKE... LIKE I'VE LOST HIM TWICE, IF THAT MAKES ANY SENSE.
IT DOES.
I GREW UP NEVER KNOWING OLLIE. I DIDN'T GET THE CHANCE TO SPEND MUCH TIME WITH HIM BEFORE HE WAS GONE.
"FLIGHTS OF ANGELS SING THEE TO THY REST."

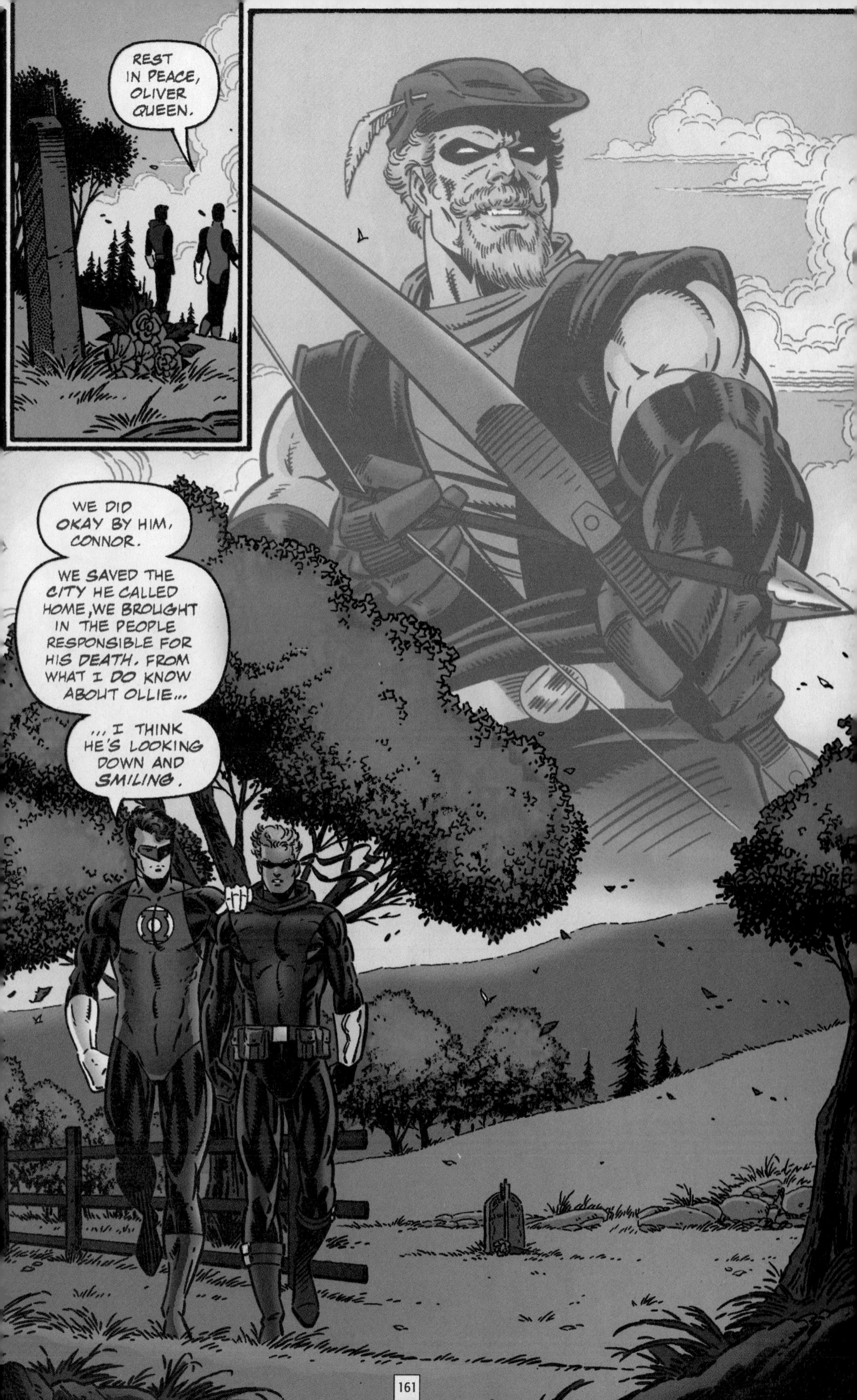
REST IN PEACE, OLIVER QUEEN.
WE DID OKAY BY HIM, CONNOR.
WE SAVED THE CITY HE CALLED HOME, WE BROUGHT IN THE PEOPLE RESPONSIBLE FOR HIS DEATH. FROM WHAT I DO KNOW ABOUT OLLIE...
...I THINK HE'S LOOKING DOWN AND SMILING.

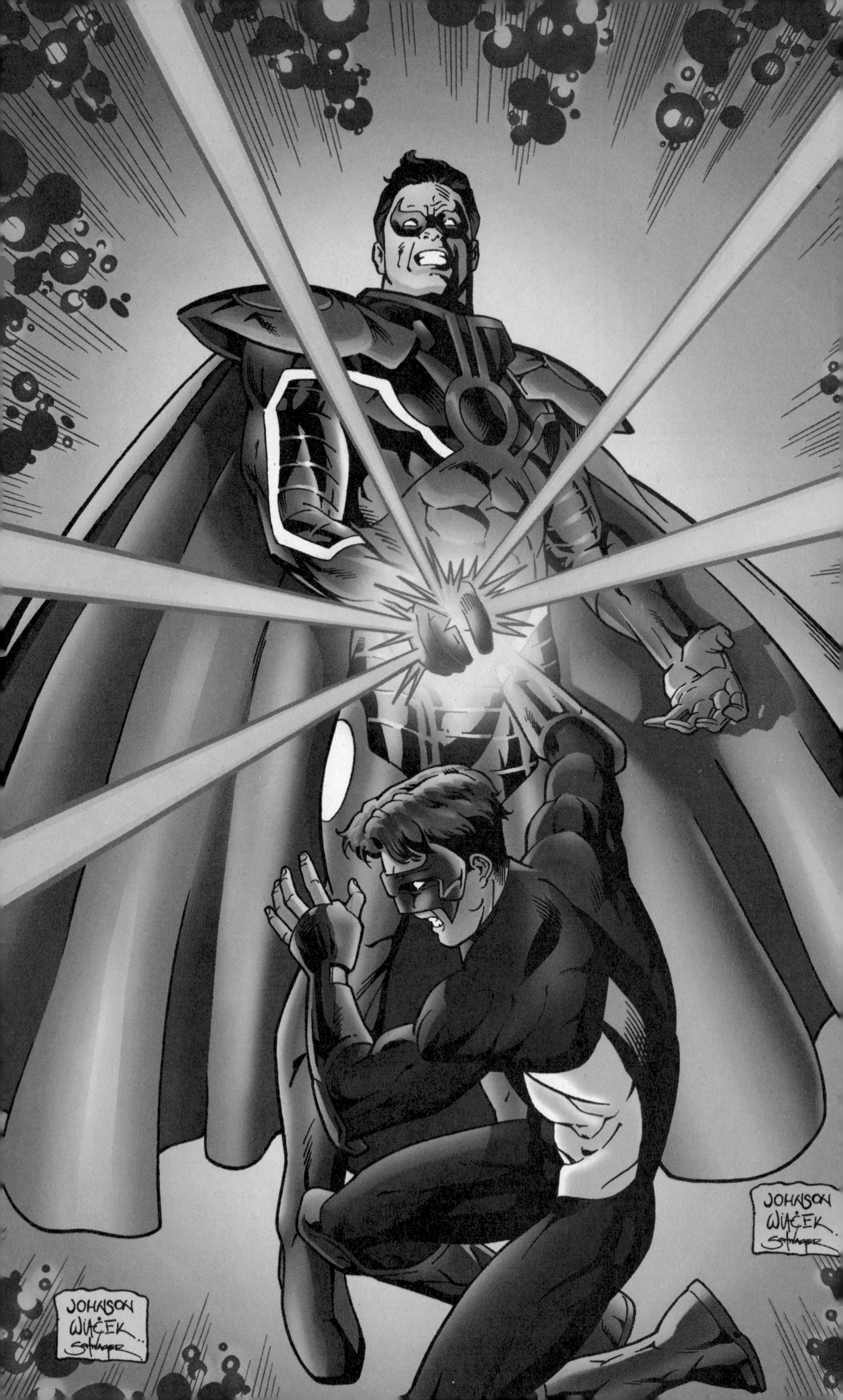
JOHNSON
WIAÇEK
JOHNSON
WIAÇEK

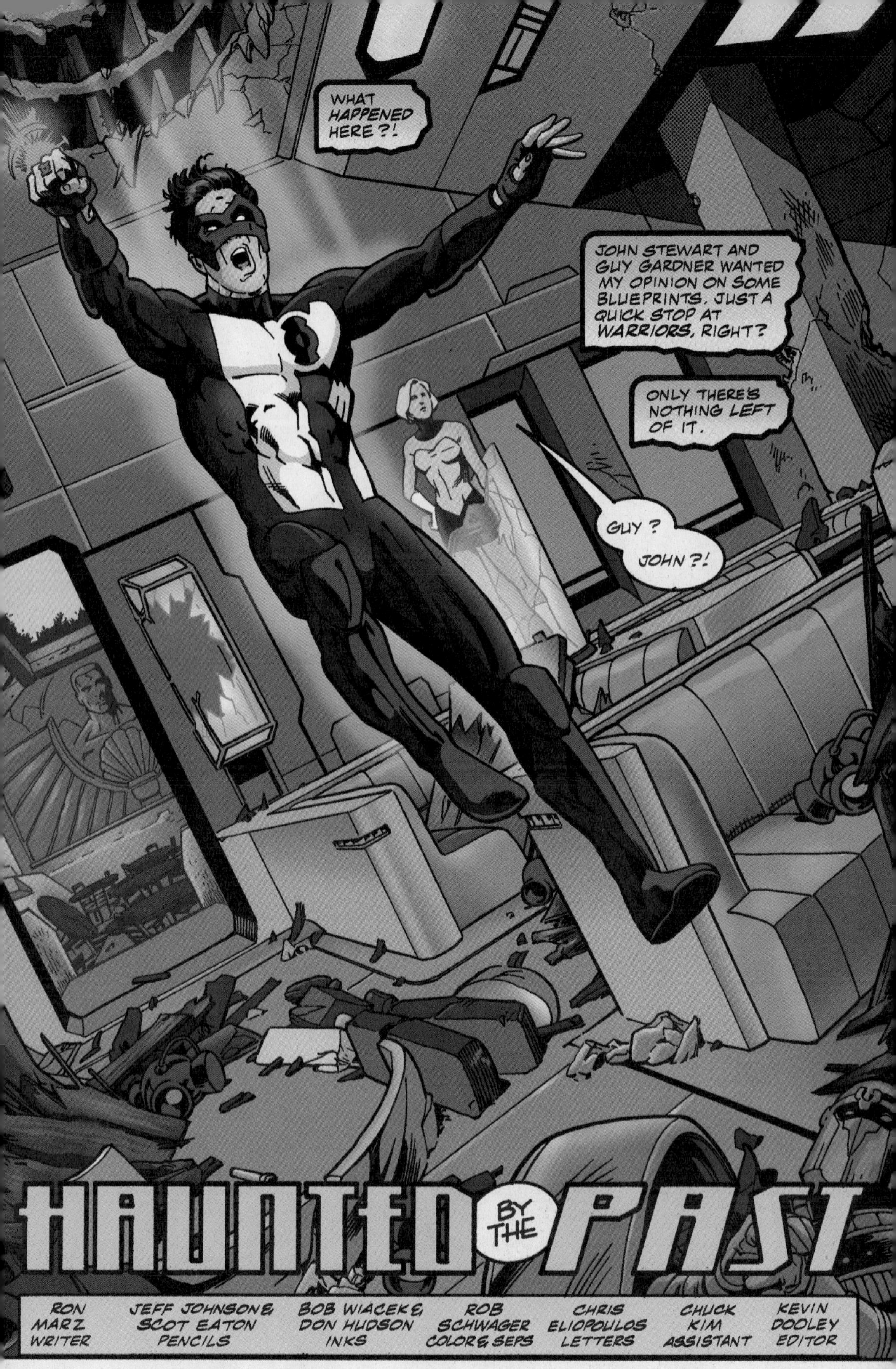
WHAT HAPPENED HERE?!
JOHN STEWART AND GUY GARDNER WANTED MY OPINION ON SOME BLUEPRINTS. JUST A QUICK STOP AT WARRIORS, RIGHT?
ONLY THERE'S NOTHING LEFT OF IT.
GUY?
JOHN?!
HAUNTED BY THE PAST
RON MARZ WRITER
JEFF JOHNSON & SCOT EATON PENCILS
BOB WIACEK & DON HUDSON INKS
ROB SCHWAGER COLOR & SEPS
CHRIS ELIOPOULOS LETTERS
CHUCK KIM ASSISTANT
KEVIN DOOLEY EDITOR

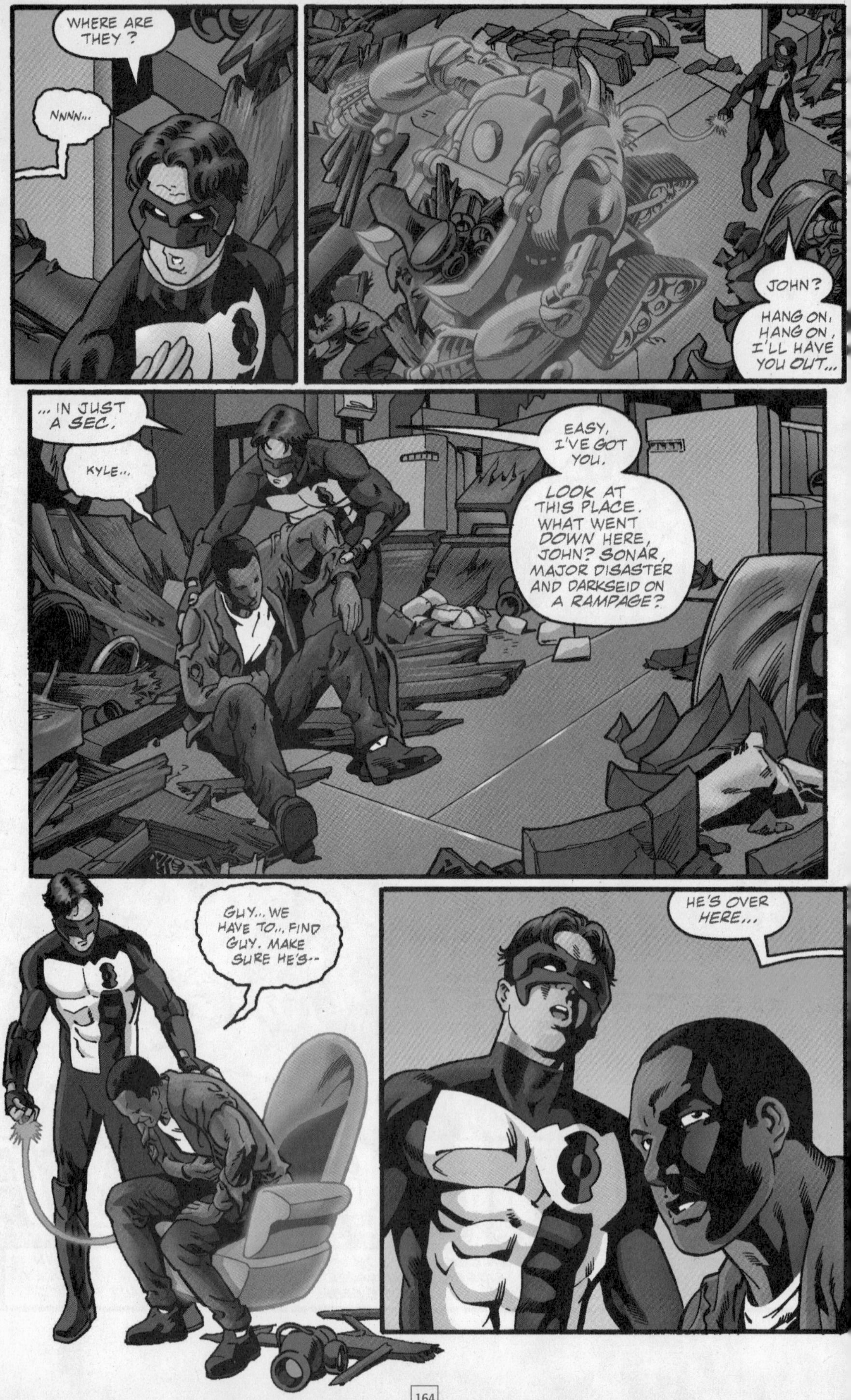
WHERE ARE THEY?
NNNN...
JOHN?
HANG ON, HANG ON, I'LL HAVE YOU OUT...
...IN JUST A SEC.
KYLE...
EASY, I'VE GOT YOU.
LOOK AT THIS PLACE. WHAT WENT DOWN HERE, JOHN? SONAR, MAJOR DISASTER AND DARKSEID ON A RAMPAGE?
GUY... WE HAVE TO... FIND GUY. MAKE SURE HE'S--
HE'S OVER HERE...

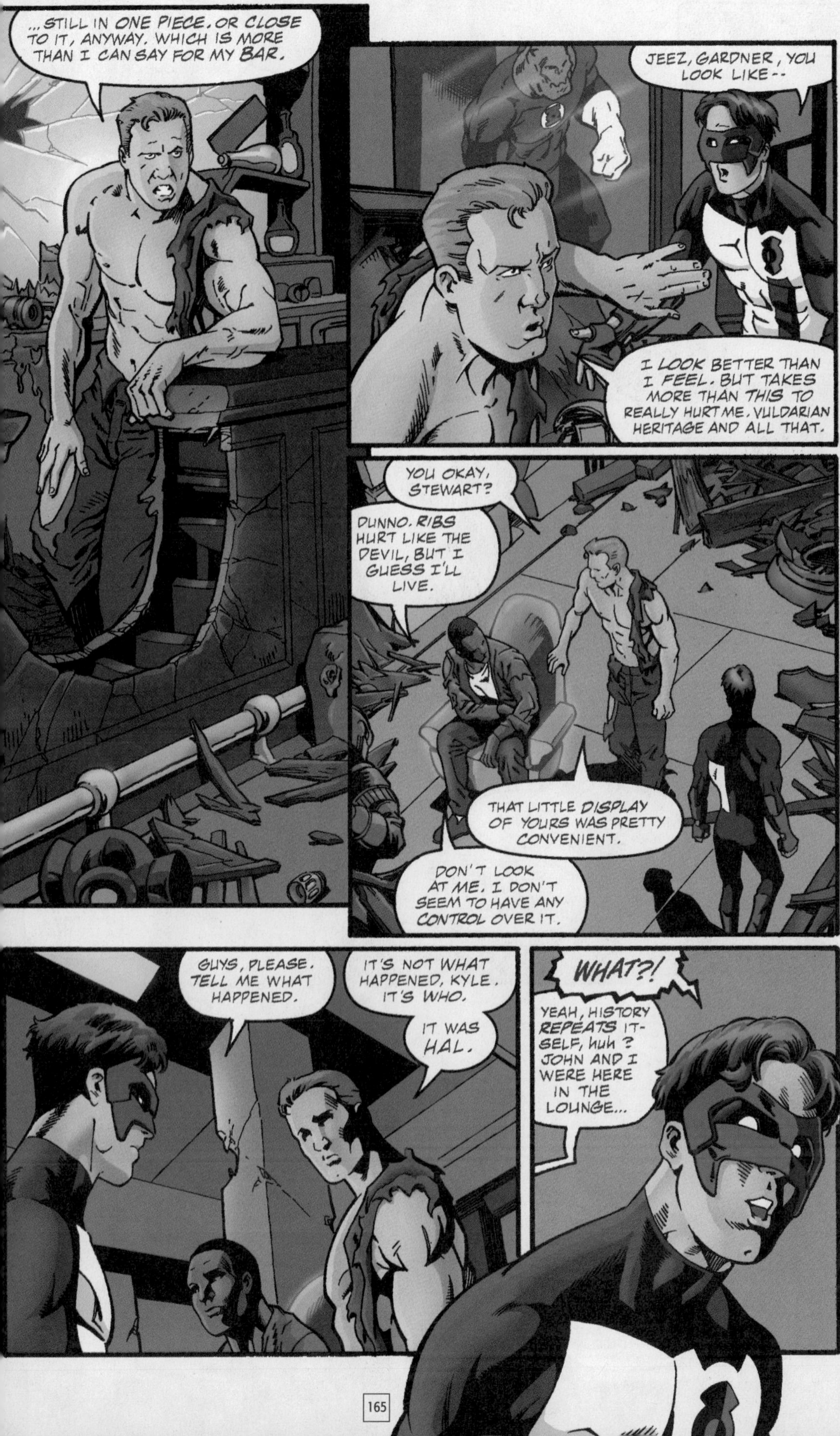
...STILL IN ONE PIECE. OR CLOSE TO IT, ANYWAY. WHICH IS MORE THAN I CAN SAY FOR MY BAR.
JEEZ, GARDNER, YOU LOOK LIKE--
I LOOK BETTER THAN I FEEL. BUT TAKES MORE THAN THIS TO REALLY HURT ME. VULDARIAN HERITAGE AND ALL THAT.
YOU OKAY, STEWART?
DUNNO. RIBS HURT LIKE THE DEVIL, BUT I GUESS I'LL LIVE.
THAT LITTLE DISPLAY OF YOURS WAS PRETTY CONVENIENT.
DON'T LOOK AT ME. I DON'T SEEM TO HAVE ANY CONTROL OVER IT.
GUYS, PLEASE. TELL ME WHAT HAPPENED.
IT'S NOT WHAT HAPPENED, KYLE. IT'S WHO.
IT WAS HAL.
WHAT?!
YEAH, HISTORY REPEATS IT-SELF, huh? JOHN AND I WERE HERE IN THE LOUNGE...

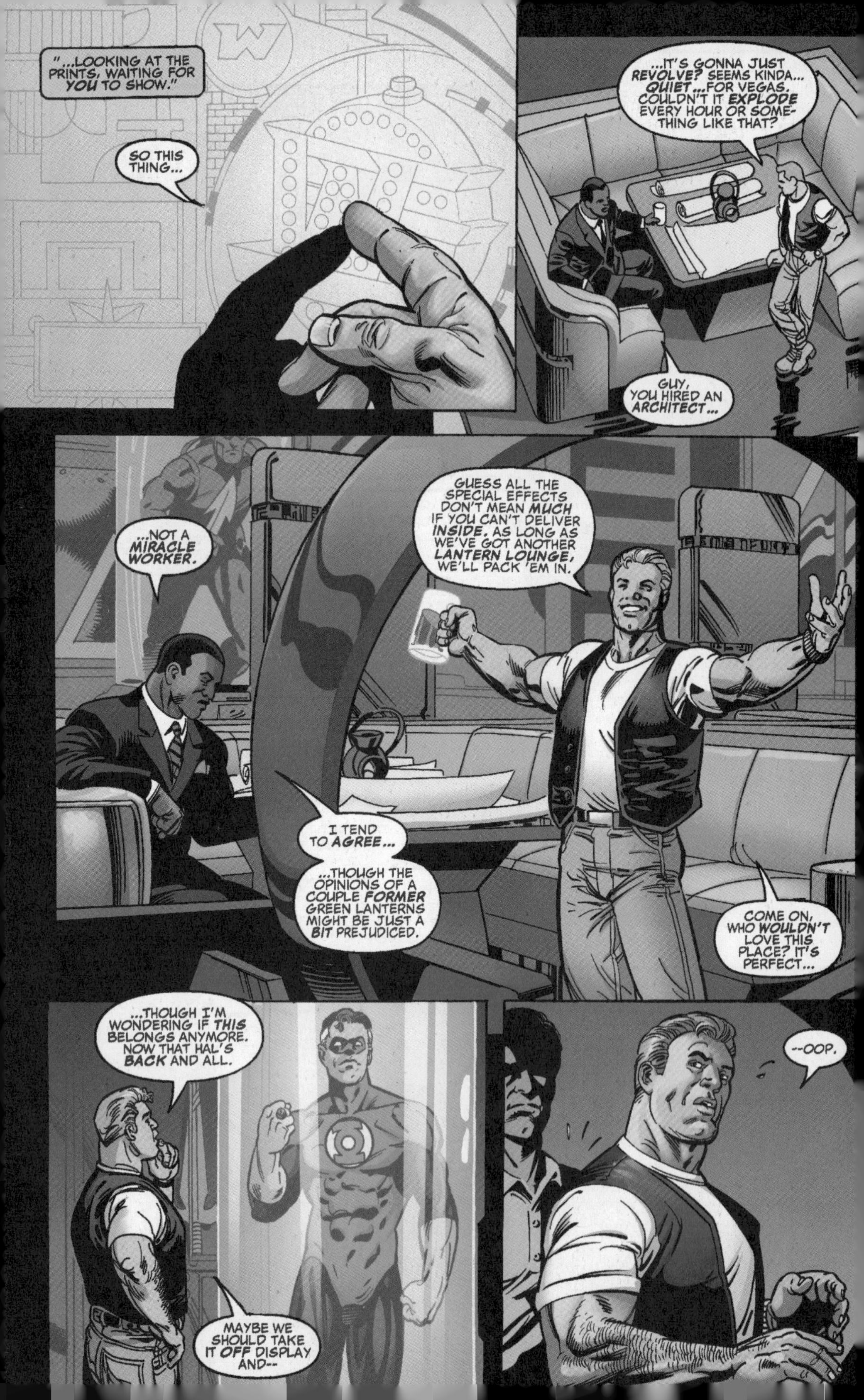
"...LOOKING AT THE PRINTS, WAITING FOR YOU TO SHOW."
SO THIS THING...
...IT'S GONNA JUST REVOLVE? SEEMS KINDA... QUIET...FOR VEGAS. COULDN'T IT EXPLODE EVERY HOUR OR SOMETHING LIKE THAT?
GUY, YOU HIRED AN ARCHITECT...
...NOT A MIRACLE WORKER.
GUESS ALL THE SPECIAL EFFECTS DON'T MEAN MUCH IF YOU CAN'T DELIVER INSIDE. AS LONG AS WE'VE GOT ANOTHER LANTERN LOUNGE, WE'LL PACK 'EM IN.
I TEND TO AGREE...
...THOUGH THE OPINIONS OF A COUPLE FORMER GREEN LANTERNS MIGHT BE JUST A BIT PREJUDICED.
COME ON, WHO WOULDN'T LOVE THIS PLACE? IT'S PERFECT...
...THOUGH I'M WONDERING IF THIS BELONGS ANYMORE. NOW THAT HAL'S BACK AND ALL.
MAYBE WE SHOULD TAKE IT OFF DISPLAY AND--
--OOP.

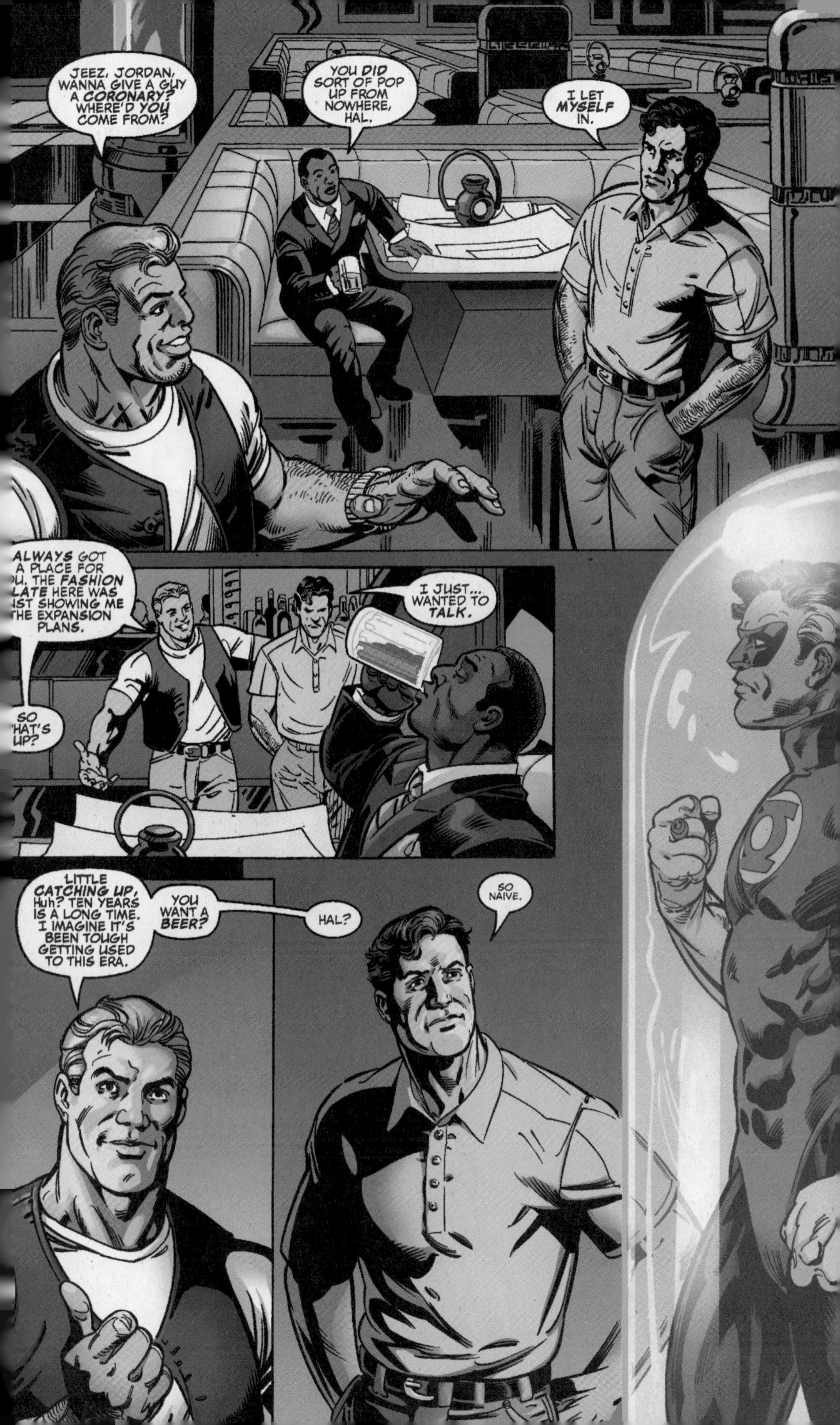
JEEZ, JORDAN, WANNA GIVE A GUY A CORONARY? WHERE'D YOU COME FROM?
YOU DID SORT OF POP UP FROM NOWHERE, HAL.
I LET MYSELF IN.
ALWAYS GOT A PLACE FOR OU. THE FASHION LATE HERE WAS IST SHOWING ME THE EXPANSION PLANS.
SO HAT'S UP?
I JUST... WANTED TO TALK.
LITTLE CATCHING UP, Huh? TEN YEARS IS A LONG TIME. I IMAGINE IT'S BEEN TOUGH GETTING USED TO THIS ERA.
YOU WANT A BEER?
HAL?
SO NAIVE.

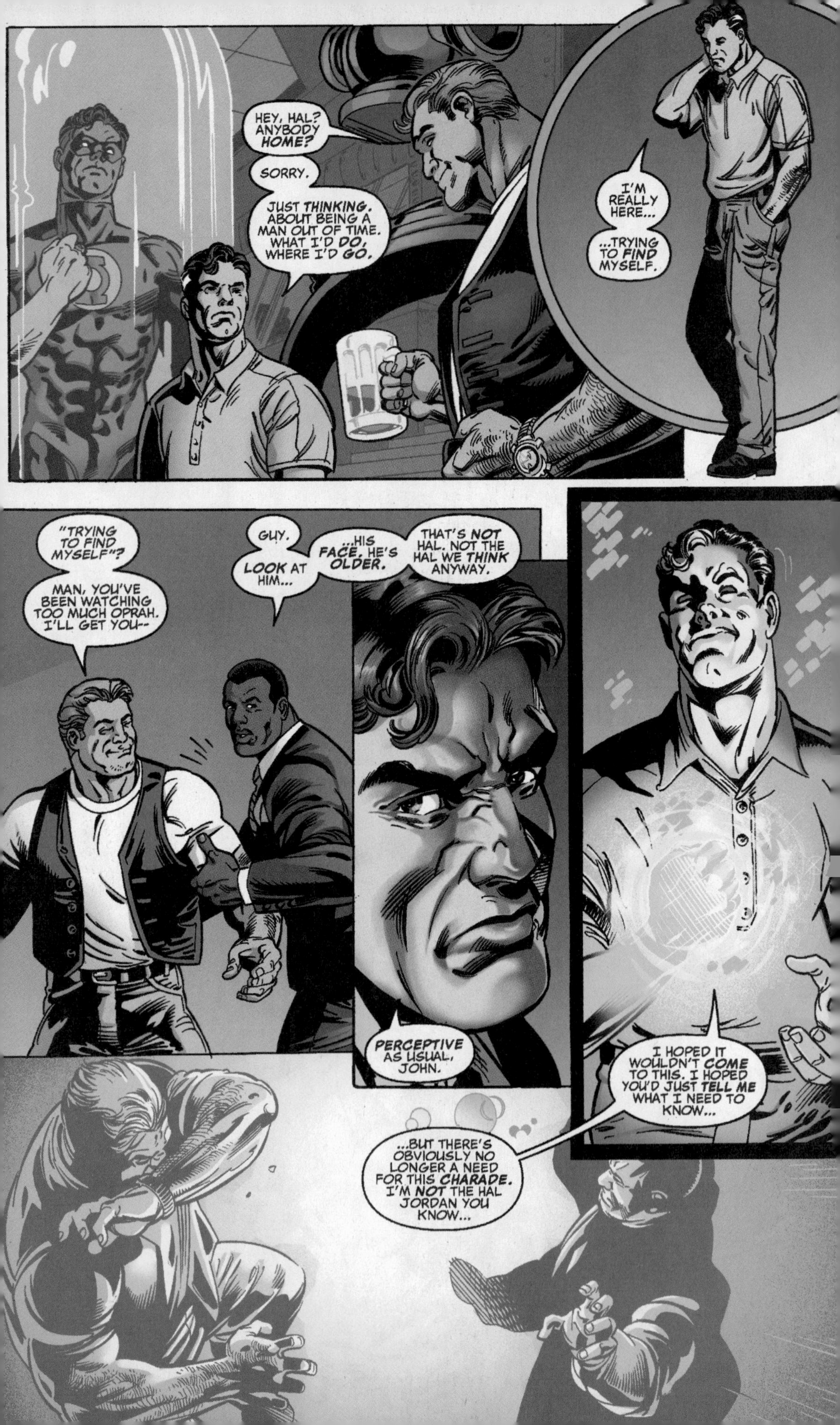
HEY, HAL? ANYBODY HOME?
SORRY.
JUST THINKING. ABOUT BEING A MAN OUT OF TIME. WHAT I'D DO, WHERE I'D GO.
I'M REALLY HERE...
...TRYING TO FIND MYSELF.
"TRYING TO FIND MYSELF"?
MAN, YOU'VE BEEN WATCHING TOO MUCH OPRAH. I'LL GET YOU--
GUY.
LOOK AT HIM...
...HIS FACE. HE'S OLDER.
THAT'S NOT HAL. NOT THE HAL WE THINK ANYWAY.
PERCEPTIVE AS USUAL, JOHN.
I HOPED IT WOULDN'T COME TO THIS. I HOPED YOU'D JUST TELL ME WHAT I NEED TO KNOW...
...BUT THERE'S OBVIOUSLY NO LONGER A NEED FOR THIS CHARADE. I'M NOT THE HAL JORDAN YOU KNOW...

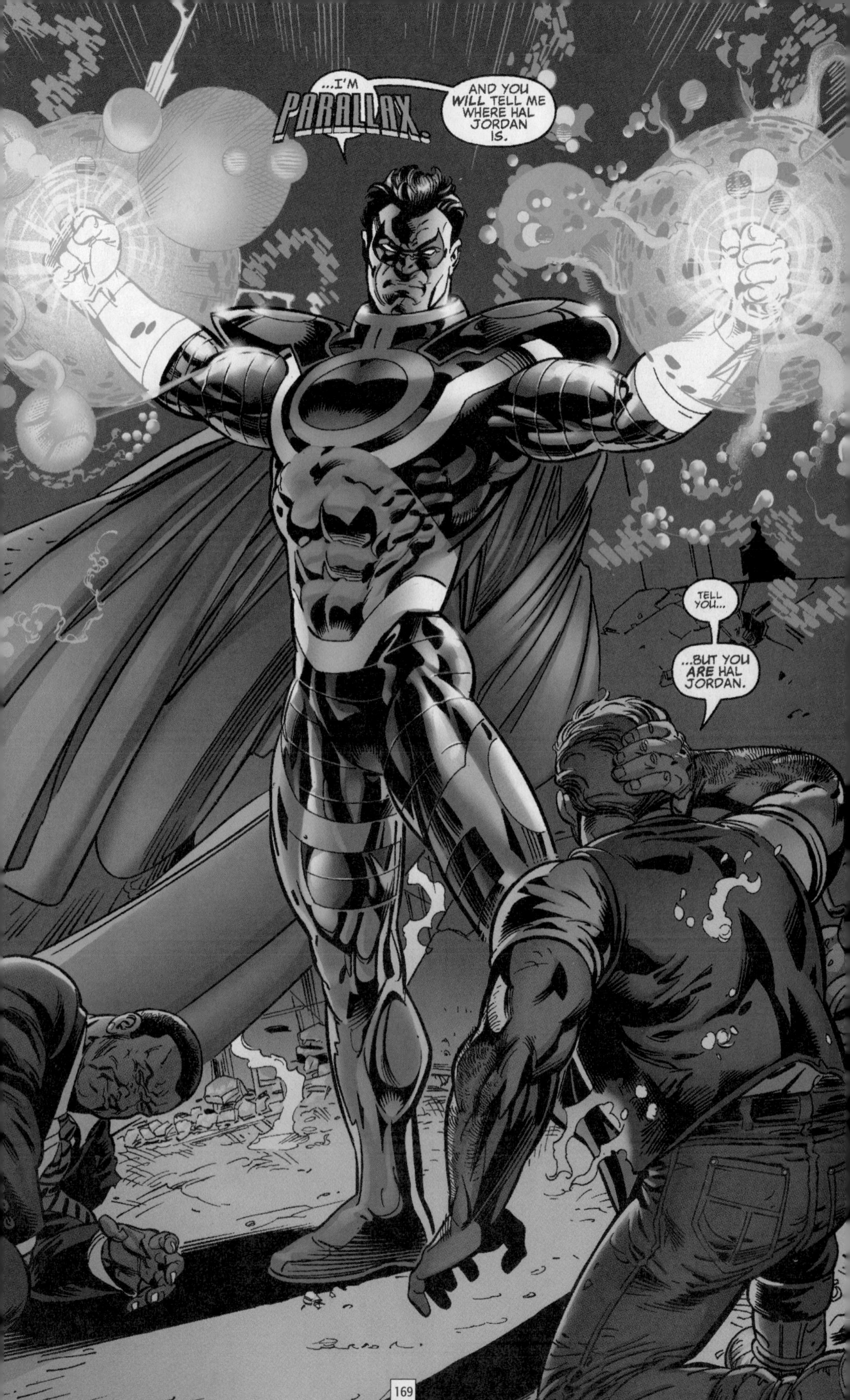

...I'M PARALLAX.
AND YOU WILL TELL ME WHERE HAL JORDAN IS.
TELL YOU...
...BUT YOU ARE HAL JORDAN.

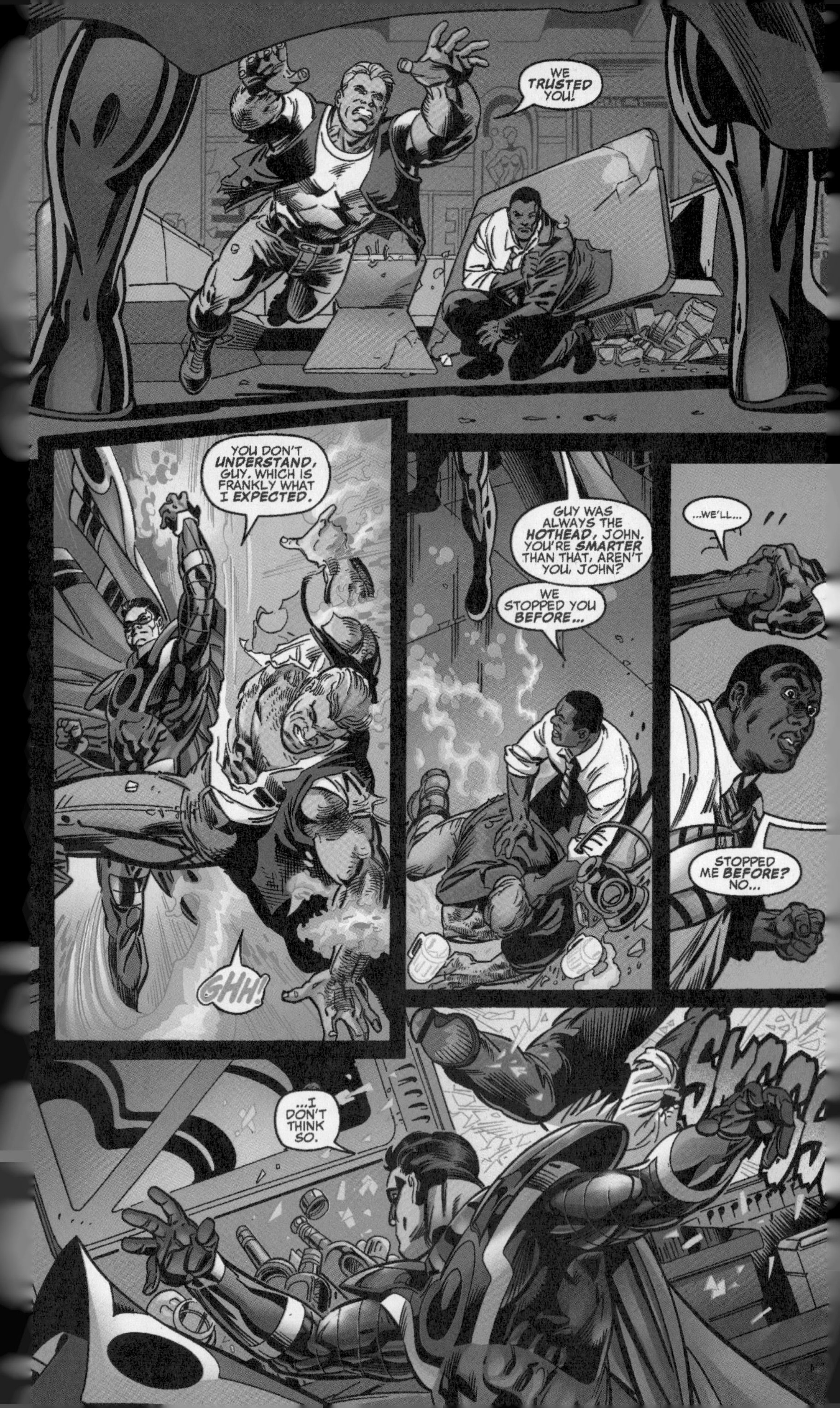
WE TRUSTED YOU!
YOU DON'T UNDERSTAND, GUY. WHICH IS FRANKLY WHAT I EXPECTED.
GHH!
GUY WAS ALWAYS THE HOTHEAD, JOHN. YOU'RE SMARTER THAN THAT, AREN'T YOU, JOHN?
WE STOPPED YOU BEFORE...
...WE'LL...
STOPPED ME BEFORE? NO...
...I DON'T THINK SO.

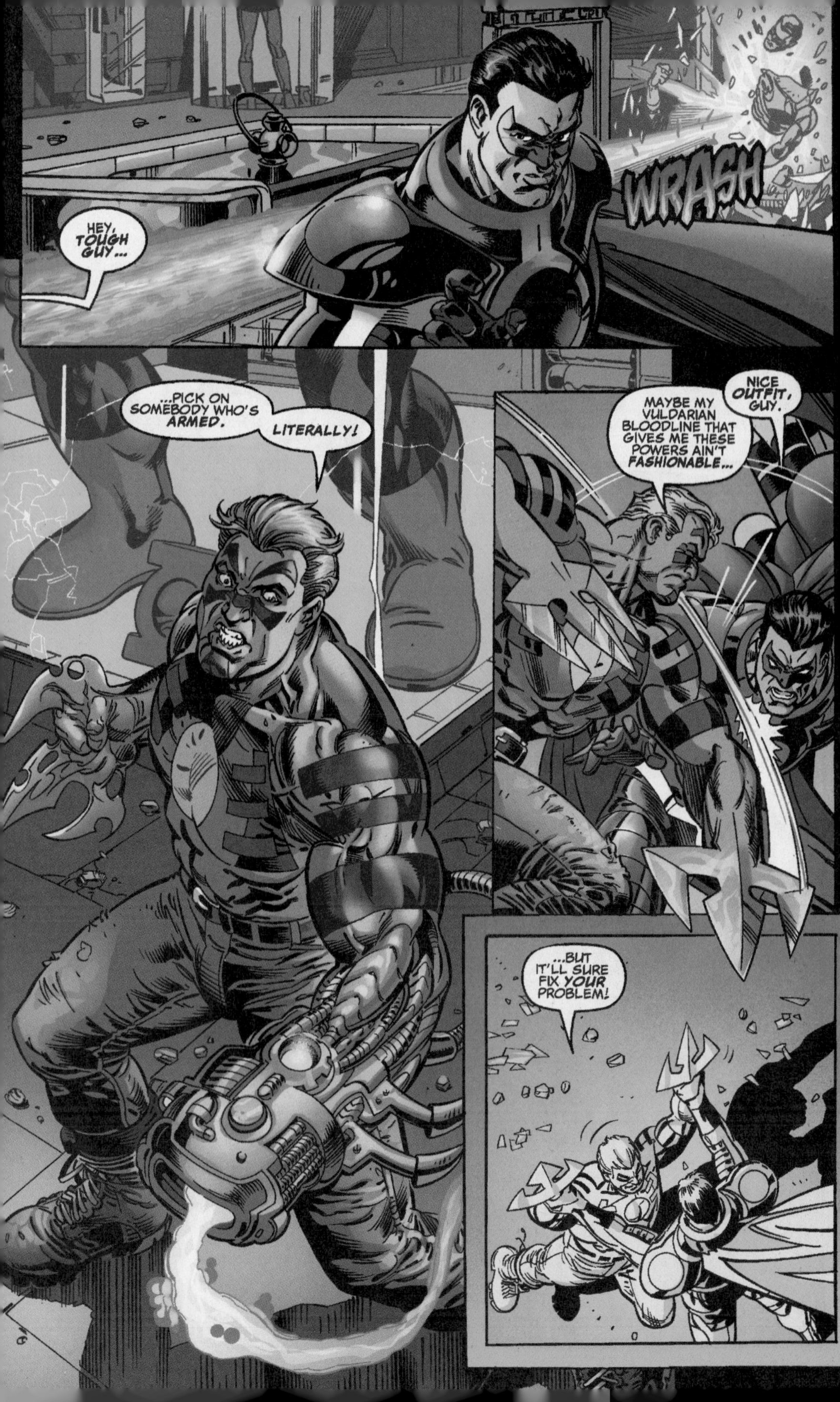

WRASH
HEY, TOUGH GUY...
...PICK ON SOMEBODY WHO'S ARMED.
LITERALLY!
NICE OUTFIT, GUY.
MAYBE MY VULDARIAN BLOODLINE THAT GIVES ME THESE POWERS AIN'T FASHIONABLE...
...BUT IT'LL SURE FIX YOUR PROBLEM!

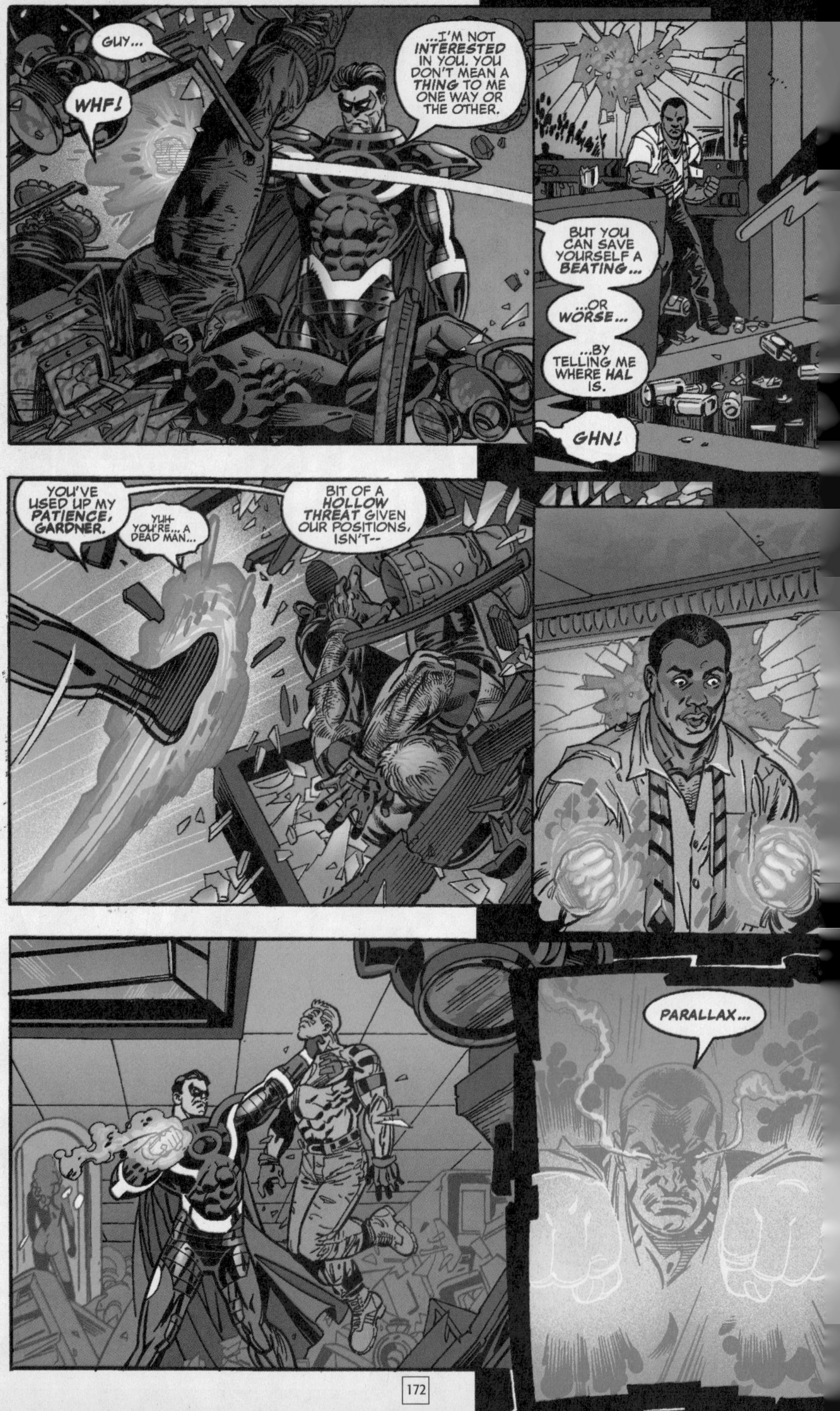
GUY...
WHF!
...I'M NOT INTERESTED IN YOU. YOU DON'T MEAN A THING TO ME ONE WAY OR THE OTHER.
BUT YOU CAN SAVE YOURSELF A BEATING...
...OR WORSE...
...BY TELLING ME WHERE HAL IS.
GHN!
YOU'VE USED UP MY PATIENCE, GARDNER.
YUH-YOU'RE... A DEAD MAN...
BIT OF A HOLLOW THREAT GIVEN OUR POSITIONS, ISN'T--
PARALLAX...

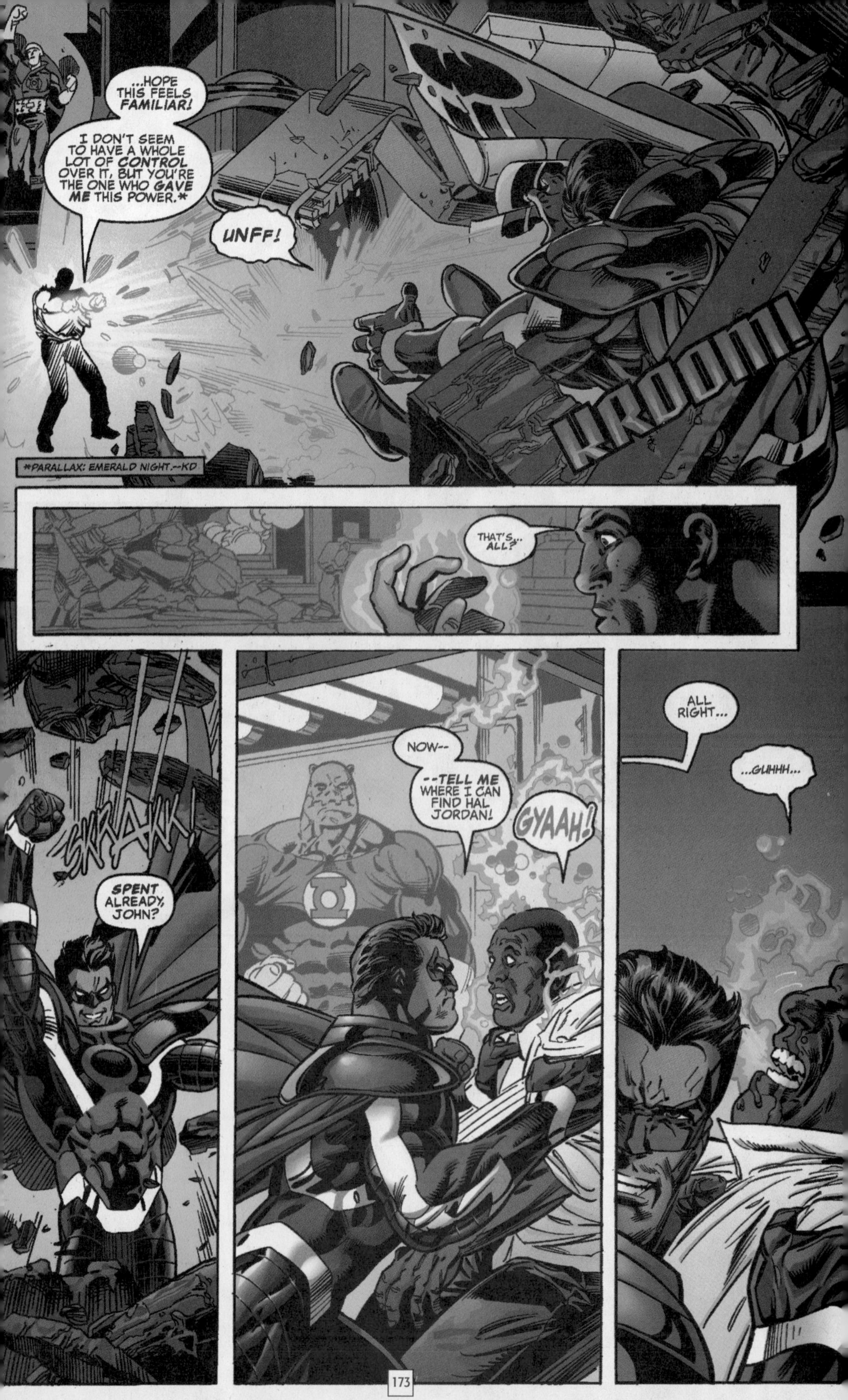
...HOPE THIS FEELS FAMILIAR!
I DON'T SEEM TO HAVE A WHOLE LOT OF CONTROL OVER IT, BUT YOU'RE THE ONE WHO GAVE ME THIS POWER.*
UNFF!
KROOM!
*PARALLAX: EMERALD NIGHT.--KD
THAT'S... ALL?
SKRAKK!
SPENT ALREADY, JOHN?
NOW--
--TELL ME WHERE I CAN FIND HAL JORDAN!
GYAAH!
ALL RIGHT...
...GUHHH...

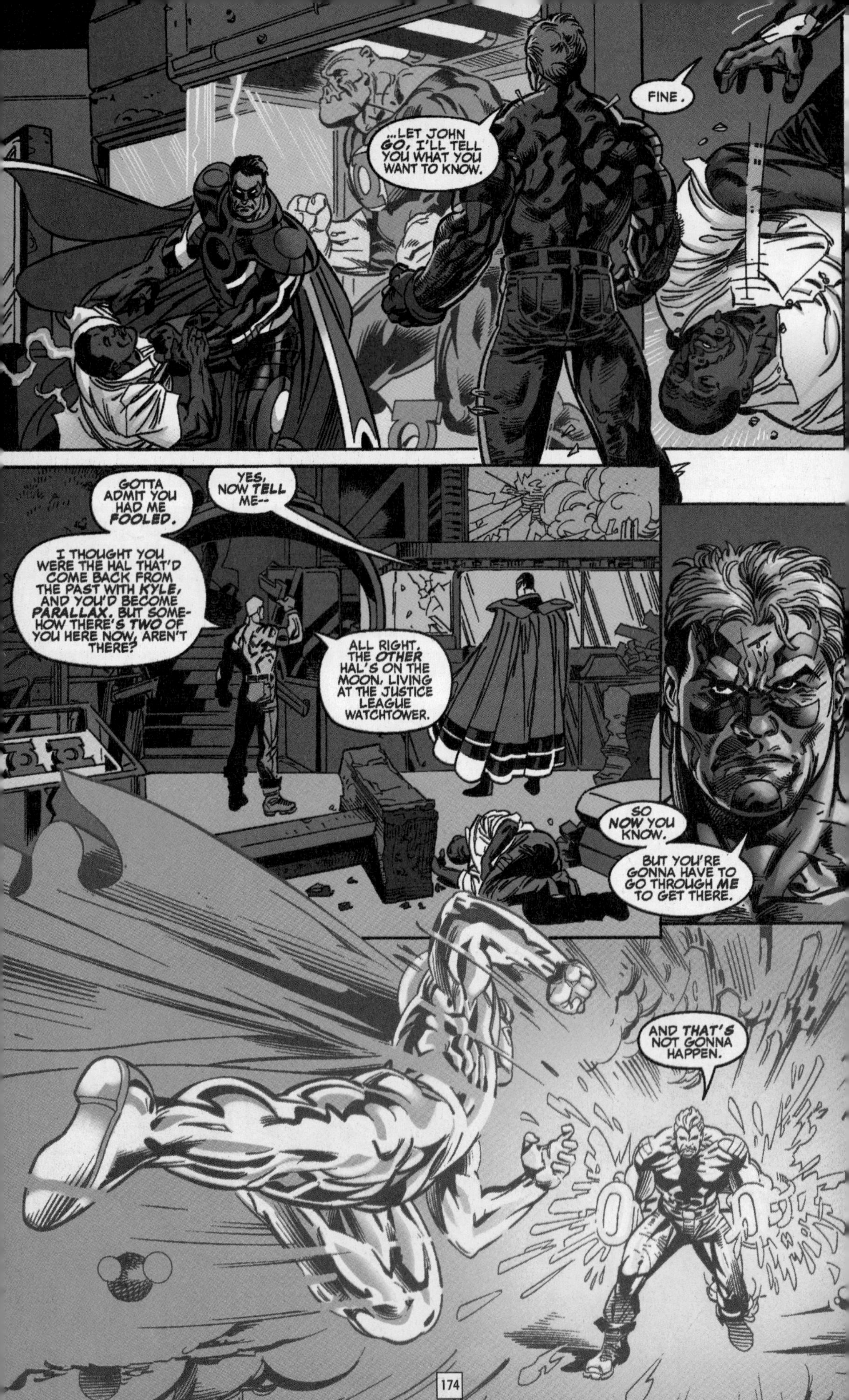
...LET JOHN GO, I'LL TELL YOU WHAT YOU WANT TO KNOW.
FINE.
GOTTA ADMIT YOU HAD ME FOOLED.
I THOUGHT YOU WERE THE HAL THAT'D COME BACK FROM THE PAST WITH KYLE, AND YOU'D BECOME PARALLAX. BUT SOMEHOW THERE'S TWO OF YOU HERE NOW, AREN'T THERE?
YES, NOW TELL ME--
ALL RIGHT. THE OTHER HAL'S ON THE MOON, LIVING AT THE JUSTICE LEAGUE WATCHTOWER.
SO NOW YOU KNOW.
BUT YOU'RE GONNA HAVE TO GO THROUGH ME TO GET THERE.
AND THAT'S NOT GONNA HAPPEN.

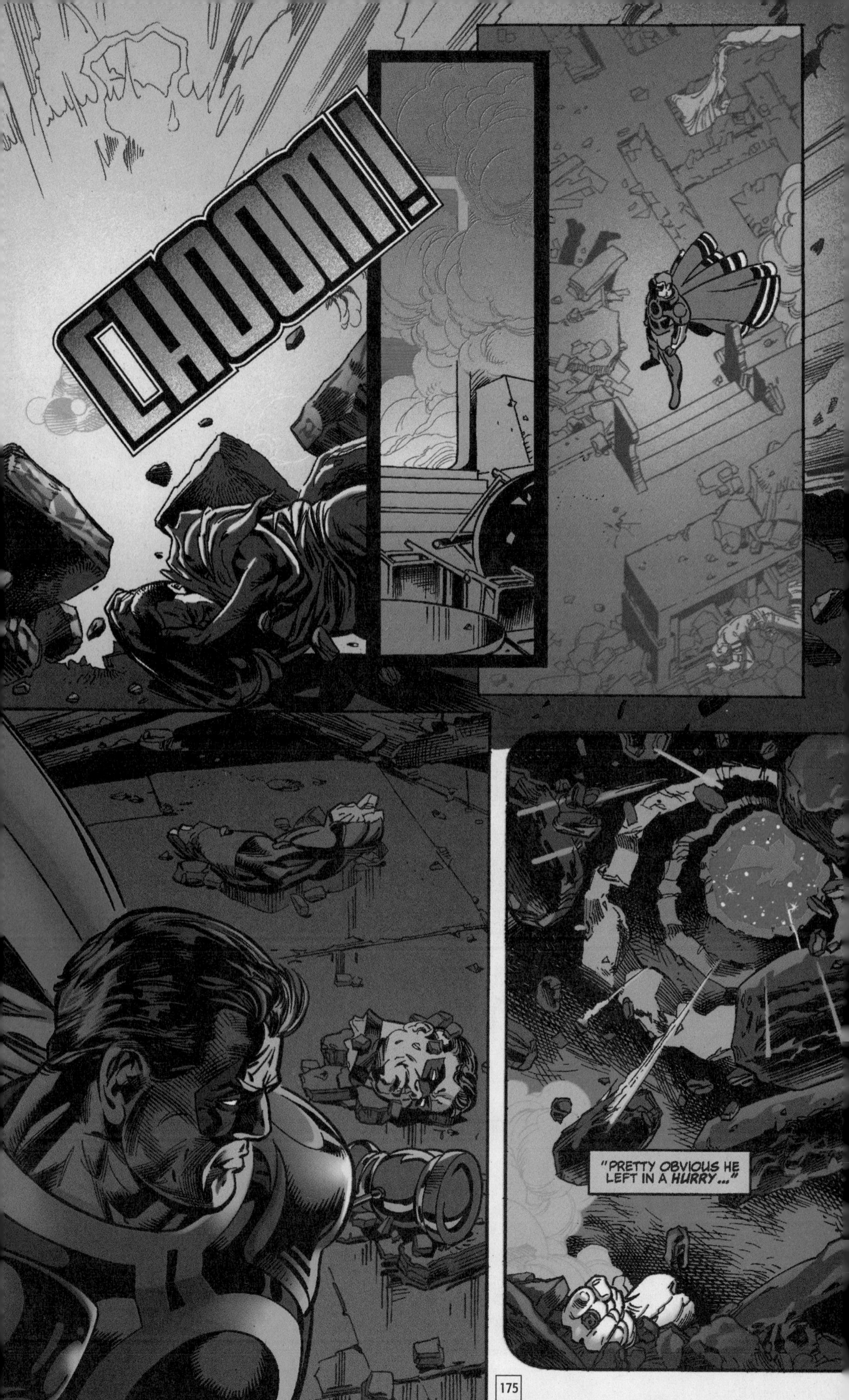
CHOOM!
"PRETTY OBVIOUS HE LEFT IN A HURRY..."

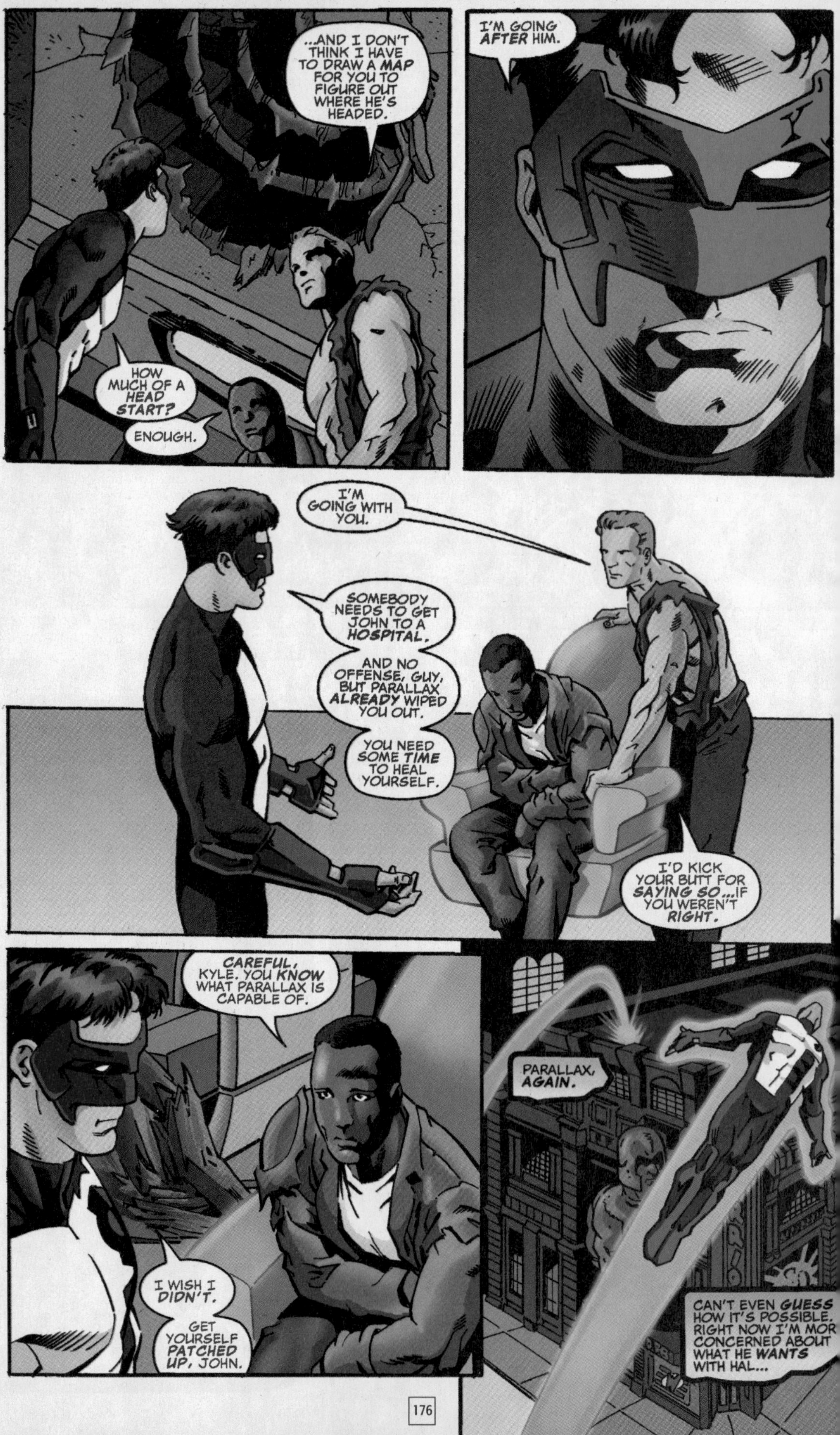
...AND I DON'T THINK I HAVE TO DRAW A MAP FOR YOU TO FIGURE OUT WHERE HE'S HEADED.
HOW MUCH OF A HEAD START?
ENOUGH.
I'M GOING AFTER HIM.
I'M GOING WITH YOU.
SOMEBODY NEEDS TO GET JOHN TO A HOSPITAL.
AND NO OFFENSE, GUY, BUT PARALLAX ALREADY WIPED YOU OUT.
YOU NEED SOME TIME TO HEAL YOURSELF.
I'D KICK YOUR BUTT FOR SAYING SO...IF YOU WEREN'T RIGHT.
CAREFUL, KYLE. YOU KNOW WHAT PARALLAX IS CAPABLE OF.
I WISH I DIDN'T.
GET YOURSELF PATCHED UP, JOHN.
PARALLAX, AGAIN.
CAN'T EVEN GUESS HOW IT'S POSSIBLE. RIGHT NOW I'M MOR CONCERNED ABOUT WHAT HE WANTS WITH HAL...

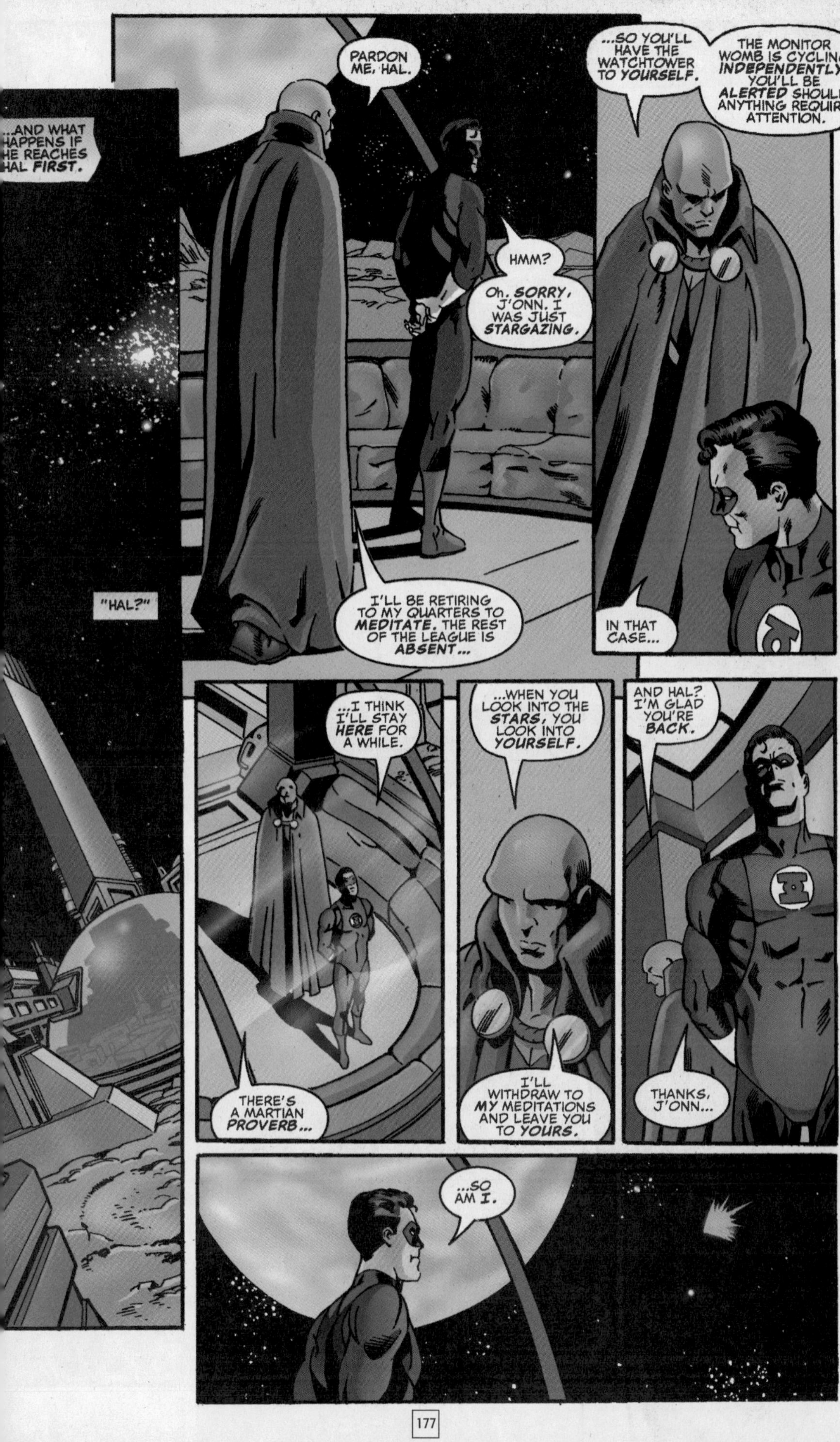
...AND WHAT HAPPENS IF HE REACHES HAL FIRST.
"HAL?"
PARDON ME, HAL.
HMM?
Oh. SORRY, J'ONN. I WAS JUST STARGAZING.
I'LL BE RETIRING TO MY QUARTERS TO MEDITATE. THE REST OF THE LEAGUE IS ABSENT...
...SO YOU'LL HAVE THE WATCHTOWER TO YOURSELF.
THE MONITOR WOMB IS CYCLING INDEPENDENTLY. YOU'LL BE ALERTED SHOULD ANYTHING REQUIRE ATTENTION.
IN THAT CASE...
...I THINK I'LL STAY HERE FOR A WHILE.
THERE'S A MARTIAN PROVERB...
...WHEN YOU LOOK INTO THE STARS, YOU LOOK INTO YOURSELF.
I'LL WITHDRAW TO MY MEDITATIONS AND LEAVE YOU TO YOURS.
AND HAL? I'M GLAD YOU'RE BACK.
THANKS, J'ONN...
...SO AM I.

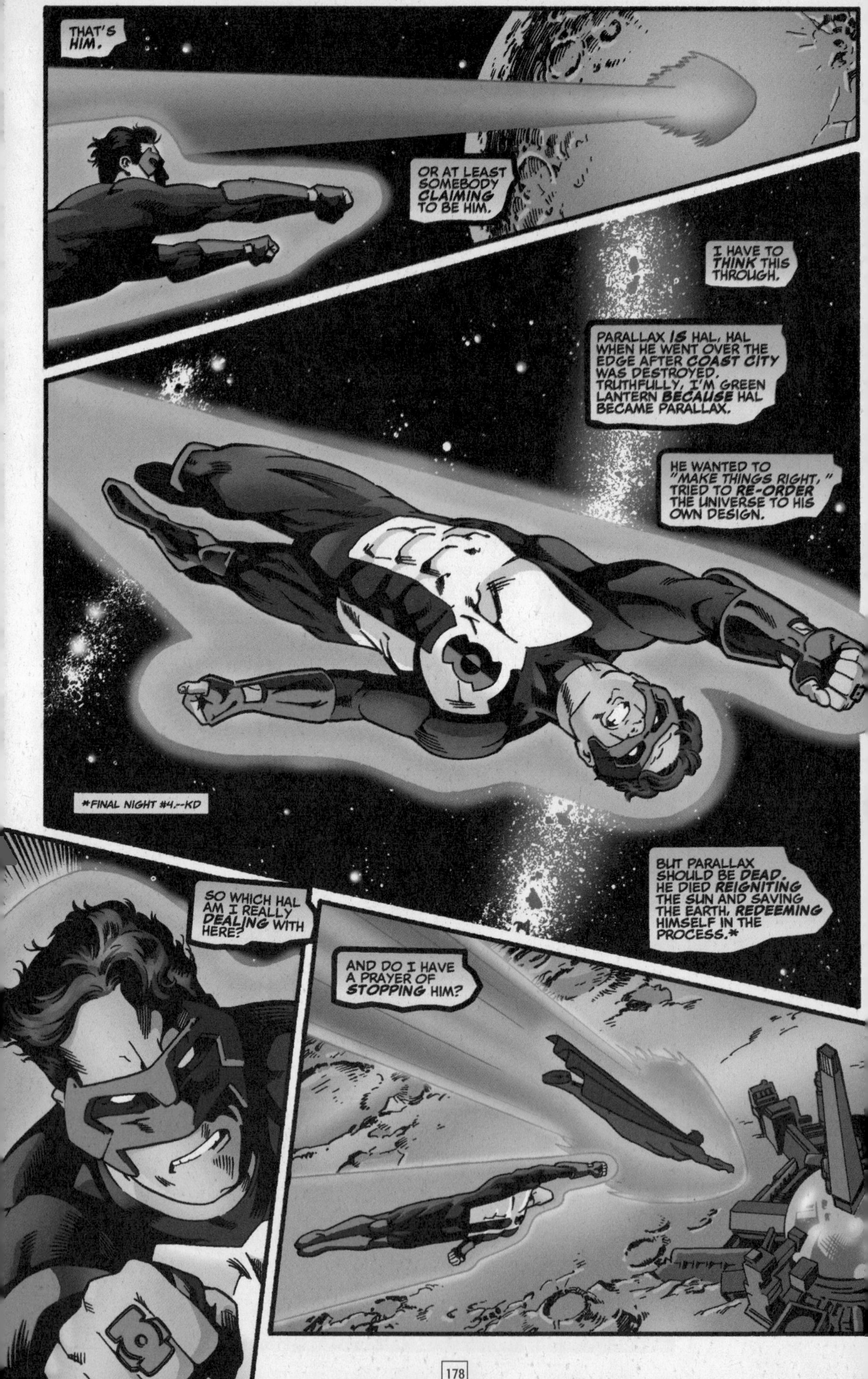
THAT'S HIM.
OR AT LEAST SOMEBODY CLAIMING TO BE HIM.
I HAVE TO THINK THIS THROUGH.
PARALLAX IS HAL. HAL WHEN HE WENT OVER THE EDGE AFTER COAST CITY WAS DESTROYED. TRUTHFULLY, I'M GREEN LANTERN BECAUSE HAL BECAME PARALLAX.
HE WANTED TO "MAKE THINGS RIGHT," TRIED TO RE-ORDER THE UNIVERSE TO HIS OWN DESIGN.
*FINAL NIGHT #4.--KD
BUT PARALLAX SHOULD BE DEAD. HE DIED REIGNITING THE SUN AND SAVING THE EARTH, REDEEMING HIMSELF IN THE PROCESS.*
SO WHICH HAL AM I REALLY DEALING WITH HERE?
AND DO I HAVE A PRAYER OF STOPPING HIM?

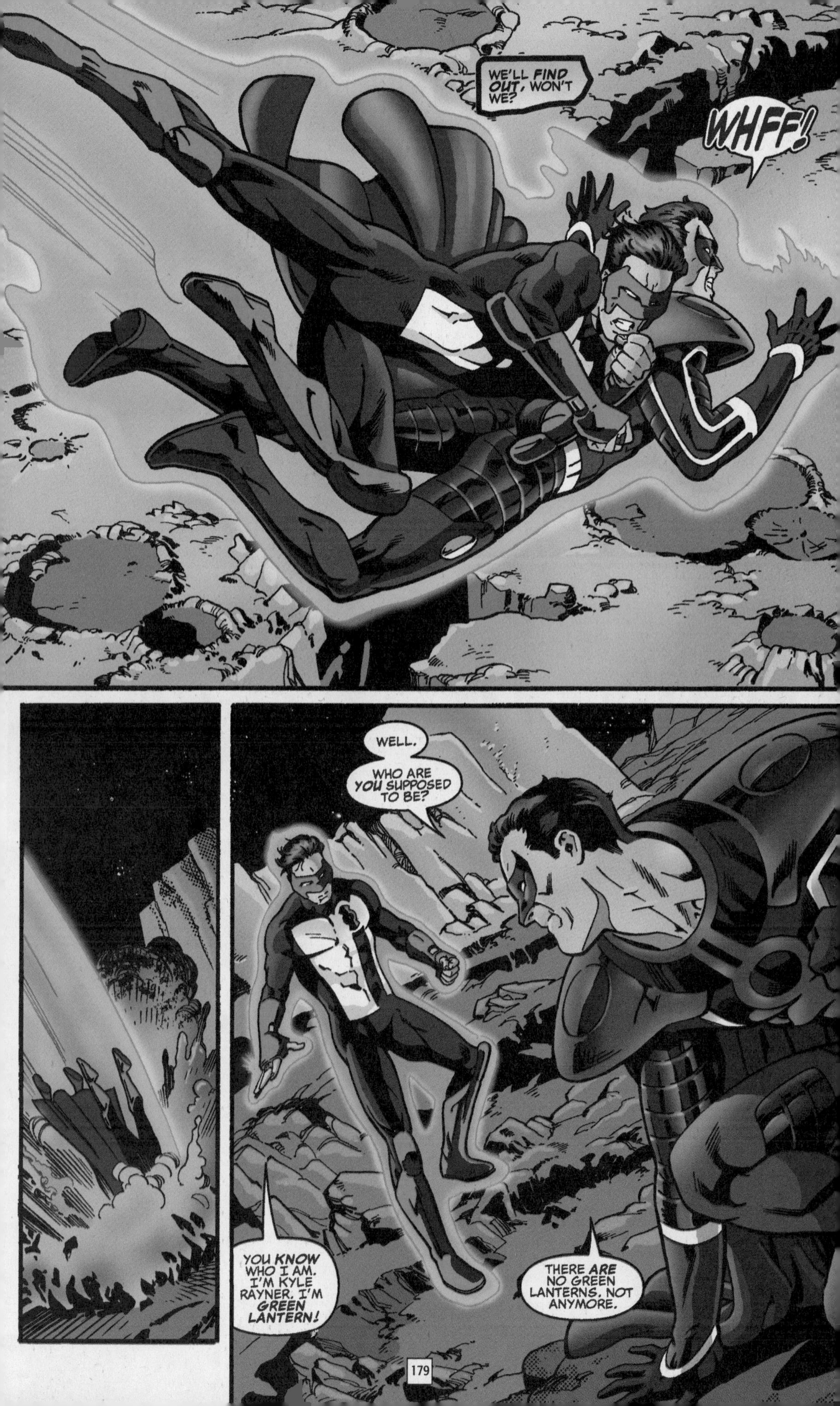
WE'LL FIND OUT, WON'T WE?
WHFF!
WELL.
WHO ARE YOU SUPPOSED TO BE?
YOU KNOW WHO I AM. I'M KYLE RAYNER. I'M GREEN LANTERN!
THERE ARE NO GREEN LANTERNS. NOT ANYMORE.

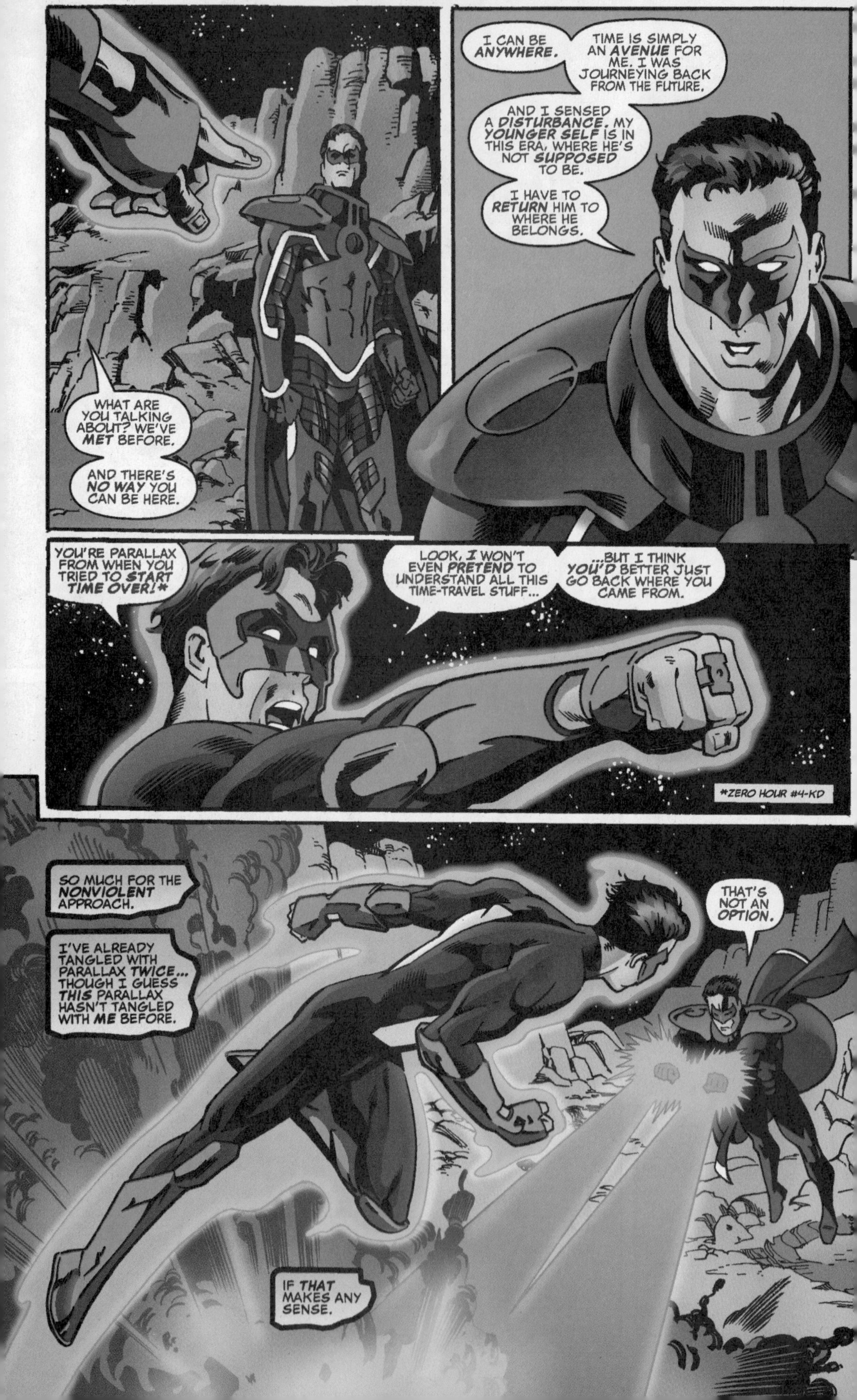

I CAN BE ANYWHERE.
TIME IS SIMPLY AN AVENUE FOR ME. I WAS JOURNEYING BACK FROM THE FUTURE.
AND I SENSED A DISTURBANCE. MY YOUNGER SELF IS IN THIS ERA, WHERE HE'S NOT SUPPOSED TO BE.
I HAVE TO RETURN HIM TO WHERE HE BELONGS.
WHAT ARE YOU TALKING ABOUT? WE'VE MET BEFORE.
AND THERE'S NO WAY YOU CAN BE HERE.
YOU'RE PARALLAX FROM WHEN YOU TRIED TO START TIME OVER!*
LOOK, I WON'T EVEN PRETEND TO UNDERSTAND ALL THIS TIME-TRAVEL STUFF...
...BUT I THINK YOU'D BETTER JUST GO BACK WHERE YOU CAME FROM.
*ZERO HOUR #4-KD
SO MUCH FOR THE NONVIOLENT APPROACH.
I'VE ALREADY TANGLED WITH PARALLAX TWICE... THOUGH I GUESS THIS PARALLAX HASN'T TANGLED WITH ME BEFORE.
THAT'S NOT AN OPTION.
IF THAT MAKES ANY SENSE.

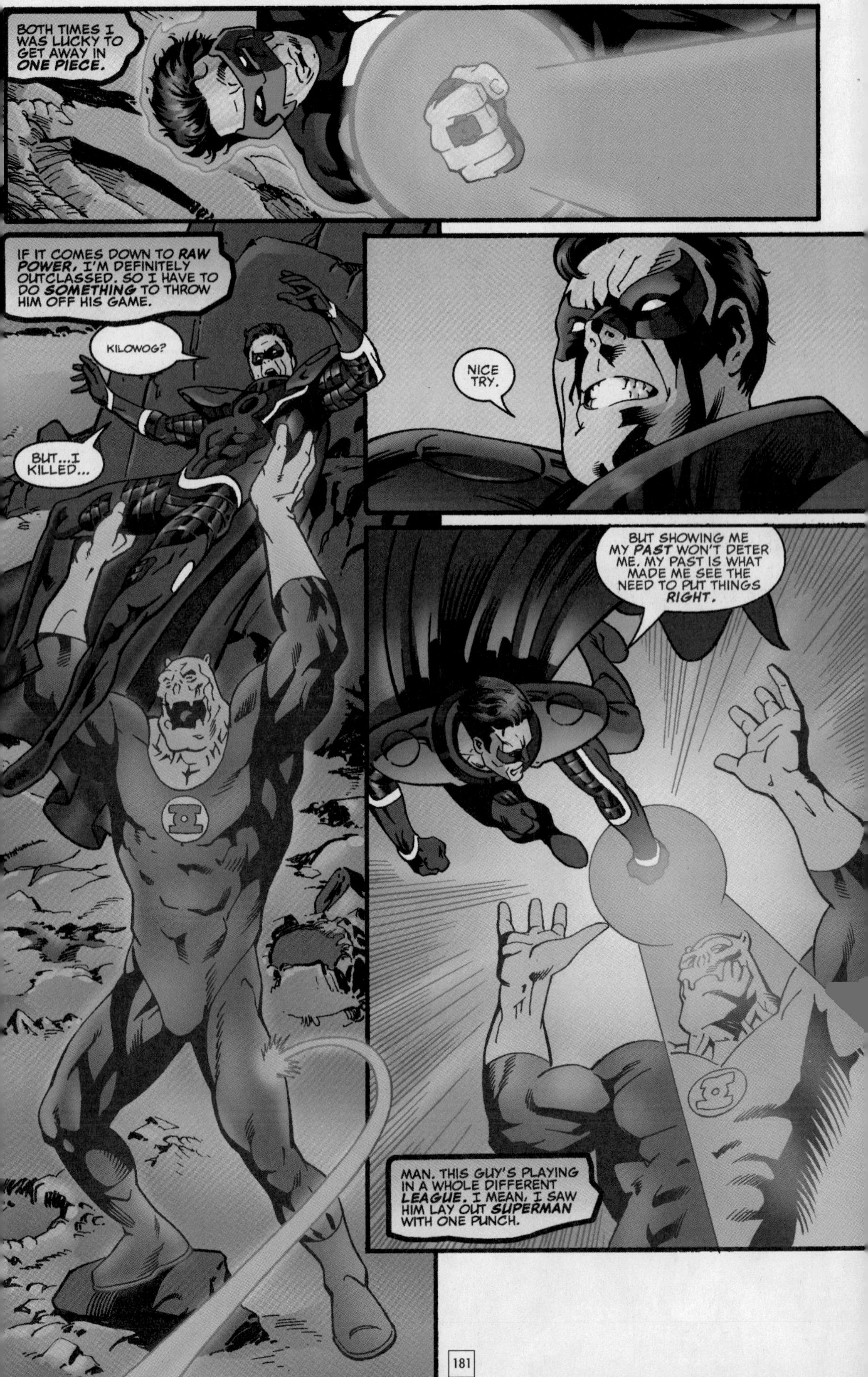

BOTH TIMES I WAS LUCKY TO GET AWAY IN ONE PIECE.
IF IT COMES DOWN TO RAW POWER, I'M DEFINITELY OUTCLASSED. SO I HAVE TO DO SOMETHING TO THROW HIM OFF HIS GAME.
KILOWOG?
BUT...I KILLED...
NICE TRY.
BUT SHOWING ME MY PAST WON'T DETER ME. MY PAST IS WHAT MADE ME SEE THE NEED TO PUT THINGS RIGHT.
MAN. THIS GUY'S PLAYING IN A WHOLE DIFFERENT LEAGUE. I MEAN, I SAW HIM LAY OUT SUPERMAN WITH ONE PUNCH.

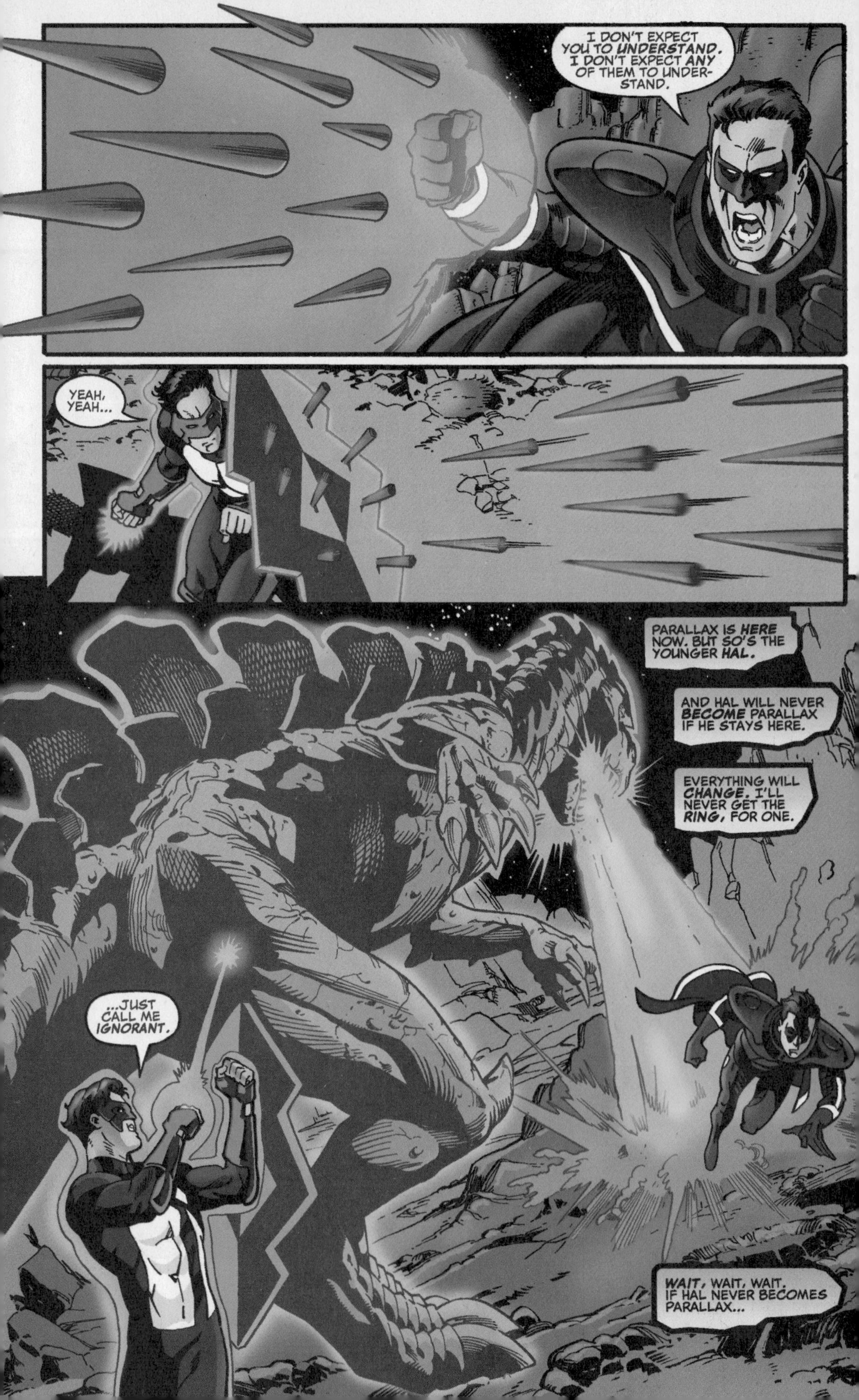
I DON'T EXPECT YOU TO UNDERSTAND. I DON'T EXPECT ANY OF THEM TO UNDERSTAND.
YEAH, YEAH...
PARALLAX IS HERE NOW. BUT SO'S THE YOUNGER HAL.
AND HAL WILL NEVER BECOME PARALLAX IF HE STAYS HERE.
EVERYTHING WILL CHANGE. I'LL NEVER GET THE RING, FOR ONE.
...JUST CALL ME IGNORANT.
WAIT, WAIT, WAIT. IF HAL NEVER BECOMES PARALLAX...

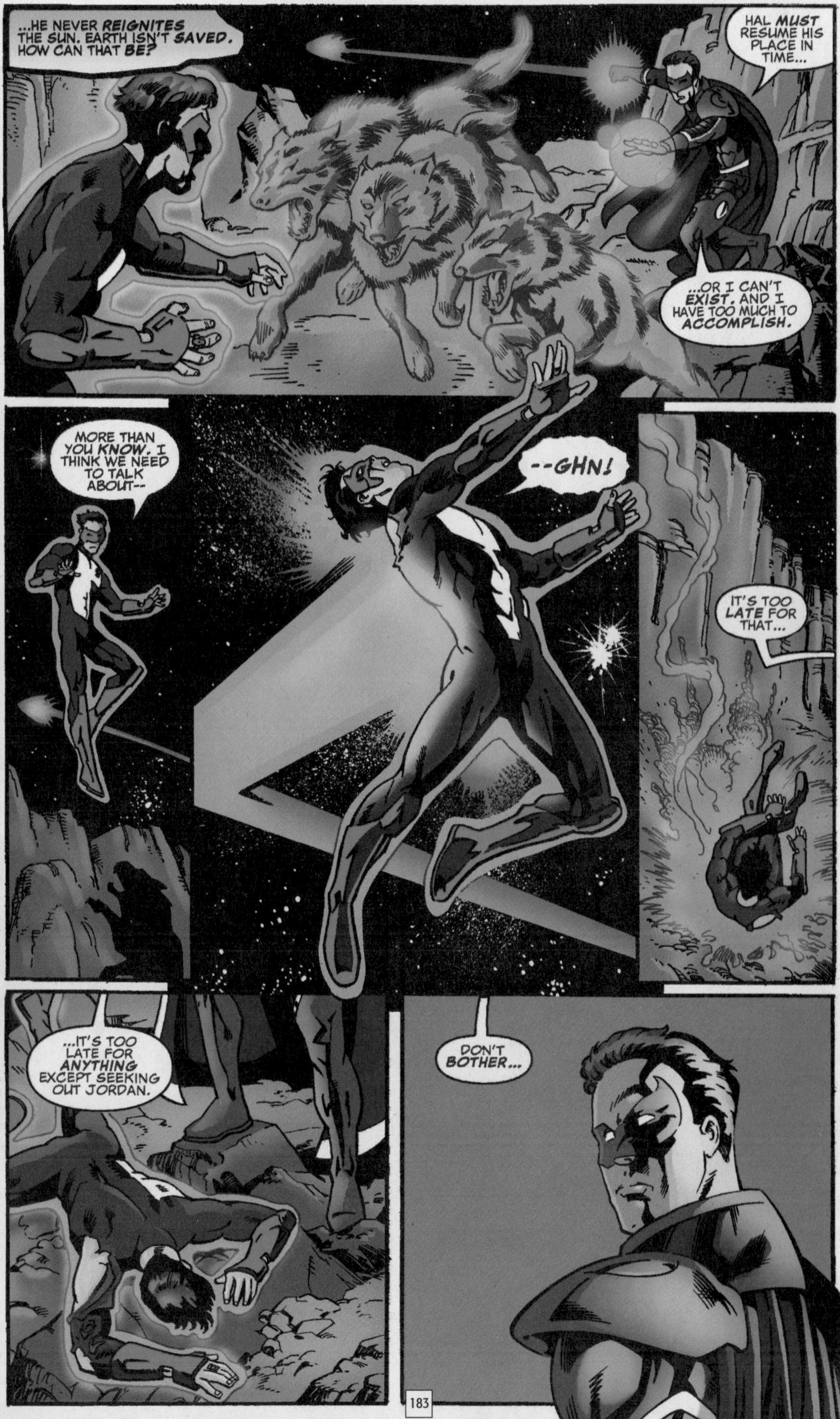
...HE NEVER REIGNITES THE SUN. EARTH ISN'T SAVED. HOW CAN THAT BE?
HAL MUST RESUME HIS PLACE IN TIME...
...OR I CAN'T EXIST. AND I HAVE TOO MUCH TO ACCOMPLISH.
MORE THAN YOU KNOW. I THINK WE NEED TO TALK ABOUT--
--GHN!
IT'S TOO LATE FOR THAT...
...IT'S TOO LATE FOR ANYTHING EXCEPT SEEKING OUT JORDAN.
DON'T BOTHER...

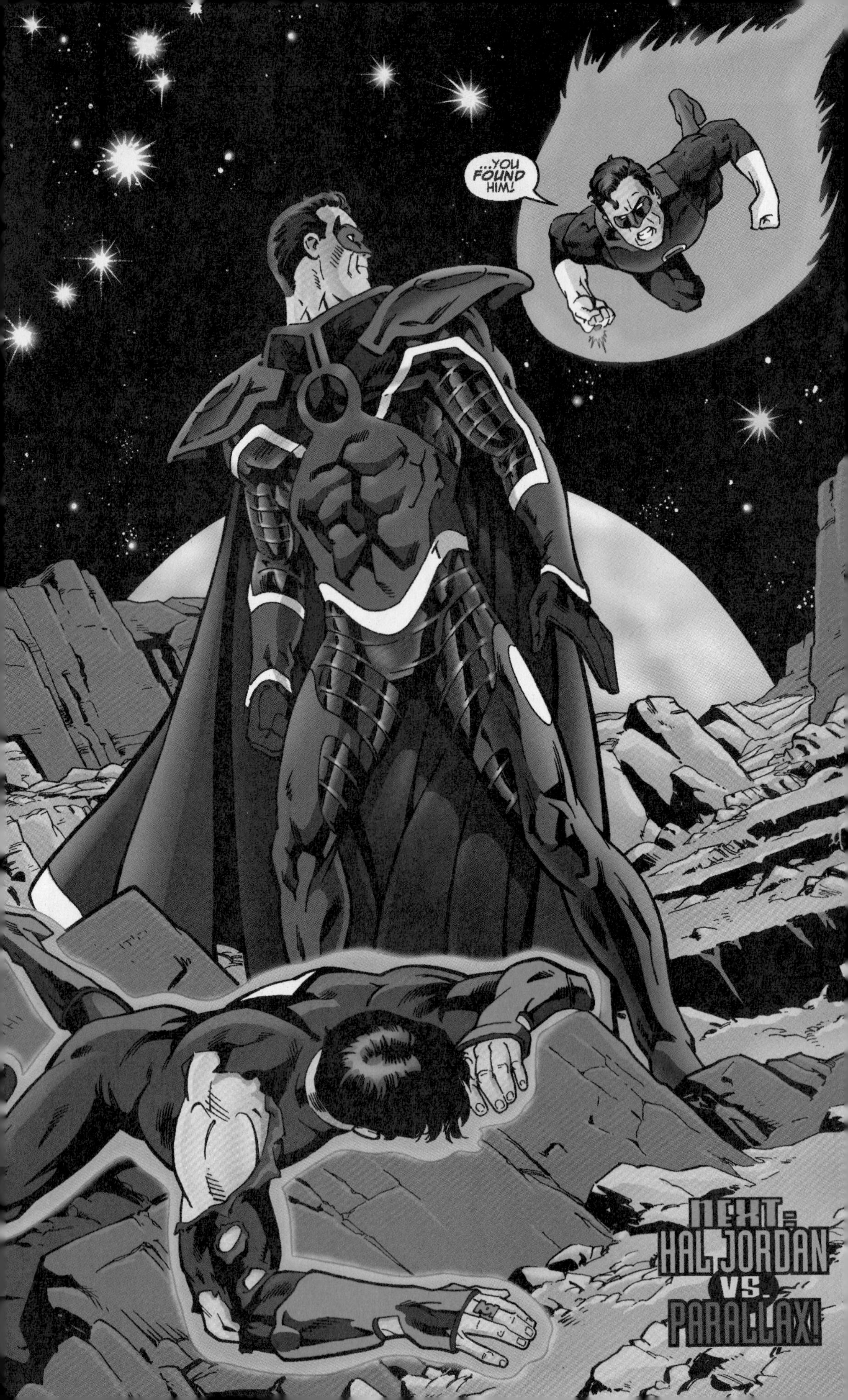
...YOU FOUND HIM!
NEXT: HAL JORDAN VS. PARALLAX!

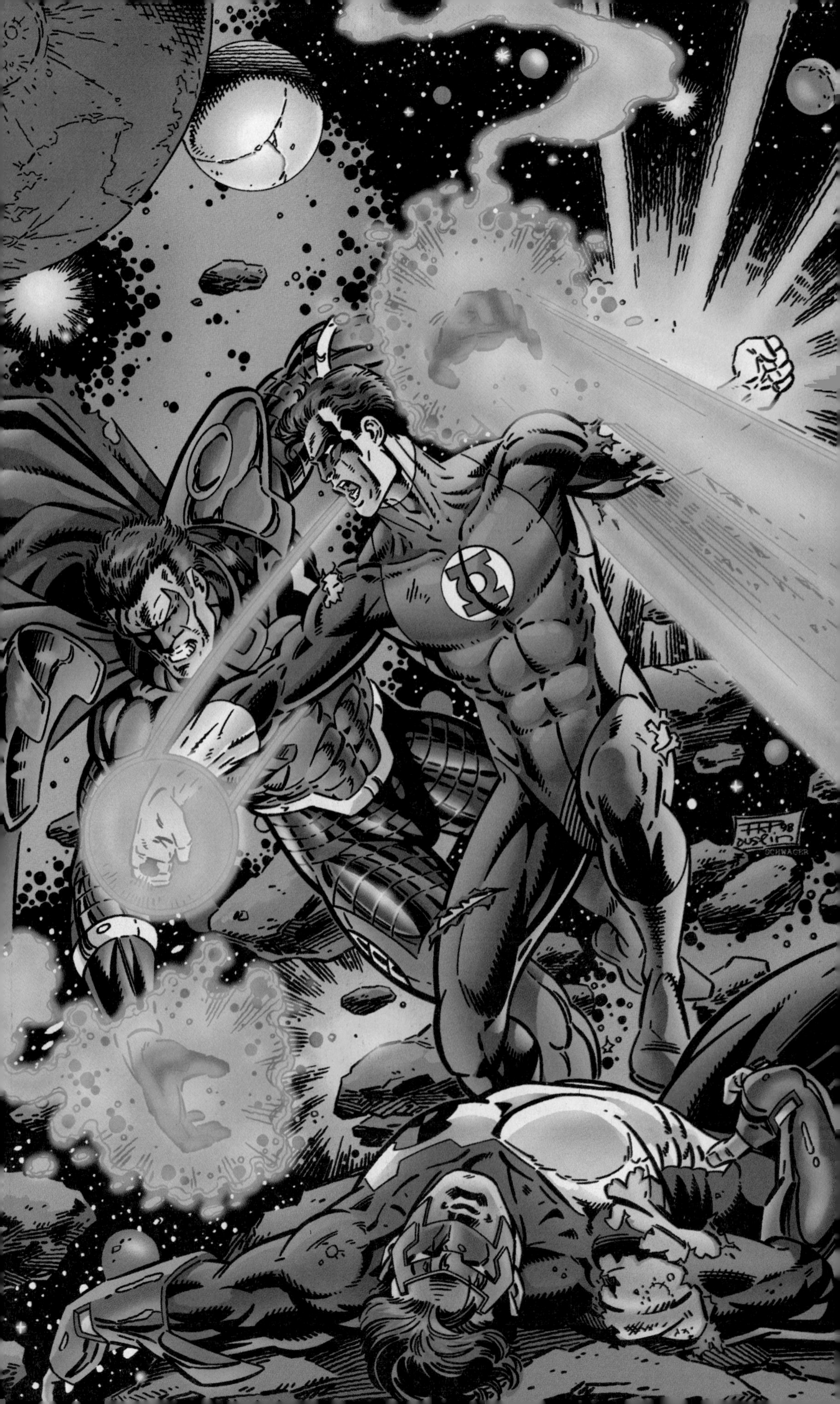
SCHWAGER

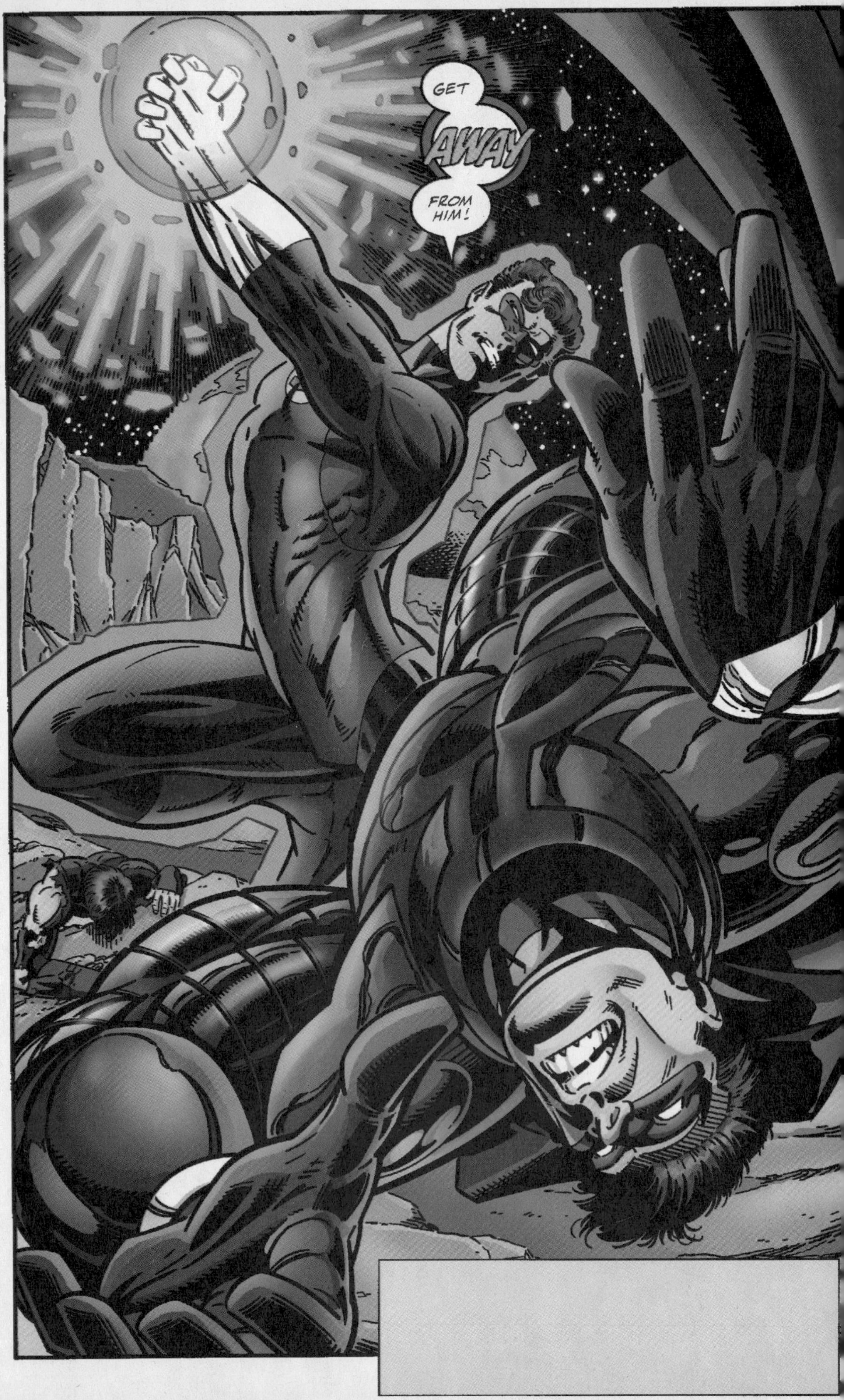
GET AWAY FROM HIM!

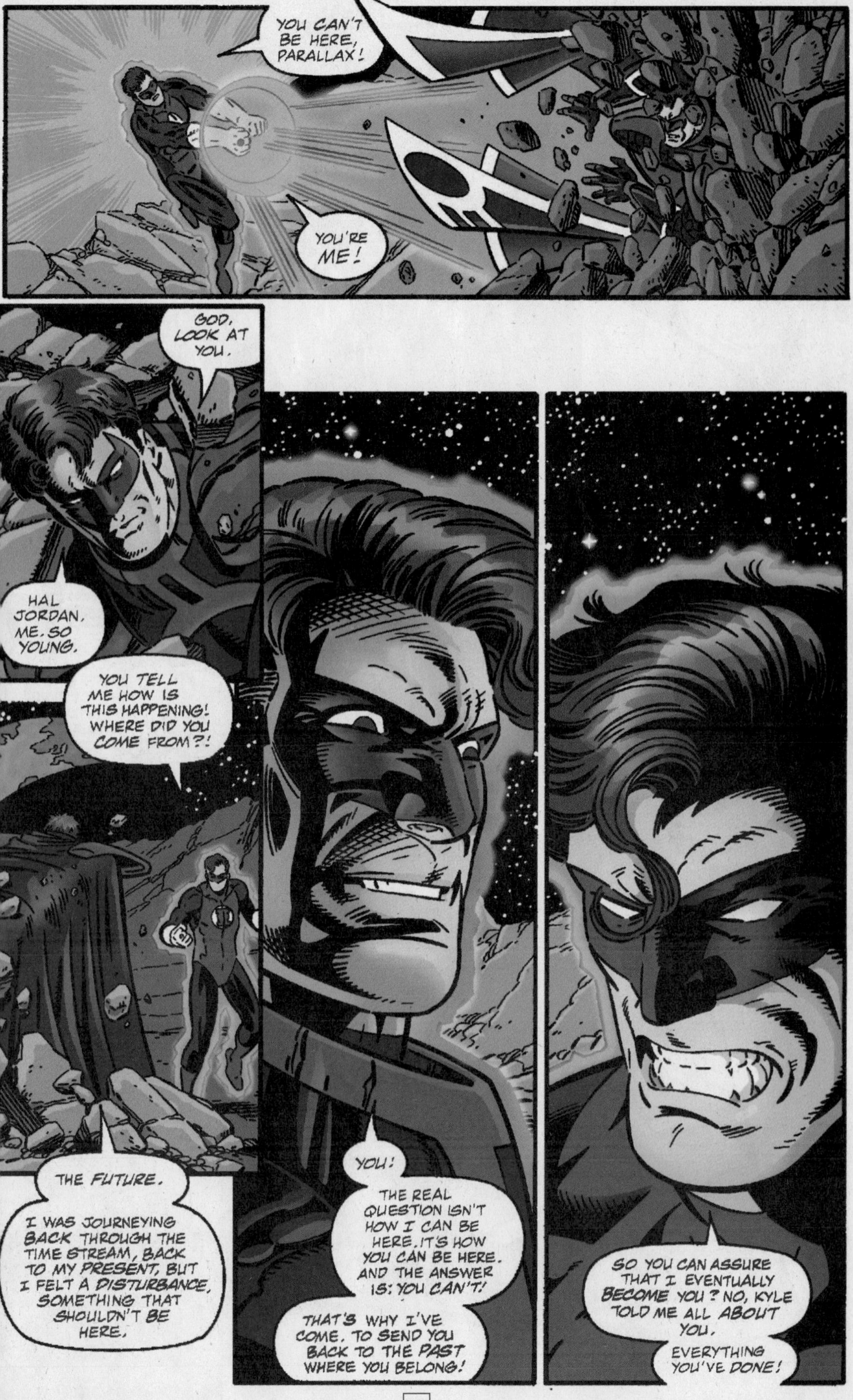

YOU CAN'T BE HERE, PARALLAX!
YOU'RE ME!
GOD, LOOK AT YOU.
HAL JORDAN, ME. SO YOUNG.
YOU TELL ME HOW IS THIS HAPPENING! WHERE DID YOU COME FROM?!
THE FUTURE.
I WAS JOURNEYING BACK THROUGH THE TIME STREAM, BACK TO MY PRESENT, BUT I FELT A DISTURBANCE, SOMETHING THAT SHOULDN'T BE HERE.
YOU!
THE REAL QUESTION ISN'T HOW I CAN BE HERE. IT'S HOW YOU CAN BE HERE. AND THE ANSWER IS: YOU CAN'T!
THAT'S WHY I'VE COME. TO SEND YOU BACK TO THE PAST WHERE YOU BELONG!
SO YOU CAN ASSURE THAT I EVENTUALLY BECOME YOU? NO, KYLE TOLD ME ALL ABOUT YOU.
EVERYTHING YOU'VE DONE!

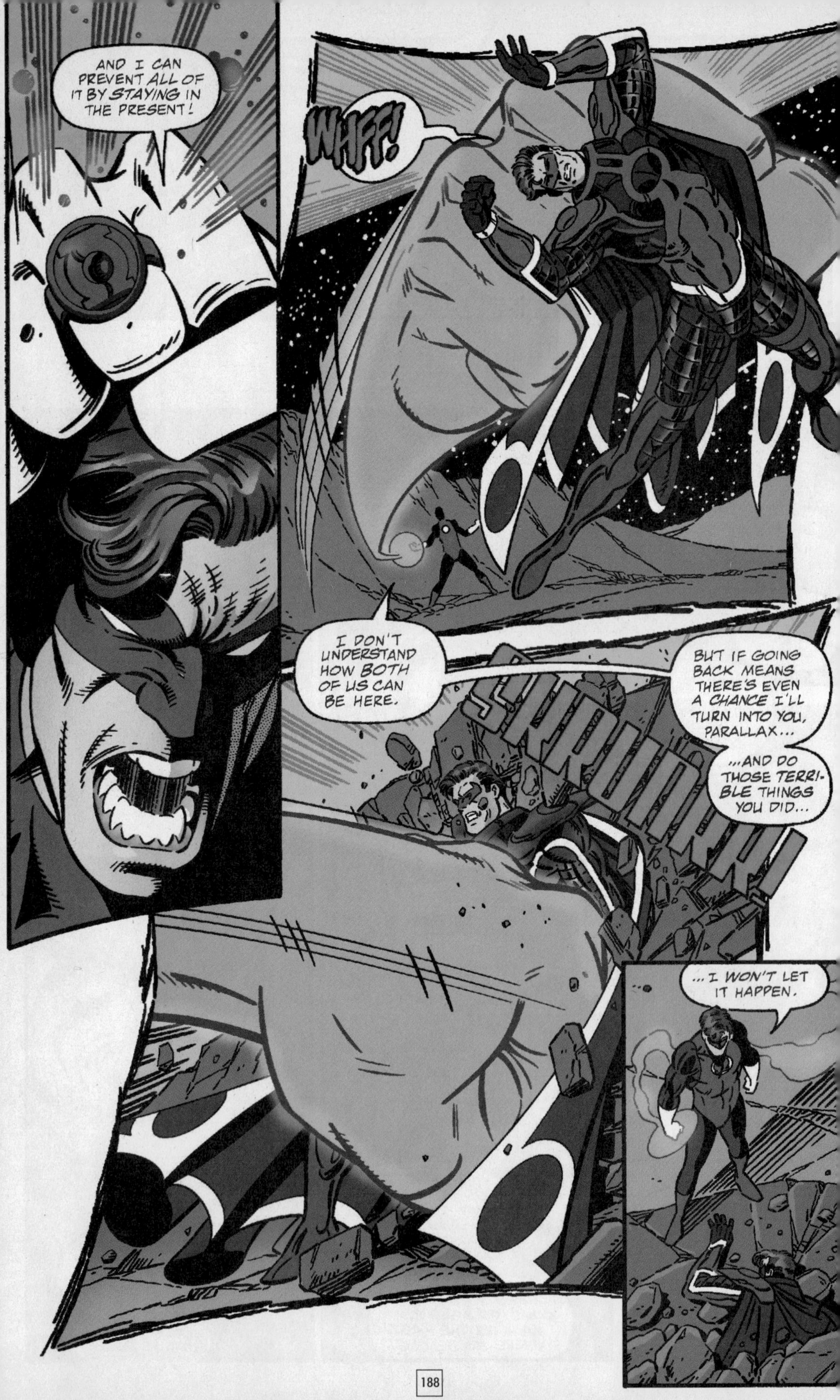

AND I CAN PREVENT ALL OF IT BY STAYING IN THE PRESENT!
WHFF!
I DON'T UNDERSTAND HOW BOTH OF US CAN BE HERE.
BUT IF GOING BACK MEANS THERE'S EVEN A CHANCE I'LL TURN INTO YOU, PARALLAX...
...AND DO THOSE TERRIBLE THINGS YOU DID...
...I WON'T LET IT HAPPEN.

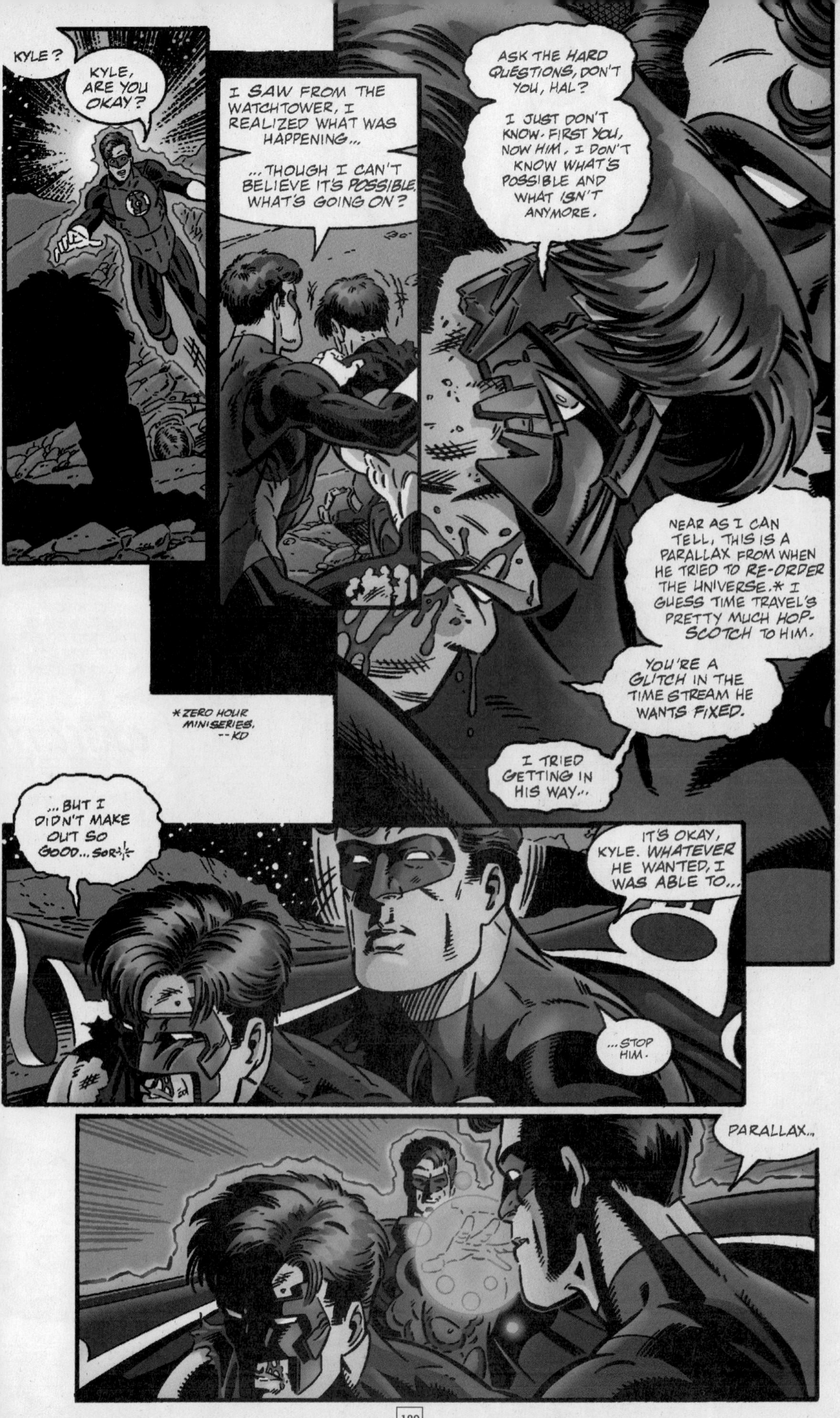
KYLE?
KYLE, ARE YOU OKAY?
I SAW FROM THE WATCHTOWER, I REALIZED WHAT WAS HAPPENING...
...THOUGH I CAN'T BELIEVE IT'S POSSIBLE. WHAT'S GOING ON?
ASK THE HARD QUESTIONS, DON'T YOU, HAL?
I JUST DON'T KNOW. FIRST YOU, NOW HIM. I DON'T KNOW WHAT'S POSSIBLE AND WHAT ISN'T ANYMORE.
NEAR AS I CAN TELL, THIS IS A PARALLAX FROM WHEN HE TRIED TO RE-ORDER THE UNIVERSE.* I GUESS TIME TRAVEL'S PRETTY MUCH HOP-SCOTCH TO HIM.
YOU'RE A GLITCH IN THE TIME STREAM HE WANTS FIXED.
*ZERO HOUR MINISERIES. --KD
I TRIED GETTING IN HIS WAY...
...BUT I DIDN'T MAKE OUT SO GOOD... SOR-!
IT'S OKAY, KYLE. WHATEVER HE WANTED, I WAS ABLE TO...
...STOP HIM.
PARALLAX...

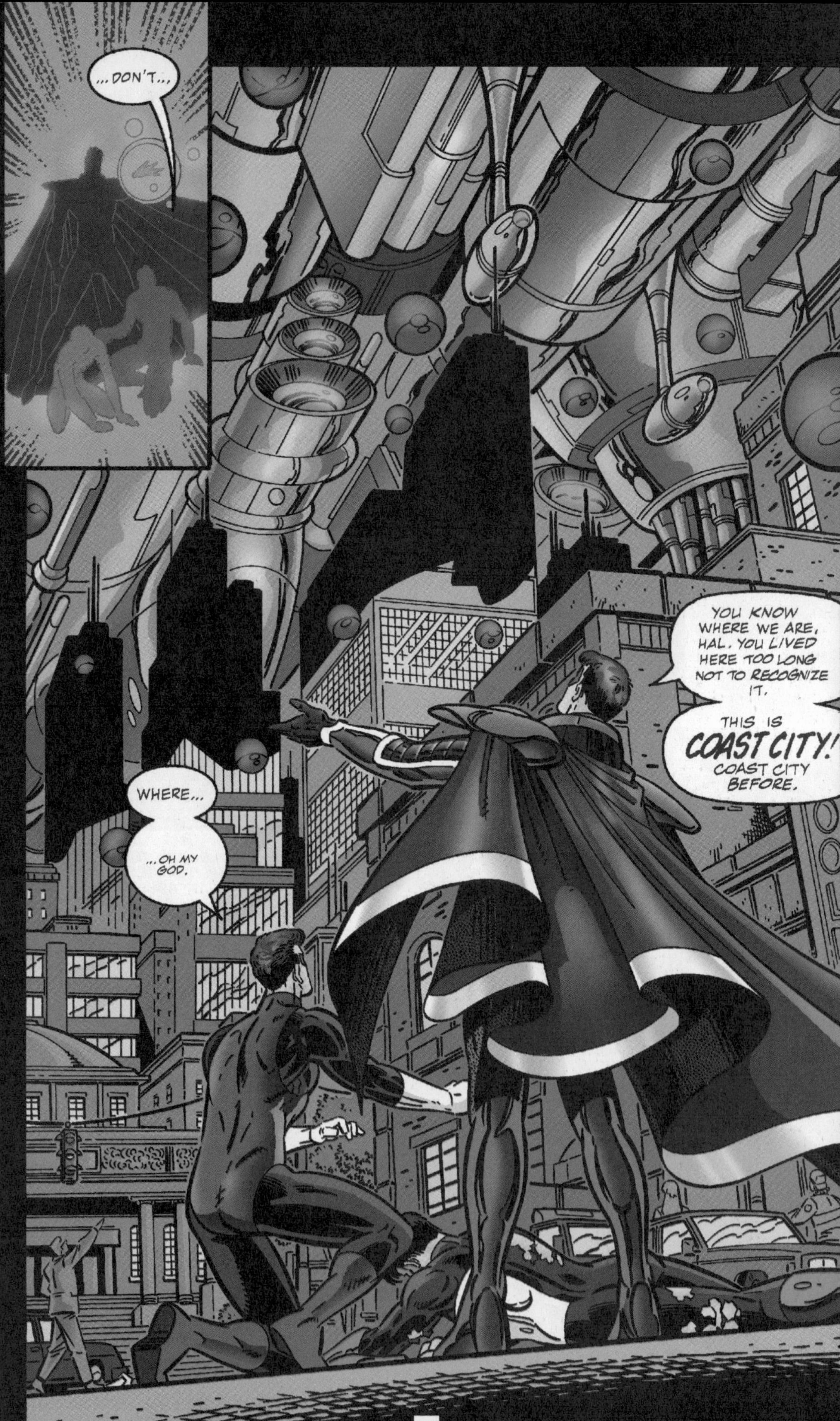
...DON'T...
WHERE...
...OH MY GOD.
YOU KNOW WHERE WE ARE, HAL. YOU LIVED HERE TOO LONG NOT TO RECOGNIZE IT.
THIS IS COAST CITY! COAST CITY BEFORE.

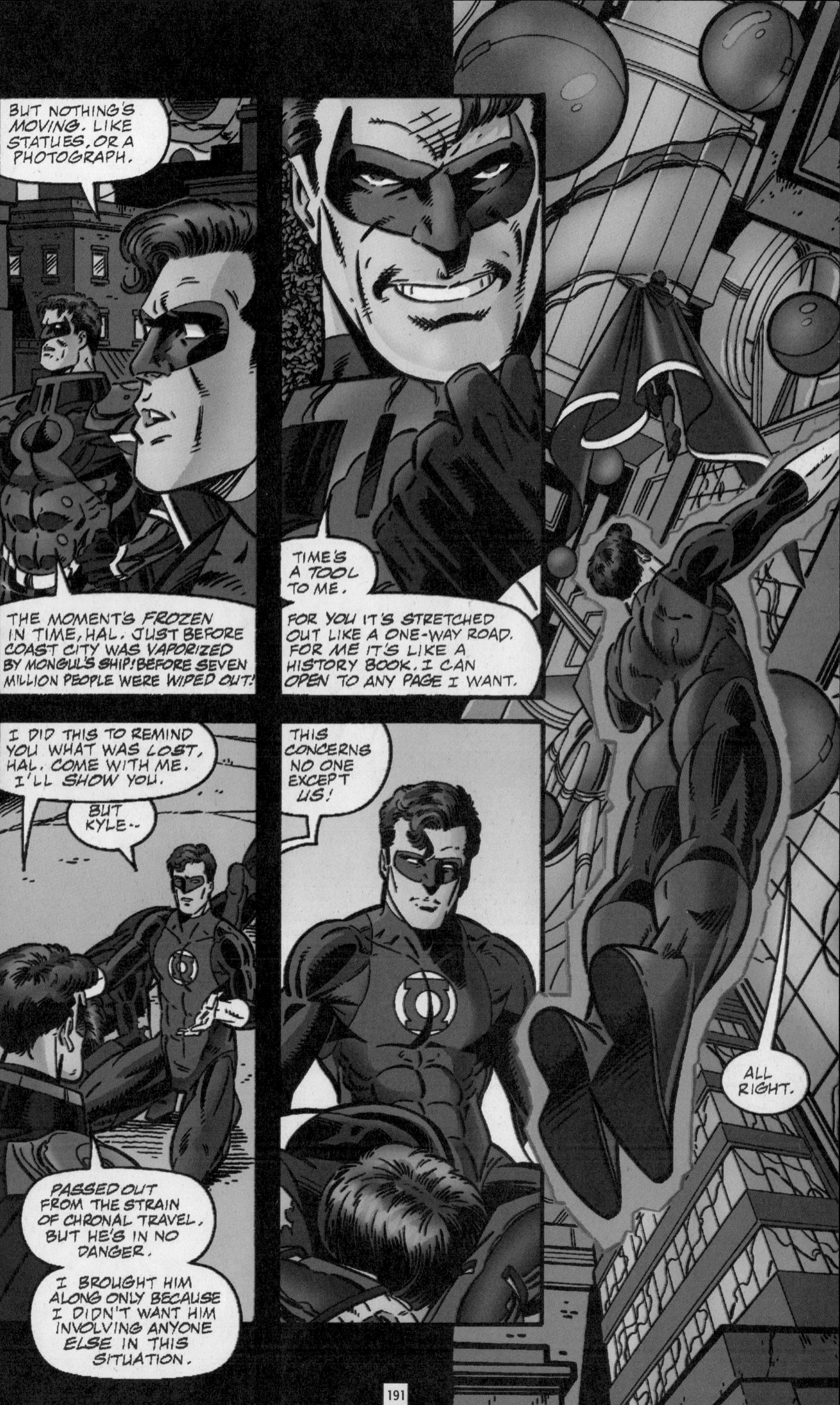

BUT NOTHING'S MOVING. LIKE STATUES, OR A PHOTOGRAPH.
THE MOMENT'S FROZEN IN TIME, HAL. JUST BEFORE COAST CITY WAS VAPORIZED BY MONGUL'S SHIP! BEFORE SEVEN MILLION PEOPLE WERE WIPED OUT!
TIME'S A TOOL TO ME.
FOR YOU IT'S STRETCHED OUT LIKE A ONE-WAY ROAD. FOR ME IT'S LIKE A HISTORY BOOK. I CAN OPEN TO ANY PAGE I WANT.
I DID THIS TO REMIND YOU WHAT WAS LOST, HAL. COME WITH ME. I'LL SHOW YOU.
BUT KYLE--
PASSED OUT FROM THE STRAIN OF CHRONAL TRAVEL. BUT HE'S IN NO DANGER.
I BROUGHT HIM ALONG ONLY BECAUSE I DIDN'T WANT HIM INVOLVING ANYONE ELSE IN THIS SITUATION.
THIS CONCERNS NO ONE EXCEPT US!
ALL RIGHT.

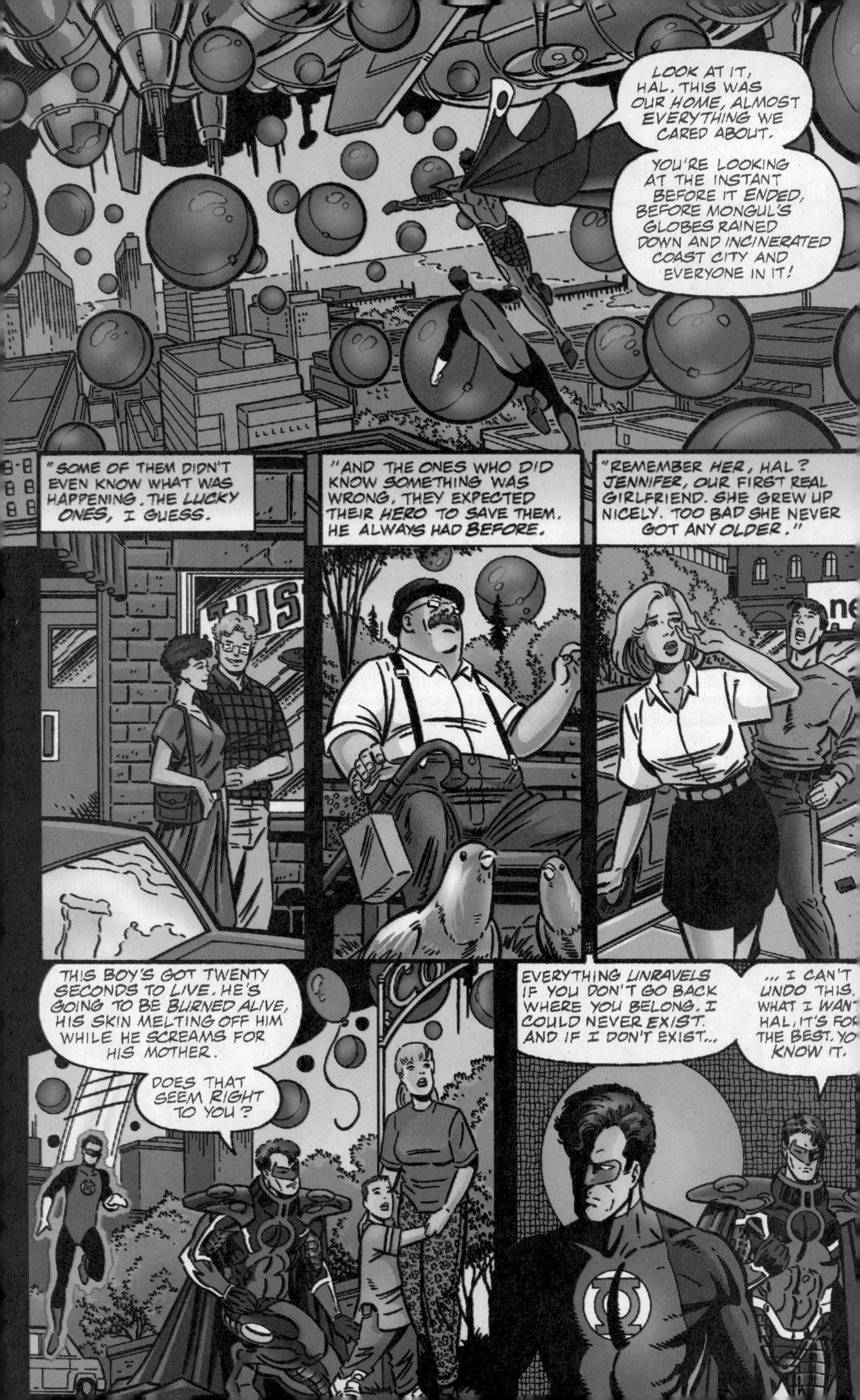

LOOK AT IT, HAL. THIS WAS OUR HOME, ALMOST EVERYTHING WE CARED ABOUT.
YOU'RE LOOKING AT THE INSTANT BEFORE IT ENDED, BEFORE MONGUL'S GLOBES RAINED DOWN AND INCINERATED COAST CITY AND EVERYONE IN IT!
"SOME OF THEM DIDN'T EVEN KNOW WHAT WAS HAPPENING. THE LUCKY ONES, I GUESS.
"AND THE ONES WHO DID KNOW SOMETHING WAS WRONG, THEY EXPECTED THEIR HERO TO SAVE THEM. HE ALWAYS HAD BEFORE.
"REMEMBER HER, HAL? JENNIFER, OUR FIRST REAL GIRLFRIEND. SHE GREW UP NICELY. TOO BAD SHE NEVER GOT ANY OLDER."
THIS BOY'S GOT TWENTY SECONDS TO LIVE. HE'S GOING TO BE BURNED ALIVE, HIS SKIN MELTING OFF HIM WHILE HE SCREAMS FOR HIS MOTHER.
DOES THAT SEEM RIGHT TO YOU?
EVERYTHING UNRAVELS IF YOU DON'T GO BACK WHERE YOU BELONG. I COULD NEVER EXIST. AND IF I DON'T EXIST...

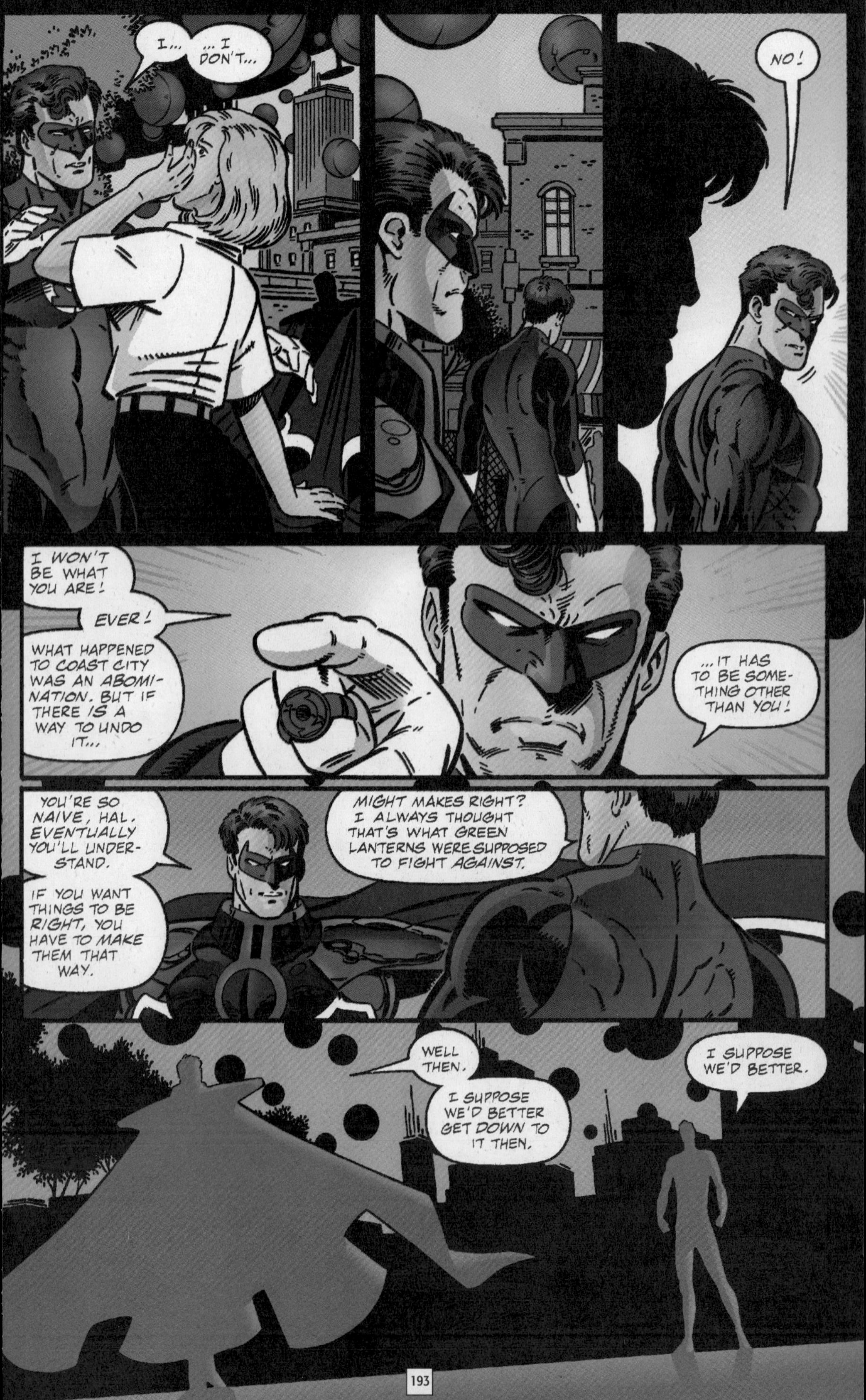
I... ...I DON'T...
NO!
I WON'T BE WHAT YOU ARE!
EVER!
WHAT HAPPENED TO COAST CITY WAS AN ABOMINATION. BUT IF THERE IS A WAY TO UNDO IT...
...IT HAS TO BE SOMETHING OTHER THAN YOU!
YOU'RE SO NAIVE, HAL. EVENTUALLY YOU'LL UNDERSTAND.
IF YOU WANT THINGS TO BE RIGHT, YOU HAVE TO MAKE THEM THAT WAY.
MIGHT MAKES RIGHT? I ALWAYS THOUGHT THAT'S WHAT GREEN LANTERNS WERE SUPPOSED TO FIGHT AGAINST.
WELL THEN.
I SUPPOSE WE'D BETTER GET DOWN TO IT THEN.
I SUPPOSE WE'D BETTER.

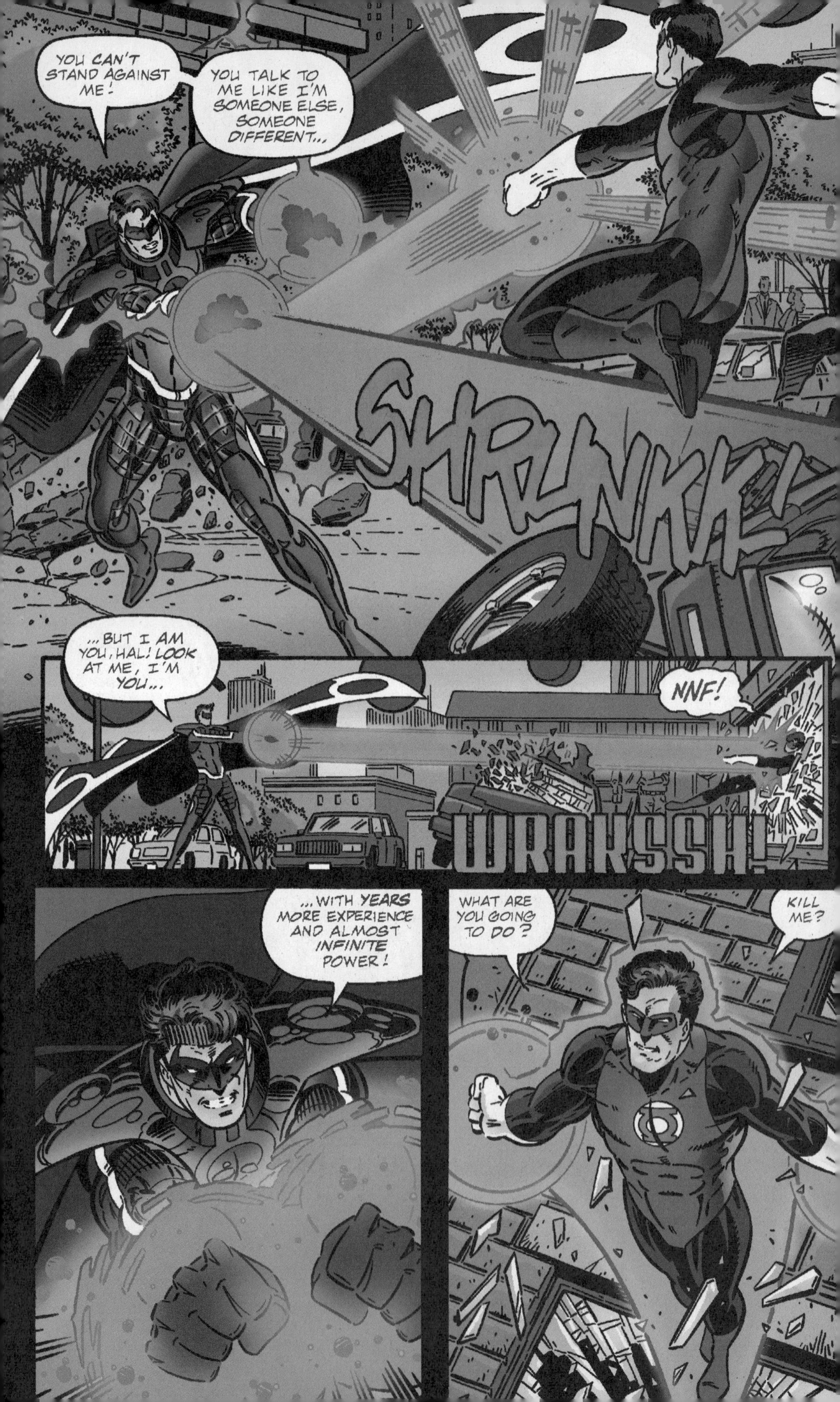
YOU CAN'T STAND AGAINST ME!
YOU TALK TO ME LIKE I'M SOMEONE ELSE, SOMEONE DIFFERENT...
SHRUNKK!
...BUT I AM YOU, HAL! LOOK AT ME, I'M YOU...
NNF!
WRAKSSH!
...WITH YEARS MORE EXPERIENCE AND ALMOST INFINITE POWER!
WHAT ARE YOU GOING TO DO?
KILL ME?

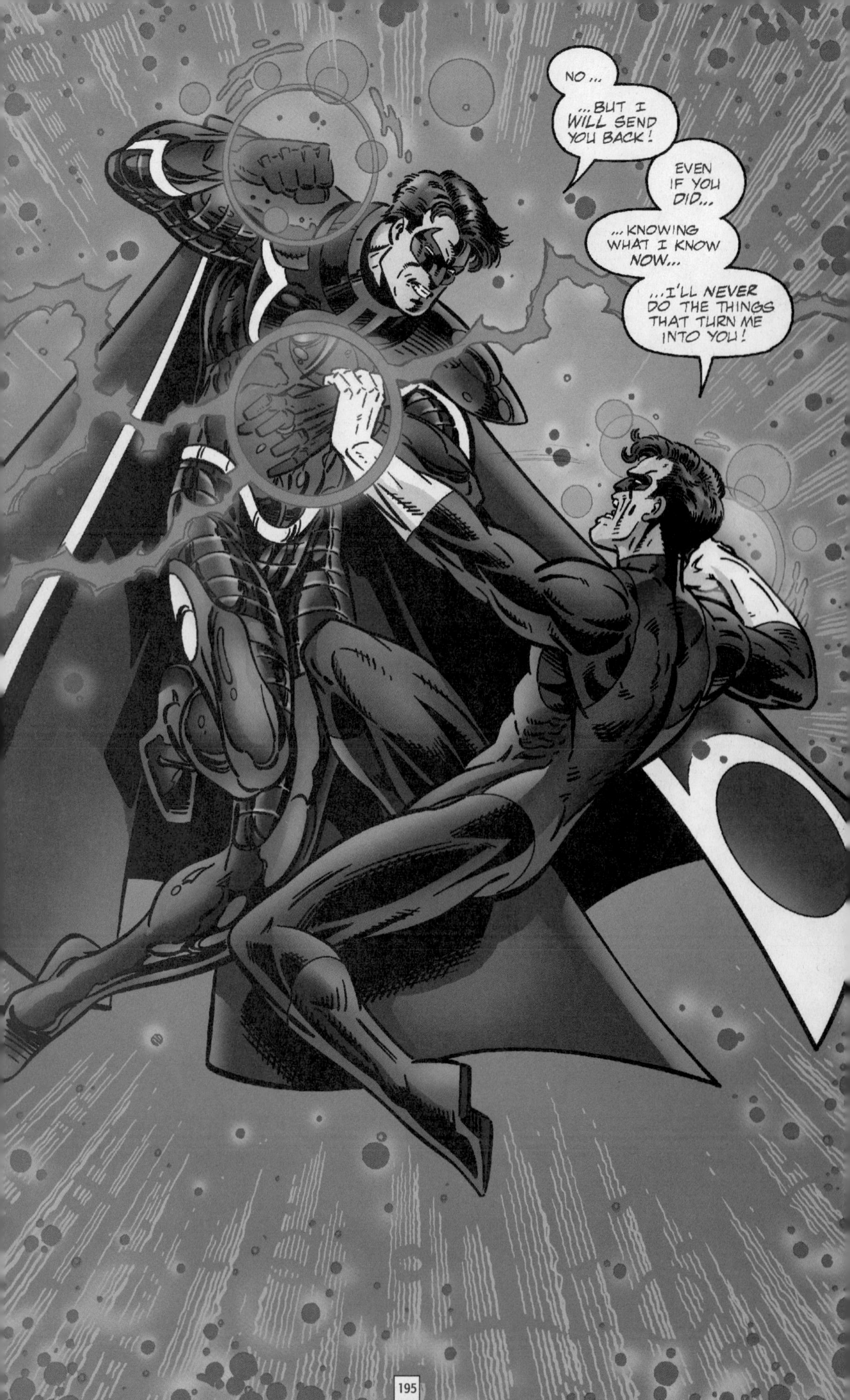
NO...
...BUT I WILL SEND YOU BACK!
EVEN IF YOU DID...
...KNOWING WHAT I KNOW NOW...
...I'LL NEVER DO THE THINGS THAT TURN ME INTO YOU!

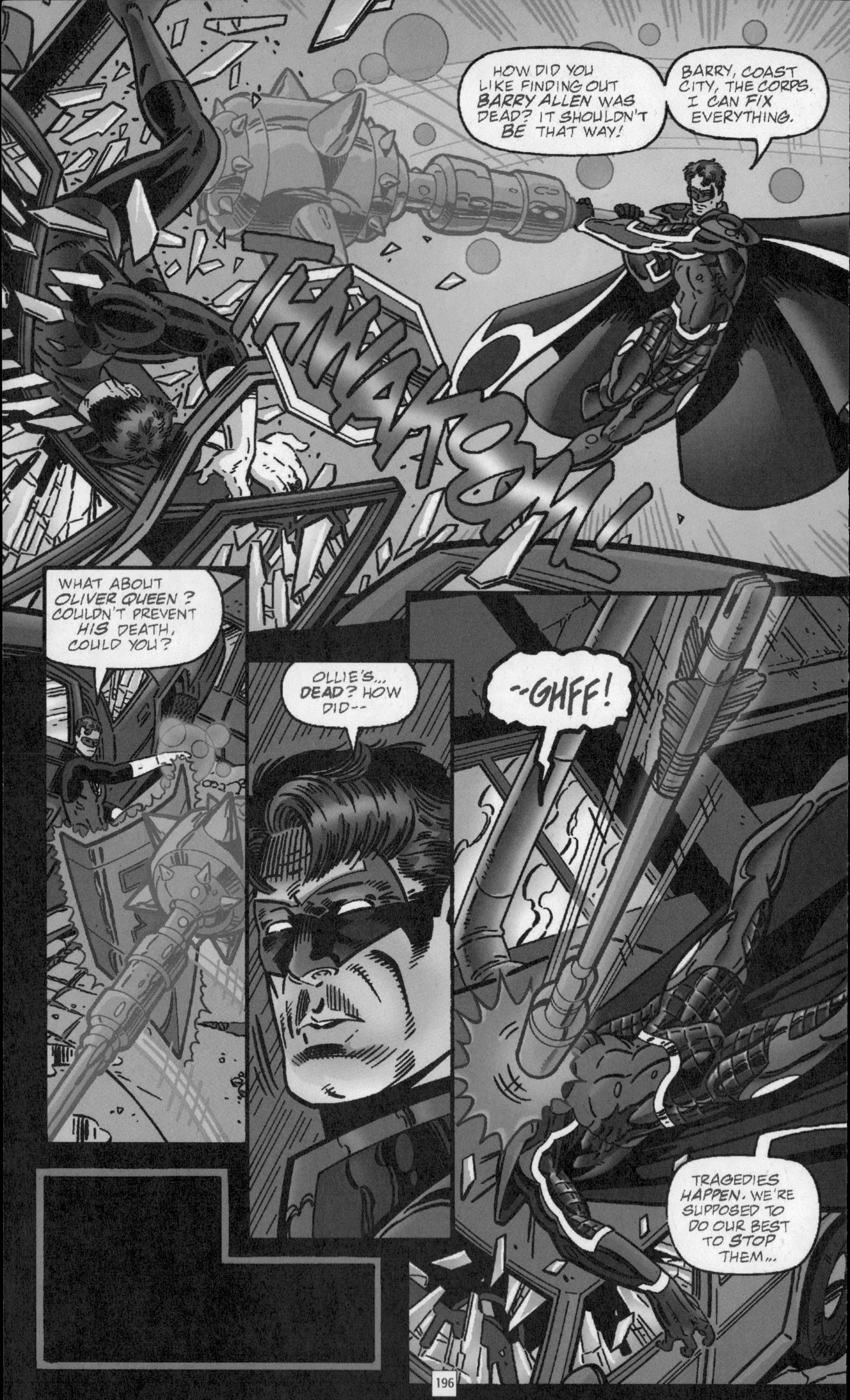
HOW DID YOU LIKE FINDING OUT BARRY ALLEN WAS DEAD? IT SHOULDN'T BE THAT WAY!
BARRY, COAST CITY, THE CORPS. I CAN FIX EVERYTHING.
THWAKOOM!
WHAT ABOUT OLIVER QUEEN? COULDN'T PREVENT HIS DEATH, COULD YOU?
OLLIE'S... DEAD? HOW DID--
--GHFF!
TRAGEDIES HAPPEN. WE'RE SUPPOSED TO DO OUR BEST TO STOP THEM...

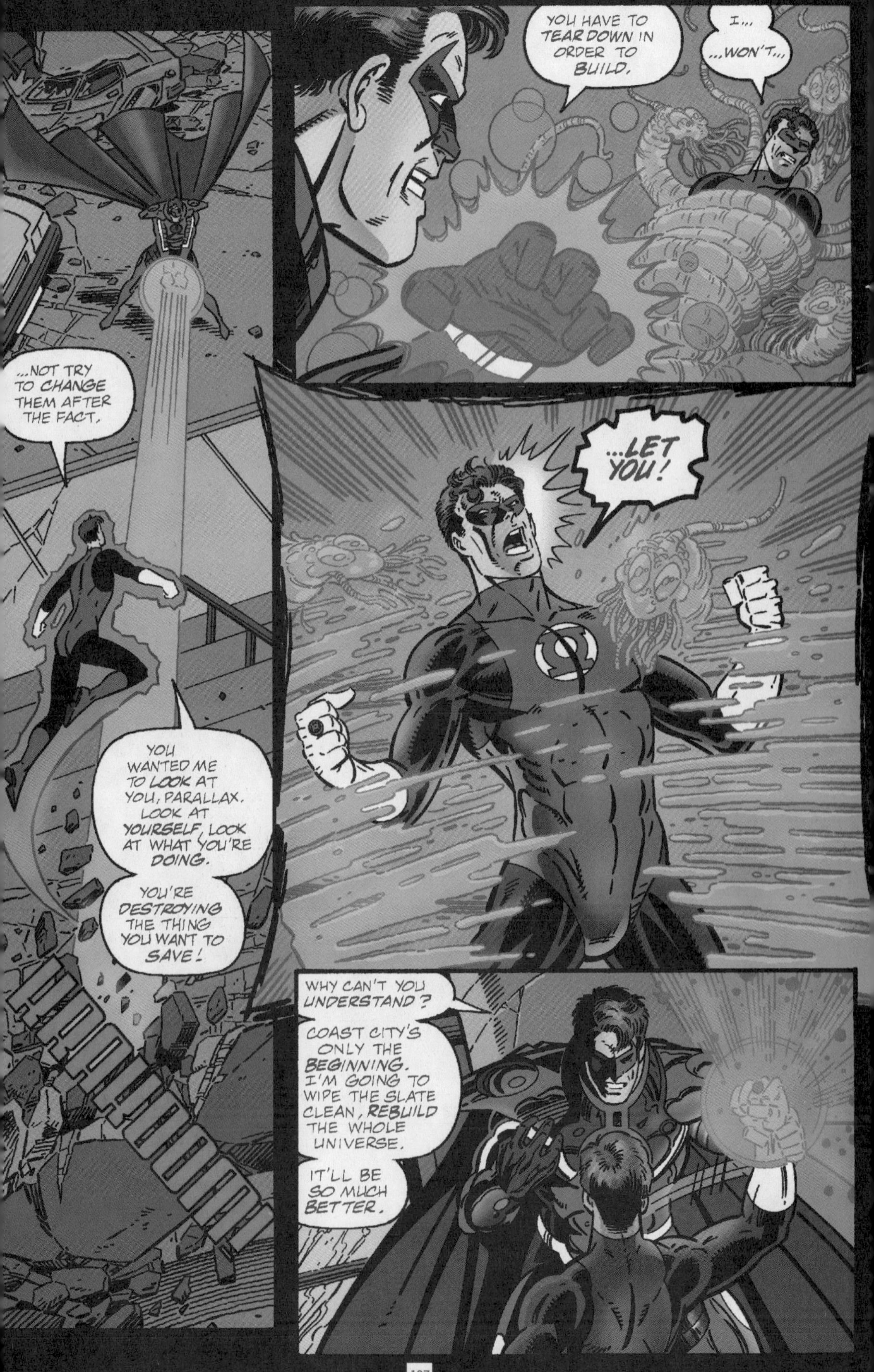
YOU HAVE TO TEAR DOWN IN ORDER TO BUILD.
I... ...WON'T...
...NOT TRY TO CHANGE THEM AFTER THE FACT.
...LET YOU!
YOU WANTED ME TO LOOK AT YOU, PARALLAX. LOOK AT YOURSELF, LOOK AT WHAT YOU'RE DOING.
YOU'RE DESTROYING THE THING YOU WANT TO SAVE!
WHY CAN'T YOU UNDERSTAND?
COAST CITY'S ONLY THE BEGINNING. I'M GOING TO WIPE THE SLATE CLEAN, REBUILD THE WHOLE UNIVERSE.
IT'LL BE SO MUCH BETTER.

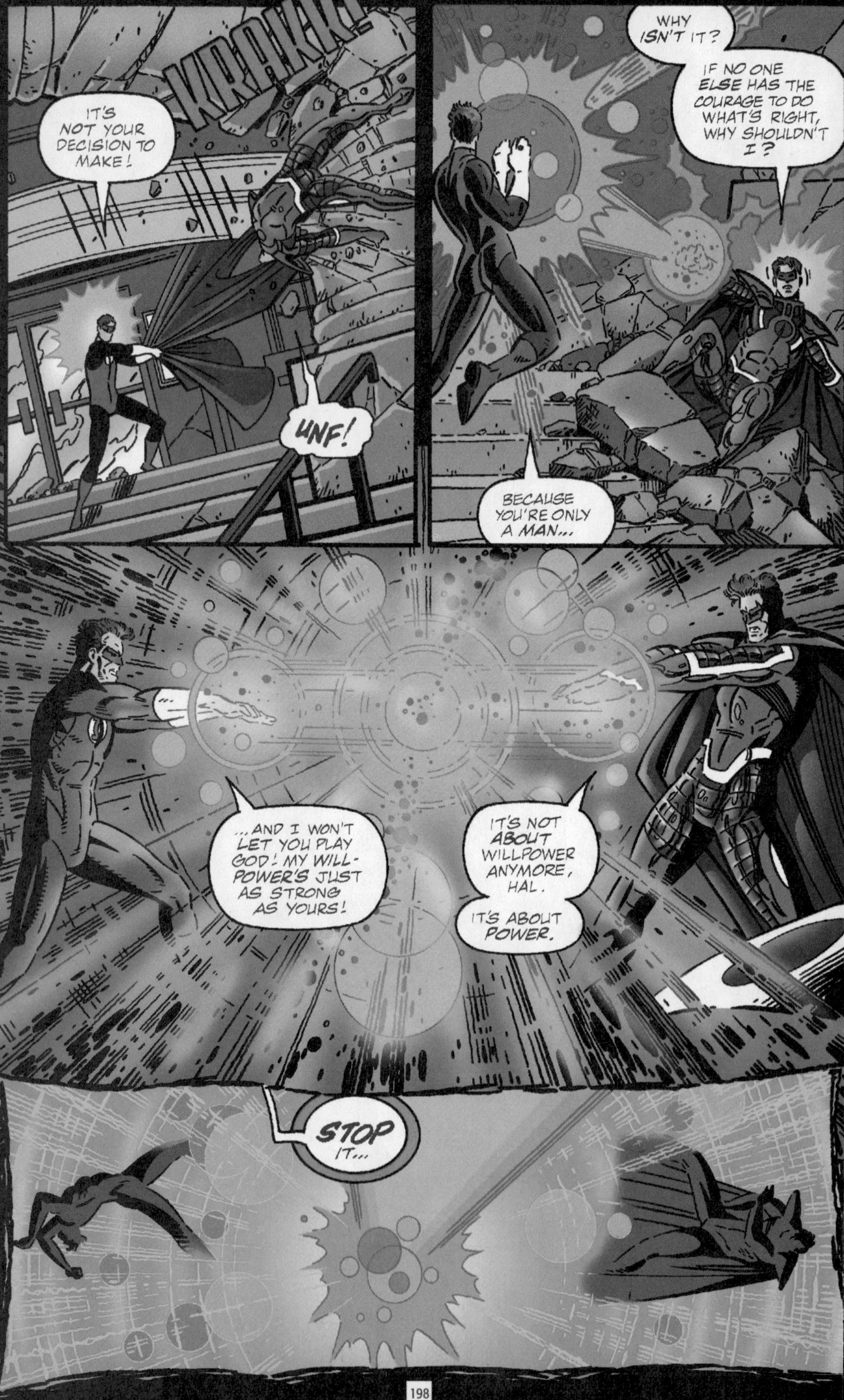
KRAKK!
IT'S NOT YOUR DECISION TO MAKE!
UNF!
WHY ISN'T IT?
IF NO ONE ELSE HAS THE COURAGE TO DO WHAT'S RIGHT, WHY SHOULDN'T I?
BECAUSE YOU'RE ONLY A MAN...
...AND I WON'T LET YOU PLAY GOD! MY WILL-POWER'S JUST AS STRONG AS YOURS!
IT'S NOT ABOUT WILLPOWER ANYMORE, HAL.
IT'S ABOUT POWER.
STOP IT...

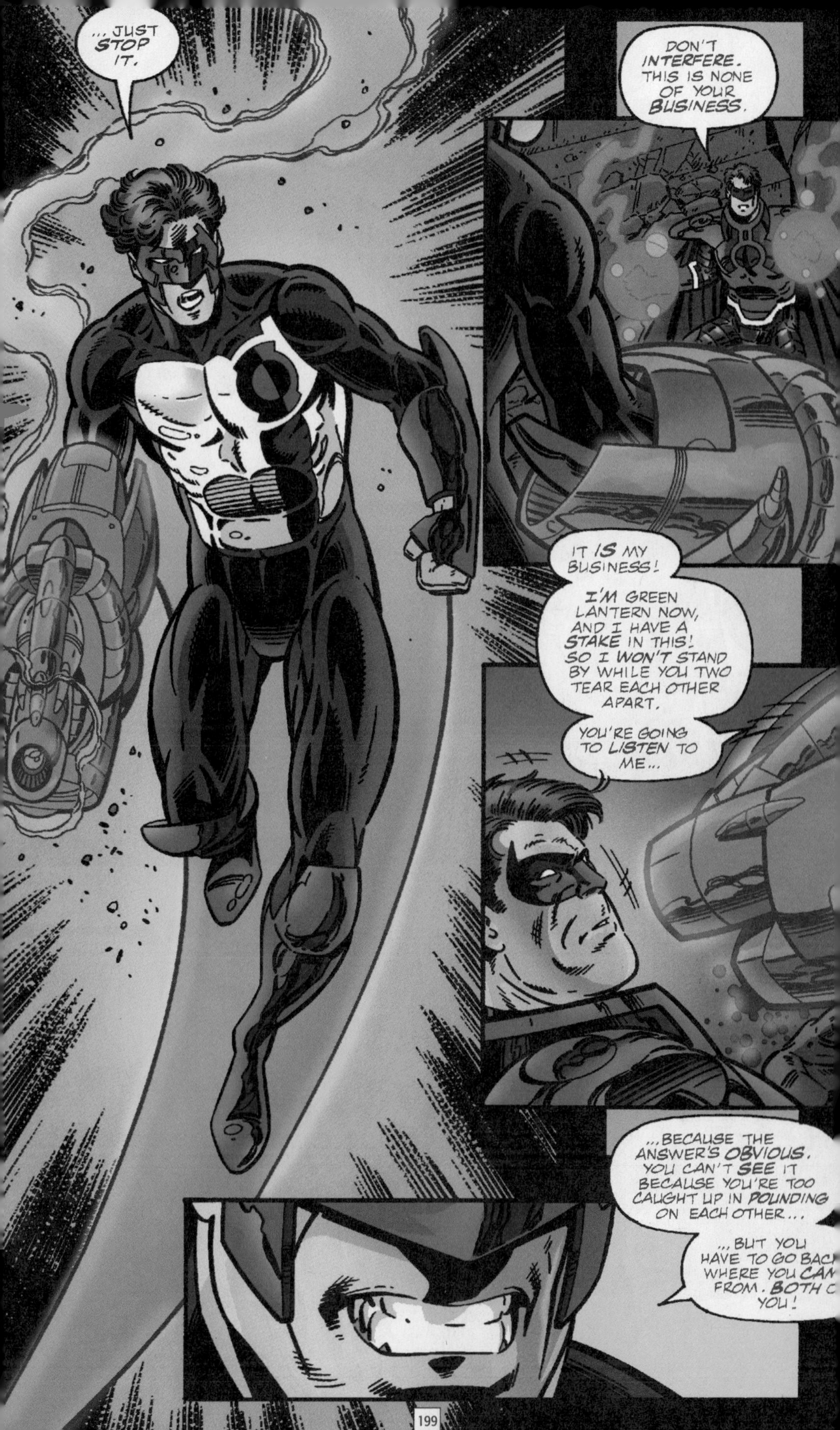

...JUST STOP IT.
DON'T INTERFERE. THIS IS NONE OF YOUR BUSINESS.
IT IS MY BUSINESS!
I'M GREEN LANTERN NOW, AND I HAVE A STAKE IN THIS! SO I WON'T STAND BY WHILE YOU TWO TEAR EACH OTHER APART.
YOU'RE GOING TO LISTEN TO ME...
...BECAUSE THE ANSWER'S OBVIOUS. YOU CAN'T SEE IT BECAUSE YOU'RE TOO CAUGHT UP IN POUNDING ON EACH OTHER...

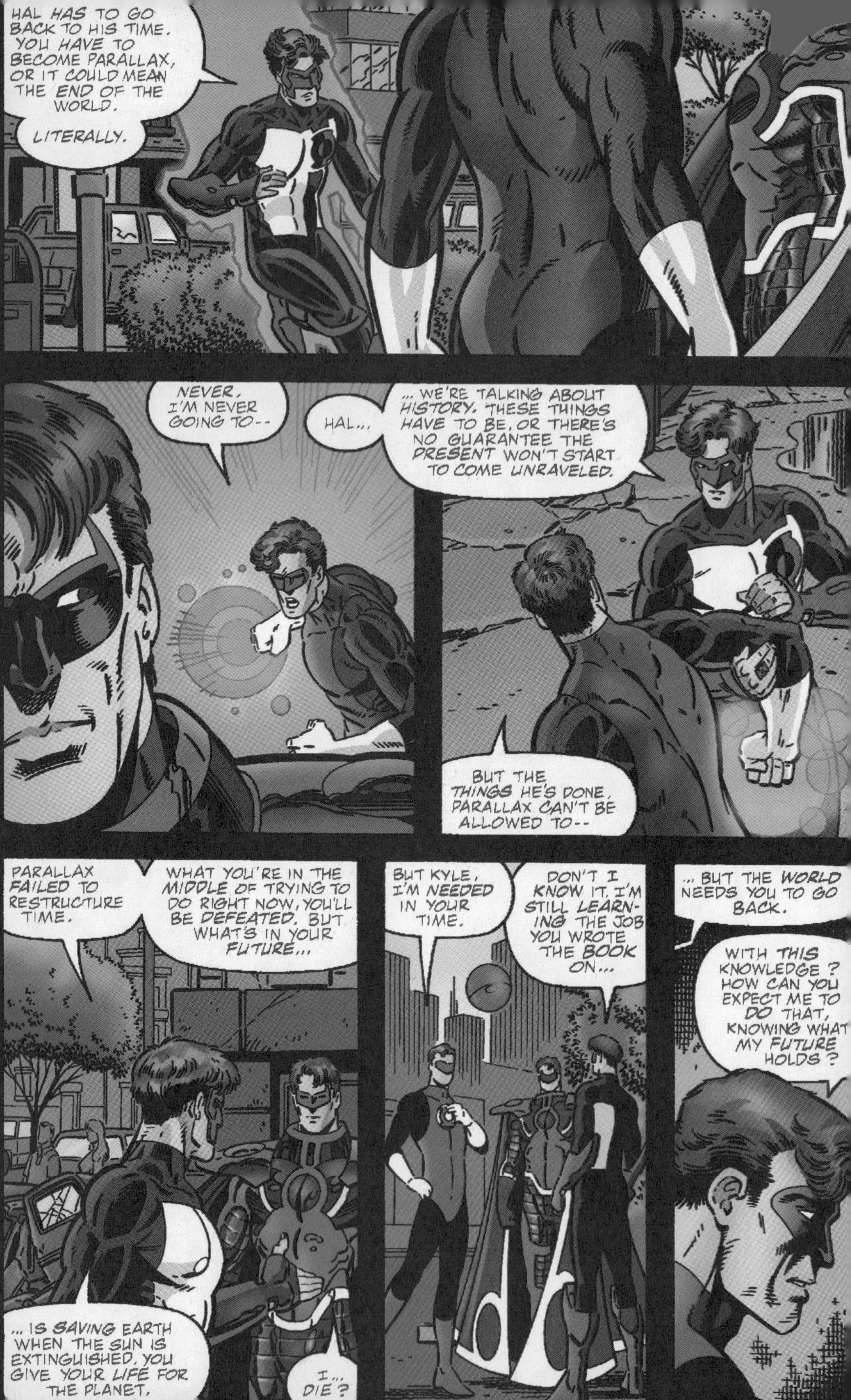

HAL HAS TO GO BACK TO HIS TIME. YOU HAVE TO BECOME PARALLAX, OR IT COULD MEAN THE END OF THE WORLD.
LITERALLY.
NEVER. I'M NEVER GOING TO--
HAL...
... WE'RE TALKING ABOUT HISTORY. THESE THINGS HAVE TO BE, OR THERE'S NO GUARANTEE THE PRESENT WON'T START TO COME UNRAVELED.
BUT THE THINGS HE'S DONE, PARALLAX CAN'T BE ALLOWED TO--
PARALLAX FAILED TO RESTRUCTURE TIME.
WHAT YOU'RE IN THE MIDDLE OF TRYING TO DO RIGHT NOW, YOU'LL BE DEFEATED. BUT WHAT'S IN YOUR FUTURE...
... IS SAVING EARTH WHEN THE SUN IS EXTINGUISHED. YOU GIVE YOUR LIFE FOR THE PLANET.
I... DIE?
BUT KYLE, I'M NEEDED IN YOUR TIME.
DON'T I KNOW IT. I'M STILL LEARNING THE JOB YOU WROTE THE BOOK ON...
... BUT THE WORLD NEEDS YOU TO GO BACK.
WITH THIS KNOWLEDGE? HOW CAN YOU EXPECT ME TO DO THAT, KNOWING WHAT MY FUTURE HOLDS?

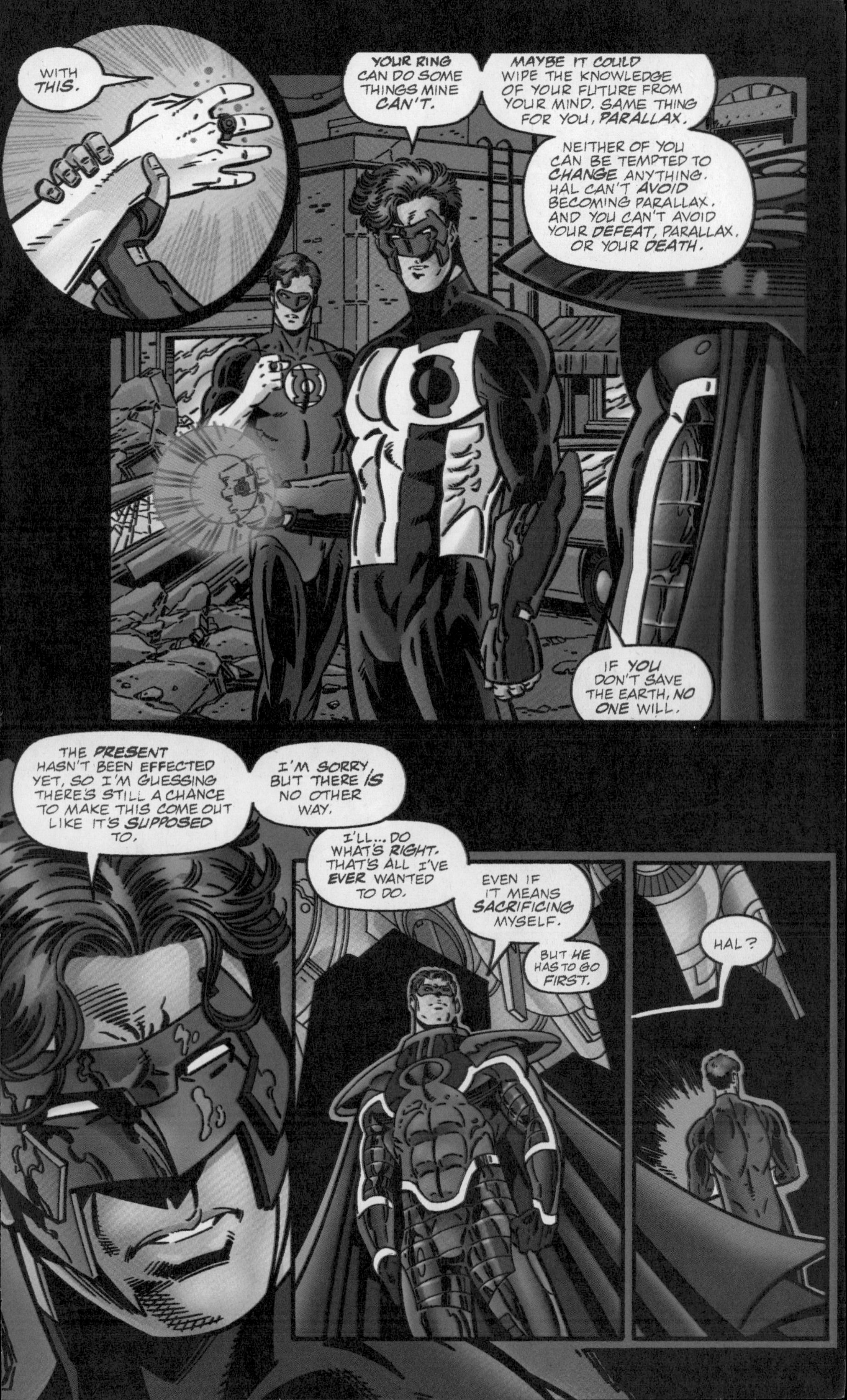
WITH THIS.
YOUR RING CAN DO SOME THINGS MINE CAN'T.
MAYBE IT COULD WIPE THE KNOWLEDGE OF YOUR FUTURE FROM YOUR MIND. SAME THING FOR YOU, PARALLAX.
NEITHER OF YOU CAN BE TEMPTED TO CHANGE ANYTHING. HAL CAN'T AVOID BECOMING PARALLAX. AND YOU CAN'T AVOID YOUR DEFEAT, PARALLAX. OR YOUR DEATH.
IF YOU DON'T SAVE THE EARTH, NO ONE WILL.
THE PRESENT HASN'T BEEN EFFECTED YET, SO I'M GUESSING THERE'S STILL A CHANCE TO MAKE THIS COME OUT LIKE IT'S SUPPOSED TO.
I'M SORRY, BUT THERE IS NO OTHER WAY.
I'LL... DO WHAT'S RIGHT. THAT'S ALL I'VE EVER WANTED TO DO.
EVEN IF IT MEANS SACRIFICING MYSELF.
BUT HE HAS TO GO FIRST.
HAL?

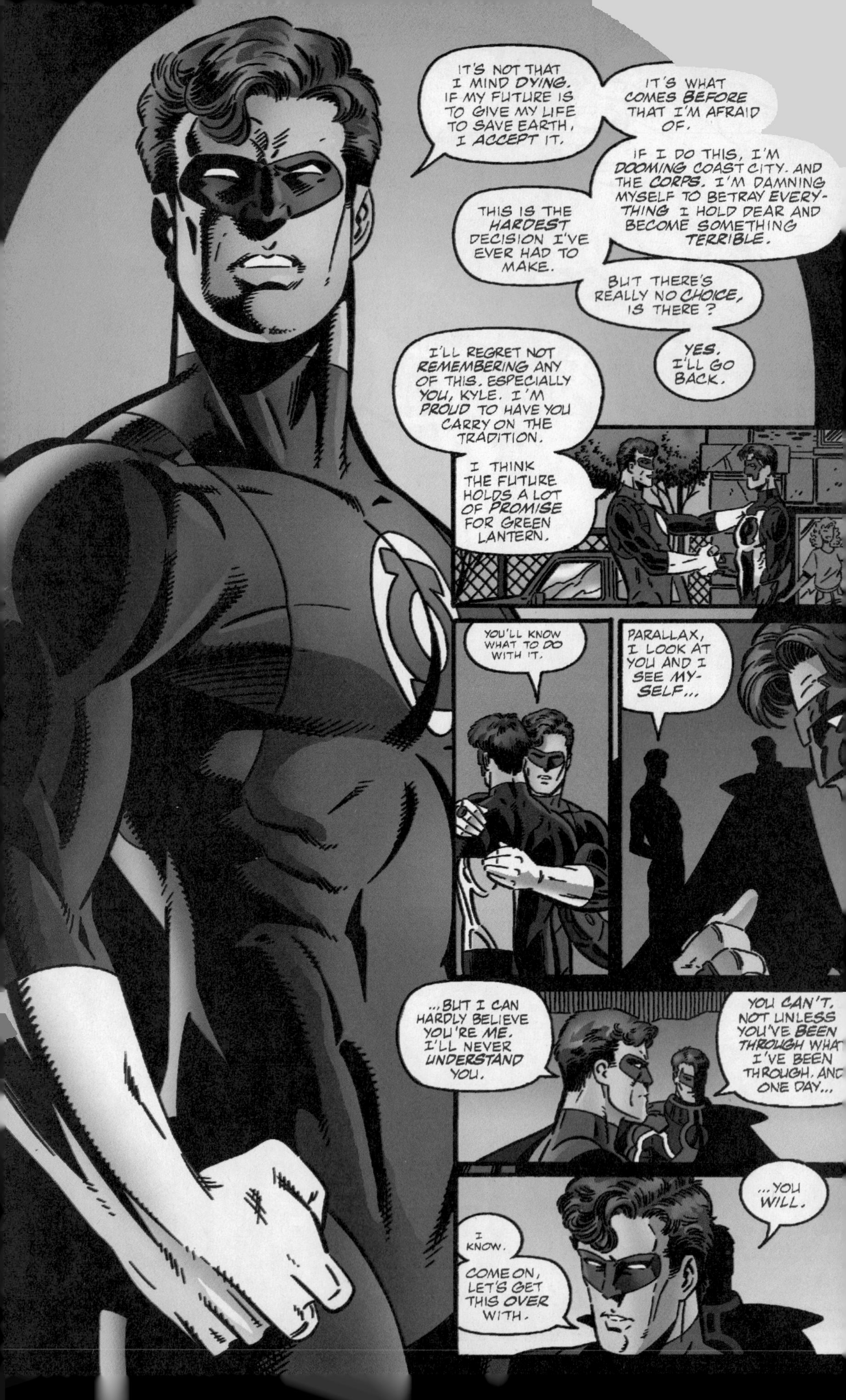
IT'S NOT THAT I MIND DYING. IF MY FUTURE IS TO GIVE MY LIFE TO SAVE EARTH, I ACCEPT IT.
IT'S WHAT COMES BEFORE THAT I'M AFRAID OF.
IF I DO THIS, I'M DOOMING COAST CITY. AND THE CORPS. I'M DAMNING MYSELF TO BETRAY EVERY-THING I HOLD DEAR AND BECOME SOMETHING TERRIBLE.
THIS IS THE HARDEST DECISION I'VE EVER HAD TO MAKE.
BUT THERE'S REALLY NO CHOICE, IS THERE?
YES. I'LL GO BACK.
I'LL REGRET NOT REMEMBERING ANY OF THIS. ESPECIALLY YOU, KYLE. I'M PROUD TO HAVE YOU CARRY ON THE TRADITION.
I THINK THE FUTURE HOLDS A LOT OF PROMISE FOR GREEN LANTERN.
YOU'LL KNOW WHAT TO DO WITH IT.
PARALLAX, I LOOK AT YOU AND I SEE MY-SELF...
...BUT I CAN HARDLY BELIEVE YOU'RE ME. I'LL NEVER UNDERSTAND YOU.
YOU CAN'T. NOT UNLESS YOU'VE BEEN THROUGH WHAT I'VE BEEN THROUGH. AND ONE DAY...
...YOU WILL.
I KNOW.
COME ON, LET'S GET THIS OVER WITH.

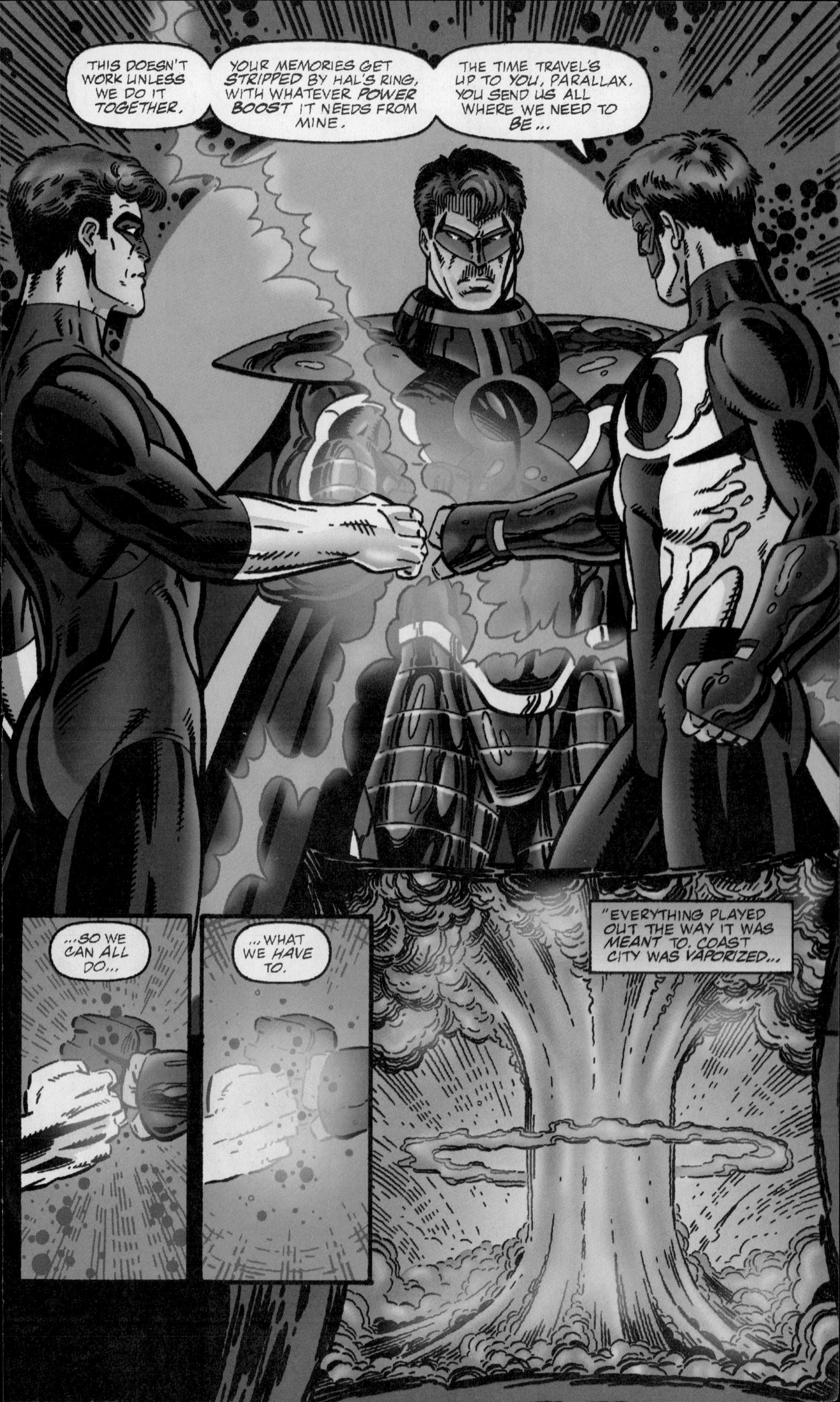
THIS DOESN'T WORK UNLESS WE DO IT TOGETHER.
YOUR MEMORIES GET STRIPPED BY HAL'S RING, WITH WHATEVER POWER BOOST IT NEEDS FROM MINE.
THE TIME TRAVEL'S UP TO YOU, PARALLAX. YOU SEND US ALL WHERE WE NEED TO BE...
...SO WE CAN ALL DO...
...WHAT WE HAVE TO.
"EVERYTHING PLAYED OUT THE WAY IT WAS MEANT TO. COAST CITY WAS VAPORIZED...

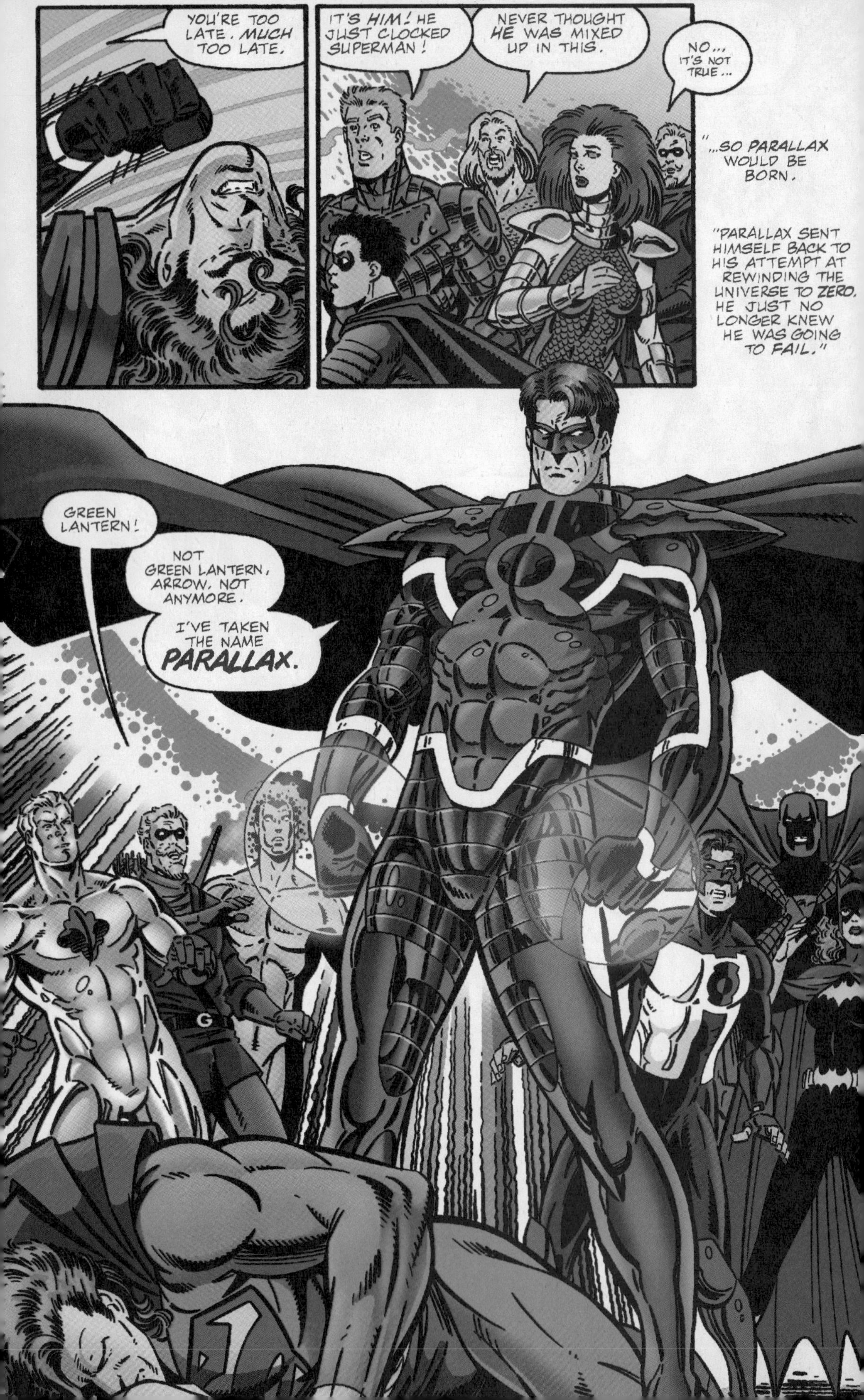
YOU'RE TOO LATE. MUCH TOO LATE.
IT'S HIM! HE JUST CLOCKED SUPERMAN!
NEVER THOUGHT HE WAS MIXED UP IN THIS.
NO... IT'S NOT TRUE...
"...SO PARALLAX WOULD BE BORN.
"PARALLAX SENT HIMSELF BACK TO HIS ATTEMPT AT REWINDING THE UNIVERSE TO ZERO. HE JUST NO LONGER KNEW HE WAS GOING TO FAIL."
GREEN LANTERN!
NOT GREEN LANTERN, ARROW. NOT ANYMORE.
I'VE TAKEN THE NAME PARALLAX.

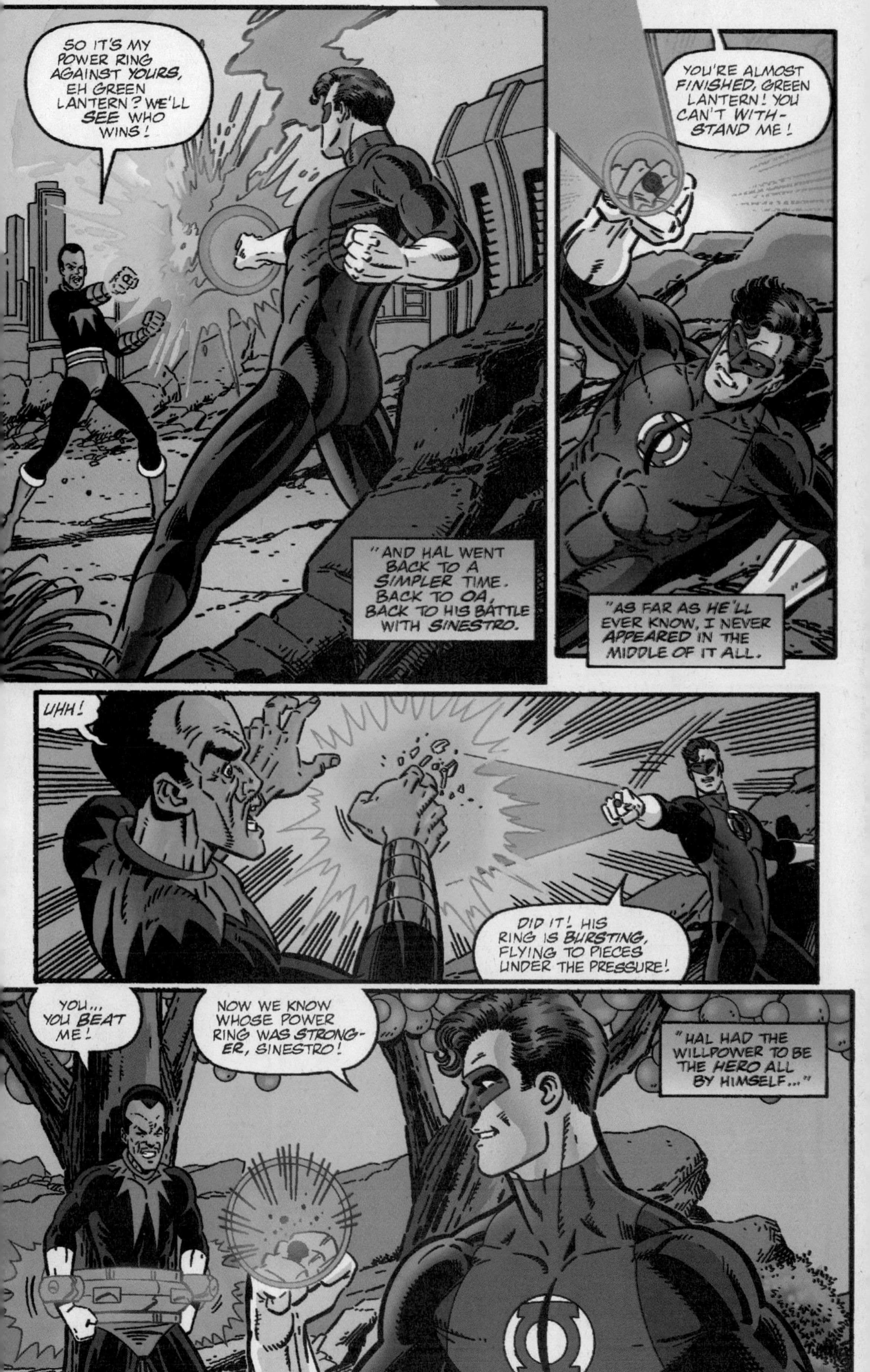
SO IT'S MY POWER RING AGAINST YOURS, EH GREEN LANTERN? WE'LL SEE WHO WINS!
YOU'RE ALMOST FINISHED, GREEN LANTERN! YOU CAN'T WITH-STAND ME!
"AND HAL WENT BACK TO A SIMPLER TIME. BACK TO OA, BACK TO HIS BATTLE WITH SINESTRO.
"AS FAR AS HE'LL EVER KNOW, I NEVER APPEARED IN THE MIDDLE OF IT ALL.
UHH!
DID IT! HIS RING IS BURSTING, FLYING TO PIECES UNDER THE PRESSURE!
YOU... YOU BEAT ME!
NOW WE KNOW WHOSE POWER RING WAS STRONG-ER, SINESTRO!
"HAL HAD THE WILLPOWER TO BE THE HERO ALL BY HIMSELF..."

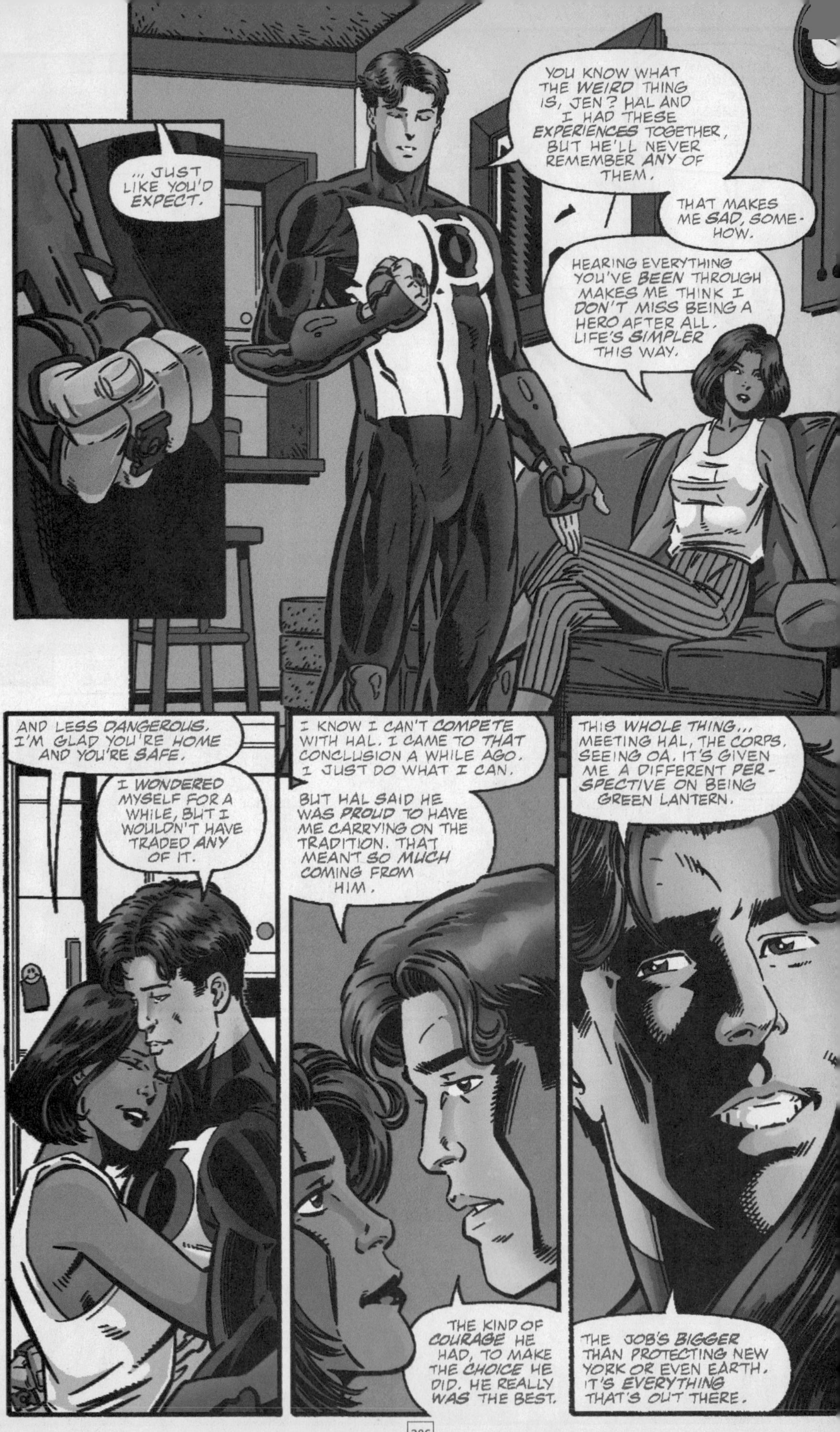
...JUST LIKE YOU'D EXPECT.
YOU KNOW WHAT THE WEIRD THING IS, JEN? HAL AND I HAD THESE EXPERIENCES TOGETHER, BUT HE'LL NEVER REMEMBER ANY OF THEM.
THAT MAKES ME SAD, SOMEHOW.
HEARING EVERYTHING YOU'VE BEEN THROUGH MAKES ME THINK I DON'T MISS BEING A HERO AFTER ALL. LIFE'S SIMPLER THIS WAY.
AND LESS DANGEROUS. I'M GLAD YOU'RE HOME AND YOU'RE SAFE.
I WONDERED MYSELF FOR A WHILE, BUT I WOULDN'T HAVE TRADED ANY OF IT.
I KNOW I CAN'T COMPETE WITH HAL. I CAME TO THAT CONCLUSION A WHILE AGO. I JUST DO WHAT I CAN.
BUT HAL SAID HE WAS PROUD TO HAVE ME CARRYING ON THE TRADITION. THAT MEANT SO MUCH COMING FROM HIM.
THE KIND OF COURAGE HE HAD, TO MAKE THE CHOICE HE DID. HE REALLY WAS THE BEST.
THIS WHOLE THING... MEETING HAL, THE CORPS, SEEING OA. IT'S GIVEN ME A DIFFERENT PERSPECTIVE ON BEING GREEN LANTERN.
THE JOB'S BIGGER THAN PROTECTING NEW YORK OR EVEN EARTH. IT'S EVERYTHING THAT'S OUT THERE.

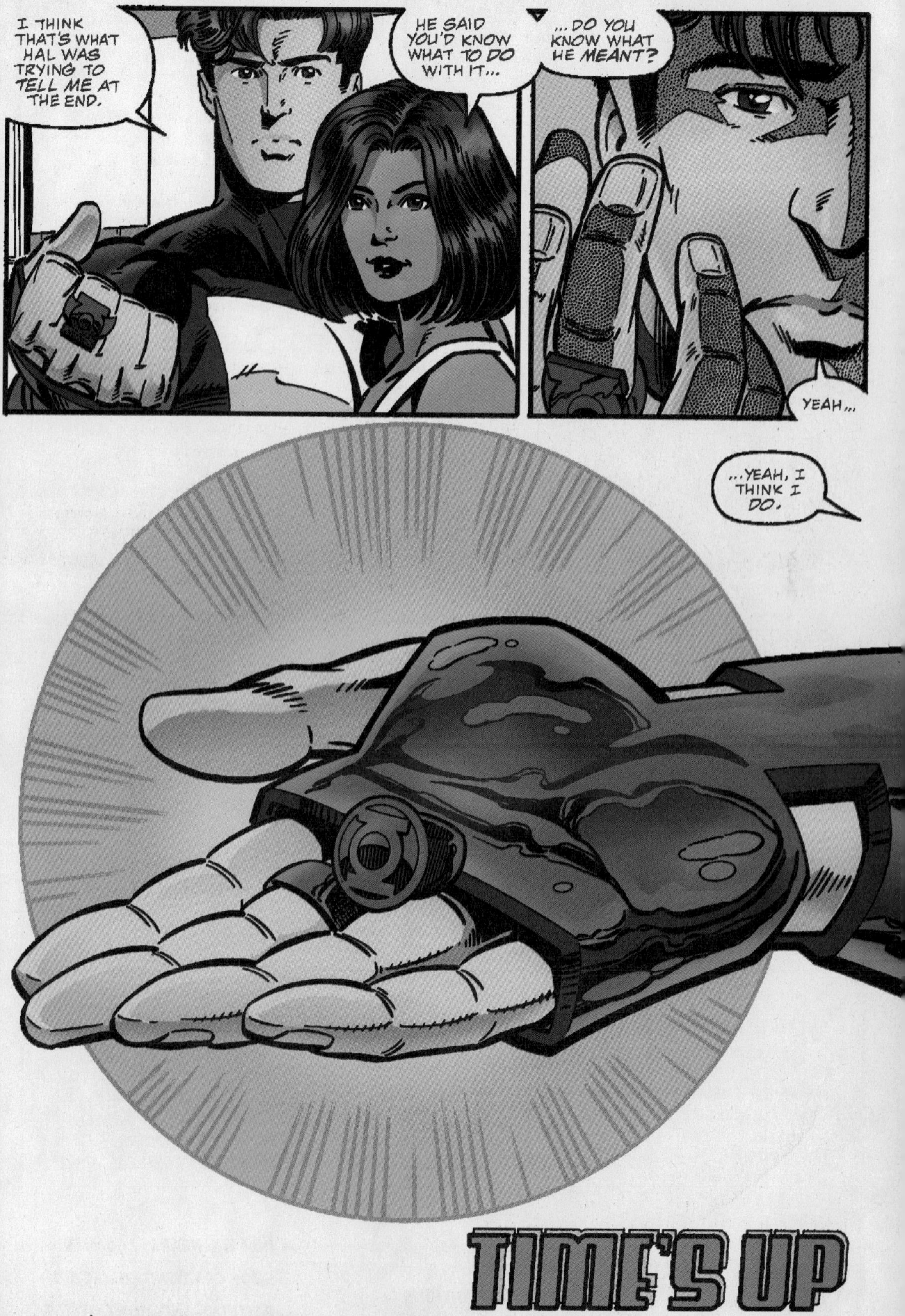
I THINK THAT'S WHAT HAL WAS TRYING TO TELL ME AT THE END.
HE SAID YOU'D KNOW WHAT TO DO WITH IT...
...DO YOU KNOW WHAT HE MEANT?
YEAH...
...YEAH, I THINK I DO.
TIME'S UP
RON MARZ WRITER
PAUL PELLETIER PENCILLER
TERRY AUSTIN INKER
ROB SCHWAGER COLOR & SEPARATIONS
CHRIS ELIOPOULOS LETTERS
CHUCK KIM ASSISTANT
KEVIN DOOLEY EDITOR

THE STARS OF THE DC UNIVERSE CAN ALSO BE FOUND IN THESE BOOKS:

GRAPHIC NOVELS

DARKSEID VS. GALACTUS: THE HUNGER
John Byrne

ENEMY ACE: WAR IDYLL
George Pratt

JLA/WILDC.A.T.S: CRIME MACHINE
Grant Morrison/Val Semeiks/Kevin Conrad

JUSTICE RIDERS
Chuck Dixon/J.H. Williams/Mick Gray

THE POWER OF SHAZAM!
Jerry Ordway

TITANS: SCISSORS, PAPER, STONE
Adam Warren/Tom Simmons/Joe Rosas

COLLECTIONS

AQUAMAN: TIME & TIDE
Peter David/Kirk Jarvinen/Brad Vancata

THE AMALGAM AGE OF COMICS:
THE DC COMICS COLLECTION
Various writers and artists

DC VERSUS MARVEL/MARVEL VERSUS DC
Ron Marz/Peter David/Dan Jurgens/
Claudio Castellini/Josef Rubinstein/Paul Neary

THE FLASH: THE RETURN OF BARRY ALLEN
Mark Waid/Greg LaRocque/Roy Richardson

THE GOLDEN AGE
James Robinson/Paul Smith/Richard Ory

THE GREATEST 1950s STORIES EVER TOLD
Various writers and artists

THE GREATEST TEAM-UP STORIES EVER TOLD
Various writers and artists

HAWK & DOVE
Karl & Barbara Kesel/Rob Liefeld

HITMAN
Garth Ennis/John McCrea

IMPULSE: RECKLESS YOUTH
Mark Waid/Humberto Ramos/
Wayne Faucher/various

JUSTICE LEAGUE: A NEW BEGINNING
Keith Giffen/J. M. DeMatteis/Kevin Maguire

KINGDOM COME
Mark Waid/Alex Ross

LEGENDS: THE COLLECTED EDITION
John Ostrander/Len Wein/John Byrne/Karl Kesel

LOBO'S GREATEST HITS
Various writers and artists

LOBO: THE LAST CZARNIAN
Keith Giffen/Alan Grant/Simon Bisley

LOBO'S BACK'S BACK
Keith Giffen/Alan Grant/Simon Bisley/
Christian Alamy

RETURN TO THE AMALGAM AGE OF COMICS:
THE DC COMICS COLLECTION
Various writers and artists

THE RAY: IN A BLAZE OF POWER
Jack C. Harris/Joe Quesada/Art Nichols

SOVEREIGN SEVEN
Chris Claremont/Dwayne Turner/Jerome
Moore/various

THE SPECTRE: CRIMES AND PUNISHMENTS
John Ostrander/Tom Mandrake

STARMAN: NIGHT AND DAY
James Robinson/Tony Harris/
Wade von Grawbadger

STARMAN: SINS OF THE FATHER
James Robinson/Tony Harris/
Wade von Grawbadger

WONDER WOMAN: THE CONTEST
William Messner-Loebs/Mike Deodato, Jr.

WONDER WOMAN: THE CHALLENGE
OF ARTEMIS
William Messner-Loebs/Mike Deodato, Jr.

WONDER WOMAN: SECOND GENESIS
John Byrne

OTHER COLLECTIONS OF INTEREST

CAMELOT 3000
Mike W. Barr/Brian Bolland

RONIN
Frank Miller

WATCHMEN
Alan Moore/Dave Gibbons

ARCHIVE EDITIONS

ALL STAR COMICS ARCHIVES Volume 1
(ALL STAR COMICS 3-6)
Various writers and artists

ALL STAR COMICS ARCHIVES Volume 2
(ALL STAR COMICS 7-10)
Various writers and artists

ALL STAR COMICS ARCHIVES Volume 3
(ALL STAR COMICS 11-14)
Various writers and artists

THE FLASH ARCHIVES Volume 1
(The Scarlet Speedster's adventures from FLASH
COMICS 104, SHOWCASE 4, 8, 13, 14, and
THE FLASH 105-108)
John Broome/Robert Kanigher/Carmine
Infantino/Frank Giacoia/Joe Giella/Joe Kubert

LEGION OF SUPER-HEROES ARCHIVES Volume 1
(The Legion of Super-Heroes' adventures from
ADVENTURE COMICS 247, 267, 282, 290, 293,
300-305, ACTION COMICS 267, 276, 287, 289,
SUPERBOY 86, 89, 98 and SUPERMAN 147)
Various writers and artists

LEGION OF SUPER-HEROES ARCHIVES Volume 2
(The Legion of Super-Heroes' adventures from
ADVENTURE COMICS 306-317 and SUPERMAN'S
PAL, JIMMY OLSEN 72)
Various writers and artists

LEGION OF SUPER-HEROES ARCHIVES Volume 3
(The Legion of Super-Heroes' adventures from
ADVENTURE COMICS 318-328, SUPERMAN'S PAL,
JIMMY OLSEN 76 and SUPERBOY 117)
Various writers and artists

LEGION OF SUPER-HEROES ARCHIVES Volume 4
(The Legion of Super-Heroes' adventures from
ADVENTURE COMICS 329-339 and
SUPERBOY 124-125)
Various writers and artists

LEGION OF SUPER-HEROES ARCHIVES Volume 5
(The Legion of Super-Heroes' adventures from
ADVENTURE COMICS 340-349)
Various writers and artists

LEGION OF SUPER-HEROES ARCHIVES Volume 6
(The Legion of Super-Heroes' adventures from
ADVENTURE COMICS 350-358)
Various writers and artists

LEGION OF SUPER-HEROES ARCHIVES Volume 7
(The Legion of Super-Heroes' adventures from
ADVENTURE COMICS 359-367 and SUPERMAN'S
PAL, JIMMY OLSEN 106)
Various writers and artists

**FOR THE NEAREST COMICS
SHOP CARRYING COLLECTED
EDITIONS AND MONTHLY TITLES
FROM DC COMICS,
CALL 1-888-COMIC BOOK.**